G U N
CONTROL

A Reference Handbook

GUN CONTROL

A Reference Handbook

Earl R. Kruschke, Ph.D.
Professor Emeritus of Political Science
California State University, Chico

CONTEMPORARY
WORLD ISSUES

ABC-CLIO

Santa Barbara, California
Denver, Colorado
Oxford, England

Library of Congress Cataloging-in-Publication Data

Kruschke, Earl R. (Earl Roger), 1934–
    Gun control: a reference handbook / Earl R. Kruschke.
      p. cm.—(Contemporary world issues)
    Includes bibliographical references and index.
    1. Gun control—Government policy—United States. 2.
Firearms—Law and legislation—United States. I.
Title II. Series
    HV7436.K78 1995   363.3'3'0973—dc20   95-10450

ISBN 0-87436-695-X

01 00 99 98 97 96   10 9 8 7 6 5 4 3 2

ABC-CLIO, Inc.
130 Cremona Drive, P.O. Box 1911
Santa Barbara, California 93116-1911

This book is printed on acid-free paper ∞ .

Manufactured in the United States of America

Contents

Preface, ix

1 Introduction, 1
    Context of the Gun Control
       Issue, 2
    The Second Amendment
       Issue, 3
        Arguing for the Collective Right
          To Bear Arms, 5
        Arguing for the Individual Right
          To Bear Arms, 8
    Is There a Need for Gun
       Control?, 15
        Types of Firearms, 18
        Public Support for Gun
          Control Legislation, 20
    How Effective Are Gun
       Control Laws?, 21
    Race, Ethnicity, and Gun
       Control Policy, 24
    Gender and Gun Control
       Policy, 30

Self-Defense in General, Gun Ownership,
and Gun Control Policy, 34
Police and Gun Control Policy, 38
Manufacturers' Product Liability and
Gun Control Policy, 42
Conclusion: Control Guns or Understand
the Causes of Crime?, 46

2 Chronology, 59

3 Biographical Sketches, 99

4 Legislation and Statistical Data, 125
Introduction, 125
Court Cases, 127
Some Cases Illustrating the Collective View, 127
Some Cases Illustrating the Individual View, 140
United States Supreme Court Opinions, 157
Constitutional Provisions on the Right To Keep
and Bear Arms, 162
Major Federal Gun Control Legislation, 170
Selected State and Local Laws Dealing with
Gun Control, 179
State Laws, 179
City Laws, 181
Selected Statistical Data—Tables, 182

5 Directory of Organizations, 189
National Organizations, 189
Selected State Organizations Interested in
Gun Issues, 218
Other Organizations Interested in Gun
Issues, 233
Selected Victims Rights Groups, 237

Selected Organizations Endorsing a
National Waiting Period for the
Purchase of Handguns, 238

6 Selected Print Resources, 241
Articles, 242
Bibliographies, 296
Books, Monographs, Theses, Symposia, 299
Periodicals, 319
Scholarly Papers and Government Reports, 326
Pamphlets, Booklets, and Reprints, 332

7 Selected Nonprint Resources, 345
Films and Videocassettes, 345
Databases, 367
CD-ROMs, 369
Educational Software, 370

Glossary, 373
Index, 391
A Note about the Author, 409

Preface

I have been interested in the subject of gun control—broadly defined—for over 35 years. The debate over gun control is perhaps most often conducted in an atmosphere of frenzied controversy and, indeed, sometimes in a context of outright hysteria by those involved. Given the recent passage of legislation by the Congress of the United States—first, the Brady Bill (which requires a five-day waiting period for the purchase of a handgun); then the Assault Weapons Ban (which ostensibly bans from private use some 19 assault-type weapons in the United States); and, finally, the Anti-Crime Bill of 1994 (which contains a veritable laundry list of provisions aimed at drastically reducing crime in the United States—the nature and extent of the debate over gun control and its impact on individual rights under the Constitution are likely to escalate even further. The last two laws mentioned above constitute some of the most sweeping and potentially litigation-inducing legislation ever to be placed in the statutes of the United States. The fever-pitch arguments that are likely to erupt as a consequence of their passage is unfortunate, because ultimately a largely unknowledgeable public will once again find itself vacillating between and among the strident positions taken by those who have determined to define the political agenda related to this matter, and then find themselves making future policy decisions based largely on emotional judgments rather than on rational conclusions.

This condition is a bit ironic in that, in addition to the generally superficial and sometimes sensational reporting of the journalistic press, there exists an increasingly large and highly sophisticated body of scholarly literature on the subject. The work of authors who have moved the understanding of the issue of gun control to unprecedented heights of historical, legal, and philosophical reason remains essentially unknown to the lay public. Be that as it may, the controversy is sure to continue.

This book appears almost exactly ten years after the publication of my *The Right To Keep and Bear Arms: A Continuing American Dilemma* (Charles C Thomas, Publisher, 1985). In that book, through a review of the historical foundations of the Second Amendment and an examination of cases dealing with the individual and collective views of the right to keep and bear arms, I attempted to build a bridge between the then-existing scholarly literature and what I hoped would be a comparatively large lay readership. I do not have the empirical evidence to draw a sound conclusion about whether my attempts to become a structural engineer succeeded. Nevertheless, in this book I again attempt to build a similar bridge from a somewhat different perspective. I attempt to create a research handbook for both the first-time inquirer with an interest in the subject and others with a more serious interest. In other words, the book is to be regarded as something of an advanced introduction rather than a comprehensive survey of the field.

In the introduction to this book, I attempt to provide context for the gun control controversy by examining a diverse—but loosely interrelated—set of issues: the Second Amendment foundations dealing with the right to keep and bear arms; the relevance of race, ethnicity, and gender to an understanding of the gun issue; police attitudes about gun ownership and use; self-defense and gun policy; the product liability problem and its relationship to the gun control issue; and, finally, the question of whether we are dealing with a crime control issue rather than a gun control issue. Chapter 2 presents a chronology of some of the major events that are directly or indirectly relevant to the current controversy. Chapter 3 presents brief biographical sketches of a few individuals, mainly scholars and politicians, who have been especially articulate on the issue. Chapter 4 lays out some of the major state and federal court cases related to gun control and right-to-arms issues, some of the major state and national laws relevant to regulating behavior in this area, constitutional provisions of both state and federal constitutions dealing with the right to keep and bear arms, and related topics. Chapter 5 provides a partial directory of organizations having a direct or tangential interest in the matter. Chapter 6 presents some of the major articles, books, monographs, theses, symposia, bibliographies, magazines, scholarly papers, pamphlets, and other materials of importance to understanding the gun control issue. Chapter 7 provides a partial list of nonprint materials available on the subject. The last part of the book provides a glossary of relevant terms.

This book was a long time in gestation. To complete it, I had the help of many people, only some of whom will be acknowledged here. My thanks go to several former students who assisted me during the very early stages of the development of this work: Ms. Jacquie Carroll, Mr. Preston Donovan, and Mr. Michael Cini. I owe a deep debt of gratitude to the National Rifle Association, and especially to Dr. Paul Blackman of that organization, for not only supplying me with information, but for directing me to places where it might be found. Similar thanks go to organizations such as Handgun Control, Inc., and the dozens of other organizations with whom I had contact. To Don B. Kates, Jr., one of the country's leading civil liberties lawyers and scholars of the gun control issue, I express particular appreciation for his immense generosity in supplying much needed guidance during the early and late stages of the writing of this book. I owe appreciation to Mr. Kates and to Professor Joseph Olson of Hamline University School of Law for their invitation to the New Orleans Scholarship Conference on the Bill of Rights' Second Amendment, which proved to be an extraordinary learning experience for me. To Mr. Henry Rasof, senior acquisitions editor at ABC-CLIO, I express my appreciation for his almost incredible patience and goodwill while the manuscript was being developed. To Amy Catala, development editor at ABC-CLIO, I owe thanks for shepherding the manuscript through the final stages. And, as always, I owe my greatest debt to my wife, Marilyn Ann Kruschke, who endured the many difficulties that both necessarily and unnecessarily result from the writing of a scholarly book. This book very likely could not have been completed without her.

For any errors of omission or commission, I alone assume responsibility.

—Earl R. Kruschke
Chico, California

Introduction[1] 1

What limitations, if any, should be placed on gun ownership by American citizens? That deceptively simple question has been the cause of one of the longest-lasting, most contentious debates in all of American politics over the past half century.

The reason that some people have been calling for controls on the ownership of guns is not difficult to understand. Violent crime in the United States has been an increasingly serious problem over the last few decades. And guns have been an important factor in the nation's recent epidemic of crime.

To deal with this issue, many citizens demand that governmental bodies more carefully monitor the kinds of guns sold and the individuals to whom they are sold. In some cases, these demands include a call for a complete ban on some types of firearms, such as handguns, "Saturday Night Specials," or semiautomatic weapons. Still others propose that security checks be carried out on prospective gun buyers or that such buyers be required to wait a certain number of days before actually being issued a weapon.

In recent years, more subtle forms of gun control have also been suggested. For example, some cities and private organizations

1

have offered to buy back firearms from gun owners, hoping to remove these weapons from public use. Some gun control groups have also suggested that product liability suits be filed against the manufacturers and sellers of guns when weapons are involved in personal injury or death. Proposals such as these are always met with vigorous opposition, however. A large segment of the U.S. population believes that gun ownership is an inalienable right guaranteed by the Second Amendment of the U.S. Constitution (and also by many state constitutions). According to this segment, any attempt to ban the sale or ownership of firearms in the United States is absolutely unconstitutional. Their fear is that any form of gun regulation is the first step leading to an outright ban on all kinds of guns.

The gun control debate is both a fascinating intellectual exercise and an emotional contest in which those with opposing views have traditionally found very little common ground. In most cases, both sides begin with essentially the same factual data. From those data, however, they are likely to draw very different conclusions. For example, the words of the Second Amendment are the same whether one believes in or opposes gun control efforts. Yet for many decades, scholars have strongly disagreed as to whether the amendment guarantees gun ownership only to organized groups of Americans (such as members of the National Guard) or to individual Americans.

Debates over the effectiveness of existing gun control laws also begin with the same laws and the same statistics concerning crime in jurisdictions with those laws. For example, both sides of the debate can cite the stiff gun control laws in effect in New York City and the statistics on violent crime in that city over the past two decades and still come to diametrically opposed conclusions about the effectiveness of gun control legislation.

The Context of the Gun Control Issue

When one enters into a discussion of gun control policy, one immediately enters into an area of controversy—often an area of controversy that seems to defy rationality. One is immediately immersed in issues of political ideology; of constitutional rights under the Second Amendment to the Constitution of the United States; of matters related to criminal justice, police power, and public authority; of one's individual rights to privacy and self-protection; and many other issues that have become snarled, for better or for worse, in the semantics of "liberal" and "conservative" arguments and that touch even on matters that are referred to today as "politically correct." To attempt to sort through these ideas and to present a view based on the best available scholarship is, to say the least, no easy task.

The matter is made more complicated by the fact that what one might assume to be generally liberal and conservative points of view on this issue have been essentially reversed.[2] Liberals, for example, although supporting government regulation of business, have been—at least since President Franklin Roosevelt's New Deal—consistently opposed to government interference with individual rights, whether it be in such areas as speech, freedom of association, personal sexual preferences and activities, search and seizure issues, rights of criminals, and, in general, those rights presumably guaranteed individuals under various sections of the Bill of Rights, notably the First, Fourth, Fifth, Sixth, Eighth, and Ninth Amendments. Civil libertarians have defended the rights of Nazis, skinheads, some of the most violent serial killers, and artists whose various creations some critics have labeled pornographic. Yet, liberals have tended not to support the individual right to keep and bear arms. Conservatives generally have tended to oppose government regulation of business and have been much more inclined to advocate and impose government rules on the conduct of individual and group behavior, whether public or private. Thus, conservatives tend to support the death penalty; oppose abortion; and advocate imposition of severe penalties for drug use, the use and distribution of pornographic materials, and participation in and advocacy of various aspects of sexual behavior that they deem aberrant. They also tend to support the individual right to keep and bear arms.

In other words, on the issue of gun control policy, liberals and conservatives find themselves taking a position different from that which might be expected in the context of their ideological orientation.

The discussion of gun control policy—at least from a contemporary legal and political perspective—must thus be understood to occur within this liberal-conservative context.

The Second Amendment Issue

At the very heart of the matter of the gun control controversy lies the Second Amendment to the Constitution of the United States and the issue of its interpretation and application.[3] The Second Amendment reads as follows:

> A well regulated Militia, being necessary to the security of a free State, the right of the people to keep and bear arms shall not be infringed.

To the casual reader, the meaning and interpretation of these words might appear obvious; yet they lie at the heart of a significant controversy among members of the legal, the scholarly, and even the lay communities.

Gun control proponents say that the Second Amendment guarantees a *collective* rather than an *individual* right. When the occasion occurs that Americans find it necessary to band together to defend their rights, they are constitutionally guaranteed the right to own the firearms they need for that purpose. Opponents of gun control argue that the Second Amendment guarantees to every individual American citizen the right to own any number or kind of firearms. Any law that bans guns in any form is, ipso facto, unconstitutional.

It is accurate to state that

> scholars, lawyers, and judges, using essentially the same body of evidence, have reached diametrically opposed conclusions on the meaning and application of the Second Amendment. The collective, or state's rights view, embraces the idea that the writers of the Second Amendment were responding to fears that the national government might attempt to disarm the state militias. Those who embrace the collective view also assert that the Second Amendment was a response to the fear of large standing armies. In short, the "people" referred to are—according to this view— to be considered those who were intended to serve in the militias. The proponents of the individual view, on the other hand, argue that the Amendment does not create a state right but instead protects a preexisting individual right. It was through an attempt to protect the individual right that protection of the militia was achieved. The "people" referred to in the Amendment are, therefore, to be viewed as the same people referred to in the first, fourth, ninth, and tenth amendments—namely, individuals.[4]

Arguing for the Collective Right To Bear Arms

Proponents of gun control measures argue that the Second Amendment does not automatically guarantee an American's right to own a gun for nondefensive reasons. They believe that even if the individual-rights interpretation were to prevail in the courts and halls of academia, restrictions on gun use and ownership—for example, registration, waiting periods, and personal background checks—would still be constitutional because Americans have many constitutionally guaranteed rights that are nonetheless regulated. For example, the First Amendment to the Constitution guarantees all American citizens the right of free speech; however, as the Supreme Court and other courts have ruled on a number of occasions, the right to free speech is not an unlimited right. As a classic example, one does not have the right to stand in a crowded movie theater and yell out "Fire!"

Furthermore, the right to free expression is often limited and regulated by the federal government. At one time, it was thought that anyone could build and operate a radio station because using the public airwaves was simply exercising the right of free speech. It eventually became obvious, however, that communication by radio waves would become impossible if everyone had an unfettered right to the airwaves. As a result, Congress established the Federal Communications Commission in 1934 to license a limited number of radio stations authorized to operate only on certain assigned frequencies. By analogy, some would argue that the federal government has the right to impose certain restrictions on gun ownership and use, *even if the right to own guns is guaranteed by the Second Amendment.*

Thus, the fact remains that a substantial number of legal scholars have argued that the Second Amendment does *not* say that Americans have a constitutionally guaranteed right to own guns. These "collectivist" scholars, like their "individualist" colleagues, go back to constitutional history to find support for their position. For example, after a review of the debate over the Second Amendment at the Constitutional Congress in 1787, Dennis Henigan, director of the Legal Action Project at the Center to Prevent Handgun Violence comes to the conclusion that

> there is no indication from the history of the 2nd Amendment that the Founders were seeking a broad guarantee of the individual right to own firearms for any purpose. On the contrary, the expressed intention of the framers

was to guarantee that state militias remained armed and viable, and the "right to keep and bear arms" must be understood as implementing that purpose.[5]

The Second Amendment, Henigan shows, grew out of colonists' fear of standing armies and their belief that militias composed of ordinary citizens were the surest guarantee of maintaining their freedom.

Like "individualist" interpreters of the Second Amendment, "collectivist" scholars point to court decisions to support their view of the amendment's "real" meaning. In fact, collectivists often use the *same* court cases in their arguments. As an example, the National Rifle Association (NRA) has pointed to the U.S. Supreme Court's decision in the case of *U.S. v. Miller* (307 U.S. 174: 1939) to support its anti-control position on gun ownership. The Court's decision, the NRA claims, supports its contention that any weapon that could conceivably be useful to a militia is constitutionally protected and that the militia is intended to mean all citizens able to bear arms. A pamphlet of the Center to Prevent Handgun Violence, however, comes to exactly the opposite conclusion. It quotes the Court's decision in *U.S. v. Miller*, as follows:

> In the absence of any evidence tending to show that possession or use of a [sawed-off shotgun] at this time has some reasonable relationship to the preservation of efficiency of a well regulated militia, we cannot say that the Second Amendment guarantees the right to keep and bear such an instrument. . . . With obvious purpose to assure the continuation and render possible the effectiveness of such forces the declaration and guarantee of the Second Amendment were made. It must be interpreted and applied with that end in view.[6]

Collectivist scholars also point to a more recent Supreme Court decision to support their case. In *Lewis v. United States* (445 U.S. 55: 1980), the court ruled specifically about laws that attempt to regulate firearms. It said that

> these legislative restrictions on the use of firearms are neither based upon constitutionally suspect criteria, nor do they trench upon any constitutionally protected liberties. . . . The Second Amendment guarantees no right to keep and bear a firearm that does not

have "some reasonable relationship to the preservation or efficiency of a well regulated militia."[7]

Even more forceful statements about the sense of the Second Amendment have been made by lower courts. For example, in 1973, the U.S. Court of Appeals for the Third Circuit ruled in *Eckert v. City of Philadelphia* (477 F.2d 610: 1973):

> Appellant's theory [*sic*] in the district court which he now repeats is that by the Second Amendment to the United States Constitution he is entitled to bear arms. Appellant is completely wrong about that. . . . It must be remembered that the right to bear arms is not a right given by the United States Constitution.[8]

And in a case brought against the Village of Morton Grove's handgun ban, the Seventh Circuit Court of Appeals ruled that

> construing [the language of the Second Amendment] according to its plain meaning, it seems clear that the right to bear arms is inextricably connected to the preservation of a militia. . . . We conclude that the right to keep and bear handguns is not guaranteed by the second amendment [*sic*].[9]

In a 1991 editorial on the subject of the Second Amendment, former chief justice of the U.S. Supreme Court Warren E. Burger wrote about "the meaning and distortion of the Second Amendment." Burger noted that, "the real purpose of the Second Amendment was to ensure that the 'state armies'—the 'militia'—be maintained for the defense of the state."

After reviewing the historical development of the amendment, Burger then concluded that

> if an 18th-century militia was intended to be "well regulated," surely the Second Amendment does not remotely guarantee every person the constitutional right to have a "Saturday Night Special" or a machine gun without any regulation whatsoever. There is no support in the Constitution for the argument that federal and state governments are powerless to regulate the purchase of such firearms so that they do not get into the hands of persons with significant criminal

records or mental impairments, or persons who are engaged in criminal activity. [10]

Burger concludes his editorial on the Second Amendment on a note that characterizes much of the debate over gun control. "Of course, some of these observations will be challenged by weapons and ammunition manufacturers and other members of the so-called 'gun lobby.' That there should be vigorous debate on this subject is a tribute to our freedom of speech and press, but the American people should have a firm understanding of the true origin and purpose of the Second Amendment." [11]

Arguing for the Individual Right To Bear Arms

Opponents of gun control argue for the individual right to bear arms. They build their argument on interpretation of U.S. history and of the Constitution, and among opponents are numerous scholars in various fields.

It is probable that members of the species have kept and borne arms since prehistory. Indeed,

> whether with stick, club, tree branch, rock, or the jaw-bone of a subdued beast, the brute which was to evolve into modern man went forth, drawing upon the experience stored in the dim recesses of his under-developed brain, to attack, to hunt, or to defend. Pre-historic man was probably born into an environment in which weapons were fundamental instruments of existence. This fact lays the [intellectual and philo-sophical] foundation . . . for those who argue that the use of weapons was evolved in the original state of nature and that, therefore, the right to keep and bear arms—particularly in defense of one's self, one's fam-ily, and one's property—is a "natural right." [12]

Individual rights advocates maintain that this natural rights philosophy was part of the entire political and intellectual appara-tus upon which the framers of the American Constitution and es-pecially those like James Madison—who was responsible for drafting the Second Amendment—based their thinking. These were widely read, intellectual, informed, and politically pragmatic men. Included in their collective intellectual experience were Plato and Aristotle; Livy and Cicero; Grotius, Vatel, and Pufendorf; Galen, Hobbes, and Rousseau; Beccaria, Machiavelli, and Montesquieu; Hume, Bodin, and Locke; Harrington, Sydney, and Voltaire; Burgh, Trenchard, Gordon, and Macaulay; and Smith, Coke, and Blackstone, among others. In general, to the colonists "books were the high road to history."[13] Each of these authors had something to say about the right and duty of citizens to keep and bear arms.

For example, the framers would have read that Plato urged that "citizens ought to practice war—not in time of war, but rather while they are at peace."[14]

In Cicero, the framers read of the natural law of self-defense:

> . . . Gentlemen, there exists a law, not written down anywhere but inborn in our hearts; a law which comes to us not by training or custom or reading but by itself; a law which has come to us not by theory but from practice, not by instruction but by natural intuition. I refer to the law which lays it down that, if our lives are endangered by plots of violence or armed robbers or enemies, any and every method of protecting ourselves is morally right. When weapons reduce them to silence, the laws no longer expect one to wait[,] for these will have to wait for justice, too. . . . Indeed, even the wisdom of the law itself, by a sort of tacit implication, permits self defense, because it does not actually forbid men to kill; what it does, instead, is to forbid the bearing of a weapon with the intention to kill.[15]

In Adam Smith they would have read:

> Men of republican principles have been jealous of a standing army as dangerous to liberty. . . . The standing army of Caesar destroyed the Roman republic. The standing army of Cromwell turned the Long Parliament out of doors.[16]

In Rousseau they would likewise have been warned of the dangers of mercenaries and of standing armies, and in Machiavelli they would have read that "the ruin of Italy has been caused by nothing else than by resting all her hopes for many years on mercenaries."[17]

In brief, the framers of the Constitution of the United States were men of both pragmatism and philosophy whose ideas were founded in classical thought and in the republican thought of the seventeenth century. Thus the Second Amendment was drafted on the basis of "the fear of standing armies and the exaltation of militias composed of ordinary citizens."[18] Republican thought was based essentially on the Florentine tradition expressed by Machiavelli, who celebrated the "citizen-warrior." "From this [tradition there] developed a sociology of liberty that rested upon the role of arms in society: political conditions must allow the arming of all citizens."[19]

But a more immediate and difficult problem faced the colonists. William Knox, who was under secretary of state for the British Colonial Office, had prepared a document entitled "What Is Fit To Be Done with America?" in which he proposed not only establishing in the colonies a ruling class loyal to the British Crown, making the Church of England the universal church in the colonies and imposing unlimited taxes, but also totally disarming all Americans. His proposal stated:

> The militia laws should be repealed and none suffered to be re-enacted, & *the Arms of all the People should be taken away*, & every piece of Ordnance removed into the King's Stores, nor should any Foundry or manufactory of Arms, Gunpowder, or Warlike Stores, be ever suffered in America, nor should any Gunpowder, Lead, arms or Ordnance be imported into it without License; they will have but little need of such things for the future, as the King's Troops, Ships & Forts will be sufficient to protect them from any danger.[20]

To this, Americans responded as follows under the leadership of James Otis and John Hancock:

> Whereas, by an Act of Parliament, of the first of King William and Queen Mary, it is declared, that the Subjects being Protestants, may have Arms for their Defence; it is the Opinion of this town [Boston], that the said Declaration is founded in Nature, Reason and sound Policy, and is well adapted for the necessary defence of the Community.
>
> *And Forasmuch*, as by a good and wholesome Law of this Province, every listed Soldier and other House-

holder (except Troopers, who by Law are otherwise to be provided) shall always be provided with a well fix'd Firelock, Musket, Accoutrements and Ammunition, as in said Law particularly mentioned, to the Satisfaction of the Commission officers of the Company; . . . *VOTED*, that those of the Inhabitants, who may at present be unprovided, be and hereby are requested duly to observe the said Law at this Time.[21]

Other statements were issued by the colonists to the effect that citizens had the right to protect themselves from armed oppression.

This threat was combined with a particularly significant influence on the framers: the tradition of English common law. "It must be emphasized, in other words, that the right to keep and bear arms was not established by the Second Amendment. It has its foundation in English jurisprudence."[22] As Richard E. Gardiner has put it,

> . . . the Bill of Rights protects against infringement or abridgement those fundamental human rights which the framers viewed as naturally belonging to each individual human being. It would be a grotesque perversion of the framers' understanding of the concept of rights to suggest that any of the rights found in the Bill of Rights, particularly the few substantive rights of the first and second amendments, were created by that document.[23]

Evidence suggests that Englishmen were armed by 602 or 603, as is illustrated, for example, in the decree of Ethelbert, King of Kent. Other evidence of this fact can be adduced by referring to the proclamations of Hlothhere and Eadric in the 600s, Alfred in the 800s, and King Cnut during the period 1020 to 1023. His laws included a provision stating that "if anyone illegally disarms a man, he is to compensate him."[24] Even further, the right and obligation of every Englishman to be armed goes to the year 870, when King Alfred established the fyrd—a military organization made up of personal troops of the king (house guards); a group known as the select fyrd (males who regularly trained and were paid out of the treasury); and, finally, the general fyrd (all those able-bodied males who were required to arm themselves at their own expense for the purpose of national defense).

Other statutes, such as the Assize of Arms of Henry II, the Statute of Winchester under Edward I, and Edward III's Statute of Northhampton also required that persons be armed to defend the nation. The nonexistence of a standing army and the absence of a police force necessitated a population who were equipped with arms. Citizens made up "trained bands" for purposes of protection. Likewise, the *posse comitatus*, organized by the sheriff, was made up of all able-bodied males who were expected to keep arms in order to deal with disturbances of a criminal nature. And citizens were expected to engage in the "hue and cry" when they observed a crime and to pursue the offender. At night, moreover, the duty of keeping the peace was rotated among citizens. They were expected to keep private arms for this purpose.

Blackstone, in his authoritative commentary on the common law, set forth what were considered the absolute rights of persons, rights that he insisted grew out of the state of nature itself and were part of the human entitlement. He suggested that there were five "auxiliary subordinate rights" to the three "great and primary rights of personal security, personal liberty, and private property." The fifth of these auxiliary rights was "having arms for their defence . . . and is indeed a public allowance, under due restrictions, of the *natural right of resistance and self-preservation,* when the sanctions of society and laws are found insufficient to restrain the violence of oppression."[25] Hawkins and Coke also took this view, and, ultimately, the right to bear arms was included in the 1689 English Bill of Rights. As the historian Joyce Lee Malcolm observes, "the right to have arms was part and parcel of that bundle of rights and privileges that Englishmen carried with them to America and which they later fought to preserve."[26]

With respect to the meaning of the word *militia* in revolutionary America, it was meant to include every able-bodied white male of every household; indeed, even the Continental Congress "defined the militia to include the entire able-bodied military-age citizenry of the United States and required each of them to own his own firearm.[27] Richard Henry Lee, a delegate to the Continental Congress from Virginia, stated, "To preserve liberty, it is essential that the whole body of the people always possess arms, and be taught alike, especially when young, how to use them." Patrick Henry proclaimed, during the Virginia convention on the ratification of the federal constitution that "the great object is that every man be armed. . . . Everyone who is able

may have a gun." James Madison argued—in *Federalist* No. 26—
that "the advantage of being armed . . . the Americans possess
over the people of all other nations. . . . Notwithstanding the military establishments in the several kingdoms of Europe, which
are carried as far as the public resources will bear, the governments are afraid to trust the people with arms." Thomas Jefferson, who was widely known for having a large number of
handguns, rifles, and shotguns in his Monticello mansion, had
said, "No free man shall ever be debarred the use of arms." And
Samuel Adams argued that the Constitution of the United States
should never be interpreted as disallowing law-abiding citizens
from the ownership of guns.[28]

Individualist scholars also point out that the original wording of the Second Amendment as drafted by James Madison read
as follows: "The right of the people to keep and bear arms shall
not be infringed; a well armed and well regulated militia being
the best security of a free country: but no person religiously
scrupulous of bearing arms shall be compelled to render military
service in person." Madison used the Virginia Declaration of
Rights as the source of his language, inserting the clause specify-
ing the "right to keep and bear arms" (language that was contained in the draft Virginia submitted to Congress) and the
language pertaining to what today would be referred to as the
rights of conscientious objectors to military service. The House
committee dealing with Madison's proposal made considerable
changes in the phraseology reversing, for example, the militia
and the right to bear arms language, and the full House, fearing
that conscientious objectors would not be required, under the
original language of the amendment, to provide substitutes for
military service, added the clause referring to rendering military
service in person. When the Bill of Rights and the Second
Amendment reached the Senate, still other changes were made.
The entire clause relating to conscientious objectors was deleted
and the phrase *for the common defence,* which had been proposed
to follow the words *bear arms,* was voted down. The Senate ultimately redrafted the amendment so that it read then as it reads
today. It is of historical interest also that the Second Amendment
was originally the fourth amendment of a total of twelve submitted to the states. The first two—one concerned with the population of congressional districts, the other with compensation for
members of Congress—were not approved. (Curiously, the
amendment referring to compensation was exhumed and ratified
in 1992.) In any event, the original Fourth Amendment proposed

by the Congress became the Second Amendment as adopted by the states.

Other eminent men of the time, such as St. George Tucker of Virginia and William Rawle of Pennsylvania, maintained the same view. And Thomas Cooley, perhaps the preeminent commentator on American jurisprudence during his time, stated the following of the right to keep and bear arms:

> The Right is General.—It might be supposed from the phraseology of this provision [the Second Amendment] that the right to keep and bear arms was only guaranteed to the militia; but this would be an interpretation not warranted by the intent. The militia . . . consists of those persons who, under the law, are liable to the performance of military duty, and are officered and enrolled for service when called upon. . . . The meaning of the provision undoubtedly is, that the people, from whom the militia must be taken, shall have the right to keep and bear arms, and they need no permission or regulation of law for the purpose.[29]

Under the Militia Act of 1792, free adult males in the United States were required by law to keep a firearm and ammunition. The framers of this law were distinctly not referring to what we might presently label the National Guard. The current Federal United States Code indicates that "the militia of the United States consists of all able-bodied males at least 17 years of age."[30] And in a recent Supreme Court decision dealing with searches and seizures, it was asserted that the right to keep and bear arms is an individual right.[31] The Supreme Court itself has held that the militia is intended to mean all citizens or all males able to bear arms. It wrote, in *U.S. v. Miller*, (307 U.S. 174, 179: 1939), that "ordinarily when called for service these men were expected to appear bearing arms supplied by themselves and of the kind in common use at the time."

It is also important to elaborate somewhat further on what was meant by the term *people* when the Second Amendment was adopted. Did the framers have in mind an individual or collective interpretation of the right of "the people" to keep and bear arms? Many leading contemporary scholars agree, given the English legal and intellectual context in which the amendment, like the Constitution itself, was written, that the framers had an individual right in mind. This was not, of course, absolute in its application, for such groups as lunatics, idiots, infants, and felons were excluded from the right to keep and bear arms.

> Given the fact that the [second] amendment is part of the Bill of Rights, and that the first, fourth, ninth, and tenth amendments have been construed to refer to individuals rather than to a collectivity, it would seem bizarre to assume that they did not have individuals in mind when they wrote the second. To rationalize a collective view, one would have to assume that the framers referred to individuals in the first amendment, to the states in the second, to individuals in the fourth, to individuals in the ninth, and then separated the states and the people in the tenth amendment, even though this was inconsistent with the wording of the second.[32]

In the words of Don B. Kates, Jr., "Any one of these textual incongruities demanded by an exclusively state's rights position dooms it. Cumulatively they present a truly grotesque reading of the Bill of Rights."[33] And Stephen P. Halbrook, in a linguistic analysis of the Second Amendment, concludes that "the syntax of the proposition that makes up the Second Amendment necessitates the construction that the right to keep and bear arms is absolute and is not dependent on the needs of the militia; the contrary view . . . commits the fallacy of denying the antecedent and is therefore a misconstruction."[34]

The Subcommittee on the Constitution of the United States Senate Judiciary Committee has stated "that the second amendment to our Constitution was intended as an individual right of the American citizen to keep and carry arms in a peaceful manner, for the protection of himself, his family, and freedoms."[35]

And so the argument goes on. Yet, of the at least 37 law review articles published on the subject since 1980, 32 appear to endorse the individual right to bear arms interpretation. The scholarly literature on the subject has now become substantial and compelling, even though it remains controversial.[36]

Is There a Need for Gun Control?

If there is one point in the gun control debate about which opponents are most likely to agree, it is this: There is too much violent crime in the United States, and guns too often are involved in such crimes. One statistic that illustrates the problem posed by guns is the nation's murder rate. In 1993, the most recent year for which national data are available, 23,271 Americans were murdered. Of that number, 16,189, or 69.6 percent, were killed by guns.[37] On average, one man, woman, or child is killed or wounded by a gun every 32.5 minutes in the United States.

Likewise, Americans use guns to a major extent in other kinds of violent crime. By violent crime, the U.S. Department of Justice means murder, forcible rape, robbery, and aggravated assault. In 1993, for example, 1,135,099 cases of aggravated assault were reported in the United States. Of this number, 284,910, or 25.1 percent, involved the use of some kind of firearm.[38]

Guns are also widely used in suicides. In 1991, for example, guns were involved in 18,526 suicides.[39] The trend in suicide cases, especially among certain groups, is even more disturbing. In the two decades preceding 1980, the percentage of suicides by children using guns increased by 299 percent, in comparison with an increase of 175 percent by other means. Comparable figures for women and non-whites were 116 percent compared to 16 percent and 160 percent to 88 percent, respectively.[40]

Guns are an especially serious cause of death and injury among children and teenagers. In 1992, 1,468 young people were killed by handguns. Although statistical data are not available, authorities believe that the number of youth injured by guns may be about a hundred times the number killed.[41] Every measure of gun use by teenagers and injuries involved has increased rapidly over the past decade. For example, the number of 10- to 17-year-olds who used a firearm to commit murder increased by 79 percent during the 1980s. In the 1990s, firearms became the first or second most common cause of death among every category of teenagers.[42] Included in this statistic is the number of teenagers who now commit suicide using a gun. According to one source, on an average, a teenager commits suicide in the United States every three hours.[43]

Proponents and opponents of gun control may acknowledge these statistics, but they then part company as to what these numbers mean and how they relate to gun control. Those who support gun control claim that the most certain way to reduce gun-related crime is to make the ownership of firearms more difficult. If fewer guns are in circulation, they are less likely to be used in the commission of a crime.

A familiar statement of this position was offered before the Senate Subcommittee on Criminal Law in 1982 by David J.

Steinberg, acting chairman of the National Council for a Responsible Firearms Policy. Steinberg first admitted that "if all handguns disappeared from the face of America at the stroke of midnight tonight and no more were ever manufactured anywhere in the world, there would still be a lot of gun-related violence in America." But, Steinberg went on to say, "Now, additional or strict gun control is not the alpha and omega of the answer that needs to be found to firearms-related violence. But it is indispensable to the answer that urgently needs to be found."[44] In other words, no matter what additional measures are taken to reduce violent crime, Steinberg believes (and most gun control advocates believe) that limitations on gun ownership are essential if the problem of gun-related violence is to be solved.

Supporters of gun control also point to the impulsive nature of many violent crimes. According to FBI statistics, about two-thirds of all killings take place between friends and acquaintances. If guns were not so readily available, many of these crimes could be avoided.

Gun control opponents interpret the statistics of violent crime differently. Enough laws already exist, they say, to prosecute and convict people who commit violent crime, whether they use guns or not. What is needed is not limitations on the ownership of firearms, but more vigorous prosecution of criminals.

As an example, those opposed to gun controls point to the period between 1937 and 1963 when gun ownership in the United States increased by about 250 percent. During that same period, however, the number of homicides, adjusted for population, decreased by 35.7 percent. If the pro-control argument were correct, opponents say, the number of homicides should have increased, and by a dramatic number, during this period.

The anti-control position was stated forcefully in March of 1982 by Neal Knox, executive director of the Institute for Legislative Action of the National Rifle Association in testimony before the Senate Subcommittee on Criminal Law. Knox said that

> gun laws fail because they do not address the issue. The issue is not possession of firearms, but misuse of firearms. We cannot expect criminals to abide by gun laws, when they have already shown a disregard to law and order by their criminal activity. The only people ever affected by gun laws are peaceful, law-abiding citizens, who never abuse their firearms right.[45]

Types of Firearms

An important consideration in the gun control debate is the distinction among various types of firearms. In a general sense, firearms can be divided into three major categories: (1) handguns, (2) long guns, and (3) automatic and semiautomatic weapons. The term *handgun* refers to any weapon that can be held with one hand. Pistols and revolvers are two kinds of handguns. Long guns are weapons that require two hands to hold. Rifles and shotguns are examples of long guns. Automatic weapons are guns that fire more than one shot with a single pull of the trigger; semiautomatic weapons fire one shot with each pull of the trigger without reloading or manually inserting another round into the firing chamber. Such weapons have been most commonly associated with military use.

In most instances, gun control advocates do not concern themselves with limitations on long guns. Such guns are used only rarely in violent crime or as suicide weapons. In 1993, for example, handguns were used in 81.9 percent of all homicides, long guns in 11.2 percent, and other types of guns in the remaining 6.9 percent of cases. These statistics are particularly striking because only about one quarter of all guns in the United States are handguns. Thus, a quarter of the guns in the country account for more than three-quarters of all homicides. These data explain why for many years the gun control effort was really an effort to control *handguns*.

A long-time target of gun control advocates is the "Saturday Night Special." Although there is no precise definition, a Saturday Night Special is usually regarded as a handgun with a barrel no longer than 3 inches, of .32 caliber or less, and for sale at less than $50. Gun control supporters argue that Saturday Night Specials have virtually no legal uses. They claim that the barrel is too short to be used for hunting and that the metal used in the gun is so cheap that it wears out too quickly for use in target practice. Also, the weapon fires such a low-velocity bullet and is often so inaccurate that it makes a poor defensive weapon. Thus gun control advocates argue that Saturday Night Specials have few legitimate uses.

Nearly every proponent of gun control makes special mention of the problems presented by Saturday Night Specials. For example, in an article for the *National Black Law Journal,* University of Pittsburgh School of Law Professor Robert Berkley Harper has written that cheap handguns, commonly categorized as a "Saturday night special" should be banned altogether. This would deny many people access to a common source of an instrument of violence, the most common weapon obtained and found in the streets of our community.[46]

The focus of gun control advocates has begun to shift somewhat over the last two decades, however, as military-type semiautomatic weapons have become more generally available in the United States. A few dramatic and widely publicized instances in which such weapons were used in mass murders have brought them to public attention. In January 1989, for example, an unemployed welder named Patrick Edward Purdy opened fire on a schoolyard full of children in Stockton, California. His weapon was a semiautomatic version of the AK-47, a military assault rifle.

Purdy's actions brought forth widespread demand for stiffer controls on semiautomatic weapons, particularly those of military types. Critics argue that these weapons have few legitimate uses. The notion that an AK-47 might be used by deer-hunters, for example, has frequently been the target of newspaper cartoonists. Maintaining that law-abiding citizens have no reason to own such powerful weapons, gun control advocates have argued that they should not be available for sale under any circumstances in the United States.

And it is in the context of military-type, semiautomatic weapons that gun control efforts have, perhaps, been most successful. Shortly after the Stockton murders, for example, the California legislature banned the manufacture, sale, or unlicensed possession of 56 military-type weapons. On a national level, President George Bush placed a ban on the importation of certain kinds of semiautomatic weapons, although he did not extend that ban to the production, sale, or ownership of domestic models.

Opponents of restrictions on semiautomatic guns—or any other kind of firearm—have a number of objections to legislation such as that adopted in California. In the first place, they point out that semiautomatic weapons have been around for nearly a century, since the Winchester Repeating Arms Company produced the first semiautomatic rifle in 1903. The current uproar about such weapons, they argue, is substantially the result of overwhelming media attention. Relatively few incidents, such as the Purdy case, have focused an inordinate amount of attention on weapons that, in fact, are used infrequently in the commission of violent crimes.

It is argued further that it is inappropriate and even dangerous to classify some firearms as "good" and some as "bad." It is not the weapon that causes the problem, but the way in which the weapon is used. If one can justify the banning of semiautomatic weapons, how long will it be before shotguns and rifles and other kinds of firearms are also banned. According to this "slippery slope" argument, restrictions on *any* kind of firearm clears the way for restrictions on *all* kinds of firearms. As writer Wayne R. Austerman has said,

> If the banners truly want to eliminate all guns capable of rapid-fire or the discharge of multiple projectiles in quick succession, then they will ultimately have to move against all revolvers, all shotguns, and all lever- and bolt-action magazine-fed rifles. . . . The end result of this campaign for public safety would likely be the prohibition of all firearms except muzzleloaders and single-shot breech-loading hand and shoulder guns.[47]

Public Support for Gun Control Legislation

In general, gun control advocates appear to be reflecting the mood of the American public. In survey after survey, respondents strongly oppose governmental attempts to *ban* gun ownership. At the same time, however, they tend to strongly support attempts to *limit* gun ownership. Depending on the way questions are asked, the percentage of respondents favoring gun laws varies, but that percentage almost always represents a majority of those surveyed.

Furthermore, recent trends seem to suggest an increase in popular support both for banning handguns and for imposing other types of sanctions on gun ownership. Between 1980 and 1991, for example, the Gallup Poll found that "should" responses increased from 31 percent to 43 percent to the question, "Do you think there should or should not be a law that would ban the possession of handguns except by the police and other authorized persons?"[48]

During the same period, Gallup respondents consistently expressed the feeling that gun laws needed to be made more severe. In response to the question, "In general, do you feel that the laws covering the sale of firearms should be made more strict, less strict, or kept as they are now?" the "more strict" response was consistently given by about 70 percent of all respondents (69 percent in 1975, 59 percent in 1980, 78 percent in 1990, and 68 percent in 1991).[49]

During the same time period, support for registration of handguns was increasing. In response to the Gallup question, "Would you favor or oppose the registration of all handguns?," favorable responses increased from 66 percent in 1982 to 80 percent in 1991.[50]

Support for handgun legislation appears to be widespread, with every demographic group within society approving of such laws. In the 1991 Gallup survey on this question, for example, 78 percent of all men and 84 percent of all women surveyed agreed with legislation that would require registration of all handguns (except for those held by law enforcement officers and other authorized individuals). Comparable patterns can be seen across age groups (18–29 years: 85 percent support; 30–49 years: 82 percent support; and 50 & older: 75 percent support), race (white: 81 percent support; black: 78 percent support), education (college graduates: 89 percent support; high school graduates: 82 percent support; and non–high school graduates: 66 percent support), political stance (Republican: 80 percent support; Democrat: 85 percent support), ideology (liberal: 89 percent support; conservative: 80 percent support), and religion (Protestant: 80 percent support; Catholic: 86 percent support; none: 66 percent support).[51]

There is evidence that many gun owners also support some types of limitations on gun ownership. In a 1990 survey commissioned by *Time* magazine, for example, 87 percent of all gun owners interviewed favored a federal law requiring a seven-day waiting period and background check for anyone wanting to purchase a handgun. At least half of those respondents also favored mandatory registration of rifles (54 percent of those asked), shotguns (50 percent), handguns (72 percent), and semiautomatic weapons (73 percent).[52] These data correspond to results reported by the Gallup Poll in 1991. In that year, 22 percent of all gun owners favored a ban on civilian handguns (compared to 58 percent for non–gun owners), and 81 percent favored gun registration (compared to 78 percent of non–gun owners).

How Effective Are Gun Control Laws?

One of the most controversial issues in the debate over gun control laws is how effectively such laws work. Many studies have attempted to answer this question, but with inconsistent results.

Some studies report that gun laws result in a reduction of gun-related violent crime, while others show that such crime continues to increase even where strict laws are in effect.

For example, a team of researchers from the universities of British Columbia, Tennessee, and Washington, under the direction of Dr. John H. Sloan, conducted one of the most famous studies on the effects of gun legislation. Sloan's researchers studied crime rates in two nearby cities, Seattle, Washington, and Vancouver, British Columbia. The two cities were chosen because they are geographically close to each other and are similar in a number of other respects, such as population size and demographic composition. The two cities differ, however, on the issue of gun regulation. Vancouver has very strict gun control laws; Seattle has lenient laws.

The Sloan team reported that during a two-year period from 1987 to 1988, 139 handgun-related homicides were reported in Seattle with a 36 percent rate of death by handguns. In Vancouver, 25 out of 204 homicides, a rate of 12 percent, were caused by handguns. Sloan's research team concluded that a Seattle resident was 1.6 times more likely to be murdered by a handgun than was a resident of Vancouver. [53]

Opponents of gun control have raised questions about the accuracy of Dr. Sloan's research. They argue that saying that the major difference between Seattle and Vancouver is the presence or absence of gun laws is gross oversimplification. In fact, they say, the two cities are different in a number of important ways. Dr. Sloan's research is, therefore, seriously flawed, they argue, and any results it produced are highly suspect. The strongest criticism of the Sloan research has probably come from Dr. Paul H. Blackman, director of research for the National Rifle Association. "There is nothing in the [Sloan] paper," Dr. Blackman has written, "that could possibly be mistaken for scientific methods by a sociologist or criminologist." [54]

Gun control organizations often point to cities and states where strict laws have been enacted to show how effective such laws can be in reducing crime. In its brochure *20 Questions and Answers*, for example, the Coalition to Stop Gun Violence argues that handgun control laws now in existence do, in fact, work. The brochure claims that "within three years of the passage of the Washington, D.C., law banning the sale of handguns, the murder rate in the District dropped 25 percent. In Boston, after two years under Massachusetts' Bartley-Fox law, homicides declined 39 percent. And in South Carolina, after handgun laws were tightened in 1975, the murder rate fell 28 percent. In each case the reduction in the handgun murder rate was even more dramatic."[55]

However, gun laws are another area in which people on opposite sides of the gun control issue can look at the same facts and come to different conclusions. With regard to the Washington gun law, for example, opponents of gun control claim that violent crime rose by 43 percent between 1976, the year before the law was adopted) and 1982. During the same period, they say that the murder rate rose by 14 percent in the District of Columbia.[56]

Similar points are made about the Massachusetts Bartley-Fox law. In the first place, control opponents say, the law really had nothing to do with gun control, but instead dealt with more severe penalties for people who used guns in the commission of a crime. In any case, they go on to say, the crime rate in Boston was very different from the rate in the rest of Massachusetts, where violent crime continued to increase under the Bartley-Fox law. Finally, although the number of murders in Boston decreased during the period in question, the number of other violent crimes committed with a gun did not.[57]

The question of gun-law effectiveness is one of the most controversial and convoluted within the general issue of gun control. Spokespersons on both sides of the issue often raise the examples of Morton Grove, Illinois, and Kennesaw, Georgia, where handguns were, in the first case, banned and, in the second case, required in every household. In fact, crime was never a serious problem in either community, nor did either community make much of an effort to enforce their laws once they were adopted. Thus, it is difficult to know how to interpret such statistics as the drop in the number of rapes in Kennesaw from three to zero and the number of homicides from one to zero in the year following adoption of the town's gun ordinance.[58]

In contrast, gun control proponents often use examples from around the world to show how effective legislation can be in reducing violent crime. A common comparison is drawn with England, a nation with whom the United States shares a long cultural tradition. Handgun ownership is severely limited in England. Traditionally, police officers have not even carried weapons. In 1983, 8 people in all of Great Britain were murdered with handguns compared to 8,092 Americans who were killed in the same way that year. Adjusting for differences in population, a British subject was 202 times less likely to be killed by a handgun than was an American.

Gun control advocates also point to Japan as an example of the effectiveness of strong gun control legislation. In that country, handguns were used in 209 crimes in 1985, 46 resulting in a person's death. Approximately two-thirds of those crimes were attributed to the *boryokudan*, organized crime groups. The handgun crime rate in Japan in 1985 was, therefore, 0.038 homicides per 100,000 citizens. In the United States, that rate was 3.14 per 100,000 citizens. The difference in these rates, according to some observers, is the very strict policy of the Japanese government regarding gun ownership. No civilian may own a handgun, and only hunters and target shooters who have passed severe exams are allowed to purchase rifles.

Critics of gun control legislation point to a number of flaws in the preceding argument. In the first place, they say, comparisons between cultures as different as that of the United States and Japan can be very deceiving. While it may be true that the rate of violent crime in Japan is low, one author has written, the reason is that Japanese people operate under severe controls in all parts of their lives. "Japan's low crime rate has almost nothing to do with gun control and everything to do with people control," he has written. The nation may be a "gun-banner's dream," he says, but it is also "a civil libertarian's nightmare."[59]

International comparisons also depend, gun control opponents say, on the nation selected for comparison. Gun control legislation in both Australia and Jamaica, for example, has been a complete failure; violent crime has not decreased in either nation, according to some writers.[60] Even the comparison between the United States and England is open to question. After all, gun control opponents point out, the rate of armed robberies in England involving the use of handguns increased by 700 percent between 1974 and 1986, at a time when the comparable rate in the United States was decreasing by 17 percent.[61]

Race, Ethnicity, and Gun Control Policy

Opponents of gun control raise a number of arguments in their favor. One of them is that gun control contributes toward the suppression of minorities.

Some scholars suggest that gun control policy in many parts of the world has served the purpose of suppressing "undesirable" minorities or cultures and even of committing genocide against them. Indeed, in each of the at least seven major genocides perpetrated during the twentieth century, government gun control laws have impaired racial, ethnic, or other minority groups from protecting themselves against destruction or virtual elimination. One is reminded of the Holocaust in Nazi Germany as one of the most blatant of these genocidal efforts, but there have been others; for example, under the Ottoman Turkish Penal Code, the Soviet Criminal Code, the Chinese Criminal Code, the Cambodian Penal Code, as well as those in Guatemala and, very recently, efforts in such places as the former Yugoslavia and Rwanda. Although the assertion is, of course, controversial, one observer has pointed out that

> gun control leads to genocide. This is strongly evidenced . . . by the circumstances of the major genocides committed in this century in which an estimated total of some 50 to 60 million people have perished. Other genocides are probably in progress today, in Europe and Africa, and these also are made possible by government gun control.[62]

With respect to the United States, evidence suggests that gun control policy has had, among other objectives, the intent of keeping blacks—and especially poor Southern blacks—in a condition of defenselessness (although in the increasingly large literature on gun control in the United States, this type of discussion has been comparatively neglected). This oppressive aspect of anti-gun policy has applied not only to blacks; it has also been applied to other racial minorities, ethnic groups (especially Italians), Native Americans, some immigrants, and those who have been engaged in labor union and agrarian reform movements at one time or another.

It is known, for example, that the "slave codes" prohibited, with some narrow exceptions, both slaves and those blacks who were free, from owning guns. In the antebellum South, moreover, these laws re-emerged as "black codes" and once again subjected blacks to a status of relative defenselessness. The Supreme Court itself upheld denying guns to blacks on the basis that they were not citizens. Perhaps one of the best examples of this is found in the case of *Dred Scott v. Sanford* (60 U.S., 19 How.), decided in 1856. Chief Justice Taney declared that if free blacks were to be regarded as citizens, "it would give to persons of the negro race . . . the right to enter every other State whenever they pleased, . . . full liberty of speech in public and in private upon all subjects upon which its own citizens might speak; to hold public meetings upon political affairs, and to keep and carry arms wherever they went." The passage of the Civil Rights Act of 1866 and the Fourteenth Amendment likewise did not prevent Southern states from keeping guns out of the hands of blacks. The states simply banned particular types of weapons, specifically inexpensive handguns, which were the only types of guns poor blacks could afford to buy. And, even with the passage of the Fifteenth Amendment to the Constitution of the United States, Southern states were able to deny blacks the right to have arms by making available to them in this instance only the most expensive weapons— weapons that most blacks could not afford to purchase. Thus the Southern states had it both ways: they legally banned cheap handguns and gave the freed negroes the right to buy expensive weapons that they could not purchase because of their high price. Heavy taxes on sales were also imposed. In the context of the 1980s and 1990s, the attempts to ban cheap weapons—sometimes referred to as "Saturday Night Specials"—continues effectively to disarm a segment of society that arguably most needs firearms as a means of self-protection. It is of interest to note that "[t]he term *Saturday Night Special* itself has a racist origin, rooted as it is in the Southern elite's derogatory descriptions of the revelry on a "Nigger-Town Saturday Night."[63]

Thus,

> [the Second Amendment] . . . poses important questions about social stratification, cultural bias, and constitutional interpretation. Do courts really protect rights explicit or implicit in the Constitution, or is the courts' interpretation of rights largely a dialogue with the elite, articulate sectors of society, with the courts enforcing those rights favored by dominant elites and ignoring those not so favored?
>
> Many of the issues surrounding the Second Amendment debate are raised in particularly sharp relief from the perspective of African-American history. With the exception of Native Americans, no people in American history have been more influenced by violence than blacks.[64]

Justice Buford declared in his concurring opinion construing a Florida gun control law: "I know something of the history of this legislation. The original Act of 1893 was passed when there was a great influx of negro laborers in this State drawn here for the purpose of working in turpentine and lumber camps. The same condition existed when the Act was amended in 1901 and the Act was passed for the purpose of disarming the negro laborers."[65] He went on to say that there was never ". . . within my knowledge, any effort to enforce the provisions of this statute as to white people, because it has been generally conceded to be in contravention of the Constitution and non-enforceable if contested."[66]

Under such an interpretation, blacks obviously could not fully exercise their rights of citizenship. As indicated above, even free blacks were denied the right to keep arms. As early as 1640 "the first recorded restrictive legislation passed concerning blacks in Virginia excluded them from owning a gun."[67] Similar practices occurred in North Carolina, South Carolina, and Mississippi, for example.

In the North, gun laws passed between 1901 and 1934 appear to have been especially severe in reaction to black civil rights efforts, union organization movements, and to the activities of various other social and political agitators.[68] Xenophobic reactions to foreign immigrants were nothing particularly new in the United States, but during the period between the 1870s and the 1930s, fear of anarchism and violence was focused especially on immigrants from eastern and southern Europe. These "undesirables" were the object of particular concern on the part of the Immigration Protective League and the American Protective Association, as well as some business groups, which advocated the banning of guns—especially handguns—to aliens. In New York City, for example, the police vigorously attempted to disarm the Italian population and, as two authorities have argued, the passage of the Sullivan Law was aimed in part at continuing the effort to make it illegal for aliens to have guns "in any public place."[69] Today, comparatively few gun permits are issued to blacks, persons of low income, and to minorities in general.

Gun control has also been forced upon Native Americans. The taking of Indians' guns was often accompanied by other oppressive measures and, indeed, some have argued that there was at one time in American history a possibly overt attempt to exterminate them as a people. It was not until 1979 that the national government actually lifted its restrictions on the sale of guns to Native Americans. American gun control policy has frequently been based upon prejudices that assume that certain minorities and the poor should be denied the ownership and use of guns because they are allegedly more likely to commit crimes with them if they have them in their possession. Even some anti-gun advocates recognize this point.[70]

In America's British colonies, white males were likewise viewed as constituting those who should be armed in order to provide protection against the potential dangers posed by indigent groups. Although laws regarding arms in early America varied from colony to colony—for example, Virginia required extending arms to white men at public expense and denied to blacks the right to carry weapons ranging from simple clubs to firearms, while Massachusetts prohibited blacks from participating in militia exercises—the overall intention of such laws was essentially to maintain white domination over the ownership and use of firearms.

Some observers assert that residues of this policy remain today in many states and among some police departments. Thus, some law-abiding blacks and others who reside in minority communities throughout the United States and who are disproportionately the victims of crime, and especially of violent crime, are often denied the right to own guns even though they might benefit most from such ownership for purposes of self-protection against the violence they face in their communities on a regular basis. As several scholarly observers have pointed out,

> Two gun-control methods more or less try this approach (that banning guns will control crime). One is New York City's stringent permit law, which dates back to 1911. All New Yorkers need a permit for a handgun on their own premises and a permit to carry a gun wherever they go. One would think that there would be far fewer "carry permits" than "premises permits," but one would be wrong. According to [Don B.] Kates, there are only about 3,000 premises permits in New York, and 25,000 carry permits. Street corner grocers have a harder time getting a gun permit than do upper class whites.
>
> Another gun law that works more against poor people than against criminals is the campaign, waged with varying success in Richmond, Va., Portland, Ore., and Chicago, Ill., to ban guns from public-housing projects. This is a straight-up disarming of the poor. It goes hand-in-hand with the more disturbing proposals . . . to cordon off some housing projects and establish checkpoints to stop and search those going in and out of the neighborhood. Such authoritarianism in the name of security is social engineering with a vengeance.[71]

Cottrol and Diamond argue that

> The history of blacks, firearms regulations, and [the] right to bear arms should cause us to ask new questions regarding the Second Amendment. These questions will pose problems both for advocates of stricter gun controls and for those who argue against them. Much of the contemporary crime that concerns Americans is in poor black neighborhoods and a case can be made that greater firearms restrictions might alleviate this tragedy. But another, perhaps stronger case can be made that a society with a dismal record of protecting a people has a dubious claim on the right to disarm them. Perhaps a re-examination of this history can lead us to a modern realization of what the framers of the Second Amendment understood: that it is unwise to place the means of protection totally in the hands of the state, and that self-defense is also a civil right.[72]

And Tahmassebi writes: "By prohibiting the possession of firearms, the state discriminates against minority and poor citizens. In the final analysis, citizens must protect themselves and their families and homes."[73]

Black supporters of gun control do not disagree with this analysis. There is no question that gun control in the United States was long used as a means of keeping blacks in a subservient position. But, according to those who favor gun control, one must also consider the situation in which blacks find themselves today. After all, the major threat to most black lives today is no longer the Ku Klux Klan or other bigoted members of the white community, but blacks themselves. In 1994, for example, firearms were the leading cause of death among black males in the age group 15–34 and among black females in the age group 15–29. And in the majority of those homicides, the perpetrator of the crime was also black. As Professor Robert Berkley Harper, of the University of Pittsburgh's School of Law, has written, "Black violence directed against blacks [is] thus in many ways accomplishing what the Klan could not accomplish."[74] Solving the problem of black-on-black crime will be a complex challenge, Harper suggests, but one basic element in that solution will have to be the imposition of some kind of limitations on gun ownership.

Gender and Gun Control Policy

Opponents of gun control argue that gun ownership by women is a deterrent to crimes against women. Gun control laws, they maintain, hinder efforts by law-abiding women to protect themselves.

Women, who have been shown as a group to be particularly vulnerable to violence in American society, are often defenseless against their attackers. Hundreds of thousands of women are raped—or barely escape being raped—every year in the United States. Close to 2 million women are assaulted every year, and hundreds of thousands are robbed. As one author has pointed out, "If you are over the age of twelve and female, be prepared to be criminally assaulted some time in your life. If you are about thirty years old now, there's a fifty-fifty chance of your being raped, robbed, or attacked."[75]

Like all other Americans, women have the right to be secure from personal attack. Yet, evidence suggests that both police and courts are not capable of fully protecting people in general against crime (and it should be noted that the police have in fact no legal obligation to protect individual citizens against crime and violence), let alone protecting women from the offenses perpetrated specifically against them. The courts have ruled that the police cannot be sued for negligence if they do not respond to calls for assistance. Two celebrated examples may serve as illustrations of this point.

In Washington, D.C., three women were raped, assaulted, robbed, beaten, and sodomized. Even after they had called the police, in one instance the officers left when they received no answer at the door, and in the second instance they did not arrive at all. When the women sued the District of Columbia police, they lost their case, the Court of Appeals judges finding that "the District of Columbia appears to follow the well-established rule that official police personnel and the government employing them are not generally liable to victims of criminal acts for failure to provide adequate police protection . . . this uniformly accepted rule rests upon the fundamental principle that a government and its agents are under no general duty to provide public services, such as police protection, to any particular individual citizen." But the court did offer its "sympathy" to the "tragic victims."[76]

A second example involves the New York Transit Authority, which was sued for not attempting to correct conditions in its subways—conditions that presented dangers to train riders. A woman had been raped in a subway station that had frequently been the scene of similar acts, and a school board official had been robbed and injured by assailants using knives in a place where 13 separate robberies—most of them involving knives wielded by the assailants—had occurred in less than a year. But the relevant court held the Transit Authority free from liability because it was of the same genre as any other municipality or agency of the government. It had no obligation to protect persons on its premises nor did it have to increase the level of protection for its passengers.[77] (It is of interest to note that the principle that police have no legal duty to protect individuals evolves out of the fact that, historically, there were no police in the United States—indeed, police are an "invention" of the mid-19th century—and that citizens were expected to defend themselves. Police were feared as much as standing armies. But, given that people were increasingly unwilling or incapable of dealing with all of the crime in their environment, police came into being as a way of augmenting citizen forces. But no one thought seriously at the time of doing away with the citizen's right of self-defense).

And, of course, the examples of *non*-intervention by private citizens when women—or, for that matter, men as well—are being attacked in situations where others might come to their assistance have been widely documented. Most people do not wish to become involved. What, then, is a woman in particular to do in the face of potential attack against her person?

Many suggestions have been made. For example, there is the suggestion that use be made of such products as mace as a deterrent, but use of this type of defensive device is not necessarily effective because it has been demonstrated that assailants are often capable of receiving the spray directly in the face and still continuing their attack. Moreover, what if the assailant is wearing glasses, and the victim has attempted to hit him or her in the eyes? If the assailant has been consuming large amounts of alcohol, the probability of successful deterrence by the substance is decreased because of the possibility that the blood alcohol level will create a chemical reaction that negates the potential effectiveness of the spray.

Others have suggested training in, and the use of, the so-called martial arts. One does not learn these self-protection measures in a short time, however, and if one's attacker has a lethal weapon or is simply "bigger," this alternative may not prove to be at all effective.

Still others have suggested use of various alarm systems that are designed to give off shrieking sounds or other types of warning signals to alert others of an attack with the expectation that nearby persons will come to the victim's assistance. Although this method of deterrence is interesting from a theoretical point of view, one could argue that the likelihood that someone will respond to the sound of such an alarm with the intention of giving aid to a person being victimized is remote at best.

In short, the entire matter of the utility and effectiveness of these and other self-protection devices cries out for greater empirical inquiry. Conclusive evidence relevant to their impact on deterrence from attack remains to be summarized.

The discussion of the right to keep and bear arms once again becomes relevant.

Although the number of cases that might be cited can be multiplied thousands of times, a specific example can be given of a San Francisco woman who was being terrorized by one of her male neighbors. The woman had been verbally abused, and the male had twice broken into her apartment, making bizarre accusations against her. The woman duly reported the events to the police, who did nothing more than file written reports. She obtained a restraining order and sought assistance from social workers and from the physician who was treating the intruder. The physician suggested that the woman protect herself "at all costs."

She therefore purchased a gun. She has been quoted as stating "I have asked for intervention," citing the fact that she had contacted police, the social workers, the landlord of her apartment complex, the man's physician, and even the courts. "I've done everything a responsible person can do. Enough is enough. From now on what I am doing is for me. If he steps into my house, I will shoot. I'll probably warn him first, but I will shoot him before he kills me, because he is a threat to my life."[78]

The woman's shooting coach notes that her "clients have changed from exclusively men to mostly women." She has been quoted further as stating that "a lot of women come to me with a feeling of total powerlessness . . . and I'm trying to empower them. . . . A gun is just a tool—it gives the edge to a smaller person."[79] Paxton Quigley is a former advocate of strict gun control who, after watching the increase in crime over the past 20 years even after enactment of further gun control laws, states in the same article, "Criminals understand the power of a gun. . . . If more women understood the power of a gun, there would be less rape. Police, courts and prisons can't protect women. We have to do it ourselves."[80]

That individuals who possess guns in their homes feel safer as a result has been widely confirmed by public opinion surveys.

"A 1990 national survey indicated that nearly all defensive gun owners feel safer because they have a gun. Among persons whose primary reason for owning a gun was self-defense, 89% replied 'yes' to the question: 'Do you feel safer because you have a gun at home?'" Previous surveys have reached the same conclusion.[81] And it has been found that "rape victims using armed resistance were less likely to have the rape attempt completed against them than victims using any other mode of resistance."[82] "In view of the robbery and assault findings indicating that gun resistance is generally more effective than armed resistance using other weapons, it would seem to be a reasonable inference that the same would be true for rape."[83] Indeed, in Orlando, Florida, for example, after a police program that trained over 2,000 women to use guns, "the rape rate decreased by 88% in 1967, compared to 1966, a decrease far larger than in any previous one-year period. The rape rate remained constant in the rest of Florida and in the United States."[84]

Specific figures as to the precise number of women in the United States who own firearms are not readily available. On the basis of public opinion surveys, however, it can be stated that the number of women who own guns has greatly increased, particularly since attempts have been made to ban or limit the sale of certain types of weapons. According to Quigley, "The National Research Opinion Center claims that 44 percent of adult women own or have access to firearms. That's forty-two million, and of those, Dr. Paul H. Blackman, research coordinator for the Institute for Legislative Action of the National Rifle Association, estimates that twenty-two million own their own guns."[85] Moreover, "more than 50 percent of the 104,000 women who responded to a March 1987 *Ladies' Home Journal* survey say they have guns in their homes, with 40 percent of them reporting that the firearms are owned strictly for protection."[86]

The best evidence available seems to suggest that a gun may be a significant deterrent to attack. Gary Kleck and Don B. Kates—both leading constitutionalists and criminologists—have suggested that would-be attackers and criminals have been driven off by women who wielded a gun.[87] And James D. Wright and Peter H. Rossi, authors of a leading and path-breaking volume on guns, crime, and violence in the United States,[88] have, in a more recent study, concluded that women who are armed are probably more likely to prevent rapes, assaults, and robberies against themselves than if they were not armed.[89]

In any event, "the threat of assault against women continues at an alarming rate; law enforcement is virtually incapable of preventing such assault; and women are arming themselves in self-defense."[90]

Self-Defense in General, Gun Ownership, and Gun Control Policy

Given the very real fear of crime that many women in the United States feel today, the argument for gun ownership has a power-ful appeal. There are risks, however, associated with owning a gun as a means of self-defense. A woman (or a man) who keeps a gun in the house for purposes of self-defense is actually more likely to injure herself, her family, or a friend than she is to ward off an attacker. The issue of gun ownership among women is, therefore, imbedded in the more general question of how effec-tive personal firearms are in protecting oneself against crimes against one's person or property.

Some groups, such as the National Rifle Association, insist that personal gun ownership for purposes of self-defense can be highly effective. Others, such as Handgun Control, Incorporated, contend that there should be limitations on the availability of handguns and bans on certain other types of weapons because such weapons allegedly cause more injury than they prevent. In addition, a number of other issues are often raised in connection with this point. For example, what are the moral and ethical is-sues involved in possession of a gun for personal defense? (The framers of the Constitution, for example, were of the opinion that the right to keep and bear arms for self-defense was a moral duty). How are we to address factors related to safety in the household, for example, accidental discharge and the resulting consequences or shootings during times of passion? What are some of the psychological implications of personal gun owner-ship with respect to the notion of self-defense?

Obviously, ownership of a gun does not in itself *assure* one of personal security. Placing a gun in a hiding place is one's home may very well cause a sense of security—but it might in fact be a *false* sense of security. Unless the owner of the weapon is able to use it in a proper way (the operation of some guns requires relatively com-plex knowledge) or, unless the owner can use it defensively from a psychological point of view (i.e., can one, in fact, readily kill or maim someone else, even under dire circumstances?), the mere presence of a gun in the home might not provide the type of self-protection that is desired.

A number of studies have pointed out the risks of keeping a firearm in the home for self-defense. One study of gun-related deaths in King County, Washington, between 1978 and 1983 found that gun owners, their friends, and family were more likely to be the victims of gun-related violence than were criminals. The study authors reported that

> for every case of self-protection homicide involving a firearm kept in the home, there were 1.3 accidental deaths, 4.6 criminal homicides, and 37 suicides involving firearms. . . . Even after excluding suicide deaths, guns in the home were involved in the death of a household member 18 times more often than in the death of a stranger.[91]

Gun accidents are also a matter of concern. Each year, about 14,000 people are killed in accidents involving the use of guns.[92] Comparable statistics for accidental gun injuries are not available, but some experts claim that as many as 183,000 times a year people are injured in such accidents.[93]

Relatively little research has been done on the number and types of accidental injuries relating to gun use. Perhaps the most famous study was carried out in Cleveland between 1967 and 1973. That study showed that a gun kept in a person's home was six times more likely to cause an accident than to be used against an intruder. In summarizing the results of their study, investigators concluded "that a loaded firearm in the home is more likely to cause an accidental death than to be used as a lethal weapon against an intruder."[94]

Still, accidents resulting from the use of motor vehicles and, indeed, even from the use of swimming pools, far exceed those caused by accidental discharge of firearms. As is often the case with statistics, they can be used and interpreted in different ways by different people.

Opponents of gun control argue that, in the event of a confrontation with an intruder in one's home, police encourage the victim to either flee the premises or call for assistance from a relatively safe place inside the house rather than attempt to deal violently with the assailant, yet police often take considerable time to respond (if they are able to respond at all), and if the telephone wires have been cut, one can hardly make a telephone call to summon help.

Studies by the U. S. Department of Justice and by careful scholars such as Gary Kleck are used to underscore this point. Kleck indicates that persons using guns to protect themselves have been shown to be at lower risk of being either attacked or injured in robbery or assault situations than persons who use other means of defense or who do not defend themselves at all from their attackers. Kleck states,

> . . . Gun use by private citizens against violent criminals and burglars is common and about as frequent as arrests, is a more prompt negative consequence of crime than legal punishment, and is more severe, at its most serious, than legal system punishments. Victim gun use in crime incidents is associated with lower rates of crime completion and of victim injury than any other defensive response, including doing nothing to resist. Serious predatory criminals say they perceive a risk from victim gun use which is roughly comparable to that of criminal justice system actions, and this perception appears to influence their criminal behavior in socially desirable ways.[95]

The concept of self-defense is a long-standing tradition in both the practice of the common law of England and in the law of the United States. The right to keep and bear arms under the common law evolved during a period when effective police protection did not exist,[96] and efforts at self-protection are today regarded by some as a form of vigilantism, but, gun control opponents argue, the fact remains that even with the existence of organized police protection and the increase in the number of laws dealing with firearms, the crime rate shows little or no evidence of decline and the number of potential and actual citizen victims of crime remains on the rise.

Edward F. Leddy makes the following observation:

> According to a 1985 NBC News survey, about one in twenty (7,500,000) Americans carry a firearm for self-defense. If the fears of anti-gun advocates were of substance this would produce millions of gun murders instead of the total of about five thousand actually committed in the U.S.A. Crimes of any kind committed by citizens having gun licenses are so rare that the police do not even bother to keep statistics. Few murders are

committed by people without prior criminal records. Of course people with criminal histories should not be licensed.[97]

Gun control opponents can cite the similar conclusions of other experts in the field. For example, Kleck, and Bordua state,

> Given the data on private citizens' use of firearms against criminals and evidence on the slight risks of legal punishment associated with most crimes, it is a perfectly plausible hypothesis that private gun ownership currently exerts as much or more deterrent effect on criminals as do the activities of the criminal justice system.[98]

The case of Florida and its enactment of a concealed weapons licensing law on 1 October 1987, is used as a case in point. In March of 1988 a Miami cab driver was accosted, his money taken, and was told by a robber that he was going to be shot. When the robber was about to pull the trigger of his own gun, the fact that he had forgotten to disengage the safety device prevented him from pulling the trigger, and the taxi driver fired and killed the assailant. Among the robber's past exploits were armed robbery arrests, gun violations, and the attempted murder of a police officer. After serving seven years of a twelve-year term in prison, he was released and once again engaged in criminal activity. Although the Florida criminal justice system had failed to keep this violent criminal off the streets, the concealed weapons licensing law enabled the taxi driver to defend himself and to preserve his own life.

In a study conducted by E. Duane Davis and Laura J. Moriarty, the authors found that over one-half of their sample held the opinion that their right to use deadly force against assailants should be broadened. Indeed, nearly 90 percent felt that an attempted murder or rape in particular should be regarded as allowing potential victims to use force, and over 75 percent felt that deadly force might be appropriate to prevent burglaries. Finally, over 50 percent were of the opinion that deadly force was appropriate in robbery and assault situations, and 20 percent felt it was appropriate even in drug-related incidents.[99]

It is necessary to point out that self-defense behavior involves personal responsibility, given the nature of the law in most states and communities. Generally speaking, deadly force may be employed in self-defense only if one is reasonably in fear of imminent bodily harm or death under specific circumstances of the crime being perpetrated. Knowledge of the law is therefore a virtual necessity if one is himself or herself not to suffer from adverse legal results as a consequence of attempted self-defense efforts. Unfortunately, the luxury of consulting a lawyer well-grounded in these matters appears unlikely when an attack on one's person or property is underway.

Police and Gun Control Policy

Police forces in the United States were originally to be un-armed—an emulation of their British counterparts. Instead, the people-at-large were to be armed; they were to own and to have the right to carry weapons in an effort to protect themselves and the community from criminal, political, and military hostility against their freedoms. The assumption was that arms would be used judiciously by all who possessed them, and that the armed citizenry would manifest responsibility in their relationships with others in the community. There was in early America a re-markable faith in citizen loyalty and in citizens' civil and law-abiding treatment of each other.

But as an increasingly hostile environment began to de-velop, law-abiding citizens—either out of disability or disinter-est—became increasingly unwilling to, or incapable of, relying solely on themselves for protection. As Frank T. Morn has stated,

> . . . There is a tantalizing dichotomy in America: Amer-icans are law-abiding people prone to violence. A cer-tain degree of violence and even criminality in America has become permissible as a moral necessity. Many heroes, especially those found in literature and media, are placed in situations in which some form of violence or criminality is condoned.[100]

The public accepted the notion that police should carry guns only reluctantly. Guns in the hands of the police were viewed as a potential means of oppression by another armed element of the government. These fears notwithstanding, by the early 1900s the police forces in the United States were armed, and their arms were then, as they are now, often displayed in a conspicuous manner on their persons.

Given the fact that police officers carry guns and are officially authorized to use them, how do they feel about the matter of gun control? The logical assumption would be that police officers, who out of necessity sometimes have to place themselves in positions of potential danger, would favor the widespread limitation of gun ownership and even the banning of some types of weapons that could prove of particular danger to themselves during the course of the performance of their official duties. Interestingly, the evidence on this issue suggests that police have not unanimously supported strict gun controls and that, in fact, many individual officers and many police professional groups have been supportive of an armed citizenry.

For example, one survey revealed that 83 percent of the members of the Boston Police Department were opposed to a ban on the possession of handguns, and 80 percent supported the right to possess handguns in one's home or business. Fewer than 10 percent held the opinion that the national government should impose legislation in the areas of licensing and registration of guns.[101] Moreover, results of the Crime Control Research Survey that was conducted among police chiefs, county sheriffs, and police officers in general, indicated that if police were "ordinary citizen[s]," over 80 percent of them would own a gun to protect their families and their homes. And over 90 percent of these respondents agreed that if handgun ownership were banned, such weapons would continue to find their way into the hands of criminals throughout the United States. Over 60 percent of them believed that the ownership of guns by private law-abiding citizens helped to deter crime.[102] And in another survey, it was found that over 80 percent of police officers indicated that they did not believe that state and local legislation aimed at controlling guns actually did very much to control crime.[103] Similar attitudes have been expressed in the official statements of the National Sheriffs' Association, the American Federation of Police, and the National Police Officers' Association of America. Each of these organizations has taken the position that law-abiding American citizens should have the right to keep and bear arms for their own protection and for the protection of their homes and families. They have also expressed the opinion that there are already sufficient laws in existence on the subject of gun control, and that many of the laws regulating firearms have been ineffective. In addition, the National Association of Chiefs of Police and the American Federation of Police have endorsed the Firearms Owners Protection Act.[104]

Furthermore, many police departments have advocated the ownership of handguns by citizens for their self-protection and have conducted training sessions to teach private citizens the proper use of such weapons.

This fact notwithstanding, one aspect of the gun control debate which has not often been addressed is the broad philosophical and theoretical issue of disarming, or dearming, the police themselves. As one student of the subject states, "If the police showed leadership in disarming or 'de-arming' themselves, more private citizens, including gun owners, might view firearms as unnecessary in their own lives."[105] Still, one is hard-pressed to find among those who urge the banning or control of handguns and other firearms among private citizens a similar suggestion respecting the possession of such weapons on the part of police officers. Indeed, even in such communities as Morton Grove, Illinois—a village that gained national attention for its banning of handguns—police were exempted from the law's provisions. James B. Jacobs asks, "Why should the police be armed and the general citizenry or various discrete groups of citizens be disarmed? Four plausible reasons are: 1) personal safety; 2) arrest powers; 3) deterrence of crime; and 4) superior training and judgment."[106]

Jacobs addresses each of these points. With respect to the personal safety factor, for example, he points out that if the issue of gun possession involves that of self-defense, then perhaps a case can be made that everyone should possess guns to defend himself, not just police officers. And, he suggests, police might in fact be in no "greater danger than other citizens." Moreover, he points out, police are able to utilize a larger number of alternative means to protect themselves from violence and are more effectively trained in their use against assailants as compared to private citizens.[107] With respect to the power to arrest, Jacobs asks, "Does the authority and responsibility to make arrests support a special claim to carry firearms?"[108] He points out that many police work in environments that actually never require them to use a firearm in situations that involve confronting violent criminals, and that most police probably never use their guns at all. He asserts that "proof is lacking . . . on the extent to which police officers do need handguns in order to take suspects into custody,"[109] and he cites the examples of the British and Japanese police, who rarely use their weapons in the arrest process. He also argues that "a police firearms policy that required a showing of need [on the part of the police officer] before a firearm was issued would reflect a powerful societal commitment to restrict the use of handguns."[110] Finally, he presents as an interesting alternative to that of police "de-arming"—that is, decreasing the firepower of weapons and bullets used by police instead of increasing the power and lethality of the weapons they use.[111]

With respect to the proposition that an armed police force deters crime, he points out that an armed citizenry will probably be as effective—and has been as effective or even more effective—than an armed police force in deterring actual or potential criminals. Finally, with respect to the proposition that police officers receive special training in the use of firearms and are therefore more likely to be more careful and responsible in weapons use than private citizens would be, he suggests that given the often low level of their training upon entry into the police force and the frequent off-duty accidents and shootings on their part, police may not necessarily be more competent than well-trained civilians in the use of weapons. He asks, "If private citizens were willing to submit to the same training as police, and to abide by the same rules (or even more stringent ones) on the use of deadly force, could the police officer still claim to be more reliable in possessing and carrying a handgun than is the private citizen in keeping a handgun at home?"[112] And he concludes by stating, "The best strategy toward handgun disarmament may not be to chip away at peripheral owners, but to change the attitudes, values, and practices of the core ownership group—the police, other law enforcement personnel, and private security forces."[113] Jacobs has raised valid questions relevant to the entire gun debate.

Despite the historical attitudes of law enforcement officials supporting private gun ownership, a significant number of these officials now believe that some form of gun control may be necessary. One factor that has contributed to this attitude has been the spread of powerful weaponry, such as semiautomatic weapons, among the general populace. Peace officers in many jurisdictions now complain that they are out-armed by the very criminals they are attempting to control.

Another factor has been the development of armor-piercing or "cop-killer" bullets. These bullets have the ability to break through the protective clothing that many police officers wear while on duty. Many law enforcement groups broke ranks with the National Rifle Association, which opposed the ban of such bullets, on this issue.

Today, a number of law enforcement organizations have taken stands in support of some form of limitation on gun ownership. In testimony on the Brady Bill in 1989, for example, a representative of the 198,000-member Fraternal Order of Police said that "if the seven-day waiting period will insure just one life—the life of a law enforcement officer or a citizen—then [Congress's] work will be successful. Our prediction is that a 'cooling off' period will save hundreds of lives."[114]

Additional support for this position came from the International Association of Chiefs of Police in testimony before the House Judiciary Subcommittee on Crime on 24 February 1988. That testimony concluded with the following statement: "We totally support H.R. 975 [a bill requiring a seven-day waiting period before the purchase of a firearm can be completed]. We do not suggest that this type of legislation is a panacea for all violent crimes but we do feel that it serves a legitimate purpose and will help law enforcement fight crime and will help protect innocent citizens and law enforcement officers from senseless violence."[115]

Manufacturers' Product Liability and Gun Control Policy

Another aspect of the gun control debate is manufacturers' product liability. For the past two decades proponents of gun control have been suing gun manufacturers—and even gun merchants—for the deaths or injuries resulting from either the criminal or accidental misuse of their products. In other words, those persons who accidentally misuse guns, or criminals or madmen who use guns in pursuit of the completion of their crimes, would no longer necessarily be held responsible for their acts. The companies that produce the guns that have been misused or the gun shop owners who sell them would instead be held accountable for death or injury.

This is a highly disputatious legal, political, and philosophical issue, for if the principle of manufacturers' or merchants' product liability can be applied to guns, the same principle can undoubtedly be applied to virtually any other product. One can readily give examples of a wide range of products—such as knives, drugs, alcohol, tobacco, motor vehicles, ammunition, lawnmowers, tree pruners, perfumes, and a host of others—which, if somehow "misused," could cause their manufacturers or purveyors to be held liable for any resulting injury. Obviously, the vast majority of persons who use or consume products such as those are not injured by them—either accidentally or intentionally. Consumer responsibility in their use is assumed; manufacturers have generally not been held accountable for the misuse of their products. Likewise, the vast majority of individuals who purchase guns or other weapons do not use them for criminal purposes, nor are the vast majority of weapons owners and users accidentally injured by the use of such weapons.

The principle of consumer responsibility for the use of manufactured products, however, appears to be eroding. Although product liability law, as an element of the law of torts, is hardly a new field of litigation, it is true that a significant shift of responsibility for the misuse of a product from its purchaser or possessor to that of the manufacturer or seller of the product presents a highly controversial and, indeed, significantly destabilizing element in the application of the law. Who can predict the ultimate use to which any manufactured product might be put? Yet the courts have begun to accept the notion that individuals or groups may blame the business—manufacturers can be sued—for alleged misuse, injury, or death resulting from products they have manufactured. And numerous law review articles and books can be cited as illustrative of the trend and the parameters of the debate.[116]

Suits against gun manufacturers that have proven to be especially successful have focused on the alleged defects in the design and manufacture of such weapons. In addition, litigation against manufacturers of guns—especially handguns—has emphasized the argument that handguns are *inherently* potentially dangerous even in the absence of design defects and that, consequently, the manufacturers of these weapons should be held liable for any harm resulting from their use. In the widely cited case of *Kelley v. R. G. Industries, Inc.,* for example, the Maryland Court of Appeals held the manufacturer of Saturday Night Specials liable for their use.[117] The court based its decision on the arguments that the risk of the product outweighed its usefulness to society, the knowledge or foreseeability that the product was to be used primarily in criminal behavior, and the relative degree of fault resulting from its use as between the victim and the manufacturer or seller of the weapon. The manufacturer, thus suffering a grievous economic blow, subsequently went out of business. Shortly after the court issued its decision in this case, the State of Maryland set up a Handgun Review Board.

An increasingly large number of both policy makers and organized interest groups have become involved in this controversial effort, and their tactics include such devices as research, information and propaganda efforts, regulation and legislation, as well as litigation in the courts.[118] Gun shop owners have likewise not escaped litigation. For example, in a recent case involving a deranged man who took 33 people hostage in a Berkeley, California, bar and grill, ultimately killing one and wounding nine others by use of an automatic weapon, parents filed suit against the gun shop owners on the grounds they were negligent in selling the automatic weapons to a person who was emotionally and mentally disturbed. In this particular case, the court held that the gun shop owners could not be held liable because they had no way of knowing that the purchaser was mentally unstable. In Oakland, California, in a similar suit, a widow whose husband had been shot while driving in that city sued the gun shop who had sold the weapon. In that case, the gun shop owners avoided going to trial by paying a $400,000 settlement fee.[119] The issue of manufacturer liability for the resulting use to which their products are put was raised to another level on 10 April 1995, when a San Francisco Superior Court judge refused to dismiss a series of lawsuits against the manufacturers of guns and ammunition used in the killing of eight people and the wounding of six others in offices located at 101 California Street in San Francisco. Gian Luigi Ferri burst into the law firm of Pettit & Martin and, using three guns and hundreds of rounds of ammunition, sprayed the offices with bullets and then turned a gun on himself. The case is complicated by the fact that the guns were legally manufactured in Florida and sold in Nevada where "assault weapons" were not banned at the time. Thus, according to attorneys for the manufacturer—Navegard, Inc.—the company did nothing wrong in California. Whatever the final outcome of the judge's ruling, the decision is likely to stimulate an increasingly large number of suits against the manufacturers of guns and ammunition.

The real issue involved in the manufacturer liability controversy lies, of course, in an interpretation of the appropriate application of the law of torts and the question of the ultimate personal responsibility one undertakes in the use of products and especially in the use of guns. The entire controversy is neatly summarized in two law journal articles, one by Andrew J. McClurg, the other by Philip D. Oliver.[120] McClurg takes the position that handguns "as products" are unreasonably dangerous per se. He argues that manufacturers of these weapons should be liable for the deaths and injuries of persons affected by handguns when one of their products is actually used for such purposes. He states unequivocally that he is opposed to the policy that permits access to handguns, weapons capable of destruction, even though such weapons may be those of "solace" and "recreation" for many.

As Oliver puts it, however, "the assertion that strict liability against suppliers of well-made guns follows from existing principles of tort law must be roundly rejected. The underlying principles of products liability law require a defect before liability is to be imposed. Simply stated, a well-made handgun is free from defect."[121] He points out, in conclusion, that

> courts tempted to impose gun control through tort law should recognize that they are ill-suited to carry out carefully calibrated regulatory schemes, and that manifest injustice would result from imposing liability on suppliers who have done nothing that was not fully sanctioned by society. Courts should also recognize . . . that imposition of liability would be inconsistent with all legitimate doctrines of products liability law. Virtually no precedent, in gun cases or other product liability cases, would support such a step.[122]

Still, a number of observers from both within and without the legal field believe that a case can be made against gun manufacturers for the damage caused by the weapons they produce and sell. As an example, a grocer named Olen Kelley was shot in March 1981 by a burglar who was carrying a Saturday Night Special. Kelley survived and then decided to sue the manufacturer of the gun. His argument was that Saturday Night Specials have little or no practical use except in the commission of a crime. The manufacturers should have been aware, therefore, that some reasonable probability existed that the gun would be used to shoot someone like Kelley. The plaintiff's argument was adopted by the Maryland Supreme Court whose decision set a precedent for product liability decisions against gun manufacturers.

The Center to Prevent Handgun Violence has now established a Legal Action Project whose goal is to introduce suits like Kelley's against gun manufacturers for wrongful damage resulting from the use of a firearm. The center is attempting to establish a nationwide system of attorneys who will bring such suits and then to provide those lawyers with the information they need to prosecute their cases successfully.

Conclusion: Control Guns or Understand the Causes of Crime?

The question of whether we should spend our efforts on controlling crime or on controlling guns remains.

Probably no one on either side of the gun control debate would argue that we should not try to control crime and to understand the causes of criminality and violence, as long as the means justify the ends. The focus of the debate on gun control would then change substantially. This focus might result in efforts to devote greater time and research on the issue of the *causes* of crime and to what alternative solutions might prove useful from a public policy perspective. To be sure, any discussion of the causes of crime can itself degenerate into controversy, but perhaps greater progress might be forthcoming than under the current context in which the issue has been couched.

Some researchers and analysts have suggested that a greater emphasis of an examination of the crime control problem be focused on sociological, economic, psychological, and even biological perspectives. An understanding of the crime problem may ultimately lie in discovering why the vast majority of persons *conform* to a society's norms, values, and laws and some others do *not*. Some analysts have therefore suggested that research in two general areas of the theory of crime causation might be of particular use: (1) the psychological and possibly biological underpinnings of criminal behavior and (2) the socioeconomic conditions in the environment that lead to specific behaviors the society has deemed criminal. This observation is hardly pathbreaking. Indeed, over 2,000 years ago the ancient Greeks are known to have speculated on these aspects of the field of study that would later come to be called criminology. The actual founders of criminology, however, were members of the Italian School: Cesare Lombroso, Enrico Ferri, and Raffaele Garofalo, who lived and wrote between 1835 and 1934.

Early psychobiological approaches were widely attacked and discredited by other scholars, particularly in the period during and after World War II. But in recent years, biological origins of criminal behavior have once again become an area of serious study. Factors such as nutrition, genetics, neurology, endocrinology, and other physical dysfunctions or abnormalities have stimulated renewed scientific interest.

A recent report by a panel of the National Academy of Sciences, for example, has suggested that violence, including gun violence, might be related to "neurobiological markers." One report of the findings states, "Research links aggressive acts with chemicals in the brain. Among key findings: Violent persons have a notably lower level of a substance called serotonin . . . abnormal brain activity . . . and high levels of minerals like manganese in their hair."[123] Moreover, "the new view neither negates social factors nor suggests that there is a 'violence gene,' a 'bad seed.'"[124] It does, however, take into account the possibility of brain dysfunction. Pharmacological techniques may thus be an area of application in treating criminal behavior.[125]

Some psychologists have maintained that human behavior is the result of early personality formation and that abnormal psychological development can lead to personality types that have been labeled psychopathic, sociopathic, or antisocial. Such persons are said to be unable to control their impulses, incapable of experiencing human emotions described as normal (such as love), and are unable to learn from their social experiences.

Some sociologists involved in the study of crime have argued that the criminal's personality—like everyone's personality—is the product of the social environment. One such theory, popularized by Emile Durkheim, asserts that some level of crime is a natural part of social existence. Durkheim suggested that a condition of anomie—a situation in which the rules regulating social behavior have weakened or dissolved—develops, and as a result some people are unable to discern what is expected of them, and this may lead to deviant behavior.

Other theories have been set forth, such as Sutherland's differential association theory (in which he argued that criminal behavior was learned as a consequence of association with those whose activities placed high value on illegal activities, for example), or Tanenbaum's labeling theory (in which he argued that criminal behavior is that which is labeled as such by various social groups and social-control agencies such as the police or departments of correction that have the authority to define acts that place some individuals outside of the expected community norms; this authority to define criminal behavior enables them to "create" criminals. But these theories, too, have been criticized as being unsupported by empirical evidence and as being vague and speculative.

There is therefore no consensus among researchers on the causes of criminal behavior. Until one has been reached and a way is found to control crime in other ways from controlling guns, proponents and opponents alike of gun control will undoubtedly remain locked in vigorous debate.

Notes

1. This introduction and significant parts of some of the chapters to follow rely heavily on Earl R. Kruschke, *The Right To Keep and Bear Arms: A Continuing American Dilemma* (Springfield, IL: Charles C Thomas, Publisher, 1985). The material, both quoted and paraphrased from that work, are used herein with permission of the publisher.

2. For one discussion of this fact, see, for example, Gary Kleck, Chap. 1 in *Point Blank: Guns and Violence in America* (New York: Aldine De Gruyter, 1991).

3. For a detailed examination of the amendment, see Don B. Kates, Jr., "Handgun Prohibition and the Original Meaning of the Second Amendment," *Michigan Law Review* 82, no. 2 (November 1983). See also Joyce Lee Malcolm, "The Right of the People To Keep and Bear Arms: The Common Law Tradition," *Hastings Constitutional Law Quarterly* 10 (1983): 305–306.

4. Kruschke, *op. cit.*, 12.

5. Dennis A. Henigan, "The Right To Be Armed: A Constitutional Illusion," *San Francisco Barrister* (December 1989): 11–12.

6. Quoted in "Exploding the NRA's Second Amendment Mythology," Center to Prevent Handgun Violence, 1994, 9–10.

7. Ibid., 18.

8. Ibid.

9. Ibid.

10. Warren E. Burger, "The Meaning and Distortion of the Second Amendment," *The Keene* [N.H.] *Sentinel* (26 November 1991): 10.

11. Ibid.

12. Kruschke, *op. cit.*, 4.

13. H. Trevor Colbourn, *The Lamp of Experience; Whig History and the Intellectual Origins of the American Revolution* (Chapel Hill University of North Carolina Press, 1965), 9.

14. Plato, *Laws,* Book VIII, translated by Jowett, in *Great Books of the Western World,* Vol. 7 (Chicago: Encyclopaedia Britannica, Inc., 1952), 732.

15. Michael Grant, trans., *Political Speeches of Cicero* (Baltimore: Penguin Books, 1969), 222.

16. Adam Smith, *An Inquiry into the Nature and Causes of the Wealth of Nations*, in *Great Books of the Western World*, Vol. 39 (Chicago: Encyclopaedia Britannica, Inc., 1952), 308.

17. See Jean Jacques Rousseau, *A Discourse on Political Economy*, in *Great Books of the Western World*, Vol. 38 (Chicago: Encyclopaedia Britannica, Inc. 1952,) and Nicolo Machiavelli, *The Prince*, in *Great Books of the Western World*, Vol. 23 (Chicago: Encyclopaedia Britannica, Inc., 1952), 18.

18. Robert E. Shallope, "The Ideological Origins of the Second Amendment," *The Journal of American History* 69, no. 3 (December 1982): 601.

19. Ibid. See also Stephen P. Halbrook, "The Second Amendment as a Phenomenon of Classical Political Philosophy," in Don B. Kates, Jr., ed., *Firearms and Violence: Issues of Public Policy* (San Francisco: Pacific Institute for Public Policy Research; Cambridge: Ballinger Publishing Company, 1984).

20. H. Peckman, ed., *Sources of American Independence* (1978): 176, as cited in Stephen P. Halbrook, "The Arms of All the People Should Be Taken Away," pamphlet, (Washington, DC: NRA Institute for Legislative Action).

21. Ibid., 2–3.

22. Kruschke, *op. cit.*, 7.

23. Richard E. Gardiner, "To Preserve Liberty—A Look at the Right To Keep and Bear Arms," *Northern Kentucky Law Review* 10, no. 1 (1982): 64.

24. See Dorothy Whitelock, ed., *English Historical Documents 500–1042*, Vol. 1 (New York: Oxford University Press, 1955), 358.

25. William Blackstone, *Commentaries on the Laws of England*, George Chase, ed. (New York: Banks & Brothers, 1884), 81–84, 141–144.

26. Malcolm, *op. cit.*

27. Don B. Kates, Jr., "Handgun Prohibition and the Original Meaning of the Second Amendment," *op. cit.*, 216.

28. See "The Right To Keep and Bear Arms," Report of the Subcommittee on the Constitution of the Committee on the Judiciary, United States Senate, 97th Congress, Second Session (Febuary 1982).

29. Thomas Cooley, *The General Principles of Law in the United States of America* (Boston: Little, Brown and Company, 1880), 271.

30. United States Code, Title 10, Section 311(a).

31. *U.S. v. Verdugo-Urquidez* (494 U.S. 259: 1990).

32. Kruschke, *op. cit.*, 11.

33. Don B. Kates, Jr., "Handgun Prohibition and the Original Meaning of the Second Amendment," *op. cit.*, 218.

34. Stephen P. Halbrook, *That Everyman Be Armed: The Evolution of a Constitutional Right* (Albuquerque: University of New Mexico Press, 1984), 66.

35. "The Right To Keep and Bear Arms," Report of the Subcommittee on the Constitution of the Committee on the Judiciary, *op. cit.*, viii.

36. See Sanford Levenson, "The Embarrassing Second Amendment," *Yale Law Journal* (1989): 99; Joyce Lee Malcolm, *To Keep and Bear Arms: The Origins of An Anglo-American Right* (Cambridge: Harvard University Press, 1994). For the major articles endorsing the individual rights interpretation see: Glenn H. Reynolds and Don B. Kates, "The Second Amendment and States' Rights: A Thought Experiment," *William and Mary Law Review* 36 (1995); Jeremy Rabkin, Review, *Journal of Criminal Law & Criminology* 86 (1995); Robert J. Cottrol and Raymond T. Diamond, "Never Intended To Be Applied to the White Population: Firearms Regulation and Racial Disparity, The Redeemed South's Legacy to a National Jurisprudence," *Chicago-Kent Law Review* (1995); Don B. Kates and Daniel D. Polsby, "Of Genocide and Disarmament," *Journal of Criminal Law & Criminology* 86 (1995); Glenn H. Reynolds, "A Critical Guide to the Second Amendment," *Tennessee Law Review* 62, no. 3 (1995); Nicholas J. Johnson, "Shots Across No Man's Land: A Response to Handgun Control, Inc.'s Richard Aborn," *Fordham Urban Law Journal* 22 (1995); Robert J. Cottrol and Raymond T. Diamond, "The Fifth Auxiliary Right," *Yale Law Journal* 104 (1994); David Vandercoy, "The History of the Second Amendment," *Valparaiso Law Review* 28 (1994); Richard J. Aynes, "On Misreading John Bingham and the Fourteenth Amendment," *Yale Law Journal* 101 (1993); John Schoon Yoo, "Our Declaratory Ninth Amendment," *Emory Law Journal* 42 (1993); Gerard V. Bradley, "The Bill of Rights and Originalism," *University of Illinois Law Forum* (1992); Stephanie A. Levin, "Grass Roots Voices: Local Action and National Military Policy," *Buffalo Law Review* 40 (1992); James Pope, "Republican Moments: The Role of Direct Popular Power in the American Constitutional Order," *University of Pennsylvania Law Review* 139 (1991); Akhil Reed Amar, "The Bill of Rights as a Constitution," *Yale Law Journal* 100 (1990); Joyce Lee Malcolm, "The Right of the People To Keep and Bear Arms: The Common Law Tradition," *Hastings Constitutional Law Quarterly* 10 (1983); Robert Dowlet, "The Right To Bear Arms," *Oklahoma Law Review* 36 (1983); Stephen P. Halbrook, "To Keep and Bear Their Private Arms," *Northern Kentucky Law Review* 10 (1982); Alan Gottlieb, "Gun Ownership: A Constitutional Right," *Northern Kentucky Law Review* 10 (1982); Richard Gardener, "To Preserve Liberty—A Look at the Right To Keep and Bear Arms,"*Northern Kentucky Law Review* 19 (1982); Stephen P. Halbrook, "The Jurisprudence of the Second and Fourteenth Amendments," *George Mason Law Review* 4 (1981); and Don B. Kates, Jr., "Gun Control: Separating Reality from Symbolism," *Journalism of Contemporary Law* 20, no. 2 (1994). See also the bibliographical list contained in Wayne LaPierre, *Guns, Crime, and Freedom* (Washington, DC: Regenery

Publishing, Inc., 1994), 237–240. Important articles that endorse the collective right interpretation are: Andrew D. Herz, "Gun Crazy: Constitutional False Consciousness and Dereliction of Dialogic Responsibilities," *Boston University Law Review* 75 (1995); George Anastaplo, "Amendments to the Constitution of the United States: a Commentary," *Loyola-Chicago Law Journal* 23 (1992); Keith A. Ehrman and Dennis A. Henigan, "The Second Amendment in the 20th Century: Have You Seen Your Militia Lately?" *University of Dayton Law Review* 15 (1989); Warren Spannaus, "State Firearms Regulation and the Second Amendment,"*Hamline Law Review* 6 (1983); Sam Fields, "Guns, Crime and the Negligent Gun Owner," *Northern Kentucky Law Review* 10 (1982); Note, "The Constitutional Implications of Gun Control and Several Realistic Gun Control Proposals," *American Journal of Criminal Law* 17 (1989); and Daniel Abrams, Note, "Ending the Other Arms Race: An Argument for a Ban on Assault Weapons," *Yale Law and Policy Review* 10 (1992).

37. Federal Bureau of Investigation, U.S. Department of Justice. *Uniform Crime Reports for the United States, 1993*. Washington, DC: Government Printing Office, 4 December 1994, Table 2.10.

38. *Uniform Crime Reports, op. cit.*, Table 2.24.

39. "Guns: Changing Our Lives," *USA Today* (29 December 1993): 1A.

40. Data summarized from *Vital Statistics of the United States, 1960* and 1980, as reported in Franklin E. Zimring and Gordon Hawkins, *The Citizen's Guide to Gun Control* (New York: Macmillan Publishing Company, 1987), Tables 6.1–6.3.

41. John Ritter, "A Shot Fired, A Life Changed," *USA Today* (29 December 1993): 3D.

42. "Guns Killed 50,000 Youths from '79 to '91, Group Reports," *San Francisco Chronicle* (21 January 1994): A3.

43. Handgun Control, Inc., "Facts about Teen Suicide and Handguns."

44. *Gun Control: The Information Series on Current Topics.* (Wylie, TX: Information Plus, 1993), 99–100.

45. Ibid., 103.

46. Robert Berkley Harper, "Controlling and Regulating Handguns — A Way To Save Black Lives," *National Black Law Journal* 9, no. 3, 250.

47. Wayne R. Austerman, "Controlling Assault Weapons Would Not Reduce Crime," in Charles P. Cozic, ed. *Gun Control* (San Diego: Greenhaven Press, 1992), 73.

48. George Gallup, Jr., *The Gallup Poll: Public Opinion 1993.* (Wilmington, DE: Scholarly Resources Inc., 1994), 50–51.

49. Ibid., 50.

50. George Gallup, Jr., *The Gallup Poll Monthly 1991.* (Wilmington, DE: Scholarly Resources Inc., 1992).

51. Ibid.

52. Jonathan Beaty, Michael Riley, and Richard Woodbury, "Under fire," *Time* (29 January 1990), 16–21.

53. John H. Sloan, et al., "Handgun Regulations, Crime, Assaults, and Homicides: A Tale of Two Cities," *New England Journal of Medicine* 10 (November 1988): 1256–1262.

54. Paul H. Blackman, "Handgun Regulations, Crime, Assaults, and Homicide: A Tale of Two Cities," *New England Journal of Medicine* (4 May 1989): 1214–1215.

55. *20 Questions and Answers,* brochure published by National Coalition to Ban Handguns (now the Coalition to Stop Gun Violence), Washington, DC, 1981.

56. "The Myths about Gun Control," pamphlet published by the National Rifle Association, n.d.

57. Ibid.

58. William E. Schmidt, "Pressure for Gun Control Rises and Falls, but Ardor for Arms Seems Constant," *New York Times* (25 October 1987): E5.

59. David B. Kopel, "Japanese Gun Control Laws Are Oppressive," in Charles P. Cozic, ed. *Gun Control* (San Diego: Greenhaven Press), 252.

60. William Calates, "Jamaican Gun Control Laws Have Not Reduced Gun Violence" and Ned Kelly, "Australian Gun Control Measures Are Ineffective," in Charles P. Cozic, ed. *Gun Control* (San Diego: Greenhaven Press), 269–277 and 260–268.

61. "The Myths about Gun Control," *op. cit.*

62. Jim Benson, "Gun Control and Genocide . . . ," *American Survival Guide* (April 1994): 6. Benson is referring to information provided in a videotape, *Gun Control: Gateway to Genocide, A Capital Hill Briefing,* by Jay Simkin, who heads the organization Jews for the Preservation of Firearms Ownership.

63. Terence Moran, "Capital Accounts," *Legal Times* (20 May 1991): 19.

64. Robert J. Cottrol and Raymond T. Diamond, "The Second Amendment: Toward an Afro-Americanist Reconsideration," *Georgetown Law Journal* 80, no. 2 (December 1991): 318. See also Don B. Kates, Jr., "Gun Control: Separating Reality from Symbolism," *Journal of Contemporary Law* 20, no. 2 (1994); and Clayton E. Cramer, "The Racist Roots of Gun Control," *The Kansas Journal of Law and Public Policy* 4, no. 2 (Winter 1995).

65. *Watson v. Stone* (148 Fla. 516, 524, 4 So.2d 700, 703: 1941).

66. Ibid.

67. Lee Kennett and James LaVerne Anderson, *The Gun in America: The Origins of a National Dilemma* (Westport, CT., Greenwood Press, 1975), 50.

68. See Stefan B. Tahmassebi, "Gun Control and Racism," *George Mason University Civil Rights Law Journal* 2, no. 1 (Summer 1991).

69. Lee Kennet and James LaVerne Anderson, *op. cit.*, 177–178.

70. See, for example, Barry Bruce-Briggs, "The Great American Gun War," *The Public Interest* 45 (1976) and Robert Sherill, *The Saturday Night Special* (New York: Charter House, 1973).

71. See Terence Moran, *op. cit.*

72. Robert J. Cottrol and Raymond T. Diamond, *op. cit.*, 361.

73. Stefan B. Tahmassebi, *op. cit.*, 99. See also Don B. Kates, Jr., "Gun Control: Separating Reality from Symbolism," *op. cit.*; Clayton E. Cramer, "The Racist Roots of Gun Control," *op. cit.*; and T. Markus Funk, "Gun Control and Economic Discrimination: The Melting-Point Case-in-Point," *The Journal of Criminal Law and Criminology* 85, no. 3 (Winter, 1995).

74. Robert Berkley Harper, "Gun Control Would Reduce Crime against Blacks," in Charles P. Cozic and Carol Wekesser, eds., *Gun Control* (San Diego: Greenhaven Press, 1992), 33.

75. See Paxton Quigley, *Armed and Female* (Paxton Quigley Productions, 1989), excerpts from article retitled as "Handguns Are an Effective Form of Self-Defense for Women," as reprinted in Charles P. Cozic and Carol Wekesser, eds., *Gun Control* (San Diego: Greenhaven Press, Inc., 1992), 163.

76. See *Warren v. District of Columbia* (444 A.2d 1, D.C. Ct. of Appeals: 1981). For similar cases, see, for example, *Keane v. City of Chicago* (98 Ill. App.2d 460, 240 N.E.2d 321: 1968) and *Chapman v. City of Philadelphia* (434 A.2d. 753, Sup. Ct. Penn.: 1981), among dozens of others.

77. "A Question of Self-Defense," pamphlet of the National Rifle Association, Institute for Legislative Action (1992), 2.

78. See the report in the *San Francisco Chronicle* (30 September 1992): A10.

79. Quoted in Ibid.

80. Quoted in Ibid.

81. See Gary Kleck, *Point Blank: Guns and Violence in America* (New York: Aldine de Gruyter, 1991), 120.

82. Ibid., 126.

83. Ibid.

84. Ibid., 134.

85. Paxton Quigley, *Armed and Female, op cit.,* 167.

86. Ibid.

87. Gary Kleck, *Point Blank: Guns and Violence in America, op. cit.,* and Don B. Kates, Jr., "Guns, Murders, and the Constitution: A Realistic Assessment of Gun Control" (San Francisco: Pacific Research Institute for Public Policy, 1990), copyright Pacific Research Institute and Don B. Kates, Jr., 1990.

88. See James D. Wright and Peter H. Rossi, *The Armed Criminal in America: A Survey of Incarcerated Felons* (Washington, DC: National Institute of Justice, U.S. Government Printing Office, 1985).

89. See James D. Wright and Peter H. Rossi, *Armed and Considered Dangerous: A Survey of Felons and Their Firearms* (New York: Aldine de Gruyter, 1986). For other pertinent data on this point, see, for example, Massad Ayoob, *In the Gravest Extreme;* his "Armed and Alive," Second Amendment Monograph Series (Second Amendment Foundation, 1982); *Women's Views on Guns and Self Defense,* Second Amendment Monograph Series (Second Amendment Foundation, 1983); *Sourcebook on Criminal Justice Statistics,* Department of Justice, annually; and Paxton Quigley, *op. cit.*

90. Paxton Quigley, *op. cit.*

91. A. L. Kellerman and D. T. Reay, "Protection or Peril: An Analysis of Firearms-Related Deaths in the Home," *New England Journal of Medicine* (June 1986): 1557–1559.

92. *Information Please Almanac Atlas & Yearbook, 1995,* 48th edition. (Boston: Houghton Mifflin Company, 1995), 846.

93. James D. Wright, Peter H. Rossi, and Kathleen Daly, *Under the Gun: Weapons, Crime, and Violence in America.* (New York: Aldine Publishing Company, 1983), Chapter 9.

94. N. B. Rushforth, C. S. Hirsch, A. A. Ford, and L. Adelson, "Accidental Firearm Fatalities in a Metropolitan County," *American Journal of Epidemiology,* 499–505.

95. Gary Kleck, "Crime Control through the Private Use of Armed Force," *Social Problems* 35, no. 1 (February 1988): 16–17. See also Paul H. Blackman, "Carrying Handguns for Personal Protection: Issues of Research and Public Policy," a paper presented at the annual meeting of the American Society of Criminology, San Diego, California, 13–16 November 1985; and his "The Law and Practice of Self Protection: The People and Bernie Goetz vs. the Media Elite," a paper presented at the annual meeting of the Academy of Criminal Justice Sciences, San Francisco, California, 4–8 April 1988). The opposing viewpoints have suggested that crime often cannot be effectively deterred by firearms because the crime takes place in locations where possession or ownership of a gun would

not deter the crime and that the law-breakers involved in the commission of crime are actually not shot very often by their intended victims. See the data presented by George D. Newton and Franklin E. Zimring, *Firearms and Violence in American Life: A Staff Report to the National Commission on the Causes and Prevention of Violence* (Washington, DC: U.S. Government Printing Office, 1969); Matthew G. Yeager, Joseph D. Alviani, and Nancy Loving, *How Well Does the Handgun Protect You and Your Family?* (Washington, DC: United States Conference of Mayors, 1976). Yeager, Alviani, and Loving also argue that because of the alleged low probability of being involved in a robbery, assault, or rape, there is some question as to whether Americans should keep guns in their homes or carry them personally. Patrick Caddell has also reported, in a survey carried on by Cambridge Reports, Inc., of Cambridge, Massachusetts, in 1978, (*An Analysis of Public Attitudes towards Handgun Control*) that self-defense use of firearms is low and essentially ineffective because such weapons are rarely used, and that handgun accidents have been somewhat higher than weapons used in self-defense. For other "anti" views on this subject see Robert F. Drinan, "Gun Control: The Good Outweighs the Evil," *Civil Liberties Review* 3 (1976); Philip J. Cook, "The Role of Firearms in Violent Crime: An Interpretative Review of the Literature," *Criminal Violence,* ed. Marvin E. Wolfgang and Neil A. Weiner, 1982.

96. Colin Greenwood, *Firearms Control: A Study of Armed Crime and Firearms Control in England and Wales* (London: Routledge, 1972).

97. Edward F. Leddy, "The Ownership and Carrying of Personal Firearms and Reduction of Crime Victimization," in *The Gun and Its Enemies,* William R. Tonso, ed. (Bellingham, Washington: The Second Amendment Foundation, 1990), excerpts from the article retitled as "Gun Owners Protect Themselves from Crime," as reprinted in Charles P. Cozic and Carol Wekesser, eds., *Gun Control* (San Diego: Greenhaven Press, Inc., 1992), 152.

98. Gary Kleck and David Bordua, "The Factual Foundations for Certain Key Assumptions of Gun Control," *Law & Policy Quarterly* 5 (1983).

99. E. Duane Davis and Laura J. Moriarty, "Citizens' Attitudes concerning Firearms: Self-Protection and Crime Prevention," conference paper (n.d.).

100. Frank T. Morn, "Firearms and the Police: A Historic Evolution of American Values," citing John Cawelti in "Myths of Violence in Popular Culture," *Critical Inquiry* 3 (1975), in Don B. Kates, Jr., ed., *Firearms and Violence: Issues of Public Policy, op. cit.,* 489.

101. See Alan M. Gottlieb, *Gun Rights Fact Book* (Bellevue, WA: Merril, 1988), 112.

102. Ibid., 112–113.

103. Ibid., 113.

104. For an analysis of lobbying efforts on the part of some police *favoring greater restrictions,* see Paul H. Blackman, "Law Enforcement Lobbying and Policymaking on 'Gun Control': An Essay," a paper presented at the annual meeting of the Academy of Criminal Justice Sciences, Washington, DC, 1 April 1989.

105. James B. Jacobs, "Exceptions to a General Prohibition on Handgun Possession: Do They Swallow Up the Rule?" *Law and Contemporary Problems* 49, no. 1, copyright 1986 Duke University School of Law, as reprinted in Charles P. Cozic and Carol Wekesser, eds., *Gun Control* (San Diego: Greenhaven Press, Inc., 1992), 43.

106. Ibid., 44.

107. Ibid., 44–46.

108. Ibid., 46.

109. Ibid.

110. Ibid., 47.

111. Ibid.

112. Ibid., 48.

113. Ibid., 49.

114. As quoted in "What You Should Know about the Brady Bill," published by Handgun Control, Inc., n.d.

115. As quoted in "We Should Mandate a National Waiting Period," in Gary E. McCuen, *Firearms and Social Violence: The Other Arms Race* (Hudson, WI: Gary E. McCuen Publications, 1991), 138.

116. See, for example, M. Stuart Madden, *Products Liability* (1988); *Kelley v. R. G. Industries, Inc.* (304 Md. 124, 497 A.2d 1143: 1985); *Sindell v. Abbott Laboratories* (607 P.2d 924, Cal.: 1980); *Addison v. Williams* (546 So. 2d 20, La. Ct. App.: 1989); *O'Brien v. Muskin Corp.* (463 A.2d 298, N.J.: 1983); *Amijo v. Ex. Cam, Inc.* (843 F.2d 406, 10th Cir.: 1988); *Shipman v. Jennings Firearms, Inc.* (791 F.2d 1532, 11th Cir.: 1986); and *Martin v. Harrington and Richardson, Inc.* (743 F.2d 1200, 7th Cir.: 1984), among hundreds of others.

117. See *Kelley v. R. G. Industries, Inc.* (304 Md. 124, 497 A.2d 1143: l985).

118. Some examples of leading journal literature on this topic—product liability—include: Joshua Horowitz, "At Issue: Strict Liability: Should Assault Weapon Makers Be Liable for Gun Injuries? Yes: Justice for Victims," *A.B.A.J.* 77 (July 1991); Don B. Kates, Jr., "Some Remarks on the Prohibition of Handguns," *St. Louis Law Journal* 23 (1979); Sam Fields, "Handgun Prohibition and Social Necessity," Ibid.; Richard C. Miller, "New Perspectives in Litigation: Smoking Guns," *Trial* 27 (July 1991); Dean Prosser, "The Assault upon the Citadel (Strict Liability to the Consumer)," *Yale Law Journal* 69 (1960) and "The Fall of the Citadel (Strict

Liability to the Consumer)," *Minnesota Law Review* 50 (1966); Andrew O. Smith, "The Manufacture and Distribution of Handguns as an Abnormally Dangerous Activity," *University of Chicago Law Review* 54 (1987); Note, "Handguns and Product Liability," *Harvard Law Review* 97 (1984); Windle Turley, "Manufacturers' and Suppliers' Liability to Handgun Victims," *Northern Kentucky Law Review* 10 (1982); David T. Hardy, "Product Liability and Weapons Manufacture," *Wake Forest Law Review* 20 (1984); and the Kelley case cited above.

119. See article, *San Francisco Chronicle,* 18 September 1992.

120. See Andrew J. McClurg, "Handguns As Products Unreasonably Dangerous Per Se," *University of Arkansas at Little Rock Law Journal* 13 (1991) and Philip D. Oliver, "Rejecting the 'Whipping-Boy' Approach to Tort Law: Well-Made Handguns are Not Defective Products," *University of Arkansas at Little Rock Law Journal* 14 (1991).

121. See Philip D. Oliver, *op. cit.,* 6.

122. Ibid., 35.

123. See *U.S. News & World Report* 23 (November 1992): 46.

124. See Lois Timnick, "Violence: Its Key May Lie in the Brain," *Los Angeles Times* (26 June 1993).

125. Ibid.

Chronology 2

The debate over the issue of gun control rages on and will continue to do so. Indeed, the stage is being set for a review by the United States Supreme Court. The following chronology attempts to lay out only a few of the most obvious, and most widely cited, developments in the long history of the debate over the right to own and bear arms.

ca. 380–370 B.C.	Plato, in his *Republic,* lauded the establishment of an elitist oligarchy and the deprivation of the citizens of their weapons. He recognized that, if a democracy were to develop, common citizens would have to be armed, but he advocated that the state maintain a monopoly on arms, e.g., "Do you mean that the despot will dare to lay hands on this father of his and beat him if he resists? Yes, when once he has disarmed him." In his *Laws,* moreover, Plato advocated compulsory military training, yet citizens would not have their own arms, and they would engage in military exercises only once a month.

380–
370 B.C.
cont.

The philosophers of the American Constitution had read Plato and had realized that he advocated use of arms only at the command of the state; citizens would therefore be ruled by despots, even if the despots turned out to be "philosopher kings." The framers of the American system took the writings of Plato into consideration when they advocated an armed populace to protect citizens from a potentially despotic government.

ca. 384–
322 B.C.

Aristotle, in his *Politics,* differed with Plato, arguing that a polity should rightly consist of a great middle class (part of his concept of a "golden mean") "the members of which are those who bear arms." Aristotle pointed out, for example, that confining the possession of arms to one group would result in oppression: "the farmers have no arms, the workers have neither land nor arms; this makes them virtually the servants of those who do possess arms." Tyranny was a real potential when standing armies were permitted, and Aristotle argued that citizens should possess arms not provided by the state. Having read Aristotle's work, the framers of the American political system were influenced by his warning and took it into consideration while debating and writing during the events that led up to the drafting and signing of the Constitution and the ultimate inclusion of the Second Amendment in the Bill of Rights.

53 B.C.

The Roman orator Cicero defended Titus Annius Milo, a fellow republican, who had been accused of the murder of one of Caesar's allies and who was being tried in a highly accusatory political environment. Cicero stated, "It is impossible to argue that every act of homicide must necessarily deserve punishment, since in certain circumstances the laws themselves place a sword in our hands to inflict death upon our fellow-men. There are, in fact, many occasions on which homicide is justifiable. In particular, when violence is needed in order to repel violence, such an act is not merely justified but unavoidable." Later, Cicero cited natural and moral law as a defense. "I refer to the law which lays it down that, if our lives are endangered by plots or violence or armed robbers or enemies, any and every method of protecting ourselves is morally right. . . . Indeed, even the wisdom of the law itself, by a sort of tacit implication, permits self-defence, because it does not actually forbid men to kill. . . . When, therefore, an inquiry passes beyond the mere question of the weapon and starts to consider the motive, a man who has used arms in self-defence is not regarded as having carried them with a homicidal aim." The philosophical and legal scholar-politicians who were instrumental in drafting the Constitution and the Bill of Rights had read—and had been influenced by—Cicero's analysis.

A.D. 165   The distinguished Roman physician Galen, in a treatise on anatomy, suggested that man is anatomically equipped to defend himself. Man has "hands, instruments necessary for every art and useful in peace no less than in war. . . . He could grasp in his hand a weapon better than a horn; for certainly swords and spears are larger weapons than horns and better suited for inflicting wounds. . . . A man's weapons are effective at a distance as well as nearby. . . . Such is the hand of man as an instrument of defense." Galen had been read by the colonial leaders active in drafting the rights of Americans.

500–1066   The Germanic Saxons, who conquered Britain and ruled the island until 1066, left writings that were of interest to colonial intellectuals and politicians. Under Saxon law, for example, every freeman was required to join the army, and landowners were required to keep armor and weapons. Specific times were set out for instruction in the use of their armaments, and there was an annual military exercise for the purposes of review.

871–899   The Laws of Alfred recognized that every man had the right to keep and bear arms, but the laws proscribed the use of arms in the case of murder,

871–899
cont.

disturbing the peace, intent to commit crimes, and in other areas.

1020–1023

The Laws of Cnut recognized the right to keep and bear arms, the right to self-defense, and the fining of an individual for illegally disarming another. The right of an individual to hunt on his own land was also protected.

1181

The Assize of Arms of Henry II, recognizing the need of an armed populace as the foundation of a militia, extended to every knight and freeman the right to have weapons, such as a hauberk, a helmet, a shield, and a lance, and to the burgesses and freemen the right to have iron headpieces and doublets, a type of close-fitting outer garment worn by men. These arms could be inherited. Their holders had to take an oath of allegiance to the king to bear these arms to defend the realm.

1215

The barons of England forced King John—who had disarmed noblemen and commoners—to grant rights and freedoms to all freedmen in such matters as jury trials, consent to taxation, and religious freedom. A militia was restored and the possession of arms by the people for the defense of all and against government tyranny were included in the list. Signed at Runnymede, a meadow on the bank of the River Thames, west of London, the Magna Carta became one of the most significant foundations of individual rights and one of the widely recognized pillars of freedom upon which the colonists relied during their later interpretations of the rights of citizens. The American Bar Association erected a small monument commemorating the ceremony of the signing of the Magna Carta near the supposed site of the event.

1230

Henry III presented an edict reaffirming the Assize of Arms of Henry II.

1252

Henry III issued another edict reaffirming the Assize of Arms. This time the breadth of the assize was expanded so that it included villeins (serfs) among the categories of citizens, burgesses, and free tenants between the ages of 15 and 60 who were to be armed. It also included a statement that required armed men to guard the city during the night, to arrest strangers, and to raise the "hue and cry" to other residents if the intruders resisted arrest or attempted to escape.

1285   The Statute of Winchester was issued by Edward I. It provided for the arming of the whole people. Inasmuch as there was no standing army, it was recognized that the whole people, fittingly armed, would constitute the means by which resistance to both foreign aggression and the internal tyranny of the monarch could be undertaken. Arms were to be reviewed twice a year by an official, and a fine would be imposed on those who failed to help in the detention of lawbreakers.

1328   The Statute of Northampton was issued by Edward III. The statute limited the classifications of persons—specifically the servants and ministers of the king—who could appear with arms before the justices, and provided further limitations with respect to the bearing of arms during the day and night. The statute was directed in large part at controlling the activities of errant knights and the presence of arms in public places. It should be noted that the statute did not call for the disarming of the entire population, but permitted self-defense and defense of property against intruders and marauders.

1485   Henry VII attempted to maintain order and to repress potential rebellions against the Crown by passing a law forbidding hunting.

1503   Henry VII decreed that no person could shoot with a crossbow except to protect his property and land. This law, too, while focusing on hunting privileges, nevertheless preserved the right of the people to protect their own homes.

1511   Henry VIII, one of England's most ruthless kings, ruled that men had the obligation to keep long-bows and arrows in their homes for their own use. He provided for this even while imposing stringent measures in other areas of law. He increased the property qualification required for the firing of crossbows. The pronouncement also included the requirement that fathers should teach their sons between the ages of 7 and 14 to shoot the longbow.

1523   Henry VIII lowered the property qualification and permitted the shooting of crossbows and handguns to all those who were qualified in their use. Some others were permitted to maintain these weapons in their homes and to use them against the king's enemies.

1531   Niccolo Machiavelli published his *Discourses on the First Ten Books of Titus Livy,* a treatise in which he discussed at some length the role of arms in a political system. He argued that an unarmed people is easily vanquished by attackers, and that in a republic a ruler must "arm oneself with one's own subjects." He pointed out that "when states are strongly armed, as Rome was and the Swiss are, the more difficult it is to overcome them the nearer they are to their homes. . . . I say . . . that a ruler who has his people well armed and equipped for war, should always wait at home to wage war." He expressed similar views in his *The Art of War* and in *The Prince,* where he states "Rome and Sparta were for many centuries well armed and free. The Swiss are well armed and enjoy great freedom." Ultimately, he argued, free nations rest upon "good laws and good arms." Indeed, he insisted that it would be impossible to have "good laws where there are not good arms." Thus, Machiavelli was among the earliest to advocate a people's militia and oppose standing armies.

1541   Henry VIII provided limitations on the lengths of guns that private citizens could possess. He was aware, too, that citizens used firearms for sport and for defense regardless of his heavy-handed efforts to restrain them. Thus, all persons were allowed to keep guns in their homes as long as the length of such guns did not violate the rules provided by Henry's legislation, and they were prohibited from carrying loaded guns only in their travels on the king's highways or elsewhere. In effect, there remained only a skeleton of earlier, much more rigid gun control laws. Henry recognized, perhaps, that if he were to retain even a modicum of control over the possession and use of firearms, he would have to provide for their legal use and reduce the penalties for violations of the gun laws. He recognized also that an armed citizenry was valuable for defense.

1557   Mary Stuart proclaimed a statute that laid out the weapons requirements for those in about 18 property categories. Depending upon the amount of property owned, varying numbers of horses, pikes, longbows, arrows, and harquebutts were required; other weapons included such items as helmets, skulls, steel caps, etc.

1606   Jean Bodin wrote *Six Bookes of a Commonweale,* in which he defended political absolutism. He argued that if monarchists were to maintain their power, they had to disarm the masses. Thus, to forestall social change and maintain the feudal order, subjects could not be trusted with arms of their own. Bodin's work was among the many influential treatises read by the writers of the Declaration of Independence and the Constitution.

1625   Hugo Grotius, in his *On the Law of War and Peace,* suggested that all persons should have arms for self-defense and for the protection of family and friends who might be injured by armed intruders. He argued that if no one wore arms, crime and evil would follow. He drew from the words of Aristotle and Galen, among others. Grotius was among the authors read by American lawyer-intellectuals who were instrumental in the drafting of the basic documents of the United States.

1642   Parliament declared a law that allowed officers of the government to enter homes of Papists, and of others who had come to the aid of the Crown or who had publicly declared themselves in opposition to the proceedings of Parliament, in order to confiscate arms, horses, and ammunition.

1651   Thomas Hobbes published *Leviathan,* a defense of monarchies and their right to the exclusivity of maintaining an arsenal. Hobbes also recognized, however, that each individual must ultimately be responsible for protecting himself if the sovereign failed to do so. This is true especially when criminals or the state itself seek to do harm to citizens. Indeed, Hobbes wrote that "the right men have by Nature to protect themselves, when none else can protect them, can by no Covenant be relinquished."

1656   Marchamont Nedham published *The Right Constitution of a Commonwealth,* in which he defended and advocated a militia made up of the people.

1659   Upon the death of Oliver Cromwell in 1658, an ordinance was passed, requiring that every householder in London deliver a precise list of all arms and ammunition owned and allowing for the search and seizure of all arms in possession of any "Popish recusant, or other person that hath been in arms against the Parliament, or that have adhered to the enemies thereof, or any other person whom the Commissioners shall judge dangerous to the Peace of this Commonwealth. . . ."

1662   Charles II legislated a bill that permitted the search for, and the seizure of, all weapons in possession of those persons deemed potentially dangerous to maintaining peace.

1663   Charles II continued to employ the Militia Act to seize the weapons of anti-Royalists and nonconformists, made up largely of Puritans, Quakers, and Anabaptists.

1670   Charles II, in An Act for the Better Preservation of Game, deprived all persons not possessing lands or leases of a given value from keeping or using guns and bows. This was in reality a blatant act aimed at suppressing the masses and the emerging professionals and bourgeoisie, placing them in a position of subjugation to the king and the aristocracy by disarming them and denying them the means of insurrection. This was the first time in English history that the common law right to keep arms—with the exception of knives and swords—was prohibited.

1671   Parliament not only disarmed persons having "incorrect" sympathies toward the Crown but also broadened the scope of its power to disarm under the Unting Act all individuals who did not own real estate worth at least 100 pounds on the basis of an annual rent. Thus, the poor in particular were unable to keep and bear arms.

1685–1688   James II continued the policy of disarming the people, especially Protestants, and increased the size of the standing army.

1686   *Rex v. Knight* was decided. The defendant, Sir John Knight, was accused of violating the Statute of Northampton by walking the streets and entering a church while armed. The justice interpreted the statute as one that applied to those who went armed "to terrify the King's subjects." Consequently Knight was found innocent and the intent of the statute was clarified.

John Locke published *Two Treatises on Government*, a landmark in the development of human rights and a work that was instrumental in bringing William and Mary to the English monarchy. The leaders of revolutionary America and the framers of the Declaration of Independence, the Constitution of the United States, and the Bill of Rights were deeply influenced by Locke's writings relevant to individual freedom. Arguing that a social

1686 *cont.*   contract governs the relationships between people and their government, and that each individual must give his consent to the formation of a civil society, Locke insisted that the people retain, as part of their sovereignty, the right to change or to abolish government that becomes oppressive. Thus, each individual has the right to life, liberty, and property, and retains the right of self-defense against those persons who and a government that might attempt to take them away. These rights evolve out of the original state of nature. He recognized government as only an institution possessing powers delegated by the sovereign people, powers that the sovereign people could take back upon undue provocation. Among his comments with respect to arms, he says, "Mankind will be in a far worse condition than in the state of nature, if they shall have armed one, or a few men, with the joint power of a multitude to force them to obey at pleasure the exorbitant and unlimited decrees of their sudden thoughts." Thus, he argued, the sovereign people have the right to resist aggression, and private individuals maintain the "right to defend themselves and recover by force what by unlawful force is taken from them."

1688   The Glorious Revolution (during which not one life was lost) occurred in England under William and Mary. A main objective of the Glorious Revolution was to do away with the standing army and to restore to Protestants the right to keep and bear arms.

1689   The Declaration of Rights, an Act of Parliament, was passed when William and Mary became monarchs of England. In that Declaration it was noted that James II had subverted the laws and liberties of England by, among other things, disarming the Protestants. The Declaration of Rights therefore negated James' act, stating "that the Subjects which are Protestants, may have Arms for their Defence suitable to their Condition, and as are allowed by Law." The law referred to was the common law tradition. This provision was duly noted by framers of colonial bills of rights and by the framers of the Constitution of the United States. Legal scholars have likewise since relied upon it in their analysis of the origins of the right of the people to keep and bear arms. Another major right that was guaranteed in the English Bill of Rights was the right of petition. It is of particular interest to note that these two rights were repeated as Amendments I and II of the Bill of Rights attached to the American Constitution in 1789.

1697   The Whig John Trenchard and Walter Moyle, a member of the British Parliament, wrote *An Argument Showing That a Standing Army Is Inconsistent with a Free Government.* Especially attacked was the disarmament of the people and the more recent proposals on the part of the king to establish temporary standing armies.

1698   Andrew Fletcher, a Scottish Whig, published *A Discourse of Government with Relation to Militias.* He vociferously argued for the right of all subjects to keep and bear arms, and he advocated a militia separate from the monarchy and one composed of all men. This, he felt, would prove formidable to tyrannous governments. Those who did not possess arms he considered slaves.

Algernon Sidney, an English philosopher, wrote in his book *Discourses concerning Government* that "the body of the People is the public defense, and every man is armed and disciplined." He insisted that "swords were given to men, that none might be Slaves, but such as know not how to use them." Like Locke, Sidney maintained the natural freedom of men and that they possess the right to life, liberty, and property, together with the freedom to do away with governments that are tyrannous. Writers of the American state constitutions and the Constitution of the United States had read Sidney, and he significantly influenced their thinking.

1721–1722   John Trenchard and Thomas Gordon jointly published a series of essays known as *Cato's Letters.* Two

1721–1722
cont.

Whigs who were particularly vocal on the issue of standing armies and who expressed vehement opposition to their existence, Trenchard and Gordon attacked not only standing armies but the entire concept of a disarmed populace. Tyrants, they proclaimed, could rule absolutely over an unarmed citizenry. In these attacks on standing military power, Trenchard and Gordon deeply influenced such thinkers as John Adams and Thomas Jefferson, who, with others of their time, brought these opinions to bear during the American Revolution and the period of the drafting of the Constitution and the Bill of Rights.

1739

Rex v. Gardner, a case brought under the game laws, held that the law did not forbid a man from possessing a gun for purposes of self-defense. Thus, the right to keep a gun was construed as a liberty.

1742

The House of Lords passed a declaration indicating a clear and unmistakable individual right to keep and bear arms.

1744

Malloch v. Eastly, another case brought under the game laws, this one for killing a pheasant, held that the possession of a gun was no violation of the game laws, and that a man had the right to own a gun for self-defense and the defense of his family and property.

1748

Baron de la Brede et de Montesquieu, noted French philosopher, published his *Spirit of the Laws*. In this widely read treatise, he underscored the right of self-defense, which he considered a natural right. As part of his legal theory, he questioned laws that punished individuals for bearing arms if they did not have an evil intent to use them. He believed that persons who use their weapons to perpetrate violence should be treated as criminals and punished.

1752

Wingfield v. Stratford, a case brought under the game laws, held that it was not the objective of the law to disarm the people; rather, a gun may be possessed for self-defense, defense of property, and other purposes within the law.

1762   Jean Jacques Rousseau published *The Social Contract*. He advocated a republicanism similar to that advanced by Machiavelli, expressing his views of the necessity to maintain an armed citizenry who were the ultimate sovereign. His opposition to the concept of standing armies was also widely known. His thoughts especially were part of the intellectual arsenal of the thinkers of seventeenth and eighteenth century America, and carried an influence long beyond that time.

1764   Cesare Beccaria published *On Crime and Punishments*. This volume advocated changes in the criminal punishment laws and constituted a major element in the general prison reform movement then underway, a movement largely stimulated by Beccaria himself. Among his views were those advocating the right of individuals to keep and bear arms, for the law-abiding citizen had the right to defend himself from those who would harm him. He wrote, for example, "False is the idea of utility that sacrifices a thousand real advantages for one imaginary or trifling inconvenience; that would take fire from men because it burns, and water because one may drown in it; that has no remedy for evils, except destruction. The laws that forbid the carrying of arms are laws of such a nature. They disarm those only who are neither inclined nor determined to commit crimes. . . . Such laws make things worse for the assaulted and better for the assailants; they serve rather to encourage than to prevent homicides, for an unarmed man may be attacked with greater confidence than an armed man."

1768   A meeting, led by James Otis, Samuel Adams, John Hancock, and Samuel Cushing, was held in September in Faneuil Hall, Boston, protesting, among other things, standing armies. Those present

1768 *cont.*   passed a resolution (1) noting that under an Act of Parliament during the reign of William and Mary it had been declared that Protestants in England had been permitted arms for their own defense, and (2) declaring that every soldier and housekeeper in Massachusetts should be supplied with a firelock, musket, and ammunition, in accordance with the law, especially since many colonists feared a war with France.

In December, the British House of Lords passed a resolution declaring that the proceedings undertaken in Boston in September of that year were illegal and unconstitutional and that they were aimed at inciting sedition and insurrection.

1769   In February, the British House of Commons approved the resolution adopted in 1768 by the House of Lords and rebuked the proceedings undertaken in Boston by the colonists.

1770   After further protests by the Massachusetts colonists over the infringement on, and denial of, many of their rights, the "Boston Massacre" took place, in which British soldiers fired upon unarmed colonists in a crowd who had been throwing snowballs. This event served to further galvanize colonial resentment and opposition to both standing armies and the erosion of colonial liberties as guaranteed by the English Bill of Rights.

1774   James Burgh, in his much-quoted and highly relied-upon *Political Disquisitions,* wrote that standing armies gave ministers courage to do things that they probably would not have done if the people were armed, that is, if a people's militia were in existence. Using examples from history and writings from both classical authors and more contemporary debates in Parliament, he strongly endorsed an armed people, insisting, as others had, that the possession of arms insured their continued freedom. The colonists, especially their leading politician-intellectuals, had carefully read Burgh and cited him on frequent occasions.

George Mason and George Washington formed the Fairfax County, Virginia, Militia Association. Those who volunteered had to keep a firelock, 6 pounds of gun powder, and 20 pounds of lead on hand at all times. This idea of a militia was adopted colony-wide.

1774–1775   This period was notable for its almost methodical efforts on the part of the British to disarm their American subjects, efforts that in part constituted the colonial rationale for the Revolutionary War. Protests were lodged with British General Gage and the colonists continued to arm themselves, re-taking their firearms in Cambridge, for example, after the British Army had confiscated them and after several people had been killed in skirmishes.

1775   The Revolutionary War began in part because colonial militiamen refused to surrender their arms while exercising at Lexington. Later, when British General Gage struck a bargain with the inhabitants that they would be able to leave Boston if they surrendered their arms, the people complied, but Gage reneged on his agreement to a truce and proclaimed martial law, saying he would pardon those who would give up their arms. He would not, however, pardon Samuel Adams or John Hancock, and he continued to seize the weapons of the citizens of Boston. On 6 July 1775, the Continental Congress issued the Declaration of Causes of Taking up Arms. The war between the colonists and the British raged on.

1776   Adam Smith published *Wealth of Nations*. In this book, Smith spent considerable space and time discussing the dangers of standing armies. He lamented the fact that economic conditions had caused a slow transition from the notion that every man be armed in order to maintain a public militia to a situation where standing armies had come to the rise. He also pointed out that the American militia had great potential power against the organized forces of the British army. His voice was not

1776 *cont.*   unheard during the early years of the formation of the American nation.

The colonies declared their independence from Great Britain in the famous and unique Declaration of Independence in Congress Assembled, 4 July 1776.

Virginia adopted a Bill of Rights, the first colony to do so. Known as the Virginia Declaration of Rights, it became the model for bills of rights subsequently adopted by the remaining colonies. Its arms provision read as follows: "That a well regulated Militia, composed of the Body of the People, trained to Arms, is the proper, natural, and safe Defense of a free State; that standing Armies, in Time of Peace, should be avoided, as dangerous to Liberty."

Pennsylvania adopted its Constitution, calling it the Declaration of Rights of 1776. Its Bill of Rights is taken virtually verbatim from the Virginia Bill of Rights. Pennsylvania was the first state to explicitly decree that its people have the *right to bear arms.* The arms provision of its Constitution read: "That the people have a right to bear arms for the defense of themselves, and the state; and as standing armies, in the time of peace, are dangerous to liberty, they ought not to be kept up; and that the military should be kept under strict subordination to, and governed by the civil power." The document also protected hunting rights.

North Carolina adopted its Declaration of Rights, in which it was stated: "That the People have a Right to bear Arms for the Defense of the State; and as standing Armies in Time of Peace are dangerous to Liberty, they ought not to be kept up."

Maryland adopted a Declaration of Rights. The background of the adoption process in this colony was complicated by the Catholic-Protestant political differences that were rooted in England, and that were to some extent exacerbated by the Declaration of Rights of 1689. In Maryland, Catholic ministers were accused of attempting to disarm Protestants while Papists remained armed. Some Protestants had forcibly taken the arms of Catholics in Maryland as a consequence of the Glorious Revolution's provisions that re-armed Protestants. The Maryland Council ordered such weapons to be returned, however, and also passed a law assuring the right of all individuals, regardless of religion, to keep arms. Although the rights of Catholics in this matter were disputed again later, the arms confiscation actions by British General Gage in Massachusetts ultimately resulted in agreement that all the populace should be armed. In its Declaration of Rights, therefore, Maryland rejected the notion of standing armies and provided "that a well-regulated militia is the proper and natural defence of a free government."

Delaware adopted a Declaration of Rights. Relying on the language contained in the declarations of Virginia, Maryland, and Pennsylvania, the Delaware provision dealing with arms stated: "That a well regulated Militia is the proper, natural and safe Defense of a free Government."

1777   Colonial Undersecretary William Knox presented a proposal entitled "What Is Fit To Be Done with America?" In it he advocated not only the establishment of a state church, a standing army, and an aristocracy that was to govern the colonies, as well as a total power to tax, but also the repeal of the militia laws, the confiscation of all arms of the people, and the prohibition of the production of arms or gunpowder, and the prohibition of the importation of gunpowder, lead, or any arms or ordnance without a specific license.

Vermont adopted a Declaration of Rights. It adopted its right to bear arms clause verbatim from that of Pennsylvania: "That the people have a right to bear arms for the defence of themselves and the State; and, as standing armies, in the time

1777 *cont.*   of peace, are dangerous to liberty, they ought not to be kept up." The hunting provision was also copied: "That the inhabitants of this State, shall have liberty to hunt and fowl, in seasonable times, on the lands they hold" as well as on other lands that had not been enclosed.

1780   Massachusetts adopted its Declaration of Rights. As drafted by Samuel Adams, the arms provision of the Constitution read: "The people have a right to keep and bear arms for the common defence. And as, in time of peace, standing armies are dangerous to liberty, they ought not to be maintained without the consent of the legislature; and the military power shall always be held in an exact subordination to the civil authority, and be governed by it." The word *standing* before *armies* was deleted after debate on the proposal.

1784   Dr. Richard Price, a British philosopher, published *Observations on the Importance of the American Revolution*. In that work, he expressed horror over the possibility that standing armies might ever be established in America. He maintained that if states are to be free, they should be made up of duly armed citizens who were always prepared to quell rioting and to fight for peace and a proper execution of the laws. He noted that these characteristics described the citizens of America. His views had a wide following among colonial American leaders as well as among the people in general.

New Hampshire approved a Declaration of Rights. It was the last state of the Revolutionary period to adopt such a declaration. A number of constitutional conventions had been held in the state during the period 1781–1783, and after much debate, a significant portion of which was focused on the role of a militia, a Declaration of Rights was implemented in 1784. The language pertaining to arms read: "A well regulated militia is the proper, natural, and sure defence of a state. Standing armies are dangerous to liberty, and ought not to be raised or kept up without the consent of the legislature." Language protecting conscientious objectors was also included in the document.

1787   Noah Webster wrote *An Examination of the Leading Principles of the Federal Constitution*, in which he defended adoption of the proposed Constitution. He noted that the only way a standing army could rule was if the people had been disarmed. This is what had happened throughout most of Europe. In America, he said, domination by an oppressive government would likely be impossible because the people are armed and their force would be superior to the regular troops. Having written in response to requests from some of the delegates to the Constitutional Convention, his words had a wide-ranging effect on debate undertaken there.

Tench Coxe, one of the leading Federalists of the period, wrote *An American Citizen*, in which he lauded a people's militia and stated that such a militia would ultimately prove to be more powerful and effective than a standing army and would prove to be a potent restraint against oppression.

Richard Henry Lee, in his *Letters from the Federal Farmer*, argued strongly against adoption of the Constitution without a Bill of Rights, fearing, among other things, that without such a bill, a standing army would soon be established through taxation of the people.

The Constitution of the United States of America was adopted, and with the submission of it to the states for ratification, Anti-Federalists expressed concern that any state militia might be victimized by a standing army. Thus, a Bill of Rights would be necessary, and one of the rights should, they argued, be that the people shall always have the right to keep and bear arms.

1787–1788   *The Federalist*, by Alexander Hamilton, James Madison, and John Jay, appeared in the newspapers of

1787–1788 *cont.*	New York City. Essentially a collection of 85 letters written to the public in defense of, and advocacy for, the adoption of the Constitution of the United States, the letters contain references to the right to keep and bear arms, especially with the right to engage in revolution against a government engaging in tyranny, and to the value of a people's militia. Hamilton in *Federalist* Numbers 28 and 29, and Madison in No. 46, are cases in point. The entire series of letters was written under the pseudonym of Publius. The papers as a group constitute one of the great American contributions to political theory.
1788	Richard Henry Lee, in his *Additional Letters from the Federal Farmer,* powerfully declared that if liberty was to be preserved, then it was absolutely necessary that all citizens have arms and that they be taught how to use them. The people were to take up arms not only to preserve their property, but to protect their rights as free citizens as well. Patrick Henry and George Mason, at the Virginia ratifying convention, vehemently attacked the notion of keeping a standing army. Henry, in particular, insisted that "the great object is, that every man be armed."
1789	James Madison, in the House of Representatives, submitted an amendment to the Constitution—one of a series of twelve to be considered—that read as follows: "The right of the people to keep and bear arms shall not be infringed; a well-regulated militia being the best security of a free country: but no person religiously scrupulous of bearing arms shall be compelled to render military service in person." The present wording of the amendment was approved by both houses of Congress in September of 1789. Before that the Senate had specifically disapproved of language that would add the phrase "for the common defense" after the words "to keep and bear arms." The first clause of the original amendment was thus in particular be taken into account. In other words, the right to keep and bear arms was

not originally intended to be for militia purposes only, but was regarded as a right of the entire people. Militia, at that time, meant the whole body of the people who were armed.

The entire Bill of Rights was approved on 25 September, and was recommended to the states for adoption. The debates over ratification continued through 1791.

1792   The Militia Act of 1792 was adopted. This act recognized an organized militia and an enrolled militia. The enrolled militia was made up of members who were free white males and who would appear with their own arms—muskets, firelocks, bayonets, and ammunition—but were not in the organized service; they were to assist in defense should it become necessary, or to protect against a standing army and conceivably against even the organized militia itself should the government become tyrannous.

1806   *Rex v. Dewhurst* was decided. The case involved the advocacy of parliamentary reform on the part of an armed group protesting a massacre. The judge indicated that ordinary persons had the right to protect themselves when going about their usual business, but that did not permit them to carry weapons to a public meeting where harm might more readily be committed. In other words, weapons were permitted as long as they were not used to intimidate other persons.

Noah Webster published his *Compendious Dictionary of the English Language*. This was the predecessor to his later dictionary, and can be used to understand the meaning of such terms as *people, bear,* and *arms* in the context of framing of state bills of rights, of the Constitution of the United States, and, ultimately, the Second Amendment as adopted in 1789. His definitions reflect common and legal understanding of the terms during the revolutionary period.

1820   *Houston v. Moore* was decided by the U.S. Supreme Court. The Court held in this case that states had the power to order men who were able-bodied to supply themselves with military weapons as declared in the Federal Militia Act of 1792.

1828   Noah Webster published *An American Dictionary of the English Language.* This dictionary became the standard reference work for an understanding of the language and was relied upon in England as well. His definitions of terms relevant to the understanding of the individual right to keep and bear arms are crucial to the analysis of their application today. For example, *militia* means "the able bodied men"; *regulated* means "adjusted by rule, method or forms; put in good order; subjected to rules or restrictions"; *people* means "the commonalty, as distinct from men of rank"; *bear* means "to carry" or "to wear"; *arms* means "weapons of offense, or armor for defense and protection of the body." If one is to understand the way in which terms were understood during the period of the drafting of the Constitution and of the Second Amendment, Webster's dictionary stands as perhaps the leading authority.

1837   The first ban on handguns went into effect in Georgia. In *Nunn v. State* this ban was later voided as a violation of the Second Amendment's right to keep and bear arms.

1854   Blacks were the focus of disarmament. Some courts in the antebellum period, as in the case of North Carolina, for example, disarmed blacks by noting that only citizens could have the right to bear arms; slaves could not go about "armed with a gun." They argued, further, that the adoption of the Second Amendment had not prohibited states from passing such laws.

1857   In *Dred Scott v. Sanford*, an exceedingly important Supreme Court case, Chief Justice Taney insisted that the Bill of Rights had not in fact been written to protect the rights of blacks. Indeed, he argued that if this were the case, "it would give to persons of the negro race . . . full liberty of speech, to hold public meetings . . . and to keep and carry arms wherever they went." The ruling in that case was to have deep repercussions throughout the nation, especially with respect to civil rights and the right explicated in the Second Amendment.

1865   Various so-called Black Codes came into existence. These codes limited access of members of the Negro race to land, to arms, and to the courts. In Mississippi, for example, freedmen—Negros or mulattos freed from slavery—were prohibited from keeping or carrying any types of firearms.

President Abraham Lincoln was assassinated.

1866   The Fourteenth Amendment, the Freedman's Bureau Act, and the Civil Rights Act of 1866 were adopted. Each of these acts was aimed in part at the application of the Second Amendment in the states. Congress voted three times to make certain that the right to keep and bear arms on the part of individual citizens could not be violated by states. The Freedman's Bureau Act specifically mentioned the rights guaranteed under the Second Amendment. When introducing the Fourteenth Amendment, Senator Jacob M. Howard stated that personal rights guaranteed by the first eight amendments to the Constitution specifically included the right to keep and bear arms.

1869   Congress acted to abolish the formation of southern white militia units. These militias had acted systematically in efforts to disarm blacks. Congressional legislation thus temporarily slowed the power of the states to maintain militias. The concern of Congress was the maintenance of the right of the people to keep and bear arms.

1871   The National Rifle Association was established. Spearheaded by former Union Army officers, the

1871 *cont.*   drive to form the association was undertaken especially by Colonel William C. Church, editor of the *Army-Navy Journal*. Rifle practice was to be a particular objective of the association, largely in response to the concern about preparedness, safety, and defense and in recognition of the inadequacies demonstrated by some of the younger Union troops during the Civil War.

1876   *U.S. v. Cruikshank* was decided. In this Supreme Court case, Ku Klux Klansmen had been convicted, in part, of depriving "persons of color" of their rights "to keep and bear arms." This was in principle a civil rights case. Nevertheless, the U.S. Supreme Court took the position that the Second Amendment protects an individual's right against the national government, not against actions of some private group; for this type of protection, persons had to look to the police power of the states. The Court also held that the right to keep and bear arms existed independent of the Constitution.

1879   *Dunne v. People* was decided by the Illinois Supreme Court. In that case, which arose out of a labor dispute, the court ruled that Congress, as the result of an amendment to the United States Constitution that had been approved by the states, does not have the power to infringe on the right of the people "to keep and bear arms," inasmuch as the states had the power to legislate respecting a militia even before the Constitution of the United States was adopted.

1881   President James Garfield was assassinated.

1886   *Presser v. Illinois* was decided by the Supreme Court. In this case, the Supreme Court reaffirmed the holding in the Cruikshank case, but it declared also that the states do not have the power to void the right of the people to keep and bear arms. In the words of the Court, "It is undoubtedly true that all citizens capable of bearing arms constitute the reserved military force or reserve militia of the

United States as well as of the States, and in view of this prerogative of the general government, as well as of its general powers, the States cannot, even laying the constitutional provision in question of view, prohibit the people from keeping and bearing arms, so as to deprive the United States of their rightful resource for maintaining the public security and disable the people from performing their duty to the general government." Although not directly stated, the findings in the Presser case also indicate that the Second Amendment was deemed applicable to the states by way of the Fourteenth Amendment.

1901   President William McKinley was assassinated.

1908   New York enacted the first law that required a hunting license. Revenues raised by this license were used in wildlife management programs. Every state eventually required a hunting license, and the funds so collected have continued to support such programs.

1911   New York City enacted the well-known Sullivan Law. It required a permit to purchase a gun. The law has been said to have been directed at disarmament of anti-Tammany politicians (Tammany Hall was the popular name for the Democratic political machine in Manhattan) and also Italian immigrants who were suspected of increasing the crime rate in the city. The law has in fact done little if anything to reduce crime in New York City.

1919   Congress enacted an excise tax on weapons. This law was rationalized as a revenue-raising device after World War I, and was the first entry on the part of the federal government in the areas of the manufacture and sale of firearms.

1927   A law was passed by the federal government prohibiting the mailing of concealable firearms in the United States. The law is still in effect.

1930   The debate between the protections provided by
          the Second Amendment and gun control became
          heated. Submachine guns, as they were used espe-
          cially during the Prohibition period, came under
          severe attack. Gun registration likewise became a
          major issue of debate in the United States. The na-
          tion's press in particular began its role as outspo-
          ken and sometimes strident advocate of gun
          control measures while largely ignoring the Sec-
          ond Amendment. Most journalists had no knowl-
          edge of guns and their use. Calvin C. Goddard,
          who was the director of the Scientific Crime De-
          tection Laboratory at Northwestern University,
          suggested that there was in fact no correlation be-
          tween gun control and the reduction of crime. It
          can be effectively argued that Goddard's words re-
          main particularly true today, given the passage of
          a large number of gun control laws and the relative
          absence of data showing a negative impact on the
          commission of crime.

1934   The National Firearms Act of 1934 was passed. It
          was aimed at restricting "gangster-type" weapons,
          and came on the heels of an attempt to assassinate
          President Franklin Delano Roosevelt and in re-
          sponse to increased killings perpetrated by
          organized crime elements. Among the major pro-
          visions of the act were the taxation of the manu-
          facture, sale, and transfer of weapons and
          weapons accessories as defined in the act. It also
          required the purchaser to undergo a background
          check by the Federal Bureau of Investigation, re-
          quired a seller to pay a transfer tax of $200.00
          (which was ultimately passed on to the buyer in
          terms of costs), and required the purchaser of a
          weapon to have approval of a local law enforce-
          ment officer. The act thus banned the over-the-
          counter sale of machine guns, and it provided for
          registration, licensing, and taxation of fully auto-
          matic firearms, short-barreled rifles, and even
          shotguns so that law-abiding citizens could pur-
          chase them. Under the provisions of the law, one is
          required to submit a photograph and fingerprints

to the national government so a background check can be made. If the application is approved by the federal government, the person is also required to obtain approval from local law enforcement agencies in order to take the weapon into a local jurisdiction. Since the act passed, approximately 175,000 automatic firearms have been licensed by the Bureau of Alcohol, Tobacco, and Firearms (the federal agency responsible for administration of the law), and evidence suggests that none of these weapons has ever been used to commit a violent crime. Because this was the first piece of firearms law having a national impact, the act was vehemently opposed as infringing the rights of states. The category of handguns was removed from the act.

Congress passed the so-called Migratory Bird Hunting Stamp Act, which required hunters to purchase a stamp, which was valid for one year, to hunt waterfowl. Fees collected by the sale of these stamps have underwritten the cost of purchasing and managing wetlands throughout the United States.

1937   *Palko v. Connecticut* was decided by the Supreme Court. The Court held that the due process clause of the Fourteenth Amendment applied the guarantees of the Bill of Rights to the states. The Second Amendment has not yet been incorporated by a direct decision of the Supreme Court as have, for example, the Fourth, Fifth, and Sixth Amendments.

The Wildlife Restoration Act was passed by Congress. This act imposed a 10 percent tax on guns and ammunition. The act won strong support among the hunting community. The funds so raised were ostensibly used for wildlife conservation. The law was later amended in the 1970s to increase the tax to 11 percent and was expanded to include archery equipment. The training of hunters and the development of rangelands were also included in the areas to which collected funds were allocated.

1938   The Federal Firearms Act of 1938 was passed. The purpose of this law was, essentially, to control the interstate commercial sales of weapons. The law therefore required that gun manufacturers, gun dealers, and importers of firearms and ammunition for pistols and revolvers acquire licenses. The Internal Revenue Service was responsible for collecting the license fees. The act also prohibited delivering a gun to a known criminal, to someone who was under indictment, or to those who did not meet the licensing laws of local jurisdictions.

1939   The Supreme Court decided *U.S. v. Miller.* This is a much misunderstood case. The Supreme Court stated that the Second Amendment guarantees an individual right to keep and bear arms, and that the militia is composed of all able-bodied males, who, when called for duty, were to bring their own arms. Thus, the right to keep and bear arms was independent of service in the militia itself. The Court raised the question as to whether ownership of a firearm of the type involved in this case was a type suitable for use in a militia. It held that there was no evidence in the record that a sawed-off shotgun was a weapon used by the militia. Inasmuch as such evidence was not submitted to the Court, it remanded the case back to the lower trial court for an evidentiary hearing. The hearing was never held. It should be noted, too, that neither counsel for the defense nor the defendants themselves appeared before the Court, and no brief was filed that might have enlightened the Court with respect to the ruling of the lower trial court.

1949   The National Rifle Association entered into a hunter safety program with the State of New York. It was the first of these types of programs.

1954   The Mutual Security Act came into effect. This act gave the president power to exercise control over the flow of firearms and the sale of ammunition. The responsibilities for enforcement were given over to the Office of Munitions Control of the Department of State.

1958   The Federal Aviation Act was passed. This law prohibited the carrying of firearms, whether concealed or not, on or about any individual flying on a passenger aircraft.

1963   President John F. Kennedy was assassinated.

1965   *Maryland for the Use of Levin v. United States* was decided by the Supreme Court. In that case, the Court held that states may mandate that their militias may arm themselves with the same weapons used by the National Guard. Thus, Congress cannot deny possession of weapons that states require for their militias and that citizens keep in their homes and then bring with them for service.

1967   The President's Commission on Law Enforcement and Administration presented a report on the country's crime problem. Among many recommendations were national handgun registration and the prohibition of commerce, on an interstate basis, of handgun sales.

1968   Dr. Martin Luther King was assassinated.

Senator Robert Kennedy was assassinated.

The Omnibus Crime Control and Safe Streets Act of 1968 was passed. After the assassinations of Dr. Martin Luther King, Jr., and Senator Robert Kennedy, sentiment was high for passing more stringent gun legislation. This law was considerably more comprehensive than those previously enacted.

The Gun Control Act of 1968 was passed. It consists of Titles IV and VII of the Omnibus Act. The Gun Control Act aimed at the expansion of provisions of the Omnibus Crime Control and Safe Streets Act.

1969   The National Commission on the Causes and Prevention of Violence released a report that included recommendations for a national law requiring registration of handguns and for a national law that would eventually require a license for all who purchase handguns.

1970   The Organized Crime Control Act of 1970 was enacted. This act restricted the manufacture of various explosives and made federal crimes of defined bombings and arsons. The act placed these matters under the jurisdiction of the Alcohol, Tobacco, and Firearms Division of the Internal Revenue Service.

1972   The Alcohol, Tobacco, and Firearms Division of the Internal Revenue Service was given full bureau status in the Department of the Treasury. Its jurisdiction embraced impeding the illegal use and traffic in firearms, the arrest of those who were repeat firearm offenders, and the seizure of firearms used by drug dealers. It was also given the mission of investigating bombings and arsons, and acquired the power to regulate manufacturers of explosives and firearms, and to trace guns that had been recovered by law enforcement personnel.

     The Senate of the United States passed a bill to prohibit the manufacture and sale of non-sporting handguns. The legislation was known as the Bayh Bill, inasmuch as it was initiated by Senator Birch Bayh of Indiana.

1973   The National Advisory Commission on Criminal Justice Standards and Goals recommended, among other things, that by the year 1983 the private ownership of handguns be prohibited.

1974   Senate Bill 1401 was debated, resulting in the rejection of proposed amendments similar to those in the Bayh Bill passed in 1972. The bill would have required handgun registration, licenses for ownership, and the banning of the manufacture of all handguns that did not have a sporting purpose.

1977   *Moore v. East Cleveland* was decided. This was a
                case in which the United States Supreme Court
                stated that the right to keep and bear arms is one
                of the "specific guarantees" contained in the Con-
                stitution of the United States. The Court included
                in these "guarantees" the rights to "freedom of
                speech, press, and religion; the right to keep and
                bear arms; the freedom from unreasonable
                searches and seizures; and so on."

                The District of Columbia, site of the nation's capi-
                tal, imposed a freeze on the possession of hand-
                guns. Acquisition, purchase, or possession of a
                handgun after 5 February 1977 was deemed ille-
                gal. Shotguns and some types of rifles could be re-
                tained by residents of the District under the law,
                but they must have been registered, kept and
                stored unloaded, locked, or disassembled.

1978   The Bureau of Alcohol, Tobacco, and Firearms
                suggested new regulations concerning the manu-
                facture and sale of firearms. Such matters as a ser-
                ial number system, dealer reporting of sales and
                the serial numbers of weapons sold, and the re-
                porting of thefts and losses were included.
                The House of Representatives passed an appropri-
                ations bill that banned implementation of the
                above proposals and eliminated over $4 million it
                was estimated would be necessary to implement
                the proposals. The Senate later agreed.

1979   The Treasury Department withdrew its proposals
                for the serial numbering system and periodic re-
                porting of gun sales by licensed dealers.

1980   *Lewis v. U.S.* was decided by the Supreme Court.
                The Court held in this case that federal govern-
                ment laws that deny felons possession of firearms
                did not infringe upon provisions of the Second
                Amendment with respect to the right to keep and
                bear arms, nor did they transgress the equal pro-
                tection clauses of the Fifth Amendment.

1981–1984   In such places as Morton Grove, Evanston, and Oak Park, Illinois, a number of laws were passed providing for a total prohibition of handguns by persons in those communities. These provisions included both the sale and possession of such guns. During this time period, attempts were made in Skoki and some other suburbs of Chicago to implement similar laws, but they were defeated. On the other hand, the city of Kennesaw, Georgia, passed a law that required gun ownership on the part of its residents. Statistics have demonstrated that the number of armed crimes dropped dramatically in that city upon enactment of the law.

1981   The Village of Morton Grove, Illinois, passed Ordinance No. 81-11, "an Ordinance regulating the Possession of Firearms and Other Dangerous Weapons." The ordinance stated that "in order to promote and protect the health and safety and welfare of the public it is necessary to regulate the possession of firearms and other dangerous weapons." The ordinance went on to state that "no person shall possess, in the Village of Morton Grove, the following: (1) Any bludgeon, black-jack, slug shot, sand club, sand bag, metal knuckles or any knife, commonly referred to as a switchblade . . . ; (2) Any weapon from which 8 or more shots or bullets may be discharged by a single function of the firing device, any shotgun having one or more barrels less than 18 inches in length...or any bomb, bomb-shell, grenade, bottle, or other container containing an explosive substance . . . ; (3) Any handgun, unless the same has been rendered permanently inoperative." Exceptions to this ordinance were made.

The United States District Court for the Northern District of Illinois, Eastern Division, held that the Morton Grove Ordinance was constitutional.

A report was released by the United States Attorney General's Task Force on Violent Crime. It proposed, among other things, that commercial handgun purchases should require police clearance; that the importation of unassembled handgun parts should be prohibited, if, when assembled, such parts would result in weapons that would otherwise be banned; more intensive prosecution of felons in possession of a handgun; and, in the case of a federal felony, mandatory sentencing when firearms were used.

1982   Voters in California defeated Proposition 15, which would have imposed stringent handgun controls, e.g., registration of handguns and freezing their number. Some 63 percent of California voters opposed the measure.

Owners of handguns in Morton Grove, Illinois, appealed the decision of the District Court with respect to Ordinance 81-11. The case went before the United States Court of Appeals, Seventh Circuit, as *Victor D. Quilici, Robert Stentl, et al., George L. Reichert, and Robert E. Metler, Plaintiffs-Appellants, v. Village of Morton Grove, et al., Defendants-Appellees.* The decision was upheld by a vote of 2 to 1. Judge Coffey dissented on the grounds that the matter was actually one that should be "properly resolved by state action . . . that the Ordinance is invalid under the home rule provision of the Illinois Constitution . . . [and] Third, I believe that [the Ordinance] . . . impermissibly interferes with individual privacy rights" and the right to defend one's home.

1983   The Supreme Court of the United States chose not to hear an appeal in the Morton Grove decision.

1984   The Armed Career Criminal Act was passed, amending the Gun Control Act of 1968. It provided, among other things, that any person convicted of a felony; any person dishonorably discharged from the Armed Services; any person who has been adjudged mentally incompetent; any person who has renounced his citizenship; and any person who is an alien or is unlawfully in the United States who receives, possesses, or transports a firearm, shall be fined not more than

1984 *cont.* $10,000 or imprisoned not more than two years, or both. It provided 15-year sentences and a $25,000 fine for those who have had three previous convictions for robbery or burglary or both.

President Reagan signed an appropriations bill that contained a title related to crime control. The title included measures to do away with probation or suspended sentences for those committing a federal felony with any firearm, and which required a 15-year penalty for possession of a firearm by robbers and burglars who were repeat offenders. Other provisions were included.

Kalodimos v. Village of Morton Grove was decided. The judgments of the appellate and circuit courts in the Morton Grove handgun ban case were affirmed by the Illinois Supreme Court.

1985   The United States Senate passed an amended version of the Firearms Owners Protection Act, otherwise known as the McClure-Volkmer bill. On roll call votes, the bill was changed to eliminate restrictions on the interstate sale of handguns and the requirement of a 14-day waiting period for the delivery of a handgun acquired by interstate sale, and it maintained the provision that licensed dealers receive notice before they receive compliance inspections.

1986   The McClure-Volkmer Firearms Owners Protection Act came into force. Among its major provisions were those that (1) decreased from a felony to a misdemeanor violations dealers made in their paperwork with respect to gun transactions; (2) permitted the interstate sale of long guns by gun dealers; (3) required certain minimum and mandatory penalties for misuse of firearms; and (4) provided for penalties for those engaged in drug-trafficking offenses if they were carrying a firearm. The amendment by Representative William Hughes (Democrat of New Jersey) effectively banned the purchase of automatic firearms by civilians if such firearms were produced after the enactment of the act.

The Law Enforcement Officers Protection Act was passed. It prohibited manufacture or importation of certain types of so-called armor-piercing ammunition. Inasmuch as many police officers wear bulletproof vests, this law was directed at protecting them in particular.

The Armed Career Criminal Act was amended. Persons with three previous convictions under provisions of the act would receive $25,000 fines or imprisonment of 15 years, and the courts could not suspend the sentence or grant probation.

1988   The State of Nebraska adopted a constitutional provision guaranteeing the right to keep and bear arms. It was the 43rd state to do so.

The Terrorist Firearms Detection Act was signed into law by President Reagan. This act banned the importation, sale, manufacture, or possession of firearms, e.g., plastic handguns or other devices that could not be detected by security equipment.

The Anti-Drug Abuse Act called for the attorney general of the United States to develop a procedure for firearms dealers that would make it easier to identify felons attempting to purchase guns.

1989   The Congress of the United States received from the United States Attorney General a report on the study of felon identification programs that had been conducted by the Department of Justice. In terms of policy implications, it was essentially identical to the proposal published earlier.

A violent and deranged criminal who had previously been arrested seven times but who had had charges dropped against him or eliminated on the basis of plea bargains, shot and killed five schoolchildren on a playground in Stockton, California.

The State of California adopted a law that banned semiautomatic firearms. Known popularly as the

1989 *cont.*   Roberti-Roos Assault Weapon Act, it also banned unrestricted sales by unlicensed dealers at gun shows throughout the state. The type of weapon used in the Stockton killings was not included on the list of banned weapons. The law also banned guns that did not exist.

The State of Florida enacted a law requiring a background check for those purchasing guns from gun dealers. Also enacted was a law that required owners of guns to keep the weapons locked so children could not have access to them. Other states—e.g., Maryland, Oregon, and Virginia—and some local jurisdictions enacted laws requiring bans of, or waiting periods for, purchase of assault weapons, background checks for purchasers, and similar measures.

1990   The Congress of the United States received from the United States attorney general a study dealing with the development of a means for identifying persons prohibited from owning handguns (even though they were non-felons) before commercial handgun transfers could take place.

The United States Senate passed an omnibus crime control bill. It banned the importation of any semiautomatic weapon under the definition of "assault weapons." It also prohibited the possession and transfer of such weapons if they were not already legally owned by the time of the enactment of the law.

In the State of California, a bill was passed that extended the state's 15-day waiting period to sales of all firearms. In addition, multi-burst trigger activators were outlawed.

The State of Connecticut passed a law that extended the 14-day waiting period to sales of all firearms. In addition, a law aimed at preventing children's accidents with guns was passed. It required that all weapons be sold only if they had trigger locks.

The Indiana Supreme Court ruled that the mayor of Gary, Indiana, had been "arbitrary and carpricious" when he denied handgun permits to Gary residents; thus the court returned to the citizens the right to keep and bear arms. The 1871 Civil Rights Act (the so-called Anti-Ku Klux Klan Act) was used in reaching the decision.

The State of Iowa passed a law that required background checks for all persons purchasing handguns. It also required owners of gun shops to keep guns in places away from children and prohibited "exotic" trigger mechanisms.

Many other states passed legislation limiting or prohibiting assault weapons and requiring waiting periods of varying durations for purchase and possession of handguns, background checks of gun purchasers, protections for children, and other provisions affecting the ownership and possession of firearms.

The president signed the Crime Control Act of 1990, which prohibited manufacture in the United States of some types of semiautomatic long guns if the parts used in such manufacture were imported.

United States v. Verdugo-Urquidez was decided by the Supreme Court. This case arose under the Fourth Amendment provisions dealing with search and seizure. The Court also stated, however, that " 'the people' seems to have been a term of art employed in select parts of the Constitution. . . . The Second Amendment protects 'the right of the people to keep and bear Arms,' and the Ninth and Tenth Amendments provide that certain rights and powers are retained by and reserved to 'the people.' "

Perpich v. Department of Defense was decided by the Supreme Court. This case had to do with the role of the National Guard as part of the armed forces of the United States. Although the Court did not mention the Second Amendment as such, it inferred

1990 *cont.*   that the concept of "the people" in the Second Amendment referred to individuals.

1991   The Comprehensive Crime Control Act of 1991 was passed by the House of Representatives. It prohibited the domestic assembly of any semiautomatic rifle or shotgun from imported parts if any such weapon was identical to a rifle or shotgun already prohibited from being imported under the Gun Control Act's "sporting purposes test."

1994   The Brady Handgun Violence Prevention Act was passed. This act provides that "it shall be unlawful for any licensed importer, licensed manufacturer, or licensed dealer to sell, deliver, or transfer a handgun to an individual who is not licensed . . . unless. . . ." At this point several exceptions are listed. The act provides that "whoever knowingly violates [its provisions] shall be fined not more than $1,000, imprisoned for not more than one year, or both." Other matters are included.

The Assault Weapons Ban Bill was passed. The primary emphasis of this legislation was to make illegal the sale, manufacture, importation, or possession of some 19 assault weapons. Other provisions were included in the bill.

The Violent Crime Control and Enforcement Act was passed by Congress. This was one of the most sweeping pieces of legislation dealing with crime ever passed by the United States Congress. Its provisions ranged from outright gun controls to the building of more prisons, placing more police officers on the street, and providing "midnight basketball" to help deter persons from committing crime. Many of its provisions—defined especially as "pork"—were immediately under attack. The law will be subject to revision in future sessions of Congress and to varying interpretations by enforcement agencies.

1995   *United States v. Lopez* was decided by the Supreme Court. In this case, San Antonio high school student

Alfonso Lopez, Jr., challenged his conviction for carrying a concealed weapon to school on the basis that the Gun-Free School Zone Act enacted by Congress was unconstitutional. The deliberation attended to the constitutional limitation of congressional power to regulate interstate commerce. Because the respondent's actions were independent of any interstate economic activity, the Court ruled in his favor in order to maintain the distinction between federal and local government.

Biographical Sketches

T he following biographies include individuals—lawyers, philosophers, politicians, and activists—that have had a significant impact on the issue of gun control, whether for or against it. The time period covered reaches as far back as colonial times in America, when it was commonplace to own a gun, and continues up through the present with its increasing controversy.

Richard Aborn (n.d.)

The president of Handgun Control, Inc., Richard Aborn is a long-time opponent of gun ownership and a vocal proponent of the regulation and banning of firearms. During his remarks on the adoption of the Brady Bill, he suggested that one of the reasons the National Rifle Association opposed the bill was because it represented the nose of the camel under the tent of more extensive regulations. At a news conference held on 8 December 1993, Aborn proclaimed his intention of telling "what the rest of the camel looks like." His comments were directed at revealing the contents of what has come to be referred to as "Brady II"—an extensive list of objectives that would involve the imposition of particularly strong regulations on gun owners and manufacturers, and that would require, among other things, taxation on gun dealers, guns, and ammunition.

Mr. Aborn insisted that the objectives of Brady II could be accomplished.

James Jay Baker (b. 1953)

James J. Baker has been director of the Governmental Affairs Division of the National Rifle Association (NRA) Institute for Legislative Action. He has testified before the Subcommittee on Crime of the House Judiciary Committee on a number of issues related to gun control policy.

One of the NRA's most recent concerns has been efforts by some members of Congress and pressure organizations to ban the allegedly nondetectable pistol known as the Glock 17. Mr. Baker has suggested that the statements related to the gun's alleged undetectability are founded largely on inaccurate stories appearing in the media. He has argued that the Glock 17 is in fact detectable: its steel components and lower receiver (which is made largely of plastic) are detectable by airport security systems. It is probable that keys commonly carried by passengers and such devices as a screwdriver would be more undetectable given the security systems currently in use at some airports.

The issue lies not in the gun's "undetectability," but in the failures of airport security systems and, sometimes, in the complete absence of training on the part of airport personnel to use detection devices adequately.

The legislation obfuscates the realities of the situation by calling upon vague fears of terrorism. Terrorists do not necessarily need access to an aircraft while they are carrying destructive weapons. Baker points out that a terrorist could as easily apply for and get a job in a so-called sterile area of an airport and perform his activities there and simply ignore inspecting baggage, or passing it through, knowing that it contains a weapon or other explosive device. What is needed is to upgrade security measures. The proposed legislation is "piecemeal" and rests on an incorrect rationale.

In a related hearing, Mr. Baker stated, for example, that "nothing will have been done about the problems created by an overburdened and crumbling criminal justice system and the ravages caused by drug trafficking. Additional gun control is a media quick-fix solution to a very complex drug and criminal justice problem."

Michael K. Beard (b. 1941)

Michael Beard was President of the National Coalition to Ban Handguns when he presented his testimony before the Committee of the Judiciary of the United States Senate. His testimony had to do with opposition to the McClure-Volkmer amendments to the Gun Control Act of 1968.

Beard argued that

1. The amendments would prohibit the Bureau of Alcohol, Tobacco, and Firearms from doing inspections of whether licensed firearm dealers are in compliance with the law
2. The changes would create "a preferred class of criminal defendants"
3. The amendments would protect persons who use a gun in a felony, even though they do not shoot anyone
4. The resulting new bill would allow individuals to escape their own state's firearms laws by buying guns in other states.

Hence, Beard suggested, the McClure-Volkmer amendments could not be viewed as "responsible." He argued that felons would ultimately be the beneficiaries.

Joseph R. Biden, Jr. (b. 1942)

Joseph Biden is a U.S. senator from Delaware, his term having begun in 1972. He received a bachelor's degree from the University of Delaware and a J.D. degree from Syracuse University. He has served as chairman of the Senate Judiciary Committee and is a member of the Senate Foreign Relations Committee. He is widely known for his support of liberal and left-of-center policies, among them advocacy of stringent anti-gun measures.

Biden was a particularly vocal supporter of the assault weapons ban and the crime bills, both of which passed Congress in 1994, and of the Brady Bill, which requires a five-day waiting period for a purchase of a weapon. He maintained his position even in the face of evidence presented by witnesses before Congress, suggesting, for example, that David Kopel, an expert on criminal use of firearms and the intention of the framers of the Second Amendment, was consistently incorrect with respect to the points he had presented. Kopel is associated with the independent Cato

Institute, and in his testimony before Biden's committee he used Bureau of Alcohol, Tobacco, and Firearms data.

Senator Biden lost his position of Chair of the Senate Judiciary Committee as a result of the 1994 congressional elections that brought Republicans control of the Senate.

Sir William Blackstone (1723–1780)

Sir William Blackstone's significance to the issue of the right to keep and bear arms can hardly be overestimated. His *Commentaries on the House of England* was immensely influential for the development of early American law and the teaching of American lawyers about issues related to English common law. Not only did he have views on the subject of a people's militia and on the broad subject of hunting as a natural right (and efforts by the Crown to use hunting laws as a means of disarming the people), but he also insisted that "the fifth and auxiliary right of the subject . . . is that of having arms for their defence, suitable to their condition and degree and such as are allowed by law. Which is also declared . . . and is indeed a public allowance, under due restrictions, of the natural right of resistance and self-preservation. . . ." Blackstone's writings made the understanding of common law legal education comprehensive and understandable. His lectures, published as commentaries, became some of the most widely read intellectual treatises of the day. Since his works appeared, virtually every budding lawyer—and even those long in the profession—were drawn to his work, from which the only conclusion that one could reach (relevant to the right to keep and bear arms) was that it was one's legal and perhaps even moral obligation to own firearms as a defense against a potentially tyrannous government.

Barbara Boxer (b. 1940)

Barbara Boxer is currently serving as United States senator from California. She received a B.A. from Brooklyn College in 1962 and has been a stock broker and a journalist. She has also served as congressional aide to the representative from the 5th Congressional District in San Francisco and has been a member of the Marin County Board of Supervisors. She served as a member of the 98th–100th Congresses from the 6th District of California. She was one of the founding members of the Women's Political Caucus and was president of the Democractic New Members Caucus.

She is generally known for her liberal political agenda and her vocal anti-crime and anti-gun positions. She was a strong supporter of the Brady bill, the assault weapons ban, and the crime bill.

Sarah Brady (b. 1942)

Sarah Brady is the wife of former presidential press aide James Brady. Mrs. Brady is a widely known gun control activist. After many years of effort, first as a member and then as the president of Handgun Control, Incorporated, she saw adopted the Brady Law, which requires a five-day waiting period for the purchase of all handguns in the United States. Her work against guns stems largely from the result of serious wounds her husband received outside the Washington Hilton Hotel during an attempt by a gunman to assassinate President Ronald Reagan.

Aside from the implementation of the five-day waiting period, Mrs. Brady has also recommended the adoption of a national gun registration program, the requirement of a Federal Handgun Owner License, the banning of semiautomatic weapons, an increase on the tax on handguns, banning ammunition magazines over ten rounds, banning gun sales at gun shows, banning all non-sporting ammunition, banning so-called Saturday Night Specials, increasing the tax on handgun ammunition, making firearms dealers liable for victims of gun violence, and the restriction of all gun purchases to one a month. She has been a vehement opponent of the National Rifle Association (NRA).

She argues that gun laws work and that criminals buy firearms in stores that sell them. A background check on purchases would therefore serve to deal with this problem. On this issue, she has frequently testified before committees and subcommittees of Congress.

Sarah Brady has a B.A. in Education from the College of William and Mary and has been a former teacher and assistant campaign director for the National Republican Congressional Committee. She has served as an aide to Representatives Mike McKevitt and Joseph J. Maraziti, and as a Republican National Committee activist.

William Jefferson Clinton (b. 1946)

President of the United States and former Arkansas Governor William Jefferson Clinton was born in 1946. He received a bachelor's degree in international affairs from Georgetown University in 1968, attended Oxford University from 1968 to 1970, and received a J.D. from Yale University in 1973. He served as a professor in the University of Arkansas law school and practiced law privately in Arkansas, where he also served as attorney general. He served as chairman of the Education Commission of the States of the Carnegie Foundation, and was chairman of the Democratic Leadership Council.

Clinton is widely known for his strong support of gun control and anti-crime bills and of stringent limitations on the sale, possession, and use of guns as means by which crime reduction can be achieved, even at the risk of possibly violating the provisions of the Second Amendment and the prohibitions in the Fourth Amendment dealing with unreasonable searches and seizures. He has expressed support for sweeping residence searches with the purpose of confiscating guns, presumably to prevent their use in future crimes, particularly in inner-city residential complexes.

Following a 1994 shooting incident aimed at the White House, initiated from beyond the iron fence that surrounds the residence, Clinton proclaimed a renewed and even greater support for the banning of assault weapons as a means to reduce violent crime.

Thomas M. Cooley (1824–1898)

A conservative justice of the Michigan Supreme Court, Thomas M. Cooley argued that ". . . the right [to keep and bear arms] is general.—It may be supposed from the phraseology of this provision [the Second Amendment] that the right to keep and bear arms was only guaranteed to the militia; but this would be an interpretation not warranted by intent. . . . The meaning of the provision undoubtedly is, that the people, from whom the militia must be taken, shall have the right to keep and bear arms, and they need no permission or regulation of law for the purpose." He drew these conclusions from an examination of the history of the development of the Second Amendment, noting that it was taken to some extent from the English Bill of Rights, and he insisted that any more narrow interpretation of the amendment could simply not be justified by the facts. His works were highly influential in the interpretation of the Constitution, especially of the applicability of the Fourteenth Amendment and also in the law of torts and taxation.

Robert Dole (b. 1923)

Robert Dole is a United States senator from Kansas and, as a result of 1994 congressional elections, the majority leader of the Senate. Speaking on the issue of gun control, Dole has repeatedly recognized its intensely controversial nature and that it constitutes a significant area of concern for the criminal justice system as well as for its impact on fundamental issues dealing with rights guaranteed under the Second Amendment.

Dole has favored changes in the Gun Control Act of 1968 in order to make more efficient the administration of the law and to protect law-abiding citizens from both illegal and politically motivated incursions by the government. Reasonable restraints, however, could and should, in his opinion, be applied in the area of ownership and use of firearms. Those having criminal intent must be dealt with especially harshly.

He particularly commended Senator McClure and Representative Volkmer for their leadership in amending the 1968 law so that it better reflects accuracy and efficiency in the protection of individual rights while at the same time punishing those who engage in criminal excesses through the use of firearms. He offers some of his own suggestions on changes in the law as forthcoming legislative proposals, including abolishing the assault weapon ban.

Barbara Fass (b. 1940)

Barbara Fass was mayor of Stockton, California, in 1989 when five children were killed on that city's Cleveland School campus during a rampage by Patrick Purdy, an unstable felon who had been arrested on a variety of charges before the incident, but who was not held imprisoned on an extended basis for his prior crimes.

Fass testified before the Subcommittee on Crime of the House Judiciary Committee, not only representing the City of Stockton but also representing the United States Conference of Mayors. She testified that since 1986 she had seen killings with "high-powered, rapid fire, semiautomatic assault weapons" rise dramatically but that not much was done about this until the 17 January 1989 incident at Cleveland School. She suggested that assault weapons had to be done away with as a way of reducing the potential of such tragedies.

Suggesting that she could be arrested for carrying a club down the street, be legally prohibited from driving a tank down the street, or prevented from owning a nuclear bomb, Fass asked that the right to keep and bear arms be limited in such a way that military assault weapons not be permitted under its interpretation. These weapons, she argued, were designed to be used on battlefields. She made several suggestions on behalf of the Conference of Mayors, including the suspension of the importation of firearms, the registration of firearms, and the prohibition of mail order sales of all firearms and ammunition to juveniles and out-of-state residents.

Dianne Feinstein (b. 1933)

Born in San Francisco in 1933, Dianne Feinstein is now serving as one of two Democratic United States senators from California. She holds a B.S. from Stanford University and an honorary law degree from Golden Gate University, as well as various honorary doctorates from a number of universities. She has served as mayor of San Francisco, as a member of the executive committee of the U.S. Conference of Mayors, and was the Democratic nominee for the governorship of California. She holds many public service awards in a wide variety of activities, and is a member of the Trilateral Commission.

Widely known for her anti-gun philosophy and her support of rigorous anti-crime bills, Feinstein was highly instrumental in the passage of the national Anti Assault-Weapons Bill and the Crime Bill of 1994. She urged the banning of some nineteen different types of so-called assault weapons, and many of the provisions she advocated have been included in the anti-gun and anti-crime bills that have now passed the Congress of the United States.

George Gekas (b. 1930)

George Gekas is a Republican representative to the House of Representatives from the State of Pennsylvania. He has often spoken out on the gun control issue, taking the position that the sale of handguns to convicted felons is already prohibited and that felons are also legally prohibited from owning such weapons.

Gekas's argument is that even though proponents of the Brady Bill—which requires a five-day waiting period for the purchase of a handgun—insisted that it will help to prevent "crimes of passion," the facts are that the bill does not impose a background check on handgun buyers by local police. It does, however, require more paperwork and an exemption in those states that have a point of purchase background check. It is his argument that these facts negate the goals of a uniform national standard.

He has suggested that the Brady proponents have argued that this "common sense" law should be passed—even if it saves just one life. In response to arguments raised by proponents of the Brady bill, Mr. Gekas used the State of Maryland's statistics, which show that in doing background checks ". . . the police manpower and financial resources . . . have so far resulted in three felons being denied a weapon for at most six months." He has argued that the Brady Bill might prove to be counterproductive given the limitations on state and local budgets. He believes that more effective and efficient use of police and financial resources will go further than the Brady alternative offers.

Alan Gottlieb (b. ca. 1945)

Alan Gottlieb is chairman of the Citizens Committee for the Right to Keep and Bear Arms. The founder of the Second Amendment Foundation, he is a prolific writer on issues related to gun control. His articles have appeared in magazines such as *Guns and Ammo, Guns,* and *Gun Week.* In addition, his work has appeared in newspapers such as *The Washington Post, The San Francisco Chronicle, The Chicago Tribune,* and other well-known newspapers and professional journals.

A major defender of Second Amendment rights, he was given a commendation by the Kentucky House of Representatives for leadership in the preservation of freedom. He has made hundreds of appearances on both radio and television programs. His published works, aside from those in journals and newspapers, include his particularly well-known *The Gun Grabbers* (Merril Press, 1986) and *The Rights of Gun Owners* (Green Hill Publishers, Inc., 1983).

Stephen P. Halbrook (b. 1947)

Stephen Halbrook is one of the country's leading authorities on the history of the Second Amendment and the range of issues involved in the gun control policy debate. He is an attorney at law in Fairfax, Virginia, and holds both J.D. and Ph.D. degrees from Georgetown University and Florida State University, respectively. He has served as a professor of philosophy at Tuskegee Institute, Howard University, and George Mason University. The author of many scholarly articles in the leading law journals, Halbrook has also written some of the most widely quoted books on the subject. Examples include *That Every Man Be Armed: The Evolution of a Constitutional Right* (University of New Mexico Press, 1984) and *A Right To Bear Arms: State and Federal Bills of Rights and Constitutional Guarantees* (Greenwood Press, 1989).

In one of his prepared statements submitted to the Subcommittee on Crime of the House Committee on the Judiciary, Halbrook gave testimony opposing the banning of "miniature, unrecognizable, and nonmetal firearms." He was particularly concerned with the vagueness of such terms as *readily, commonly, diminished,* and *substantially,* as they relate to inclusion in a criminal statute, which the Committee was considering. His concern also focused on the arguments about airport detection devices and the inaccuracies expressed by some members of Congress about the allegations that plastic guns cannot be detected; he cited evidence to suggest that they are detectable. Moreover, some guns that are not constructed of plastic materials have evaded detection devices; these are not often mentioned by those who would propose to ban such guns as the Glock.

Second Amendment provisions are clearly at stake in attempts to ban these weapons, and have been expressed in Congress with respect to the Firearms Owners Protection Act of 1986. There are also implications related to the provisions of the Fourth and Fifth Amendments to the Constitution.

Halbrook concluded his testimony on this issue by suggesting alternatives that are viable and applicable to proposals aimed at increasing regulations on airlines and improving the training of security officers and police. He maintains that it is the airport security problem that should be addressed in detail, and that hypothetical issues and other alleged solutions should be set aside as hypothetical.

David Hardy (b. ca. 1924)

David Hardy has published widely in the law journals and is a long-time scholar in the area of firearms law on the local, state, and national levels. In some of his testimony before Congress, he pointed out that the provisions of the Gun Control Act can easily be abused because they are vague, technical, and *mala prohibita*— that is, they require no proof of evil motive or intention. Persons who quite unintentionally, or without full knowledge of the law violate its provisions, are thus turned into criminals because of the commission of a felony in which they had no intention of engaging. Of particular concern are such matters as routine inspections of dealerships, which Hardy feels should be limited; the protection of sales of a dealer's personal collection; the barring of revocation for a dealer who has been acquitted of previous charges; the requirement of proof that a violation of the law has been committed willfully; the payment of attorney's fees; mandatory sentencing; and interstate firearms sales.

Hardy's testimony on this issue was not as a member of any group, although he is a member of both the American Civil Liberties Union and the National Rifle Association. Ultimately, he says, the questions related to gun control do not relate to firearms alone. They involve civil liberties issues touching upon millions of Americans who conduct themselves lawfully in the use of legitimately acquired firearms. Criminal acts should be defined narrowly and precisely so that the rights of law-abiding citizens are protected.

Orrin Hatch (b. 1934)

Orrin Hatch is a Republican senator from Utah long known as a staunch defender of Second Amendment rights to keep and bear arms. The following are illustrative of his comments to the Committee on the Judiciary of the United States Senate.

Hatch has "constantly been amazed" by the hostility given the Second Amendment in the face of James Madison's authorship of that amendment and its approval virtually without debate, while, on the other hand, the First Amendment, which was vigorously debated, is now construed favorably by the courts in a number of detailed and lengthy cases.

Moreover, Jefferson, he argued, who had by the standards of the time essentially an arsenal of weapons in his home Monticello, and who told his nephew to pursue hunting as his major sport, would likewise be astonished to fathom the claims of civil liberties supporters that the provisions of the Second Amendment—specifically the right to firearms ownership—would be rigorously restricted. He has made similar comments about Samuel Adams, Patrick Henry, and other writers of the Constitution and the Bill of Rights who would probably find today's attempts to deny the people their rights to keep and bear arms a complete violation of the founders' intentions.

Noting that over 20 decisions of the courts of the states have recognized the individual rights guaranteed by the Second Amendment and that many of these have ruled against abridgement of such rights, many persons have attempted "to construe this right out of existence." Their arguments that the right of the people mean, in fact, the right of the state, especially in the context of the definition of the people in the rest of the amendments, is completely inconsistent. Indeed, the whole comment on the militia relates to the right of all of the people to have arms so that when they are called they can, in fact, form a militia to defend themselves and the country against attack.

Hatch has stated, "I have long regarded the right of Americans to keep and bear arms as among the most vital rights recognized in the Bill of Rights. I say 'recognized,' not 'created,' because in my view that right, the right of free men to be armed and to defend themselves, their families, and their free institutions, is a gift of the Creator, not of the First Congress, as the Declaration of Independence clarifies."

One of his conclusions is that "what we have here is fundamentally a conflict between two views of human nature and the proper role of government. One view is that the government is the giver and repository of responsibility, and the citizen someone whom the government properly distrusts and, in many cases, disciplines for his own good. This is not my view, nor was it the view of the men who organized our nation and drafted its Bill of Rights. The other view holds that the citizens of our nation are responsible individuals, individuals with unalienable rights guaranteed by the Constitution. Those who freely choose to do good, or avoid harmful acts, expect and deserve to be left alone."

Thomas Jefferson (1743–1826)

The third president of the United States, Thomas Jefferson is known as having a virtual arsenal in his home. After the outbreak of hostilities at Lexington, he wrote in the Virginia Constitution that "no free man shall be debarred the use of arms within his own land." In the Declaration of Independence, moreover, he declared that, should the government no longer recognize that it receives its powers from the consent of the governed, "it is the right of the people to alter or abolish it." This included the use of force.

He had long expounded the view that the British government had no authority in colonial America; only voluntary allegiance held the colonies and Britain together. Generally recognized as one of the great intellectuals and statesmen of his time—he was a scholar, scientist, architect, philosopher, statesman, and politician—his ultimate concern was with maintaining a free people,

and this meant, if necessary, doing away with oppressive government by the force of arms—arms held by the people.

Emanuel Kapelsohn

Emanuel Kapelsohn was the executive director of the American
Shooting Sports Coalition when he submitted a prepared statement
to the Subcommittee on Crime. The American Shooting Sports
Coalition works to promote the objectives of the shooting sports industry and to work on behalf of those persons who use guns lawfully. The organization promotes legislation to benefit the firearms
manufacturers of the country, and fights proposals that would im-
pede the legal manufacture of firearms, and their use and sale. It
seeks appropriate reforms in the criminal justice system and rigid
sentences on those who use guns in the commission of crimes. The
organization likewise supports victims' rights. It has other objectives, including those involving combating the illegal use of drugs.

The coalition opposed the prohibition of semiautomatic
weapons, shotguns, and handguns that are owned by millions of
law-abiding citizens. The coalition maintained that such weapons in the possession of legimate gun owners are used legally for
purposes of self-defense, target shooting, collecting, and various
recreational activities. To restrict the rights of such individuals is,
in the opinion of the coalition, unconstitutional. It takes the position that the country must pass and enforce laws that will effectively keep weapons out of the hands of criminals. The
organization has created and supports a procedure by which all
purchases could be checked by use of a telephone system con-
nected to a central database.

Don B. Kates, Jr. (b. 1941)

Don Kates is undisputably one of the nation's leading authorities
on the right of individuals to own guns and of the history and
analysis of the Second Amendment. A graduate of Reed College
in Oregon, he holds a law degree from Yale University. He has
been an active civil rights worker in the South, especially during
the height of racial violence and the marches conducted by
African Americans and their white supporters. Once a professor
in St. Louis University Law School, he is currently an attorney
specializing in civil liberties cases in Navato, California.

A prolific author and editor of books, Kates has likewise
written widely for legal journals and the popular press, ranging

from magazines dealing with hunting and firearms to such scholarly periodicals as *Law & Policy Quarterly, Law and Contemporary Problems,* and the *Michigan Law Review.* He is editor of such books as *Restricting Handguns: The Liberal Skeptics Speak Out* and *Firearms and Violence: Issues of Public Policy.* Kates is the author of the major article on the Second Amendment in the authoritative *Encyclopedia of the American Constitution.*

Kates has testified on numerous occasions before congressional committees on legal, political, and gun-related social issues, and about the major bills on gun control and firearms regulations. He has also submitted an amicus brief to the United States Supreme Court on behalf of several groups supporting Second Amendment rights.

Neal Knox (b. 1935)

Neal Knox is the director of the Firearms Coalition. He has testified before the Subcommittee on Crime of the House Judiciary Committee on a number of issues related to gun control policy. The following points are taken from his testimony relating to the detection of firearms containing plastic or other non-metallic parts.

He pointed out that the Bureau of Alcohol, Tobacco, and Firearms (BATF) and the Federal Aviation Administration have both stated that in their judgment all firearms made commercially are in fact detectable by use of existing screening equipment. These two agencies have also stated that equipment is being developed to aid in the detection of disposable firearms, such as those produced by the Soviet KGB.

Knox has pointed out that one of the problems in detection is that airport equipment "is as much as 20 years behind the state of the art." Airports simply have not kept up with or installed the equipment that is already capable of dealing with sophisticated developments in the evolution of firearms and other explosive devices, and even more sophisticated devices are being developed. Moreover, the technicians who operate the detection devices are often poorly trained. Inasmuch as the airline industry is responsible for buying and maintaining detection equipment, it has not been able to install the equipment because of its cost.

Polymers will increasingly be used in the production of both private and military firearms in the years ahead simply because of their advantages over metals alone. Manufacturers are also attempting to improve the detectability of their weapons.

The proposed bills dealing with so-called plastic guns are unacceptable because they do not actually provide a solution to the detection problem, do not require advanced systems of detection, and would allow the BATF to set the standards of detectability—thus opening an area of potential abuse of which the BATF has frequently been guilty in the past. Knox maintains that the bills' arbitrary provisions would lead to behavior that is unconstitutional with respect to the rights of gun owners and the provisions of the Second, Fourth, and Fifth Amendments.

David B. Kopel

David Kopel is a former assistant district attorney for the borough of Manhattan and an expert on firearms and firearms policy. He is currently a practicing attorney in Denver. He has testified on a variety of gun control issues before the United States Senate and is a well-known author on the subject of the failures of gun control legislation. Among other elements in the lengthy list of his credentials are a University of Michigan law degree, a degree from Brown University, and a prize from the National Historical Society for his thesis on historian Arthur M. Schlesinger, Jr.

Kopel is the author of *Trust the People: The Case against Gun Control* (Cato Institute, 1988) and *The Samurai, the Mountie, and the Cowboy: Should America Adopt the Gun Control of Other Democracies* (Cato Institute, 1994). His pieces on social policy, not confined to gun control and Second Amendment rights, have appeared in a wide variety of newspapers and popular journals. He is also a consultant on firearms policy for the National Association of Chiefs of Police.

The comments extracted below are from testimony he gave before the United States Senate Subcommittee on Crime, Committee of the Judiciary, as a representative of Guardian International Group (a New York security consulting and research organization). The testimony was presented also on behalf of the National Association of Chiefs of Police (an organization made up of some 10,000 police chiefs, sheriffs, and others) and the American Federation of Police (a crime-fighting group composed of some 78,000 persons in law enforcement and security that is especially concerned with training police officers).

Testifying that gun restrictions or bans dealing with semiautomatic weapons will actually increase violence against citizens, Kopel pointed out that criminals will ignore or evade such laws and that such laws are a clear violation of the Second Amendment provisions guaranteeing the right to keep and bear arms.

He observed that gun control laws have never had the effect of preventing terrorists, rioters, or gangsters in general from obtaining firearms. He argued that in order to "repulse attacks by large numbers of criminals, citizens need semiautomatic firearms."

Kopel pointed out that the rights guaranteed under the Second Amendment do not include the right to have guns for hunting purposes; rather, the amendment safeguards the right to keep guns for defensive purposes. The militia provisions of the amendment mean that all adults have the legal right to own militia-type weapons. Moreover, he stated, regulations or bans of such weapons will lead to increased disrespect for the law and that, in any event, such laws will not prevent criminals from obtaining these weapons.

Wayne LaPierre (1949–)

Wayne LaPierre has been associated with the National Rifle Association (NRA) since 1978, when he became a lobbyist for the group. Currently he is its chief executive officer and one of its major spokesmen. Recent NRA growth is often associated with LaPierre.

His book *Guns, Crime, and Freedom* examines the entire gamut of the issues involved with the gun control debate. He addresses such issues as crime, the relevance of the Second Amendment, and the larger agenda of those who wish to control, and indeed, to ban, guns in the United States. The media in particular come under his examination, and he focuses on the criminal justice system as a special example of what is wrong with the effort to control crime in the United States. He is especially concerned with the right of self-defense protection.

James A. McClure (b. 1924)

James McClure is a Republican senator from Idaho. He is a graduate of the Idaho College of Law, and before his election to the Senate he was involved in state and local politics and was an Idaho representative to Congress. Together with Representative Harold Volkmer, McClure introduced the McClure-Volkmer amendments to the Gun Control Act of 1968.

McClure argued that the Gun Control Act was a failure in that it did not reduce or control crime, but that its enforcement history was one of abuses to the rights of all law-abiding American citizens. Hence, profound changes to the law were necessary.

He asserted that the redrafting of the law was a clear civil liberties necessity and was "politically ecumenical." The 1968 act was referred to as "legal flypaper" that even the most competent attorneys found incomprehensible. Behavior of citizens under the law was made "illegal simply because the government says it is." The conduct of actual criminals was not covered by the law's provisions, while many innocent, law-abiding citizens were made criminals by this law. It was vague and undefined. If the most astute lawyers of our society could not deal effectively with the law, how could one expect citizens untrained in the liturgy of the law to comprehend its many obscure, vague, and imprecise provisions? He stated that the law simply "invites abuse." The Bureau of Alcohol, Tobacco, and Firearms, the agency designated to enforce the law, has itself engaged in activities "bordering on criminality."

McClure's amendments were aimed at adjusting and eliminating the abuses of the Gun Control Act of 1968. The amendments engaged such issues as restrictions on the sales of interstate firearms; the harrassment of citizens who are innocent of charges ascribed; and the forfeiture of property or license revocation where vindication of the charges has been demonstrated. The burden of proof must rest with the government; a person is innocent until proven guilty.

The amendments addressed appropriate awarding of attorney's fees and examined dealer sales from his or her private collection. Agents would have to demonstrate a "reasonable cause" to suggest that a violation of the law had occurred; a minimum comment period for the handing down of regulations would be required; and "harrassment" of legitimate owners of guns who were traveling through states where they do not legally reside would be eliminated. The provisions of the amendments were themselves stated in the written submission to the subcommittee. The McClure-Volkmer amendments were ultimately adopted as the Firearms Owners Protection Act.

Ira William "Bill" McCollum, Jr. (b. 1944)

A supporter of a check on gun buyers, William McCollum, United States representative from Florida, was especially in favor of an immediate telephone check to determine a gun buyer's eligibility in order to carry out the check quickly and efficiently, rather than having to wait the time required under the Brady Bill. His argument was that during the waiting period, the government is denying the right of an individual to purchase a handgun; moreover, felons will not be prevented from purchasing guns. One does not want to rely exclusively on the police in one's community to protect oneself and to determine whether one has the right to purchase a gun. The decision, he insisted, should be left to the individual.

He argued that a large number of felons are not likely to be located as a consequence of the passage of the Brady measure, and that one "could do in seven minutes what we could do in seven days" if one used a telephone check process.

Vince McGoldrick (n.d.)

Vince McGoldrick is Chairman of the National Legislative Committee of the Fraternal Order of Police. This organization has some 160,000 members drawn from both active and retired police personnel.

McGoldrick has spoken strongly on behalf of "firm and swift punishment" for individuals who break clear, defined laws; laws that are "overbroad" or "vague" are difficult to enforce. Hence, he strongly supported—on behalf of both himself and the Fraternal Order of Police—the McClure-Volkmer Bill (the Firearms Owners Protection Act), which aimed to revise substantially the Gun Control Act of 1968. His argument was that the amendments proposed served to make the Gun Control Act more "rational, more clear, more narrowed, and more precise—in a phrase, more enforceable."

He pointed out that many, if not most, of the members of the Fraternal Order of Police are themselves gun owners in private life, either collectors or those who have guns for purposes of self-defense, and as such they support changes in the law that protect legitimate owners of guns and serve to punish criminal offenders. Thus, the Fraternal Order of Police supported the changes in the Gun Control Act of 1968 both from an organizational and an individual perspective.

Joseph McNamara (b. 1934)

Joseph McNamara is the former police chief of San Jose, California. He has long been known for his anti-gun position. In April 1994, however, he wrote in the *Los Angeles Times* about his opposition to a proposal presented to Attorney General Janet Reno by President Clinton to find ways to get around a federal injunction that forbade random police searches for guns and drugs in a housing development funded by federal monies in Chicago. He stated that Clinton could have assured tenants that the federal government would do all it could to provide whatever level of policing was needed to stop the violence in the complex. Instead, the president pandered to police and public impatience with rising crime. He urged the department responsible for prosecuting officers who violate people's constitutional rights to assist police in evading the Constitution. . . . Moreover, he said, "There is no need for any dilution of individual rights that took centuries to achieve. The murderers striking the most terror in the hearts of people during this century have not been serial killers like Ted Bundy. They have been governments that have killed millions of their citizens in the name of social order."

Paul J. McNulty (b. 1958)

Paul J. McNulty is acting director of the Office of Policy Development of the Department of Justice. A supporter of the Brady Bill and its waiting period provision, he argued that "the use of severe Federal penalties is the most direct form of gun control since it targets the violent offender." He stated that it is recidivists who commit the most crime and that they especially are the ones who continue to drive up the crime rate.

He pointed out, however, that the Brady Bill would not end the use of guns because it is not possible under existing rules to trace the history of criminals, and because most felons do not procure their weapons from licensed gun dealers.

James Madison (1751–1836)

The fourth president of the United States, James Madison was a member of the Virginia planter class. He strongly opposed the colonial policies of the British. A scholar with deep understanding of philosophy and politics, he helped draft the first constitution for Virginia. He is often referred to as the father of the American Constitution.

In *Federalist* No. 46, Madison argued that even though the Constitution in its language did not impose limitations on the new national government with respect to the raising and supporting of standing armies, this was not a cause of substantial difficulty. He argued that an armed citizenry, whose size far exceeded that of any standing army, would constitute the ultimate protection against such a standing force. It is also of interest to note that, when drafting the Bill of Rights (to which, incidentally, he was initially opposed), he placed the right to keep and bear arms in the same grouping with the people's right to free speech and to other individual rights, not in the section of the Constitution itself that deals with federal power over the militia. His notes suggest that, when he rose to speak about the meaning of the amendments, he was referring to private individual rights.

Lawrence D. Pratt (n.d.)

Lawrence Pratt, as a representative of Gun Owners of America, has testified against bills that would prohibit the sale, delivery, and importation of weapons known as plastic guns. His major argument, however, has not been about opposing the prohibition of invisible guns per se, but rather the entire issue of gun control.

He argues that if one is to oppose the sale of nonmetal firearms, then one must largely oppose the sale of all firearms, inasmuch as many weapons are constructed of stocks, grips, trigger guards, and other assemblages of materials made of plastic or other nonmetal substances. Handguns, for example, other than the Glock 17 (which has been the particular focus of anti-gun forces) could easily pass through electronic security devices. The detection problem has less to do with the weapon itself and more to do with the quality of the equipment doing the detecting. Given the state of technology, an all-metal gun, if disassembled, could easily pass through security devices. His argument is that minimum detection standards must be increased, not guns banned.

He argues that proposals to pass legislation banning guns will not deter terrorists; they will only serve to undermine the provisions of the Second Amendment and provide further opportunity to those criminals and those terrorists who already have the means—and who will surely develop further means—to use their techniques to penetrate security at airports and other sensitive areas around the country and around the world. He argues that each time gun control legislation has gone into effect, more crimes have been committed.

Janet Reno (b. 1938)

Janet Reno is the Attorney General of the United States under the Clinton Administration. She has been a vigorous proponent of mass gun control efforts and has urged the ultimate banning of all weapons. She has suggested that the acquisition of a gun should involve the same techniques that are required in the acquisition of a driver's license. She has advocated mandatory registration of all gun owners, a licensing card that needs to be kept with the gun, and a total ban on assault weapons. Some of the policies she has advocated have recently been adopted by Congress with the passage of the Crime Bill of 1994.

In her testimony before Congress in 1995, she admitted responsibility for the Bureau of Alcohol, Tobacco, and Firearms and FBI attack on the Branch Davidians in Waco, Texas, during which seige many children were killed and a number of civil rights possibly violated. Tanks and high-powered weapons were used against a cult, which had stimulated interest as a potentially dangerous part of a deviant subculture. The consequences of Reno's actions remain to be determined.

Charles Schumer (b. 1950)

Charles Schumer, a Democrat and a graduate of the Harvard Law School, represents the 9th Congressional District of New York and previously served as a member of the New York State Assembly. He has served on such committees as the Banking Committee (where he proposed sweeping reforms for the savings and loan industry and focused attention on the riskiness of unlimited bank deposit insurance), but his real focus is the House Judiciary Committee, whose subcommittee on Crime and Criminal Justice he chairs.

One of Schumer's major interests is gun control, and he often vigorously interrogates witnesses before his subcomittee. He has urged an outright ban on the manufacture or possession of hollow-point bullets such as the Black Talon (which the manufacturer has voluntarily withdrawn), and a so-called arsenal license for any household that posseses over 20 guns or 1,000 rounds of ammunition. He strongly supported the Brady Bill (now law), which requires a five-day delay in handgun purchases, suggesting that it was just a start in the political movement against guns, and strongly supports banning assault weapons for purchase by private citizens.

He drew an analogy between the war in the Persian Gulf and the war on guns at home. He argued that the first objective of the war against Saddam Hussein was to disarm the Iraqis and the objective here at home in the gun war should be to disarm criminals, whom he considers to be every bit the enemy that the Iraqi army was. He stated that "we need a waiting period for people to buy handguns, not for approval of the Brady Bill." He cited the

"American mood" in support of his own anti-gun opinions. In his view, the American people "have had enough" and are now psychologically ready for strong gun controls. It is his belief that a waiting period such as that included in the Brady Bill will prevent the loss of life.

Nelson T. "Pete" Shields (n.d.)

Testifying before Congress as chairman of Handgun Control, Incorporated, Nelson Shields opposed the spread of handguns in the United States. Emphasizing that his own son had been killed by a murderer using a handgun, he reaffirmed his efforts to do what he could to enhance federal laws to deal with the problem of their criminal use.

He argued that any efforts aimed at changing the Gun Control Act of 1968 had to be focused on strengthening its provisions. Thus, he supported the waiting period to purchase handguns and the ban on importation of handguns such as Saturday Night Specials. He asserted, however, that the revisions suggested to the law would take the country away from his own proposals, and he characterized the changes as destructive to efforts to lower violent crime by controlling handguns. Shields also saw the McClure-Volkmer amendments as destructive to the capacity of the states to enforce gun laws. He called the McClure-Volkmer changes "felon relief," and said that the legislation should be called "Gun Decontrol."

John M. Snyder (n.d.)

John M. Snyder has served as director of Publications and Public Affairs of the Citizens Committee for the Right to Keep and Bear Arms and is editor of its journal, *Point Blank.* He has served as associate editor of *The American Rifleman,* is treasurer of the Second Amendment Foundation, and has been honored with an award for his "outstanding support of law enforcement" by the American Federation of Police. He has bachelor's and master's degrees from Georgetown University.

A strong supporter of the McClure-Volkmer amendments to the Gun Control Act of 1968, Snyder presented Senator McClure with a number of petitions containing the signatures of 1,500,000 persons supporting McClure's early efforts to repeal outright that entire act. Snyder suggested that this was the largest number of signatures on a single issue petition that had ever been presented to Congress.

Snyder spoke strongly in support of legislation that would eliminate certain provisions from the Gun Control Act of 1968 and that would permit the purchase of firearms across state lines if such a purchase were legal under state law; would define precisely who was a gun dealer or gun collector; would permit those who are unlicensed to sell ammunition; would prevent agents of the Treasury Department from inspecting the records of dealers unless there was positive evidence to suggest an actual violation of a firearms law; would eliminate the seizure of firearms unless there were a lawful arrest of the alleged violator; and would relax federal regulations on the sale of firearms by individuals.

Snyder also lauded the Reagan Administration's efforts to eliminate the Bureau of Alcohol, Tobacco, and Firearms, and pointed out that the Gun Control Act of 1968 was passed on the heels of unprecedented rioting, assassination, burning, and pillaging in our cities, and was thus enacted hastily and without farsighted understanding of its consequences and ramifications. He was also deeply critical of the tactics used by the Bureau of Alcohol, Tobacco, and Firearms agents, which he maintains include senselessly breaking into private residences and shooting and maiming of law-abiding private citizens. When considering future gun control laws, Snyder argued, the rights of law-abiding citizens must be taken into particular account.

Snyder has argued that, in the case of Patrick Purdy (who killed five children on a Stockton, California, schoolground in 1989), the perpetrator would have been unable to purchase any type of weapon had the criminal justice system been used properly. Purdy had a long criminal record but no record of felony convictions; he could therefore elude federal firearms laws when he purchased a semiautomatic weapon in Oregon and handguns in California. He had been allowed to plea bargain and reduce the punishment for robbery. The gun problem lies not in the use of weapons by law-abiding citizens or in the banning of "particular" weapons, but in the enforcement of stringent laws and the reform of the plea-bargaining system. Snyder asked, "Why pass laws to prevent the innocent from getting the firearms they may need to protect themselves agains terrorists or other violent criminals?"

Harley O. Staggers, Jr. (b. 1907)

A former U.S. congressman, Harley Staggers has argued on behalf of a proposal that would require a background check on gun purchasers rather than a local police investigation of the applicant.

He endorsed a criminal history background, improvement of criminal history records, a nondiscriminatory system, and a law based on the Virginia Instantaneous Firearms Transaction Program, which at the time of his argument had a 2 percent error rate. He argued on behalf of a specific appeals process in the area of improvement of deficient criminal records; among other things, he advocated a toll-free number that firearms dealers must call for a background check. It would indicate only if a person were approved or disapproved or would be approved by unique transaction number. He also wrote into his proposal that within six months of its enactment the Justice Department would have to call to obtain a background check on all handgun purchases, and the Justice Department would have a toll-free number to investigate handgun purchasers. The proposal was designed to increase the criminal history information system.

David J. Steinberg (n.d.)

Mr. Steinberg has served as executive director of the National Council for a Responsible Firearms Policy and submitted a statement on assault weapons to the Subcommittee on Crime of the House Committee on the Judiciary.

Formed in 1967, the council is described as neither pro- nor antigun. Its primary objective is to prevent access to guns by persons who are not properly qualified to use them. It thus aims to accomplish public safety standards and does not have as an objective the disarming of law-abiding citizens who are legitimate gun owners.

With respect to assault weapons, the council does not advocate a ban unless such an alternative appears to be the only reasonable one available. Severe regulations on assault weapons alone might very well result in the increased use of other weapons in the commission of crime. Stern, mandatory sentences for the commission of crime with the use of guns are not to be regarded as the only appropriate alternative; indeed, far more rigid and rigorous standards of training in the possession and use of firearms appear to be a more viable suggestion, whether assault weapons or any other types of guns are involved.

Joseph Story (1779–1845)

An American jurist, Joseph Story was born in Marblehead, Massachusetts, practiced law in Salem, and was elected to the Massachusetts legislature. His extraordinary legal knowledge led him to prominence in both the legal and intellectual communities. Strongly anti-slavery, he expressed his views in several judgments. He served as a professor of law at Harvard and wrote many legal works.

Appointed as a United States Supreme Court justice by James Madison, Story in 1833 proclaimed, "The militia is the natural defence of a free country against sudden foreign invasions, domestic insurrections, and domestic usurpations of power by rulers. . . . The right of the citizens to keep, and bear arms has justly been considered, as the palladium of the liberties of the republic; since it offers a strong moral check against the usurpation and arbitrary power of rulers, and will generally, even if these are successful in the first instance, enable the people to resist, and triumph over them."

Steven D. Symms (b. 1938)

Steven D. Symms is a Republican member of Congress from Idaho. He believes that banning firearms will have no greater impact on public policy than did attempts to ban the use of liquor during the 1920s. Just as Americans who sought to drink turned to speakeasies and to hidden stills to make their own libations, so will individuals who want them acquire firearms in any way they can. Organized crime would be greatly strengthened by a ban, and the black market would become a tremendously significant source of weapons that could otherwise not be obtained by law-abiding citizens.

Symms points out that of the over 200,000,000 guns in private circulation in the United States, only about 4 percent, according to the FBI, are ever used in crimes nationally. Under the law, decent citizens have the right to own firearms. Hunting and gun collecting, as well as target shooting and other sports in which firearms are used, are legal activities. Citizens who own guns, he asserted, are probably the least likely of all Americans to break the law and to use guns in the commission of crime. Those who are opposed to the ownership and use of guns have falsely accused gun owners to be, as a class, potential murderers and killers. Law-abiding citizens have the constitutionally protected right to own firearms.

Harold L. Volkmer (b. 1931)

The Democratic representative from Missouri's 9th Congressional District, Harold Volkmer received his law degree from the

University of Missouri School of Law and was active in Missouri politics, serving as assistant attorney general. He was a leader in the adoption of the Firearm Owners' Protection Act. His efforts, together with those of Senator James McClure, became known as the McClure-Volkmer amendments, which created major revisions in the Gun Control Act of 1968.

Volkmer's efforts were aimed at correcting and clarifying provisions of the federal firearms laws, especially those provisions of the Gun Control Act of 1968 that were vague and inconsistent and worked to undermine the fundamental rights of legitimate gun owners. Because of the vagueness, inconsistencies, and omission of fundamental rights from the existing law, honest citizens had become unintentional criminals by having committed acts regarded as felonies, and even the chief enforcement agency of the law—the Bureau of Alcohol, Tobacco, and Firearms—was unable to make up its mind as to what the law in fact required. The Bureau of Alcohol, Tobacco, and Firearms was also guilty of having committed significant abuses under existing provisions of the law, as testified to in hearings before the Subcommittee on Crime of the Committee on the Judiciary. Thus, Volkmer focused his efforts on forcing the bureau to concentrate its enforcement efforts against individuals who criminally abuse the legitimate right to keep and bear arms as provided for under the Second Amendment.

Volkmer wrote into the new law procedures protecting citizens from the confiscation of their property: only those weapons actually used in the willful commission of a crime could be seized and, if seized, charges had to be filed within 120 days or the weapons had to be returned to their rightful owners. In the event of an acquittal, firearms had also to be returned, and the legislation provided for the payment of attorney fees if the owner of the weapons must sue the government for their return.

These provisions and others became a major part of the Firearm Owners Protection Act.

Legislation and Statistical Data

Introduction

This chapter provides an annotated list of selected court cases relevant to the subject of the right to keep and bear arms, as well as an annotated but highly selective list of some of the most significant legislation, constitutional provisions, and related materials dealing with the issue. Before presenting this material, however, a brief introduction to the current legal status of the right to keep and bear arms as interpreted by the courts and law-making bodies is in order.

The courts have tended to hold that the right guaranteed in the Second Amendment and the clause stating that such a right shall not be infringed is applicable to Congress. It has not been held applicable to the states because it has not been incorporated into the Fourteenth Amendment and thus has not been interpreted as applying to the states. Moreover, the courts have generally argued that the Second Amendment provision delineating the right to keep and bear arms does not necessarily constitute an individual right. Despite historical evidence produced by some legal scholars to contradict this interpretation, the courts have maintained that state or local laws regulating the possession and use of firearms do not infringe upon the right to keep and bear arms as guaranteed in the federal Constitution. The registration provisions of the National Firearms Act have also been so interpreted.

Courts have also held that provisions in various state bills of rights guaranteeing the right of their citizens to keep and bear arms (see the list of such provisions reproduced later in this chapter) refer to the collective body of citizens, not to individuals. (For a discussion of the collective and individual views on this issue, see the case decisions in the next sections.) The courts have held that arms may be borne as long as they are used in the context of a militia or other military situation, but right-to-bear-arms provisions do not prevent duly authorized legislative bodies from writing laws that regulate or even ban the use or possession of firearms or other weapons. Although persons may defend themselves and their property against violent or threatening attackers, the use of weapons in private fights or brawls can be proscribed.

The courts have also held that construing common law rules or passing any statute that does away with the right to keep and bear arms would be unconstitutional. Again, however, this interpretation does not preclude passage of legislation regulating how and which weapons may be carried. For example, carrying a concealed weapon may very well be illegal in some jurisdictions, but such regulations do not affect the right to carry firearms or other weapons that might be used in the ordinary course of warfare. Hence, such regulations have been interpreted as not in violation of the right to keep and bear arms. Gun license laws have likewise been upheld, as have bans on certain types of weapons, such as machine guns and switchblade knives. In recent months, a federal law requiring a waiting period when purchasing a handgun and a ban on certain types of so-called assault weapons have both been enacted. Weapons sales may likewise be regulated or prohibited under some circumstances, again without violating the constitutional provision of the people's right to keep and bear arms. The courts have tended to support regulation of weapons as an element of police power—defined as the capacity to legislate in the interests of the health, welfare, and morals of the people.

Having said all of this, the controversy over whether the right to bear arms is collective or individual in nature and intent continues among lawyers, legal scholars, and laypersons. The case law on the issue contains findings, both general and specific, supporting both sides of the argument. The following list of cases is only a brief sample of the thousands that have dealt with weapons over time, and is therefore virtually arbitrary. Some of the classic cases are discussed at greater length, using excerpts from the holdings of the courts themselves. These excerpts have been aggressively edited without, it is hoped, having violated the arguments presented in the original cases. There are also other cases on the issue whose holdings have been paraphrased and that are discussed more briefly. The major U.S. Supreme Court cases that have dealt—mostly indirectly—with the right to keep and bear arms are also presented in edited form. In each instance, regardless of the level at which the case has been decided, footnotes, scholarly references, case references, and other materials cited in the original court cases—unless absolutely necessary for clarity—have been omitted for purposes of brevity. The reader is directed to the appropriate court record for the complete opinion. More recent cases dealing with the issue on state and local levels and in the lower federal courts are available in the literature, and the reader is encouraged to consult the appropriate court reports.[1]

This chapter concludes with relevant statistical information dealing with the number of gun dealers, gun ownership, and gun use; the major lobby groups in support of and opposed to gun control; descriptions of the types of weapons most often sought by the Bureau of Alcohol, Tobacco, and Firearms; and the 19 so-called assault weapons banned in the 1994 Assault Weapons Law.

Court Cases[2]

Some Cases Illustrating the Collective View

Aymette v. The State
2 Humphrey (21 Tennessee) 154 (1840)

The plaintiff in error was convicted in the Giles circuit court, for wearing a bowie knife concealed under his clothes, under the act of 1837–8, ch. 137, sec. 2, which provides, "That if any person shall wear any bowie knife, or Arkansas tooth-pick, or other knife or weapon, that shall in form, shape or size resemble a bowie knife or Arkansas tooth-pick, under his clothes, or keep the same concealed about his person, such person shall be guilty of a misdemeanor, and upon conviction thereof, shall be fined in a sum not less than two hundred dollars, and shall be imprisoned in the county jail, not less than three months and not more than six months."

It is now insisted that the above act of the legislature is unconstitutional, and therefore the judgment in this case should have been arrested.

In the first article of the Constitution of this State, containing a declaration of rights, sec. 26, it is declared, "That the free white men of this State, have a right to keep and bear arms for their common defence. . . ."

[The Court then enters into a discussion of the history of the right to bear arms and definitions of the word *common*. It also discusses the types of weapons that would be useful and useless in warfare and the question of the purpose of the right to keep and bear arms.]

A thousand inventions for inflicting death may be imagined, which might come under the appellation of an 'arm' in the figurative use of that term, and which could by no possibility be rendered effectual in war, in the least degree aid in the common defence. . . .

The legislature, therefore, have a right to prohibit the wearing, or keeping [of] weapons dangerous to the peace and safety of the citizens, and which are *not* used in civilized warfare, or would not contribute to the common defence. The right to keep and bear arms for the common defence is a great political right. . . . And although this right must be inviolably preserved, yet, it does not follow that the legislature is prohibited altogether from passing laws regulating the manner in which these arms may be employed. . . .

Let the judgment be affirmed.

City of Salina v. Blaksley
83 P.619, 72 Kan. 230 (1905)

James Blaksley was convicted in the police court of the city of Salina . . . of carrying a revolving pistol within the city while under the influence of intoxicating liquor. He appealed to the district court, where he was again convicted, and this proceeding is prosecuted to reverse the judgment of the latter court. The question presented is the constitutionality of section 1003 of the General Statutes of 1901, which reads: "The council may prohibit and punish the carrying of firearms or other deadly weapons concealed or otherwise, and may arrest and imprison, fine or set at work all vagrants and persons found in said city without visible means of support, or some legitimate business."

Section 4 of the [Kansas] bill of rights is as follows: "The people have the right to bear arms for their defense and security; but standing armies, in time of peace, are dangerous to liberty, and shall not be tolerated, and the military shall be in strict subordination to the civil power."

The contention is that this section of the bill of rights is a constitutional inhibition upon the power of the legislature to prohibit the individual from having and carrying arms, and that section 1003 of the General Statutes of 1901 is an attempt to deprive him of the right guaranteed by the Bill of Rights, and, is therefore, unconstitutional and void. . . .

The provision in section 4 of the Bill of Rights . . . refers to the people as a collective body. It was the safety and security of society that was being considered when this provision was put into our Constitution. . . . [The clause immediately following dealing with standing armies and subordination of the military to the civil power] . . . deals exclusively with the military; individual rights are not considered in this section. . . .

That the provision in question applies only to the right to bear arms as a member of the state militia, or some other military organization provided for by law, is also apparent from the Second Amendment to the federal Constitution. . . .

The defendant was not a member of an organized militia, nor of any other military organization provided for by law, and was therefore not within the provision of the bill of rights and was not protected by its terms.

Strickland v. State
72 S.E. 260 (Georgia 1911)

The first question propounded by the Court of Appeals is whether "An act to prohibit any person from having or carrying about his person, in any county in the state of Georgia, any pistol or revolver without first having obtained a license from the ordinary of the county of said state, in which the party resides, and to provide how said license may be obtained and penalty prescribed for a violation of the same, and for other purposes, is violative . . . of the Constitution of this state which provides that 'the right of the people to keep and bear arms shall not be infringed, but the General Assembly shall have power to prescribe the manner in which arms may be borne. . . .' "

The second question propounded by the Court of Appeals is whether the act of 1910 is in violation of the right of a citizen under . . . the Constitution of the United States [under the Second Amendment].

[To the first question, the court responded in agreement with the contention that] the right to bear arms, like other rights of person and property, is to be construed in connection with the general police power of the state, and as subject to legitimate regulation thereunder. . . . The ruling that the Legislature may prohibit the carrying of concealed weapons essentially concedes the police power of regulation to some extent. . . . We think, upon consideration, that the regulatory provisions of the act of 1910 are not so arbitrary or unreasonable as to amount, in effect, to a prohibition of the right to bear arms, or an infringement of that right as protected by the Constitution. . . .

[To the second question, the court responded that it] . . . is not contended that anything contained in this act affects, or was intended to affect, any federal law passed in pursuance of the Constitution of the United States in regard to the regulation of militia.

Cases v. United States
131 F.2d 916 (1st Cir. 1942)

This is an appeal from a judgment of the District Court of the United States for Puerto Rico sentencing the defendant to a term of imprisonment after he had been found guilty by a jury on all four counts of an indictment charging him with violating . . . the Federal Firearms Act . . . by transporting and receiving a firearm and ammunition.

The defendant contends that the Federal Firearms Act is unconstitutional because (a) it is an ex post facto law; (b) it violates the Second Amendment by infringing the right of the people to keep and bear arms; (c) it is an undue extension of the commerce clause; (d) it creates an unreasonable presumption of guilt; and (e) it denies equal protection of the laws. In our view none of these contentions are sound. . . .

The Federal Firearms Act undoubtedly curtails to some extent the right of individuals to keep and bear arms but it does not follow from this as a necessary consequence that it is bad under the Second Amendment. . . .

The right to keep and bear arms is not a right conferred upon the people by the federal [C]onstitution. Whatever rights in this respect the people may have depend upon local legislation; the only function of the Second Amendment being to prevent the federal government and the federal government only from infringing that right. . . . [The Court then cited Supreme Court cases that support its contention and reviewed the events that occurred in Annadale's Beach Club on 30 August 1941, where the defendant used a .38 caliber Colt type revolver against another patron in the club. The Court concluded as follows]: While the weapon may be capable of military use, or while at least familiarity with it might be regarded as of value in training a person to use a comparable weapon of military type and caliber, still there is no evidence that the appellant was or ever had been a member of any military organization or that his use of the weapon under the circumstances disclosed was in preparation for a military career. . . . The only inference possible is that the appellant . . . was using the firearm and ammunition purely and simply on a frolic of his own and without any thought or intention of contributing to the efficiency of . . . [a] well regulated militia. . . . The Federal Firearms Act does not conflict with the Second Amendment to the Constitution of the United States.

United States v. Tot
1321 F.2d 261 (3d Cir. 1942)

The defendant, Frank Tot, was convicted and sentenced for violation of the statute known as the Federal Firearms Act, . . . by which it is made unlawful for any person who has been convicted of a crime of violence "to receive any firearm or ammunition which has been shipped or transported in interstate or foreign commerce. . . ." That the defendant had been previously convicted of a crime of violence . . . is undisputed. He was arrested by federal officers at his home in Newark, New Jersey, on a warrant charging theft of cigarettes from an interstate shipment. A .32 caliber Colt automatic pistol was found in his place of residence at the time of the arrest. . . .

The appellant's contention is that if the statute under which this prosecution was brought is to be applied to a weapon of the type he had in his possession, then the statute violates the Second Amendment. . . .

The contention of the appellant in this case could, we think, be denied without more under the authority of *United States v. Miller* [q.v., below]. . . . The appellant here having failed to show such a relationship, the same thing may be said as applied to the pistol found in his possession. It is not material on this point that the 1934 statute was bottomed on the taxing power while the statute in question here was based on a regulation of interstate commerce.

But, further, . . . [w]eapon bearing was never treated as anything like an absolute right by the common law. . . .

The social end sought to be achieved by this legislation, the protection of society against violent men armed with dangerous weapons, all would concede to be fundamental in organized government. . . .

The judgment is affirmed.

Harris v. State
432 P.2d 929 (Nev. 1967)

This is an appeal from the conviction of Edward Mark Harris for the possession of a tear gas weapon. . . .

On July 27, 1966 Harris entered a super market in Reno and was observed by store personnel to be shoplifting several cartons of cigarettes. A police officer was summoned. The officer placed him under arrest and searched him. The search produced a tear gas pen. He was convicted of possession of a tear gas device in violation of . . . statute. This appeal followed. We affirm.

As his first assignment of error Harris challenges the constitutionality of NRS 202.380 as an infringement of the Second Amendment of the U.S. Constitution. . . .

The amendment applies only to the Federal Government and does not restrict state action. . . . The right to bear arms does not apply to private citizens as an individual right.

In the absence of state or federal constitutional restraints authority of the states to regulate weapons comes their police powers. . . . Tear gas pens are a proper subject for state regulation.

Burton v. Sills
248 A.2d 521 (N.J. 1968)

The Law Division upheld the constitutionality of New Jersey's recently enacted "Gun Control Law" . . . and dismissed . . . plaintiff's complaint attacking it. The Appellate Division affirmed . . . and the plantiffs appealed to this court as of right. . . .

The plaintiffs are three individuals associated with sportsmen's clubs in New Jersey, two gun dealers, and a corporation organized to promote the sports of shooting and marksmanship. They filed a complaint. . . . seeking (1) a declaration that Chapter 60 of the Laws of 1966 is unconstitutional and (2) an injunction against its enforcement. Chapter 60 . . . provided . . . for the licensing of manufacturers, wholesalers, and retail dealers, and for the issuance of permits and identification cards to purchasers. . . .

We find no merit in the plaintiff's first point and deal now with their next point under which they urge that Chapter 60 is violative of the second amendment of the United States Constitution. . . .

[The Court then entered into a discursive discussion of historical events related to the development of the Second Amendment and of various court cases that have ruled that the Second Amendment was not adopted with an individual right in mind.]

The plaintiffs venture the prediction that, notwithstanding all of the foregoing, the Supreme Court will hereafter "extend the restrictions of the Second Amendment from those which protect individual rights and, as such, have been carried over into the Fourteenth Amendment . . ." the matter need not be pursued, for as the decisions indicate, regulation . . . which does not impair the maintenance of the State's active, organized militia . . . is not all in violation . . . of the terms or purposes of the Second Amendment or Art. 1, Section 8, clauses 15 and 16. . . .

Commonwealth v. Davis
343 N.E.2d 847 (Mass. 1976)

In connection with a search under warrant of an apartment for narcotic drugs, the police found firearms and ammunition evidently in the possession of the defendant, Hubert Davis. The defendant was indicted . . . for illegal possession . . . of a shotgun with a barrel less than eighteen inches long, and he was found guilty of this crime. . . . On motion for a new trial, the defendant contended that the statute defining and punishing the offense violated his constitutionally guaranteed right to keep and bear arms. . . .

Article 17 of . . . [the Massachusetts Declaration of Rights] declares: "The people have a right to keep and to bear arms for the common defence. And as, in time of peace, armies are dangerous to liberty, they ought not to be maintained without the consent of the legislature; and the military power shall always be held in an exact subordination to the civil authority, and be governed by it. . . ."

[The Court then discussed historical conditions with respect to the existence and arming of a militia.] But that situation no longer exists; our militia, of which the backbone is the National Guard, is now equipped and supported by public funds. . . . There is nothing to suggest that, even in early times due regulation of possession or carrying of firearms, short of some sweeping prohibition, would have been thought to be an improper curtailment of individual liberty or to undercut the militia system. . . .

Presumptively the statute is valid as a police measure; indeed a sawed-off shotgun seems a most plausible subject of regulation as it may be readily concealed and is especially dangerous because of the wide and nearly indiscriminate scattering of its shot. . . .

[The Court then discussed the Second Amendment's relevance to the case.] Decisions of the courts have not retreated from the view that the amendment inhibits only the national government, not the States. . . . So the amendment is irrelevant to the present case. . . .

We affirm the denial of the motion for a new trial.

United States v. Warin
530 F.2d 103 (6th Cir. 1976)

This case requires a determination of whether certain provisions of the National Firearms Act as amended by the Gun Control Act of 1968, are an invalid infringement on the right to keep and bear arms guaranteed by the Second Amendment to the Constitution. . . . Francis J. Warin willfully and knowingly possessed a . . . 9-millimeter prototype submachine gun . . . which had not been registered to him in the National Firearms Registration and Transfer Record, . . . that submachine guns are used by the armed forces of the United States, and that submachine guns contribute to the efficient operation of the armed forces of the United States . . . that submachine guns are part of the military equipment of the United States . . . and that firearms of this general type, that is submachine guns, do bear some relationship, some reasonable relationship, to the preservation or efficiency of the military forces.

The district court found that the defendant, as an adult male resident and citizen of Ohio, is a member of the "sedentary militia" of the State. It was not contended that Warin was a member of the active militia. The court also found that the defendant was an engineer and designer of firearms whose employer develops weapons for the government and . . . that the defendant had made the weapon in question, which is indeed a firearm as described in the Act. . . . The defendant testified that he had designed and built the weapon for the purpose of testing and refining it so that it could be offered to the government as an improvement on the military weapons presently in use. The weapon was not registered to him as required by law. . . . Warin argues . . . that a member of the "sedentary militia" may possess any weapon having military capability and that application of 26 U.S. Section 5861(d) to such a person violates the Second [A]mendment. We disagree. . . .

[The Court then discussed other cases it deemed relevant to Warin's contentions.]

It is clear that the Second Amendment guarantees a collective rather than an individual right. . . .

The fact that the defendant Warin . . . is subject to enrollment in the militia of the state confers upon him no right to possess the submachine gun in question. By statute the State of Ohio exempts "members of . . . the *organized* militia of this or any other state, . . ." from the provision, "No person shall knowingly acquire, have, carry, or use any dangerous ordnance.". . . There is no such exemption of members of the "sedentary" militia. . . . Thus we conclude that the defendant has no private right to keep and bear arms under the Second Amendment which would bar his prosecution and conviction for violating 26 U.S.C. Section 5861(d). . . .

U.S. v. Oakes
564 F.2d 384 (10th Cir. 1977)

This case involved the application of the provisions of the Second Amendment to a situation in which the defendant claimed a right to keep an unregistered firearm that was not demonstrated to have had any relation to the state militia, even though the defendant was technically a member of the Kansas state militia. Moreover, inasmuch as the defendant was a member of the "posse comitatus," a nongovernmental organization, to apply the strictures of the Second Amendment in such circumstances would be unjustifiable both logically and in terms of public policy. [author summary]

State v. Rupp
282 N.W.2d 125 (Iowa 1979)

This was an Iowa case in which the court asserted that the right to bear arms under the provisions of the Second Amendment is not an absolute right; the provisions of that amendment apply only where there is some "reasonable relationship" to the preservation or efficiency of a militia and not to such situations as possession or transportation of a firearm by a convicted felon. [author summary]

Application of Atkinson
291 N.W.2d 396 (Minn. 1980)

On June 1, 1978, plaintiff Berton Atkinson filed an application with the Chief of Police of the City of Bloomington for a permit to carry a pistol, . . . His application was denied for failure to demonstrate a "personal safety hazard," as required by . . . statute. . . .

Appellant Atkinson, a law-abiding citizen, seeks a handgun permit to continue his pre-1975 practice of carrying a loaded pistol in the glove compartment of his automobile "while traveling appreciable distances away from [his] home on public roads and highways."

In 1975, the Minnesota Legislature enacted legislation which requires that, in order for a person to carry or possess a pistol in a public place, he or she must first obtain a permit from the local police chief or county sheriff. . . . In order to obtain such a permit, an individual must establish that he has "an occupation or personal safety hazard requiring a permit to carry.". . .

Plaintiff here seeks to carry a loaded pistol, uncased, in his automobile for travel other than between home and work or between home and the repair shop.

Two issues are raised by this appeal:

1. Is there an absolute constitutional or common-law right to carry a loaded gun on public highways?
2. Does travel for appreciable distances on the public roads constitute a "personal safety hazard" within the meaning of the statute?

. . . Plaintiff argues that the common law has long recognized an individual right to carry weapons for self-defense. . . . Courts and legal scholars, considering the same historical documents that appellant uses to support his common-law right to carry weapons for self-defense have reached the conclusion that any such right is not absolute. . . .

There being no absolute common-law constitutional right to carry weapons abroad for individual self-defense, the state may reasonably exercise its police power to regulate the carrying of weapons by individuals in the interest of public safety.

[The Court then engaged in an extended discussion of various cases and of the police power, and returned to the second question raised in the case.]

The legislative intention to require an applicant to demonstrate a "personal safety hazard" which entitles him to a pistol permit is not unusual. . . .

In the instant case, . . . Atkinson seeks to carry a loaded gun in his car while traveling "appreciable distances" on the public highways. We find it difficult to believe that such travel was intended by the legislature to be a personal safety hazard. . . . The hazard plaintiff has identified is vague, general, and speculative. He has not made the showing of real and immediate danger which the statute requires in order to justify issuance of a handgun permit. The permit was properly denied.

Quilici v. Village of Morton Grove
532 F. Supp. 1169 (N.D. Ill. 1981)

This is a civil action challenging the constitutionality of a gun control ordinance passed by the Trustees of the Village of Morton Grove. . . . In part, the ordinance provides that "no person shall possess, in the Village of Morton Grove . . . any handgun, unless the same has been rendered permanently inoperative." The ordinance specifies various limited exceptions of certain individuals, such as peace officers, prison officials, and members of the armed forces and national guard. The ordinance also exempts licensed gun collectors and provides that handgun owners are free to retain their operative handguns for recreational use, as long as the guns are kept and used on the premises of licensed gun clubs and certain other rules are met. . . .

The plaintiffs have alleged that the enforcement of the ordinance, . . . would violate both the Illinois and United States constitutions. Both sides have moved for summary judgment on the issue of whether the ordinance, on its face, violates article 1, section 22 of the Illinois Constitution [which states that "Subject only to the police power, the right of the individual citizen to keep and bear arms shall not be infringed"], or the Second, Fifth, Ninth or Fourteenth Amendments to the United States Constitution. . . .

The plaintiffs have contended that Morton Grove's ordinance impermissibly infringes upon that right. . . .

The plaintiffs have advocated a broad and liberal interpretation of the individual right to keep and bear arms, and a restrictive view of the scope of the police power. . . .

Because the language contained in section 22 itself offers no clue as to the proper reconciliation of these two competing concepts, the court finds it necessary to examine the provision's constitutional history, the source traditionally relied upon for the clarification of ambiguous constitutional provisions. . . .

[The Court then pursued a lengthy discussion of legislative debates that led to section 22; articles in the *Chicago Tribune*; what the people thought about section 22; and cases decided in other states. The Court continued as follows:]

After carefully reviewing the constitutional history of section 22, including the actual language used in the provision, the text of the convention debates, the committee report, and the other sources . . . the court concludes that the right to arms in Illinois is so limited by the police power that a ban on handguns does not violate that right. . . .

Given that the Morton Grove ordinance is a reasonable response to the problems seen by the Trustees, it is not automatically invalid because it is a prohibition rather than a regulation.

In sum, this court concludes that the Morton Grove ordinance has as its basis the proper goals of protecting the safety and health of the people. In addition, the court finds that the ordinance does not represent a complete ban on firearms, and is reasonable and neither arbitrary nor simplistic.

[Regarding the relevance of the Second Amendment to their decision, and perhaps the most immediately relevant of the other amendments considered, using the *Presser* case and *Adamson v. California* as the crux of their argument, the Court stated:]

Although three other Justices concurred with Justice Black [in

Adamson] that the Bill of Rights, in its entirety, should be incorporated into the protections offered by the Fourteenth Amendment, that position has never been accepted by a majority of the Supreme Court. . . . That situation is underscored by the fact that some provisions of the Bill of Rights, in addition to the Second Amendment, have never been held to apply to the states. . . .

After full consideration, the court has concluded that the Morton Grove ordinance was properly enacted pursuant to the police power, and that it does not infringe upon the rights guaranteed by the United States Constitution.

Bristow v. State
418 So.2d 927 (Ala. 1982)

This Alabama case concluded that a state statute that prohibited possession of a pistol by a person after that person had been previously convicted of committing a violent crime is not unconstitutional under the provisions of the Second Amendment. [author sumary]

Sklar v. Byrne
727 F.2d 633 (7th Cir. 1984)

This case involved a Chicago handgun ordinance that made it illegal to possess handguns that were not registered prior to the effective date of the law. The court held that this requirement does not violate the provisions of the Second Amendment to keep and bear arms. [author summary]

People v. Barela
286 Cal. Rptr. 458, 234 Cal.
App. 3d Supp. 15 (1991)

This case involved carrying firearms without a license in the defendant's "place of business." The case hinged on the adequate definition of *possessory interest* in the restaurant in which the weapon was carried. The Court ruled that the definition, even though it carried "surplusage," was sufficiently clear so as to preclude reversible error, and that the results would not have changed with the removal of the surplusage. [author summary]

Some Cases Illustrating the Individual View

Bliss v. Commonwealth
12 Ky. (2 Litt.) 90 (1822)

This was an indictment founded on the act of the legislature of this state, "to prevent persons in this commonwealth from wearing concealed arms. . . ."

The indictment, in the words of the act, charges Bliss with having worn, concealed as a weapon, a sword in a cane.

Bliss was found guilty of the charge. . . . To reverse the judgment, Bliss appeared to this court.

In argument the judgment was assailed by the counsel of Bliss, exclusively on the ground of the act, on which the indictment is founded, being in conflict with the twenty-third section of the tenth article of the constitution of this state.

That section provides, "that the right of the citizens to bear arms in defence of themselves and the state, shall not be questioned. . . ."

. . . It is the right to bear arms in defence of the citizens of the state, that is secured by the constitution, and whatever restrains the full and complete exercise of that right, though not an entire destruction of it, is forbidden by the explicit language of the constitution.

If, therefore, the act in question imposes any restraint on the right, immaterial what appellation may be given to the act, whether it be an act regulating the manner of bearing arms or any other, the consequence, in reference to the constitution, is precisely the same, and its collision with that instrument equally obvious.

And can there be entertained a reasonable doubt but the provisions of the act import a restraint on the right of the citizens to bear arms? The court apprehends not. The right existed at the adoption of the constitution; it had then no limits short of the moral power of the citizens to exercise it, and it in fact consisted in nothing else but in the liberty of the citizens to bear arms. Diminish that liberty, therefore, and you necessarily restrain the right; and such is the diminution and restraint, which the act in question most indisputably imports, by prohibiting the citizens wearing weapons in a manner which was lawful to wear them when the constitution was adopted. In truth, the right of the citizens to bear arms, has been as directly assailed by the provisions of the act, as though they were forbid carrying guns on their shoulders, swords in scabbards, or when in conflict with an enemy, were not allowed the use of bayonets; and if the act be consistent with the constitution, it cannot be incompatible with that instument for the legislature, by successive enactments, to entirely cut off the exercise of the right of the citizens to bear arms. For, in principle, there is no difference between a law prohibiting the wearing [of] concealed arms, and a law forbidding the wearing such as are exposed; and if the former be unconstitutional, the latter must be so likewise. . . .

But it should not be forgotten, that it is not only a part of the right that is secured by the constitution; it is the right entire and complete, as it existed at the adoption of the constitution; and if any portion of that right be impaired, immaterial how small the part may be, and immaterial the order of time at which it be done, it is equally forbidden by the constitution.

Hence, we infer, that the act upon which the indictment against Bliss is founded, is in conflict with the constitution; and if so, the result is obvious; the result is what the constitution has declared it shall be, that the act is void. . . .

For it is emphatically the duty of the court to decide what the law is; and how is the law to be decided, unless it be known? And how can it be known without ascertaining, from a comparison with the constitution, whether there exist[s] such an incompatibility between the acts of the legislature and the constitution, as to make void the acts?. . . . The court should never, on slight implication or vague conjecture, pronounce the legislature to have transcended its authority in the enactment of law but when a clear and strong conviction is entertained, that an act of the legislature is incompatible with the constitution, there is no alternative for the court to pursue, but to declare that conviction, and pronounce the act inoperative and void. And such is the conviction entertained by a majority of the court. . . .

State v. Buzzard
4 Ark. 18 (1842)

Lacy, J., dissenting.

The defendant in the court below stands indicted by virtue of the authority of the 13th section of an act of the Legislature, prohibiting any person wearing a pistol, dirk, large knife, or sword-cane, concealed as a weapon, unless upon a journey, under the penalties of fine and imprisonment.

The question now to be determined is, does this provision

of the statute violate the second article of the amendments to the Constitution of the United States, or the 21st section of our Bill of Rights? The language in both instruments is nearly similar: the two clauses are as follows: "That a well regulated militia being necessary for the security of a free State, the right of the people to keep and bear arms shall not be infringed." "That the free white men of this State shall have a right to keep and bear arms in their common defence.". . . Now, I take the expressions "a well-regulated militia being necessary for the security of a free State," and the terms "common defence," to be the reasons assigned for the granting of the right, and not a restriction or limitation upon the right itself, or the perfect freedom of its exercise. The security of the State is the constitutional reason for the guaranty. But when was it contended before, that the reason given for the establishment of a right, or its uninterrupted enjoyment, not only limited the right itself, but restrained it to a single specific object? According to this construction, the right itself is not only abridged, but literally destroyed; and the security of a free State is made to depend exclusively and alone upon the force of the militia. . . . This construction . . . takes the arms out of the hands of the people, and places them in the hands of the legislature, with no restraint or limitation whatever upon their power, except their own free will and sovereign pleasure. . . .

Now, if the legislature had the right to forbid the people from keeping arms secretly, may they not prohibit them from carrying them openly or exposed, and if they could do this, may they not appoint the times and places when and where they shall be borne? And as the construction relied on assumes the principle that they can only be used for a specific and single purpose, then of course the whole subject matter, in regard to keeping and bearing either private or public arms, falls within the power of the legislature, and they can control or regulate it in any manner they think proper. This principle I utterly repudiate. I deny that any just or free government upon earth has the power to disarm its citizens, and to take from them the only security and ultimate hope that they have for the defence of their liberties and their rights. I deny this, not only upon constitutional grounds, but upon the immutable principles of natural and equal justice, that all men have a right to, and which to deprive them of amounts to tyranny and oppression. . . .

Has not the State a right to designate what part or portion of her citizens shall constitute this military corps? Then she can, by indirection, arm only those who are in her interest, or who are swayed by her ambition; and, by denying arms to every other class of her citizens, may she not subjugate the liberties of all, by the very means the Constitution gives for their protection and defence?. . . .

Has not every man a natural and an unalienable right to defend his life, liberty, or property, when a known felony is attempted to be committed upon either by violence or surprise? Can any laws deprive him of this right? Upon what principle has he a right to use force to repel force, and even to slay the aggressor, it he cannot make a successful repulsion otherwise? The laws of the land being unable to protect him, the laws of nature step in, and authorize him to defend himself. . . .

I cannot separate the political freedom of the State from the personal rights of its citizens. They are indissolubly bound up together in the same great bond of union. . . . Among these rights, I hold, is the privilege of the people to keep and bear their private arms, for the necessary defence of their person, habitation, and property, or for any useful or innocent purpose whatever. We derive this right from our Anglo-Saxon ancestors. . . .

In re Brickey
8 Idaho 597, 70 P. 609 (1902)

The petitioner applies to this court for a writ of habeaus corpus, and in the petition sets forth and shows that he is unlawfully imprisoned, confined, and restrained . . . at the county jail . . . of Nez Perce, in the state of Idaho; . . . under a commitment which issued out of the justice's court . . . in a criminal action wherein petitioner was convicted upon the charge of carrying a deadly weapon, to wit, a loaded revolver, within the limits and confines of . . . Lewiston . . . contrary to the provisions of the act of the territory of Idaho approved February 4, 1889. . . . From the petition and return it appears that the only offense charged against the petitioner, of which he has been convicted . . . is that he carried a deadly weapon within the limits of the city of Lewiston, in contravention of the said act. . . . The Second [A]mendment to the federal constitution is in the following language: "A well regulated militia, being necessary to the security of a free state, the right of the people to keep and bear arms, shall not be infringed." The language of section 11, art. 1, Const. Idaho, is as follows: "The people have the right to bear arms for their security and defense, but the legislature shall regulate the exercise of this right by law." Under these constitutional provisions, the legislature has no power to prohibit a citizen from bearing arms in any portion of the state of Idaho, whether within or without the corporate limits of cities, towns, and villages. The legislature may, as expressly provided in our state constitution, regulate the exercise of the police power of the state. But the statute in question does not prohibit the carrying of weapons concealed, which is of itself a pernicious practice, but prohibits the carrying of them in any manner. . . . We are compelled to hold this statute void.

State v. Rosenthal
75 Vt. 295, 44 A. 610 (1903)

Section 10 of the ordinances of the city of Rutland provides that no person shall carry within the city any steel or brass knuckles, pistol, slung shot, stiletto, or weapon of similar character, nor carry any weapon concealed on his person, without permission of the mayor or chief of police, in writing, and for violation thereof a penalty is provided by a subsequent section. A complaint was filed against the respondent in the city court for carrying *within* the city, in violation of said ordinance, a pistol loaded with powder and bullets, concealed on his person, without such permission. On demurrer to the complaint, the respondent contends, among other things, that said ordinance is illegal, for that, so far as it forbids the carrying of a pistol, it is repugnant to and inconsistent with the Constitution and the laws of this state.

Section 24 of the city charter gives the city council power to make, establish, alter, amend, or repeal ordinances, regulations, and by-laws, not inconsistent with the charter or with the Constitution or laws of the United States or of this state. . . . After the special designations is the general clause, "And said city council may make and establish, and the same alter, amend or repeal, any other by-laws, rules and ordinances which they deem necessary for the well being of said city and not repugnant to the Constitution or laws of this state." Power to make the ordinance in question was not expressly given the council, and they had no power to make it, beyond what is given under the general clause above quoted. The people of the state have a right to bear arms for the defense of themselves and the state. Const. c. 1, art. 16. But by V.S. 4922, a person is prohibited from carrying a dangerous or deadly weapon, openly or concealed, with the intent or avowed purpose of injuring a fellow man; and . . . no person can carry or have in his possession any firearm, dirk knife, bowie knife, dagger, or other dangerous or deadly weapon, while a member of and in attendance upon a school. [The court continued a discussion of various other sections of Vermont law and the ordinances of Rutland. The court concluded as follows:] By the ordinance in question, no person can carry such weapon concealed on his person within the city of Rutland in any circumstances, nor for any purpose, without the permission of the mayor or chief of police in writing. Therein neither the intent nor purpose of carrying them enters into the essential elements of the offense. Simply to carry them concealed without such permission constitutes a violation of the ordinance. But if a permission is procured from either of those officials there is no violation of the ordinance, even though the carrying of the weapon be with the intent or avowed purpose of injuring another person; and that a person is a member of a school, and in attendance upon it, forms no exception. Consequently, unless a special permission is granted by the mayor or chief of police for that purpose, a person is prohibited from carrying such weapons in circumstances where the same is lawful by the Constitution and the general laws of the state; and there is nothing in the ordinance to prevent the granting of such permission, notwithstanding it be in circumstances to constitute a crime under the general laws. The result is that Ordinance No. 10, so far as it relates to the carrying of a pistol, is inconsistent with and repugnant to the Constitution and the laws of the state, and it is therefore to that extent, void. . . .

State v. Kerner
181 N.C. 574, 107 S.E. 222 (1921)

The defendant was indicted on a first count for carrying a concealed weapon, and on the second count for carrying a pistol off his premises unconcealed. There was a special verdict which found the defendant was walking along the streets of the town of Kernersville in Forsyth county carrying some packages, when he was accosted, for the purpose of engaging him in a fight . . . that in the course of this altercation he set down his packages and went to his place of business and there procured a pistol, which he brought back with him unconcealed to the scene of the altercation. Section 3, c. 317, Public Local Laws of 1919, prohibits the carrying of such weapons off his own premises by any one in Forsyth without a permit, even though it was not concealed. The court, being of the opinion that this statute was in conflict with the constitutional provision that "the right to bear arms shall not be infringed," directed a verdict of not guilty, and the state appealed. . . .

The Constitution of this state . . . provides: "The right of the people to keep and bear arms shall not be infringed," adding, "nothing herein contained shall justify the practice of carrying concealed weapons or prevent the Legislature from enacting penal statutes against said practice." This exception indicates the extent to which the right of the people to bear arms can be restricted; that is, the Legislature can prohibit the carrying of concealed weapons but no further. This constitutional guaranty was construed in *State v. Speller* . . . in which it was held that the distinction was between the "right to keep and bear arms" and the "practice of carrying concealed weapons." The former is a sacred right based upon the experience of the ages in order that the people may be accustomed to bear arms and ready to use them for the protection of their liberties or their country when occasion serves. The provision against carrying them concealed was to prevent assassinations or advantages taken by the lawless. . . .

We know that in the past this privilege was guaranteed for the sacred purpose of enabling the people to protect themselves against invasions of their liberties. . . .

The maintenance of the right to bear arms is a most essential one to every free people and should not be whittled down by technical constructions. It should be construed to include all "arms" as were in common use, and borne by the people as such when this provision was adopted. . . .

If the people are forbidden to carry the only arms within their means, among them pistols, they will be completely at the mercy of . . . great plutocratic organizations. Should there be a mob, is it possible that law-abiding citizens could not assemble with their pistols carried openly and protect their persons and their property from unlawful violence without going before an official and obtaining license and giving bond?

The usual method when a country is overborne by force is to "disarm" the people. It is to prevent the above and similar exercises of arbitrary power that the people, in creating this government . . . reserved to themselves the right to "bear arms," that, accustomed to their use, they might be ready to meet illegal force with legal force adequate and just defense of their persons, their property, and their liberties, whenever necessary. We should be slow indeed to construe such guaranty into mere academic expression which has become obsolete. . . .

The statute in this case . . . is especially objectionable in that it requires . . . that in order to carry a pistol off his own premises, even openly, and for a lawful purpose, the citizen must make application to the municipal court . . . or to the superior court . . . describing the weapon and giving the time and purpose for which it may be carried . . . and must pay to the clerk of the court the sum of $5 for each permit and must file a bond in the penalty of $500 that he will not carry the weapon except as so authorized. In the case of a riot or mob violence, or other emergency requiring the defense of public order, this would place law-abiding citizens entirely at the mercy of the lawless element. As a regulation even this is void because an unreasonable regulation, and, besides, it would be void because for all practical purposes it is prohibition of the constitutional right to bear arms. There would be no time or opportunity to get such permit and to give such bonds on an emergency.

On this occasion, the defendant threatened with violence was forced to abandon his property. He went to his place of business where he had the right to keep his pistol, "being on his own premises," and returned with it unconcealed. He was acting in self-defense of his person and in defense of his property. The court below most properly adjudged upon the special verdict that he was not guilty.

People v. Zerillo
219 Mich. 635, 189 N.W. 927 (1922)

Defendant, an unnaturalized foreign-born resident, was convicted under a complaint charging him with possessing a revolver without a permit. . . .

The complaint was laid under the game law, but did not charge the defendant with hunting for or capturing or killing any wild bird or animal, or intending to do so. Does the game law make it unlawful for an unnaturalized foreign-born resident of the state to possess a revolver? . . .

Defendant insists that the act, so far as it deprives him of the right to possess a revolver, for a legitimate purpose, is in conflict with the provisions of the Constitution of the state, and therefore void. The Constitution of this state . . . provides: "Every person has a right to bear arms for the defense of himself and the state. . . ."

Firearms serve the people of this country a useful purpose wholly aside from hunting, and under a constitution like ours, granting to aliens who are bona fide residents of the state the same rights in respect to the possession, enjoyment and inheritance of property as native-born citizens, and to every person the right to bear arms for the defense of himself and the state, while the Legislature has power in the most comprehensive manner to regulate the carrying and use of firearms, that body has no power to constitute it a crime for a person, alien or citizen, to possess a revolver for the legitimate defense of himself and his property. The provision in the Constitution granting the right to all persons to bear arms is a limitation upon the power of the Legislature to enact any law to the contrary.

The exercise of a right guaranteed by the Constitution cannot be made subject to the will of the sheriff. The part of the act under which the prosecution was planted is not one of regulation, but is one of prohibition and confiscation. . . .

Game being property of the state the Legislature may enact laws for its protection, but under the guise of protection of game may not disarm any class, falling within the constitutional guaranty, of the right to bear arms in defense of themselves. The guaranty of the right to every person to bear arms in defense of himself means the right to possess arms for legitimate use in defense of himself, and necessarily includes the right to defend therewith, by lawful means, his property. . . .

It will be noticed that our Constitution is inclusive of the right of *every person* to bear arms . . . and not merely citizens. . . .

The part of the act making it a crime for an unnaturalized foreign-born resident to possess a revolver, unless so permitted by the sheriff, contravenes the guaranty of such right in the Constitution of the state, and is void. . . .

Under the complaint and warrant and the evidence the defendant should have been adjudged not guilty. The conviction is set aside, and defendant is discharged.

City of Las Vegas v. Moberg
82 N.M. 626 (1971)

The defendant . . . was convicted by the municipal court of the City of Las Vegas of violating the city ordinance . . . "DEADLY WEAPONS. It shall be unlawful for any person to carry deadly weapons, concealed or otherwise, on or about their persons, within the corporate limits of the City of East Las Vegas. Deadly weapons shall consist of all kind of guns, pistols, knives with blades longer than two and a half inches, slingshots, sandbags, metallic knuckles, concealed rocks, and all other weapons, by whatever name known, with which dangerous wounds can be inflicted."

The complaint charged the defendant with the violation of the ordinance by number and specifically by "carrying a concealed and deadly weapon.". . .

The evidence . . . established, without dispute, that defendant went to the booking room of the city police department of the city of Las Vegas to report the theft of certain items from his automobile. At the same time, defendant was carrying a pistol in a holster. The pistol was in plain view at all times. It appears that both parties at the trial in the district court treated the complaints as charging simply the carrying of a deadly weapon. No contention is made that the evidence supported the carrying of a concealed weapon. . . .

Defendant has appealed and challenges the constitutionality of the ordinance as it is applied to carrying arms openly and in plain view. He asserts that in this respect the ordinance is repugnant to article II, Section 6 of the Constitution of the State of New Mexico. This section provides: "The people have the right to bear arms for their security and defense, but nothing herein shall be held to permit the carrying of concealed weapons."

It is a generally accepted principle that a municipal ordinance which denies rights protected by constitutional guaranty is void to the extent, at least, that it purports to deny such rights. . . .

Ordinances prohibiting the carrying of concealed weapons have generally been held to be a proper exercise of police power. . . .

Such ordinances do not deprive citizens of the right to bear arms; their effect is only to regulate the right. As applied to arms, other than those concealed, the ordinance under consideration purports to completely prohibit the "right to bear arms."

It is our opinion that an ordinance may not deny the people the constitutionally guaranteed right to bear arms, and to that extent the ordinance under consideration is void. . . .

Espinosa v. Superior Court of San Joaquin County
123 Cal. Rptr. 448, 40 Cal.
App. 3d 347 (1975)

In this case, the petitioner was arrested in his private residence where he was lawfully in possession of weapons. He was later acquitted of a charge of assault with a deadly weapon against a police officer. Therefore, confiscation, sale, retention or destruction of his weapons were not authorized. Moreover, a writ of mandate was an appropriate proceeding by which the petitioner could obtain the return of his confiscated weapons. [author summary]

Schubert v. DeBard
398 N.E.2d 1339 (Ind. Ct. App. 1980)

Appellant, Joseph L. Schubert, applied . . . for a license to carry a handgun. . . . A hearing was held and . . . Schubert [was] . . . denied the permit. The trial court sustained . . . and this appeal follows.

The evidence disclosed that . . . appellant applied for a permit to carry a handgun for self-protection. He had previously held such permits. . . . He had carried a handgun when engaged in part-time employment in the nature of security work. He also had held a special police commission from the City of Fort Wayne and a St. Joseph's County Deputy Sheriff's commission. Both commissions had been revoked prior to his application for the license. . . .

The licensing statute, . . . provides . . . *If it appears to the superintendent that the applicant has a proper reason for carrying a handgun and is of good character and reputation and a proper person to be so licensed* [emphasis in original], he shall issue to the applicant either a qualified or an unlimited license to carry any handgun or handguns lawfully possessed by the applicant. . . .

Establishing such a licensing procedure for handguns is not violative of the right to bear arms as guaranteed by the Second Amendment or Art. 1, Sec. 32 of the Indiana Constitution.

Schubert contends, however, that the Indiana Constitution affords him the right to bear arms for his own defense. Thus, he urges that where self-defense is properly asserted as the reason for desiring a firearms license, and the applicant is otherwise qualified, the license cannot be withheld upon an administrative official's subjective determination of whether the applicant needs defending.

Our Art. 1, Sec. 32, is worded differently than the Second Amendment. It states simply and plainly, "The people shall have a right to bear arms, for the defense of themselves and the State."

It is well settled that we are to presume that constitutional language was carefully chosen to express the framers' intention. . . . The words used are to be taken in their general and ordinary sense. . . . We think it clear that our constitution provides our citizenry the right to bear arms for their self-defense. Furthermore, . . . our Supreme Court held that if it is determined . . . that the applicant has met the conditions of the statute, the superintendent has no discretion to withhold the license. . . .

In Schubert's case it is clear from the record that the superintendent decided the application on the basis that the statutory reference to "a proper reason" vested in him the power and duty to subjectively evaluate an assignment of "self-defense" as a reason for desiring a license and the ability to grant or deny the license upon the basis [of] whether the applicant "needed" to defend himself.

Such an approach contravenes the essential nature of the constitutional guarantee. It would supplant a right with a mere administrative privilege which might be withheld simply on the basis that such matters as the use of firearms are better left to the organized military and police forces even when defense of the individual citizen is involved.

We therefore hold that Schubert's assigned reason which stood unrefuted was constitutionally a "proper reason."

State v. Kessler
614 P.2d 94 (Or. Ct. App. 1980)

The defendant in this case was convicted of "possession of a slugging weapon.". . . We allowed review to consider his claim that the legislative prohibition of the possession of a "billy" . . . violates Article 1, Section 27, of the Oregon Constitution. That provision states: "The people shall have the right to bear arms for the defence . . . of themselves, and the State, but the Military shall be kept in strict subordination to the civil power.". . .

The scope of Article 1, Section 27, has not previously been analyzed by Oregon courts. The decisions construing the second amendment to the United States Constitution are not particularly helpful because the wording of the second amendment differs substantially from our state provision. The second amendment has not yet been held to apply to state limitations on the bearing of arms. The wording of Oregon's right to bear arms provision also differs from many other state constitutional provisions. . . .

If the text and purpose of the constitutional guarantee relied exclusively on the preference for a militia "for defense of the State," then the term "arms" most likely would include only the modern day equivalents of the weapons used by colonial militiamen. The Oregon provision, however, guarantees a right to bear arms "for defense of themselves, and the state." The term "arms" in our constitution therefore would include weapons commonly used for either purpose, even if a particular weapon is unlikely to be used as a militia weapon. . . .

The defendant was charged with disorderly conduct, . . . and possession of a slugging weapon. . . .

The defendant appealed to the Court of Appeals, contending first that his acts did not amount to the crime of disorderly conduct and second that the statute prohibiting possession of billy clubs, . . . violated Article 1, Section 27, of the Oregon Constitution. . . .

The defendant contends that his conviction for possession of a billy club violates his rights to possess arms in his home for personal defense. Pursuant to our previous discussion regarding the purpose and scope of the right to bear arms provision, we hold that Article 1, section 27, of the Oregon constitution includes a right to possess certain arms for defense of person and property. The remaining question is whether the defendant's possession of a billy club in this case is protected. . . .

Our historical analysis of Article 1, Section 27, indicates that the drafters intended "arms" to include the hand-carried weapons commonly used by individuals for personal defense. The club is an effective hand-carried weapon which cannot logically be excluded from this term. We hold that the defendant's possession of a billy club in his home is protected. . . .

Shettle v. Shearer
425 N.E.2d 739 (Ind. Ct. App. 1981)

John T. Shettle, Superintendent of the Indiana State Police Department appeals the trial court's order directing him to issue an unlimited handgun license to James F. Shearer. . . .

The only question in issue at the hearing was whether Shearer had a proper reason for carrying a handgun. Shearer's asserted reason . . . was a medical condition in which any assault upon his person could cause anything ranging from a brief period of incapacitation to death. In support of his testimony, Shearer presented a letter from his physician. . . .

Shettle argues that Shearer did not properly assert self-defense as his reason for requesting a handgun license. At the hearing Shearer stated that due to phlebitis in his left leg, any assault upon him could result in his death. Additionally, when asked if there were any reasons other than medical, Shearer answered, "It is clear that self-defense was the motive for the application and that the normal need for self-defense was heightened by Shearer's medical problems." . . .

Shearer's unrefuted testimony regarding his medical problems and his desire for self-defense are proper reasons for acquiring a handgun license. Absent other justifications for denial, the application should have been granted by Shettle.

Michael Kalodimos et al., Appellants, v. The Village of Morton Grove, Appellee

Filed October 19, 1984
Clerk Supreme Court
Illinois

Ryan, C. J., dissenting.

I join in the very convincing dissent of my colleague, Justice Moran. In addition, I wish to address the question of the use of police power by the village of Morton Grove to ban the ownership of handguns.

The majority opinion concedes that section 22 of article 1 of our Illinois Constitution broadened the scope of the right to arms . . . to an individual right covering a wider variety of arms and that the Illinois Constitution bestows upon individual citizens the right to possess weapons suitable for self-defense and recreation. . . .

The majority uses equal protection standards relating to statutory classification to support its statement that police regulations will be upheld if any state of facts may reasonably be conceived to justify them. . . .

I am not concerned with an equal protection question. We are here dealing with a due process question: the taking away of a constitutionally given right—the right to arms—through the exercise of the police power. . . .

This court's inquiry in reviewing the legislative exercise of the police power should be whether the legislation represents a rational means to accomplish a proper purpose. . . . Thus, the inquiry must be: First, what purpose does the legislative body seek to accomplish by depriving the residents of Morton Grove the constitutionally given right to arms? Second, is it a proper purpose; that is, one that may be constitutionally achieved by the use of the police power? Lastly, does the ordinance use a rational means of accomplishing the purpose?

As the majority opinion notes, the ordinance, in its preamble, cites certain interests of the village, such as reducing "the potentiality of firearm related deaths and injuries" caused by "the easy and convenient availability of certain types of firearms and weapons," and finds that "handguns play a major role in the commission of homicide, aggravated assault, and armed robbery, and accidental injury and death."

Although the recited purposes of the ordinance would appear to be laudable and supportive of the exercise of the police power to achieve these ends, the minutes of the meeting of the board of trustees of the village at which the ordinance was adopted do not reflect any discussion of these purposes, or that the ordinance was adopted to achieve them. . . . Statistics compiled by the chief of police did not disclose the nature of the handgun misuse. . . . Also, the statistics did not disclose if misuses were committed by residents of Morton Grove.

Meager as these statistics are, they reveal that the misuse of handguns is a very minimal problem in Morton Grove. . . .

The purposes of the ordinance cited in its preamble were therefore pure and simple litany, inserted in the ordinance for window dressing and to help withstand constitutional challenge. . . .

The majority opinion acknowledges that these statements reflect the possibility that the ordinance was passed for the sole purpose of publicizing a political viewpoint. I am in accord with that conclusion. I am shocked, however, that the majority opinion finds no significance in this possibility. If the police power can be exercised for the sole purpose of publicizing a political viewpoint, then I feel that our constitutionally guaranteed rights are in serious jeopardy. . . .

. . . If we permit the constitutionally given right to arms to be nullified by simply inserting a few "magic words" in an ordinance which gives the ordinance an appearance of being a valid exercise of the police power, when it is in fact only the assertion of a political philosophy and a publicizing of that viewpoint, then we have in effect eliminated this right that has been granted by the Constitution. . . .

The sole purpose behind the ordinance was to assert and

publicize a particular political belief, "to send a message to other legislative bodies across the country." Such a purpose is not a sufficient reason for infringing on a constitutional right by the exercise of the police power. I therefore dissent.

Michael Kalodimos et al., Appellants, v. The Village of Morton Grove, Appellee

Filed October 19, 1984
Clerk Supreme Court
Illinois

Moran, J., also dissenting:

For more than a decade, the bill of rights to the Illinois Constitution has included a provision on the right to keep and bear arms. . . . I agree with the majority opinion that the language of section 22 of article 1 indicates that the right to keep and bear arms is a qualified, not an absolute, right. Nevertheless, I disagree with the conclusion that . . . municipalities may enact flat bans on the possession of ordinary handguns. Under the opinion announced today, so long as municipalities allow residents to possess "some form of weapon suitable for self-defense or recreation" municipalities may ban all other weapons. . . . The majority's strained reading of section 22 defies logic and runs counter to the history surrounding the enactment of the right-to-bear-arms guarantee.

To the contrary, section 22 prohibits a flat ban on those types of firearms that "law-abiding citizens employ for purposes of recreation or the protection of person and property," including ordinary handguns and long guns. . . .

After considering the debates on section 22, I am of the opinion that, at most, the debates reflect a lack of consensus as to the meaning of section 22. The debates illustrate that the issue of whether Illinois' citizens should have the right to bear arms was a highly controversial and emotional issue. . . .

The lack of consensus . . . was not lost on a number of delegates. . . .

. . . The report of the convention's Committee on the Bill of Rights left the understanding that municipalities would be prohibited from enacting total bans on the possession of ordinary handguns. . . .

Moreover, the Committee on the Bill of Rights and convention delegates specifically declined to adopt proposals which would have allowed the prohibition of ordinary handguns. . . . If committee members or convention delegates had desired to give municipalities such wide-ranging power, they would not have rejected every proposal authorizing the right to prohibit handguns.

In my opinion, municipalities cannot, consistent with section 22, enact flat bans on the possession of handguns or any other firearm which is commonly used by law-abiding citizens for recreation or protection of person or property. I would therefore hold that Morton Grove's ordinance banning the possession of handguns is unconstitutional.

. . . Because the possession of firearms has traditionally been regulated by State law, and because local firearms laws like the one adopted by Morton Grove would necessarily affect persons beyond municipal boundaries, confuse law-abiding citizens and are counterproductive, I am of the opinion that this subject is of State and not local concern. I would therefore hold that Morton Grove has exceeded its home rule authority under . . . our constitution. . . .

For the above-stated reason, I must respectfully dissent.

State v. Delgado
298 Or. 395, 692 P.2d 610 (1984)

This case involved a resident of Oregon who was convicted for the violation of a statute that prohibited the possession or carrying of switchblade knives. The court reversed on the grounds that the Oregon Constitution contains a provision that the people shall have the right to bear arms for defense of themselves and of the state. [author summary]

United States v. Verdugo-Urquidez
494 U.S. 259 (1990)

Although this case involved the application of the Fourth Amendment, the statement of the Court was to the effect that the rights protected in the Second Amendment are to be applied to all law-abiding citizens. It stated that "The Second Amendment protects 'the right of the people to keep and bear Arms,' and that the Ninth and Tenth Amendments provide that certain rights and powers are retained by and reserved to 'the people.'. . . While this textual exegesis is by no means conclusive, it suggests that 'the people' protected by the Fourth Amendment, and by the First and Second Amendments, and to whom rights and powers are reserved in the Ninth and Tenth Amendments, refers to a class of persons who are part of a national community. . . ." [author summary]

Perpich v. Department of Defense
110 S. Ct. 2418 (1990)

It has been common parlance that the Second Amendment is concerned only with protecting the right of a state to keep a militia, and that this means the National Guard. In this case, the Court stated that the militia is made up of all able-bodied citizens. It stated its view of the "militia as a part-time, nonprofessional fighting force" and as "a body of armed citizens." It referred also to the 1792 Militia Act, which required that "every able-bodied male citizen . . . equip himself with appropriate weaponry. . . ."

State v. Stevens
113 Or. App. 429, 833 P.2d 318 (1992)

A statute that prohibits the carrying of a concealed knife is applicable only to knives in possession outside one's own home. Any application of such statute to a person inside his or her own home would violate provisions of the state constitution that guarantees the right to bear arms for self-defense. [author summary]

United States Supreme Court Opinions
United States v. Cruikshank
92 U.S. 542 (1876)

This was an indictment for conspiracy under the sixth section of the act of May 30, 1870, known as the Enforcement Act (16 Stat. 140), and consisted of thirty-two counts.

The *first* count was for banding together, with intent "unlawfully and feloniously to injure, oppress, threaten, and intimidate" two citizens of the United States, "of African descent and persons of color," "with the unlawful and felonious intent thereby" . . . "to hinder and prevent in their respective free exercise and enjoyment of their lawful right and privilege to peaceably assemble together with each other and with other citizens of the said United States for a peaceable and lawful purpose."

The *second* avers an intent to hinder and prevent the exercise by the same persons of the "right to keep and bear arms for a lawful purpose.". . .

The right of the people peaceably to assemble for lawful purposes existed long before the adoption of the Constitution of the United States. In fact, it is, and always has been, one of the attributes of citizenship. . . . It was not, therefore, a right granted to the people by the Constitution. The government of the United States when established found it in existence, with the obligation on the part of the States to afford it protection. As no direct power over it was granted to Congress, it remains . . . subject to State jurisdiction. . . .

For their protection in its enjoyment, therefore, the people must look to the States. The power for that purpose was originally placed there, and it has never been surrendered to the United States. . . .

If it had been alleged in these counts that the object of the defendants was to prevent a meeting for such a purpose, the case would have been within the statute, and within the scope of the sovereignty of the United States. Such, however, is not the case. . . .

The second and tenth counts are equally defective. The right there specified is that of 'bearing arms for a lawful purpose.' This is not a right granted by the Constitution. Neither is it in any manner dependent upon that instrument for its existence. The second amendment declares that it shall not be infringed; but this, as has been seen, means no more than that it shall not be infringed by Congress. This is one of the amendments that has no other effect than to restrict the powers of the national government, leaving the people to look for their protection against violation by their fellow-citizens of the rights it recognizes, to what is called, in *The City of New York v. Miln*, 11 Pet. 139, the "powers which relate to merely municipal legislation, or what was, perhaps more properly called internal police," "not surrendered or restrained" by the Constitution of the United States. . . .

We are, therefore, of the opinion that the first, second . . . counts do not contain charges of a criminal nature made indictable under the laws of the United States. . . . They do not show that it was the intent of the defendants, by their conspiracy, to hinder or prevent the enjoyment of any right granted or secured by the Constitution. . . .

Presser v. Illinois
116 U.S. 252 (1886)

Herman Presser . . . was indicted on September 24, 1879, in the Criminal Court of Cook County, Illinois, for a violation of the following sections of Art. XI. of the Military Code of that State, . . .

Section 5. It shall not be lawful for any body of men whatever, other than the regular organized volunteer militia of this State, and the troops of the United States, to associate themselves together as a military company or organization, or to drill or parade with arms in any city, or town, of this State, without the license of the Governor thereof, which license may at any time be revoked. . . . *Provided,* that nothing herein contained shall be construed as to prevent benevolent or social organizations, from wearing swords. . . .

The indictment charged . . . that Presser, on September 24, 1879, in the county of Cook, in the State of Illinois, "did unlawfully belong to, and did parade in the city of Chicago with an unauthorized body of men with arms, who had associated themselves together as a military company and organization, without having a license from the Governor, and not being a part of, or belonging to, 'the regular organized volunteer militia' of the State of Illinois, or the troops of the United States.". . .

[The evidence suggested] that Presser was thirty-one years old, a citizen of the United States and of the State of Illinois, and a voter; that he belonged to a society called the Lehr and Wehr Verein, a corporation . . . [organized] "for the purpose" . . . of improving the mental and bodily condition of its members, so as to qualify them for the duties of citizens of a republic. Its members shall therefore obtain, in the meetings of the association, a knowledge of our laws and political economy, and shall also be instructed in the military and gymnastic exercises; that Presser, in December, 1879, marched at the head of said company, about four hundred in number, in the streets of the city of Chicago, he riding on horseback and in command; and that the company was armed with rifles and Presser with a cavalry sword; that the company had no license from the governor of

Illinois to drill or parade as a part of the militia of the State, and was not a part of the regular organized militia of the State, nor a part of troops of the United States, and had no organization under the militia law of the United States. . . .

[The Court then engaged in a discussion of the contentions of the plaintiff, various constitutional provisions of the United States and Illinois, and the military code of Illinois. The Court concluded as follows regarding whether or not the military code was in violation of the second amendment of the United States.]

We think it clear that the sections under consideration, which only forbid bodies of men to associate together as military organizations or to drill or parade with arms in cities and towns unless authorized by law, do not infringe the right of the people to keep and bear arms. But a conclusive answer to the contention that this amendment prohibits the legislation in question lies in the fact that the amendment is a limitation only upon the power of Congress and the National government, and not upon that of the States. It was so held by this court in the case of *United States v. Cruikshank,* . . .

All the Federal questions presented by the record were rightly decided by the Supreme Court of Illinois. . . .

Miller v. Texas
153 U.S. 535 (1894)

[After indictment and conviction of murder, and a sentence of death, and after appeals to the Court of Criminal Appeals of Texas and affirmation by that Court of the decisions of the lower courts,] defendant thereupon sued out this writ, assigning as error that the statute of the State of Texas prohibiting the carrying of dangerous weapons on the person, by authority of which statute the court charged the jury that, if defendant was on a public street carrying a pistol, he was violating the law, infringed the right of the defendant as a citizen of the United States, providing that the right of the people to keep and bear arms shall not be infringed. . . . [The plaintiff in error also made appeals to the Court on the basis of the Fourth, Fifth, and Fourteenth Amendments.]

Without . . . expressing a decided opinion upon the invalidity of the writ as it now stands, we think there is no Federal question properly presented by the record in this case, and that the writ of error must be dismissed upon that ground. The record exhibits nothing of what took place in the court of original jurisdiction, and begins with the assignment of errors in the Court of Criminal Appeals. In this assignment no claim was made of any ruling of the court below adverse to any constitutional right claimed by the defendant, nor does any such appear in the opinion of the court, which deals with certain alleged errors relating to the impanelling of the jury, the denial of a continuance, the admission of certain testimony, and certain exceptions taken to the charge of the court. In his motion for a hearing, however, defendant claimed that the law of the State of Texas forbidding the carrying of weapons, and authorizing the arrest without warrant of any person violating such law, under which certain questions arose upon the trial of the case, was in conflict with the Second and Fourth Amendments to the Constitution of the United States, one of which provides that the right of the people to keep and bear arms shall not be infringed. . . . We have examined the record in vain, however, to find where the defendant was denied the benefit of any of these provisions, and even if he were, it is well settled that the restrictions of these amendments operate only upon the Federal power, and have reference to proceedings in state courts. . . . The writ of error is, therefore, Dismissed.

United States v. Miller
307 U.S. 174 (1939)

An indictment in the District Court Western District Arkansas, charged that Jack Miller and Frank Layton "did unlawfully, knowingly, wilfully, and feloniously transport in interstate commerce from the town of Claremore in the State of Oklahoma to the town of Siloam Springs in the State of Arkansas a certain firearm, to-wit, a double barrel 12-gauge Stevens shotgun having a barrel less than 18 inches in length . . . not having registered said firearm as required by Title 26, United States Code, . . . and not having in their possession a stamp-affixed order for said firearm . . . under . . . the . . . Act of Congress known as the 'National Firearms Act.'". . .

A . . . demurrer alleged: The National Firearms Act is not a revenue measure but an attempt to usurp police power reserved to the States, and is therefore unconstitutional. Also, it offends the inhibition of the Second Amendment to the Constitution. . . .

In the absence of any evidence tending to show that possession or use of a "shotgun having a barrel of less than eighteen inches in length" at this time has some reasonable relationship to the preservation or efficiency of a well regulated militia, we cannot say that the Second Amendment guarantees the right to keep and bear such an instrument. Certainly it is not within judicial notice that this weapon is any part of the ordinary military equipment or that its use could contribute to the common defense. . . .

[The Court then proceeded to discuss the militia provisions of the Constitution and their historical context, citing some of the major historical writers on the subject, and citing clauses from various state constitutions dealing with the right to keep and bear arms. It concluded as follows.]

Most if not all of the States have adopted provisions touching the right to keep and bear arms. Differences in the language employed in these have naturally led to somewhat variant conclusions concerning the scope of the right guaranteed. But none of them seem to afford any material support for the challenged ruling of the court below. . . .

We are unable to accept the conclusion of the court below and the challenged judgment must be reversed. The cause will be remanded for further proceedings.

Constitutional Provisions on the Right To Keep and Bear Arms[3]

Constitution of the United States

Amendment 2. A well regulated Militia, being necessary to the security of a free State, the right of the people to keep and bear arms shall not be infringed.

Alabama

Article I, Section 26. That every citizen has a right to bear arms in defense of himself and the state.

Alaska

Article I, Section 19. A well-regulated militia being necessary to the security of a free state, the right of the people to keep and bear arms shall not be infringed.

Arizona

Article II, Section 26. The right of the individual citizen to bear arms in defense of himself or the State shall not be impaired, but nothing in this section shall be construed as authorizing individuals or corporations to organize, maintain, or employ an armed body of men.

Arkansas

Article II, Section 5. The citizens of this State shall have the right to keep and bear arms for their common defense.

Colorado

Article II, Section 13. The right of no person to keep and bear arms in defense of his home, person and property, or in aid of the civil power when thereto legally summoned, shall be called in question; but nothing herein contained shall be construed to justify the practice of carrying concealed weapons.

Connecticut

Article I, Section 15. Every citizen has a right to bear arms in defense of himself and the State.

Delaware

Article I, Section 20. A person has the right to keep and bear arms for the defense of self, family, home and State, and for hunting and recreational use.

Florida

Article I, Section 8. The right of the people to keep and bear arms in defense of themselves and of the lawful authority of the state shall not be infringed, except that the manner of bearing arms may be regulated by law.

Georgia

Article I, Section 1, Paragraph VIII. The right of the people to keep and bear arms shall not be infringed, but the General

Assembly shall have power to prescribe the manner in which arms may be borne.

Hawaii

Article I, Section 17. A well regulated militia being necessary to the security of a free state, the right of the people to keep and bear arms shall not be infringed.

Idaho

Article I, Section 11. The people have the right to keep and bear arms, which right shall not be abridged, but this provision shall not prevent the passage of laws to govern the carrying of weapons concealed on the person nor prevent passage of legislation providing minimum sentences for crimes committed while in possession of a firearm, nor prevent the passage of legislation providing penalties for the possession of firearms by a convicted felon, nor prevent the passage of any legislation punishing the use of a firearm. No law shall impose licensure, registration or special taxation on the ownership or possession of firearms or ammunition. Nor shall any law permit the confiscation of firearms, except those actually used in the commission of a felony.

Illinois

Article I, Section 22. Subject only to the police power, the right of the individual citizen to keep and bear arms shall not be infringed.

Indiana

Article I, Section 32. The people shall have a right to bear arms, for the defense of themselves and the State.

Kansas

Kansas Bill of Rights, Section 4. The people have the right to bear arms for their defense and security; but standing armies, in time of peace, are dangerous to liberty, and shall not be tolerated, and the military shall be in strict subordination to the civil power.

Kentucky

Kentucky Bill of Rights, Section I, Paragraph 7. All men are, by nature, free and equal, and have certain inherent and inalienable rights, among which may be reckoned: . . . Seventh. The right to bear arms in defense of themselves and of the state, subject to the power of the general assembly to enact laws to prevent persons from carrying concealed weapons.

Louisiana

Article I, Section 11. The right of each citizen to keep and bear arms shall not be abridged, but this provision shall not prevent the passage of laws to prohibit the carrying of weapons concealed on the person.

Maine

Article I, Section 16. Every citizen has a right to keep and bear arms for the common defense; and this right shall never be questioned.

Massachusetts

Massachusetts Declaration of Rights, Part I, Article XVII. The people have a right to keep and bear arms for the common defense. And as, in times of peace, armies are dangerous to liberty, they ought not to be maintained without the consent of the legislature; and the military power shall always be held in an exact subordination to the civil authority, and be governed by it.

Michigan

Article I, Section 6. Every person has a right to keep and bear arms for the defense of himself and the state.

Mississippi

Article 3, Section 12. The right of every citizen to keep and bear arms in defense of his home, person, or property, or in aid of the civil power where thereto legally summoned, shall not be called in question, but the legislature may regulate or forbid carrying concealed weapons.

Missouri

Article I, Section 23. That the right of every citizen to keep and bear arms in defense of his home, person and property, or when lawfully summoned in aid of the civil power, shall not be questioned; but this shall not justify the wearing of concealed weapons.

Montana

Article II, Section 12. The right of any person to keep or bear arms in defense of his own home, person, and property, or in aid of the civil power when thereto legally summoned, shall not be called in question, but nothing herein contained shall be held to permit the carrying of concealed weapons.

Nebraska

Article I, Section 1. All persons are by nature free and independent, and have certain inherent and inalienable rights; among these are life, liberty, the pursuit of happiness, and the right to keep and bear arms for security or defense of self, family, home, and others, and for lawful common defense, hunting, recreational use, and all other lawful purposes, and such rights shall not be denied or infringed by the State or any subdivision thereof.

Nevada

Article I, Section 11 (XI), Paragraph 1. Every citizen has the right to keep and bear arms for security and defense, for lawful hunting and recreational use and for other lawful purposes.

New Hampshire

Part One, Article 2-a. All persons have the right to keep and bear arms in defense of themselves, their families, their property, and the state.

New Mexico

Article II, Section 6. No law shall abridge the right of the citizen to keep and bear arms for security and defense, for lawful hunting and recreational use and for other lawful purposes, but nothing herein shall be held to permit the carrying of concealed weapons. No municipality or county shall regulate, in any way, an incident of the right to keep and bear arms.

North Carolina

Article I, Section 30. A well regulated militia being necessary to the security of a free State, the right of the people to keep and bear arms shall not be infringed; and, as standing armies in time of peace are dangerous to liberty, they shall not be maintained, and the military shall be kept under strict subordination to, and governed by, the civil power. Nothing herein shall justify the practice of carrying concealed weapons, or prevent the General Assembly from enacting penal statutes against that practice.

North Dakota

Article I, Section 1. All individuals are by nature equally free and independent and have certain inalienable rights, among which are . . . to keep and bear arms for the defense of their person, family, property, and the state, and for lawful hunting, recreational, and other lawful purposes, which shall not be infringed.

Ohio

Article I, Section 4. The people have the right to bear arms for their defense and security; but standing armies, in time of peace, are dangerous to liberty, and shall not be kept up; and the military shall be in strict subordination to the civil power.

Oklahoma

Article II, Section 26. The right of a citizen to keep and bear arms in defense of his home, person, or property, or in aid of the civil power, when thereunto legally summoned, shall never be prohibited; but nothing herein contained shall prevent the Legislature from regulating the carrying of weapons.

Oregon

Article I, Section 27. The people shall have the right to bear arms for the defense of themselves, and State, but the Military shall be kept in strict subordination to the civil power.

Pennsylvania

Article I, Section 21. The right of the citizens to bear arms in defense of themselves and the State shall not be questioned.

Rhode Island

Article I, Section 22. The right of the people to keep and bear arms shall not be infringed.

South Carolina

Article I, Section 20. A well regulated militia being necessary to the security of a free State, the right of the people to keep and bear arms shall not be infringed. As, in times of peace, armies are dangerous to liberty, they shall not be maintained without the consent of the General Assembly. The military power of the State shall always be held in subordination to the civil authority and be governed by it. No soldier shall in time of peace be quartered in any house without the consent of the owner nor in time of war but in the manner prescribed by law.

South Dakota

Article VI, Section 24. The right of the citizens to bear arms in defense of themselves and the state shall not be denied.

Tennessee

Article I, Section 26. That the citizens of this State have a right to keep and bear arms for their common defense; but the

Legislature shall have power, by law, to regulate the wearing of arms with a view to prevent crime.

Texas

Article I, Section 23. Every citizen shall have the right to keep and bear arms in the lawful defense of himself or the State; but the Legislature shall have power, by law, to regulate the wearing of arms, with a view to prevent crime.

Utah

Article I, Section 6. The individual right of the people to keep and bear arms for security and defense of self, family, others, property, or the state, as well as for the other lawful purposes shall not be infringed; but nothing herein shall prevent the legislature from defining the lawful use of arms.

Vermont

Chapter 1, Article 16. That the people have a right to bear arms for the defence [sic] of themselves and the State—and as standing armies in time of peace are dangerous to liberty, they ought not to be kept up; and that the military should be kept under strict subordination to and governed by the civil power.

Virginia

Article I, Section 13. That a well regulated militia, composed of the body of the people, trained to arms, is the proper, natural, and safe defense of a free state, therefore, the right of the people to keep and bear arms shall not be infringed; that standing armies, in time of peace, should be avoided as dangerous to liberty; and that in all cases the military should be under strict subordination to, and governed by, the civil power.

Washington

Article I, Section 24. The right of the individual citizen to bear arms in defense of himself, or the state, shall not be impaired, but nothing in this section shall be construed as authorizing individuals or corporations to organize, maintain, or employ an armed body of men.

West Virginia

Article III, Section 22. A person has the right to keep and bear arms for the defense of self, family, home, and state, and for lawful hunting and recreational use.

Wyoming

Article I, Section 24. The right of citizens to bear arms in defense of themselves and of the state shall not be denied.

Note that the States of California, Iowa, Maryland, Minnesota, New Jersey, New York, and Wisconsin, do not have constitutional provisions pertaining to the right to keep and bear arms.

Major Federal Gun Control Legislation[4]

National Firearms Act of 1934
Pub. L. No. 73-474

This was a law passed after an attempt was made to assassinate President Franklin Delano Roosevelt. It attempted to respond to increases in killing and mayhem stemming from organized crime activities during the 1920s and 1930s. Its primary objective was to restrict so-called "gangster-type" weapons. Its passage had the support of the National Rifle Association.

Its provisions included the taxation of the manufacture, sale, and transfer of the types of weapons accessories designated and defined in the law. Weapons specified were sawed-off shotguns, sawed-off rifles, machine guns (fully automatic firearms), and silencers.

In addition, stringent procedures related to purchasing and licensing of such weapons by law-abiding citizens were included. Purchasers of weapons were subjected to a background investigation by the Federal Bureau of Investigation, were required to submit their photograph, and were required to undergo full fingerprinting. Each weapon purchased under the law had to be registered.

The legislation also required the seller of a weapon to pay a transfer tax in the amount of $200, a fee which was passed on to the purchaser of the weapon.

Finally, if the purchase was approved by federal authorities, the buyer needed approval from a local law enforcement officer to bring the weapon into a local jurisdiction.

Some 175,000 of these weapons have been registered since the law was enacted, and, according to the record, not one of them has ever been used to commit a crime.

Federal Firearms Act of 1938
Pub. L. No. 75-785

The primary objective of the Federal Firearms Act of 1938 was to regulate interstate commerce in firearms.

This objective was sought through the requirement of licensure for manufacturers, dealers, and importers of firearms and for ammunition for pistols and revolvers. A fee was enacted for these licenses, to be paid to the Internal Revenue Service.

The law prohibited sales and delivery of firearms to known criminals.

Mutual Security Act of 1954
Pub. L. No. 83-665

This law empowered the president to control the flow of firearms and ammunition; the provisions of the law were actually implemented under the authority of the Department of State and its Office of Munitions Control.

Federal Aviation Act of 1958
Pub. L. No. 85-726

This law prohibited the carrying of any firearm onto a passenger aircraft.

The Omnibus Crime Control and Safe Streets Act of 1968
Pub. L. No. 90-351

This law, stimulated in particular by the recent assassinations of Senator Robert Kennedy and Dr. Martin Luther King, was considerably more comprehensive than any weapons law previously passed. Among its provisions were preventing felons, fugitives from justice, illegal drug users or addicts, minors, mental defectives and those committed to mental institutions, veterans dishonorably discharged from the armed services, illegal aliens, and those who had renounced their United States citizenship from purchasing or possessing firearms. A fee schedule was also established for the licensing of manufacturers, importers, and dealers in firearms. A serial number was required on all guns, and stricter record-keeping practices had to be met. Mail order sales of guns and ammunition were prohibited. A rule was included that permitted a purchaser of a gun to make that transaction only in the state of residence. Purchasers of handguns had to be at least 21 years of age, and those who purchased long guns had to be at least 18. The importation of Saturday Night Specials was prohibited, as were some types of semiautomatic assault weapons and two types of military shotguns. Penalties were established for crimes of violence or when trafficking in drugs when carrying and using firearms. Also prohibited were those weapons identified in the National Firearms Act of 1934; machine gun framers, receivers, and "conversion kits," and the importation of surplus military firearms.

Gun Control Act of 1968
Pub. L. No. 90-618

The Gun Control Act of 1968 is actually composed of two statutes—Titles IV and VII of the Omnibus Crime Control and Safe Streets Act, 82 Stat. 225, 236, and the Gun Control Act, 82 Stat. 1213.

As stated above, the act was passed particularly in the wake of the assassinations of Dr. Martin Luther King, Jr., and Senator Robert Kennedy.

The Gun Control Act aimed at the expansion of provisions of the Omnibus Crime Control and Safe Streets Act.

It imposed limitations on persons seeking to engage in the firearms business. It raised the standards to get a license; imposed regulations on the process of transporting firearms between states on the part of those not licensed, and also increased the minimum age for the purchase of firearms.

Maximum penalties for the violation of these provisions were raised to $5,000 and imprisonment for five years.

Administered by the Bureau of Alcohol, Tobacco, and Firearms, the act regulated who can make, import, or sell firearms. For example, applications are approved if the request is made by someone who is at least 21 years old, has not been declared as being prohibited from dealing or possessing firearms or ammunition in, or affecting, interstate commerce, has not violated the provisions of the Gun Control Act, has not willfully failed to disclose information or willfully made false statements in his or her application, and has in fact a premise for conducting his or her business.

Antique firearms are excluded from the provisions of the act.

Mail order sales are prohibited under the act.

Although, in general, no records are needed for the sale of ammunition, all ammunition is covered by the act.

The act does not permit an individual to carry a firearm in the conduct of his business if contrary to state or local regulations. An unlicensed person may only purchase or sell a gun *within* his own state unless he sells to a licensee in any state, and he may purchase a rifle or shotgun from a licensee, in person, at the business premise of the licensee assuming that the transaction complies with state and local laws on such transactions. Non-licensees may transport firearms interstate provided that they are unloaded and locked in a trunk or other container (not the glove compartment or console of a vehicle). An individual who is not a gun dealer may not sell to someone who is not a resident of the same state unless the person buying the gun is licensed or the purchase is made through a licensed person in the same state as the person who is buying.

Persons who are not in the firearms business may sell guns to persons who reside in the same state as the seller.

Foreign visitors may buy guns under specific provisions of the law, and underaged persons may acquire guns through the purchase on their part by a parent or guardian.

Licensees must comply with state and local laws.

A license does not have to be acquired for the collection of modern firearms, but a license is required to engrave, to customize, refinish, or repair a firearm, and for collectors who receive guns through interstate commerce.

There are other provisions of the act that relate to ownership and registration of firearms, the portation, manufacture or dealing in firearms, changing one's state of residence, and provisions relating to demonstrated lawful registration, conversion kits, and machine guns.

Many of the provisions of the Gun Control Act have been modified or have become obsolete as a result of the passage of the Firearm Owners Protection Act. Moreover, enforcement of its provisions has become increasingly difficult because of legal interpretation of its provisions in view of passage of the Firearm Owners' Protection Act. Further redefinition, modification, and nonenforcement as a result of the passage of the Firearm Owners' Protection Act is certain to occur.

Organized Crime Control Act of 1970
Pub. L. No. 91-452

This act authorized specially designated grand juries to sit in order to return indictments against appointed public officials involving organized crime; repealed previous witness immunity laws and provided "use-immunity" instead of "transaction-immunity" to witnesses; allowed detention of witnesses until they complied with court orders, but not longer than 18 months; and provided for conviction for perjury. It also provided for protection and maintenance of witnesses and their families in cases involving organized crime; provided for use of depositions in organized crime cases; placed a limitation of five years on the period during which action by the government to obtain evidence could be challenged; and made it a federal crime to obstruct laws of the states in the cases of establishing illegal gambling. It also established increased sentences; established federal controls over interstate and foreign commerce involving explosives; and authorized the establishment of a National Commission on Individual Rights that was to review federal laws and procedures that might interfere with individual rights.

Armed Career Criminal Act of 1984
Pub. L. No. 98-473

This act amended the Gun Control Act of 1968.

It provided, among other things, that any person convicted of a felony; any person dishonorably discharged from the armed services; any person who has been adjudged mentally incompetent; any person who has renounced his citizenship; and any person who is an alien or is unlawfully in the United States who receives, possesses, or transports a firearm, shall be fined not more than $10,000 or imprisoned not more than two years, or both.

It provided 15-year sentences and a $25,000 fine for those who have had three previous convictions for robbery or burglary, or both.

Firearms Owners Protection Act of 1986
Pub. L. No. 99-308

The "Congressional Findings" clause of this act states, "The Congress finds that (1) the rights of citizens . . . (A) to keep and bear arms under the Second [A]mendment to the United States Constitution; (B) to security against illegal and unreasonable searches and seizures under the fourth amendment; (C) against uncompensated taking of property, double jeopardy, and assurance of due process of law under the fifth amendment; and (D) against unconstitutional exercise of authority under the ninth and tenth amendments; require additional legislation to correct existing firearms statutes and enforcement policies; and (2) additional legislation is required to reaffirm the intent of the Congress, as expressed in section 101 of the Gun Control Act of 1968, that 'it is not the purpose of this title to place any undue or unnecessary Federal restrictions or burdens on law-abiding citizens with respect to the acquisition, possession, or use of firearms appropriate to the purpose of hunting, trap-shooting, target shooting, personal protection, or any other lawful activity, and that this title is not intended to discourage or eliminate the private ownership or use of firearms by law-abiding citizens for lawful purposes'."

Thus, this act was passed in large part because Congress felt it necessary to more precisely state the intent of Congress expressed in the Gun Control Act 1968. The act itself suggests that the pursuit of precision was not necessarily accomplished.

Virtually every aspect of the Gun Control Act of 1968 was influenced by the Firearm Owners Protection Act. These influences concern revisions in the types of acts prohibited under the Gun Control Act; changes in the penalty clause by adding *scienter* requirements; changes in the manner in which the 1968 law is enforced; and changes in the administrative powers of the Gun Control Act. The new law also affected the interpretation and application of, for example, the National Firearms Act of 1934 and had an impact on state laws as well. Indeed, at least six Supreme Court decisions based on the 1968 Gun Control Act were negated by the Firearm Owners Protection Act, and fully one-third of the total case law dealing with the Gun Control Act of 1968 was overturned.

Crudely summarized (the act is long and complex, and a discussion even remotely resembling a full summary is impossible here), the law focused on definitions (for example, especially that dealing with what in fact constitutes the elements of engaging in gun dealing, the issue of who is nonresident, which laws must in fact be used for enforcement purposes, the state of mind of the dealer involving "willful" and "knowing" behavior, etc.); decreased from a felony to a misdemeanor penalties for violations weapons dealers make in preparing their paper work; permitted the interstate sale of long guns by gun dealers; required certain minimum and mandatory penalties for misuse of firearms; and provided for penalties for those engaged in drug-trafficking offenses if they were carrying a firearm.

Thus, the Firearm Owners' Protection Act in effect repudiated much if not all of the Gun Control Act of 1968. The Firearm Owners' Protection Act imposed limitations on time needed to complete administration of provisions of the act; dealt with inspections, forfeitures, and seizures; and shifted payment of defense attorneys' fees to the prosecuting office. Many ambiguities, unclear clauses, and political compromises are evident in the act. Other matters were also addressed—most of which effectively change the nature and tenor of the Gun Control Act of 1968.

Law Enforcement Officers Protection Act of 1986
Pub. L. No. 99-408

This law banned the further sale, manufacture, or import of armor-piercing ammunition, except in very limited circumstances.

It identified the types of banned ammunition as bullets that "may be used in a handgun" and that are made of such metals as tungsten alloys, steel, brass, bronze, iron, beryllium copper or depleted uranium.

It provided exemptions for bullets produced to meet federal and state environmental standards for purposes of hunting and certain industrial purposes and required that ammunition be marked and packages labeled as armor-piercing.

It also provided mandatory five-year penalties for infractions of the law, and stated that dealers who willfully violated the law's provisions could have their licenses revoked.

Brady Handgun Violence Prevention Act of 1993
Pub. L. No. 103-159

Enacted on 30 November 1993, the Brady Act requires a national waiting period of five days before a duly-licensed importer, manufacturer, or dealer may transfer a handgun to a nonlicensed individual. It also provides for the establishment of a national "instant criminal background check" of purchasers before a transfer of any firearm to a nonlicensed individual may take place. This provision will become effective on 30 November 1998. Violations of either of these provisions are punishable by a fine or imprisonment, or both.

Titles II and III of the law involve reporting requirements for multiple sales of handguns and thefts from dealers. Increased license fees are also imposed.

Certain alternatives to the waiting period are provided. These include immediate need of the weapon because of threats to the transferee's life or the life of any member of the transferee's household; the presentation of a state permit issued within the last five years; where an authorized government official within the state has verified that the transfer would not violate the law; where transfers of handguns have been authorized for transfer under the National Firearms Act; or where compliance with the five-day waiting period would prove to be impracticable because of rural residence, the transferee's premises remote, and where there is an absence of telecommunications facilities in the area in which a business is located.

Other provisions involve multiple sales reports, prohibitions against labeling of packages by common carriers, and written acknowledgment of receipt, theft of firearms, and license fees.

Omnibus Violent Crime Control and Prevention Act of 1994
Pub. L. No. 103-322

After long and often acrimonious debate, and after several attempts to use the technicalities involved in the legislative process, the Crime Bill was passed in August 1994. It is an extremely detailed act having some 33 titles. It incorporates the ban on certain so-called assault weapons passed earlier in 1994.

Its major provisions include:

1. The expenditure of $13.45 billion for state, local, and federal police officers, the amount including $8.8 billion for a state matching program to aid in hiring some 100,000 new law enforcement officers.

2. Life imprisonment for those committing a third violent or drug-related crime, if the third conviction is in a federal court. The law also permits the release of those who are over 70 years of age if they have served 30 years.

3. The expenditure of $9.85 billion for prisons, including moneys for state prison grants and reimbursement for states that incarcerate criminal illegal aliens.

4. The banning of 19 specifically named assault-style weapons and dozens of others defined by the government as falling largely within the same category of assault-style characteristics. This part of the bill is to go into effect immediately upon its signature. The bill would also limit magazine capacity to 10 rounds. Some 650 named types of firearms and all guns and magazines owned legally before the law took effect were exempted. Moreover, inasmuch as magazines do not have serial numbers, the burden of proof would fall on the government to demonstrate that the magazine was purchased after the law was enacted.

5. The expenditure of $6.9 billion for various crime prevention programs, so-called drug courts, violence against women, and money for shelters, and some $1.6 billion for Local Partnership Act grants.

6. Provisions for the avoidance by some nonviolent, first-time drug offenders of the mandatory minimum five- and ten-year federal sentences. These provisions would apply only to those who did not use a gun or a threat of violence in the commission of their crime and who have not served more than 90 days in prison for any other crime.

7. Establishing 60 federal crimes for which the death penalty would be required. Many of these were death penalty crimes before, but additional crimes were included under the new law, e.g., kidnappings resulting in death, hostage-taking resulting in death, genocide, willful deprivation of federal rights resulting in death, obstruction of free exercise of religious rights resulting in death, sexual abuse crimes resulting in death, murder of a juror, torture resulting in death, mailing dangerous articles where death results, wrecking trains where death is the result, slayings during car-jackings, murders resulting from drive-by shootings, murders growing out of drug trafficking even when the felon is not specifically linked to a particular death, and dozens of others.

8. A requirement that those on trial for rape be tested for the AIDS virus; the results of the test would not be disclosed to anyone except the rape victim, the defendant, and those others to whom the court deems the information relevant and necessary.
9. A requirement that released sex offenders considered likely to repeat their crimes record their address with the police, who in turn are allowed to inform the community of the person's whereabouts. This is the so-called sexual predator provision of the bill.
10. Permission to try juveniles who are 13 years of age or older as adults for certain specified violent crimes.

Other provisions of a highly detailed nature are also included in the legislation. Undoubtedly, the law will be modified both by court litigation, administrative interpretation during the course of applying its provisions, and by future amendments. Moreover, it will also undoubtedly take years for most if not all of the elements of the legislation to come into effect, particularly given the necessity to find the money to underwrite the cost of its many features.

Selected State and Local Laws Dealing with Gun Control

State Laws

The laws pertaining to firearms regulations in the states are summarized in the Bureau of Alcohol, Tobacco, and Firearms publication, *Firearms State Laws and Published Ordinances*, 1994, 20th Edition (U.S. Government Printing Office, 1994). Some examples are given below. American territories have also come under the provisions of the Gun Control Act of 1968 and legislation following passage of that act.

Alabama: 48-hour waiting period for purchase of handguns.

California: 15-day waiting period for the purchase of all firearms.

Connecticut: 14-day waiting period for the purchase of all firearms.

Delaware: 3-day waiting period for the purchase of handguns and rifles, and a background telephone check.

District of Columbia: There is a ban on the purchase of handguns. A background check must be undergone for the purchase of rifles and shotguns.

Florida: A wait of 3 business days is required for the purchase of all firearms. A background telephone check is also required.

Hawaii: There is a maximum of a 15-day waiting period for the permit to purchase all firearms so that a background check may be undertaken.

Illinois: There is a maximum 30-day waiting period for a background check for the purchase of all firearms. This is followed by a maximum of a 3-day cooling-off period for handguns and a 24-hour cooling-off period for long guns.

Indiana: A 7-business-day waiting period is in effect for the purchase of handguns.

Iowa: There is a maximum of a 3-day waiting period while a background check is undertaken for the purchase of all handguns. This is followed by a 3-day cooling-off period. The permit is not valid until 3 days after it is issued by the sheriff.

Maryland: There is a 7-day waiting period for the purchase of handguns and assault weapons.

Massachusetts: There is a maximum of a 40-day waiting period to undertake a background check for the purchase of all firearms.

Michigan: For the purchase of handguns, there is no legal time limit to conduct a background check on the purchaser.

Minnesota: There is a 7-day waiting period for the purchase of all handguns.

Missouri: There is a maximum of a 7-business-day wait for a background check for the purchase of all handguns.

Nebraska: For the purchase of handguns, there is a maximum 2-business-day waiting period for a background check.

New Jersey: There is a maximum 30-day waiting period for the purchase of all firearms in order to conduct a background check.

New York: For the purchase of handguns, there is a maximum 6-month waiting period to conduct a background check.

North Carolina: For the purchase of handguns, there is a maximum 30-day waiting period to conduct a background check.

Oregon: There is a 15-day waiting period for the purchase of handguns.

Pennsylvania: There is a 48-hour waiting period for the purchase of handguns.

Rhode Island: There is a 7-day waiting period for the purchase of all firearms.

South Dakota: There is a 48-hour waiting period for the purchase of handguns.

Tennessee: There is a 15-day waiting period for the purchase of handguns.

Virginia: A 48-hour waiting period is required for a background telephone check for the purchase of all firearms.

Washington: There is a 5-day waiting period for the purchase of handguns.

Wisconsin: There is a maximum waiting period of 48 hours plus 3 business days in addition to a telephone background check for the purchase of handguns.

City Laws

Albany, New York: Assault weapons are banned.

Atlanta, Georgia: The sale and possession of assault weapons are banned.

Berkeley, California: The sale and possession of assault weapons are banned.

Cincinnati, Ohio: Requires a 15-day waiting period for the purchase of all assault weapons.

Cleveland, Ohio: The sale and possession of assault weapons are banned.

Columbus, Ohio: Bans the sale and possession of assault weapons and large capacity magazines.

Compton, California: The sale and possession of assault weapons are banned; large capacity magazines are banned.

Denver, Colorado: The sale of assault weapons is banned.

Gary, Indiana: The sale and possession of assault weapons are banned.

Los Angeles, California: The sale and possession of assault weapons are banned.

Sacramento, California: The sale and possession of assault weapons are banned.

Santa Clara, California: The sale and possession of assault weapons are banned. Large capacity magazines are banned.

Stockton, California: The sale and possession of assault weapons are banned.

Selected Statistical Data—Tables

Table 4-1 Gun Dealers and Pawn Shops in the United States[5]

State	Gun Dealers	Pawn Shops	Total
Alaska	3,155	79	3,234
Alabama	3,265	484	3,749
Arkansas	3,107	572	3,679
Arizona	4,158	120	4,278
California	20,232	457	20,689
Colorado	4,356	245	4,601
Connecticut	3,353	24	3,377
Delaware	506	8	514
District of Columbia	37	0	37
Florida	10,017	1,081	11,098
Georgia	5,620	1,020	6,640
Hawaii	824	1	825
Idaho	2,275	182	2,457
Illinois	9,017	83	9,100
Indiana	5,867	74	5,941
Iowa	3,894	87	3,981

Table 4-1, *continued*

State	Gun Dealers	Pawn Shops	Total
Kansas	3,651	132	3,783
Kentucky	4,699	393	5,092
Louisiana	4,910	327	5,237
Maine	2,190	35	2,225
Maryland	3,206	57	3,263
Massachusetts	3,868	2	3,870
Michigan	12,074	95	12,169
Minnesota	5,764	130	5,894
Mississippi	3,091	492	3,583
Missouri	7,688	331	8,019
Montana	3,054	170	3,224
Nebraska	2,690	56	2,746
Nevada	1,949	75	2,024
New Hampshire	1,569	7	1,576
New Jersey	1,646	0	1,646
New Mexico	1,930	168	2,098
New York	9,758	15	9,773
North Carolina	6,483	497	6,980
North Dakota	1,619	32	1,651
Ohio	9,486	150	9,636
Oklahoma	4,045	485	4,530
Oregon	4,996	36	5,032
Pennsylvania	11,811	18	11,829
Rhode Island	568	3	571
South Carolina	2,346	253	2,599
South Dakota	1,547	65	1,612
Tennessee	4,778	386	5,164
Texas	18,158	1,321	19,479
Utah	2,100	130	2,230
Vermont	1,562	1	1,563
Virginia	6,965	167	7,132
Washington	5,736	210	5,946
West Virginia	3,239	221	3,460
Wisconsin	5,983	36	6,019
Wyoming	1,731	82	1,813
Total			257,668

Table 4-2 Gun Ownership in the United States[6]

Guns in Circulation Nationwide	Handguns	67,000,000 (33%)
	Rifles	73,000,000 (36%)
	Shotguns	63,000,000 (31%)
Persons Having a Gun in the House		46%
Persons Having a Loaded Gun in the House		43%
Gun Ownership by Region	Midwest	25%
	West	18%
	Northeast	13%
	South	44%

Table 4-3 Gun Lobby Spending[7] 1 January 1991–30 June 1993

Pro-Gun	
National Rifle Association	$2,917,525
Safari Club International	81,850
Gun Owners of America	16,105
Safari Club (Detroit Chapter)	179
Anti-Gun	
Handgun Control, Inc.	287,185

Table 4-4 Guns Most Often Traced by the Bureau of Alcohol, Tobacco, and Firearms[8]

Smith & Wesson .38 Special
This revolver is the most commonly produced and the most common in the marketplace. It is relatively inexpensive (under $400), is light, snub-nosed (6½ inches long), and easily concealed. It is most frequently used for self-defense and the sport known as "plinking"—using, for example, tin cans in target-shooting.

Raven Arms .25 Caliber
This is an inexpensive (approximately $75), semiautomatic, six-shot pistol, known as a "Saturday Night Special." It is small, light, and very easy to conceal. The gun is often used in robberies and in drug-related incidents. It is not accurate for target-shooting.

Davis P-380
This pistol is inexpensive (around $199) and easily concealable. It is particularly purchased by people who live in the inner cities and who feel they need protection against crime.

Smith & Wesson .357 Magnum
Priced under $500, this six-shot revolver was for a long time the weapon of choice for law enforcement officers. It is powerful, reliable, and accurate. It is reputed to be capable of incapacitating a moving vehicle.

Ruger .22 Caliber
This pistol has a ten-bullet magazine, and is a weapon of high quality and accuracy. Used in target-shooting competitions, it was also used as a pistol for military training.

Lorcin L-380
This is a semiautomatic, inexpensive (about $100) pistol discharging seven bullets. It resembles the Davis P-380, but is somewhat heavier and is less easy to conceal.

Smith & Wesson 9mm
This is a 15-inch-magazine semiautomatic pistol much used by law enforcement agencies. It is priced between $650 and $850. It is easy to use and capable of quick discharge. It is not as powerful as some pistols of larger caliber, but has less recoil.

Mossberg 12-Gauge
Priced under $300, this "shotgun" has an 18½ inch barrel and a pistol grip; its total length is 28 inches. Not highly accurate for hunting purposes, it is nevertheless useful to police as a weapon easily carried in

Table 4-4, *continued*

their vehicles and can be relatively easily concealed. It fires 8 shots, and although not legally so, it resembles a "sawed-off shotgun."

Intratec TEC-DC9

This is a 32-inch-magazine semiautomatic pistol. It is relatively inexpensive (under $400, although its price on the black market is much higher) and relatively easy to conceal. It has been misidentified as an "assault weapon" in the course of the debate on gun control. It is especially sought out by gangs and drug traffickers.

Remington 12-Gauge

This is a five-shot shotgun, ranging in price from under $300 to about $650. Not actually often used in crimes, it is nevertheless a frequent target for theft during the course of burglaries. It is the standard shotgun issued to police officers in the United States. This is one of the classic hunting firearms produced in the United States; it is not, however, to be defined as an "assault weapon" or a weapon intended to be used in self-defense.

Table 4-5 Guns Banned under the Assault Weapons Ban Law of 1994[9]

TEC-9: This U.S.-made weapon is a semiautomatic pistol with a 36-round magazine. There are approximately 200,000 of these guns known to be in circulation in the United States. The weapon costs between $100 and $300.

TEC-DC9: This gun is a variation of the TEC-9 in that it has a shroud that permits the user of the weapon to grasp the barrel.

TEC-22: This is a TEC that fires .22 caliber bullets. It is particularly useful in the military.

All of these guns are street guns, but are also used for personal defense.

Uzi: Made in Israel, this is a semiautomatic type of machine pistol that can discharge 25 rounds from a detachable magazine. Although they were legally imported between 1980 and 1989, the Gun Control Act banned them. They continue to be available nevertheless; they cost between $900 and $1800 or more, depending upon where and how they are purchased.

M-10: Made in the United States, this is a semiautomatic pistol. It has a 32-round magazine. Its cost ranges between $300 and $700.

M-11: This gun is a variation of the M-10 in that it weighs less.

M-11/9: This is another variation of the M-10 in that its firing speed is less.

M-12: The only basic difference between this weapon and the M-11/9 is its model number.

FN/FAL: This weapon, made in Belgium, is a semiautomatic variation of the machine guns manufactured by Fabrique Nationale. It has a 20-round magazine that is detachable and a pistol grip. It can accommodate a bayonet if necessary or desired, and can come with a folding stock.

FN/LAR: This is a light automatic rifle (LAR). It has a 20-round magazine and is used by the military in many nations of the world.

Table 4-5, *continued*

FNC: This variation has a 30-round magazine and is lighter than the FAL.

All of these guns are expensive; their cost can be as high as $3,000 or more.

AK-47: This is a firearm designed in the Soviet Union. It is semiautomatic and has a 30-shot magazine; 100-shot magazines are available. The weapon has either a folding stock or a solid butt. The weapon costs up to $1,000.

Galil: Made in Israel, this is a .308 caliber semiautomatic rifle. It has a folding stock, a 20-shot magazine, and a pistol grip, and it can fire grenades. Its design makes it particularly useful in desert military operations. The weapon may cost $3,000 or more.

Street Sweeper: This is a U.S.-made 12-gauge shotgun. It has a rotating chamber that holds 12 rounds that can be fired in three seconds. It has a pistol grip and a folding stock. It costs around $500.

Striker 12: This is a shotgun made in South Africa to control riots, after which the U.S.-made Street Sweeper has been largely copied.

Colt AR-15: This is a variation of the M-16 military rifle. It is a semiautomatic that can also be fired as an automatic. It has a pistol grip and a 30-round magazine. It costs up to $1,500 or more.

Sporter: This weapon is designed for target-shooting. It has a top-mounted scope and resembles the Colt AR-15.

Steyr AUG: This is a duplicate of the automatic rifle supplied to the Austrian Army. It has detachable 30- or 40-round magazines, can accommodate a bayonet, and can be used to fire grenades. Its cost is approximately $3,000.

Beretta AR-70: This is a semiautomatic variation of the automatic rifle made in Italy. It has 8- and 30-round detachable magazines and a pistol grip. Other versions of this weapon may have the capacity to launch grenades, have bayonet capacity, and a folding stock. It costs about $2,000.

Table 4-6 Firearms Prohibited from Sale in California[10]

Rifles
    Avtomat Kalshnikovs (AK) series
    Uzi and Galil
    Beretta AR-70 (SC-70)
    CETME C3
    Colt AR-15 series and CAR-15 series
    Daewoo K-1, K-2, Max 1, and Max 2
    Fabrique Nationale FN/FAL, FN/LAR and FNC
    FAMAS MAS223
    Heckler & Koch HK-91, H-93, HK-94 and PSG-1
    MAC 10 and MAC 11
    SKS with detachable magazine
    SIG AMT, SIG 500 Series, and SIG PE-57
    Springfield Armory BM59 and SAR-48

Table 4-6, *continued*

    Sterling MK-6 and SAR
    Steyr AUG
    Valmet M62, M71S and M78
    Amalite AR-180 Carbine
    Bushmaster Assault Rifle (amgun)
    Calico M-900 Assault Carbine
    Mandall THE-TAC 1 Carbine
    Plainfield Machine Company Carbine
    PJK M-68 Carbine
    Weaver Am Nighthawk
Pistols
    Uzi
    Encom MP-9 and MP-45
    MAC 10 and MAC 11
    INTRATEC TEC-9
    Mitchell Arms Spectre Auto
    Sterling MK-7
    Calico M-900
Shotguns
    Franchi SPAS 12 and LAW 12
    Gilbert Equipment Company Striker 12 and SWD Street Sweeper
    Encom CM-55

Notes

1. The reader is directed to *Corpus Juris Secundum* (Brooklyn: The American Law Book Company, 1956), Volume 94 and Pocket Supplement; *American Jurisprudence* (Rochester: The Lawyers Co-Operative Publishing Company, and San Francisco: Bancroft Whitney Company, 1975), Second Edition, Volume 79 and Pocket Supplement; *West's Federal Practice Digest 2d* (St. Paul: West Publishing Company, 1978), Volume 80 and Pocket Supplement; and *United States Code Annotated, Amendments 1 to 3, Cumulative Supplement* (St. Paul: West Publishing Company, 1983), for summaries and citations of the relevant case law on the subject.

2. Most cases presented here are drawn from Earl R. Kruschke, *The Right To Keep and Bear Arms: A Continuing American Dilemma* (Springfield: Charles C Thomas, Publisher, 1985), and used by permission of the publisher. The cases as presented in the present volume have been more severely edited than in the 1985 publication cited.

3. The list of state constitutional provisions included here is drawn from Mary Jo Volentine, "An Analysis of Initiative 403: The Impact on Existing Nebraska Statutes Restricting the Right To Keep and Bear Arms," *Creighton Law Review* 23 (1990), pp. 507–511. For other listings of state constitutional provisions on the right to keep and bear arms, see David I. Caplin, "The Right of the Individual To Bear Arms: A Recent Judicial

Trend," *Detroit College of Law Review,* Volume 1982, Winter, Issue 4; Robert Dowlut and Janet A. Knoop, "State Constitutions and the Right To Keep and Bear Arms," *Oklahoma City University Law Review* 7, no. 2 (Summer 1982); Earl R. Kruschke, *The Right To Keep and Bear Arms: A Continuing American Dilemma* (Springfield: Charles C Thomas, Publisher, 1985); Daniel J. McKenna, "The Right To Keep and Bear Arms," *Marquette Law Review* 12 (1928); Ralph J. Rohner, "The Right To Bear Arms: A Phenomenon of Constitutional History," *Catholic University Law Review* 16 (September 1966); and Legislative Drafting Research Fund of Columbia University, *Constitutions of the United States, National and State, 2nd Edition* (Dobbs Ferry: Oceana Publications, Inc., 1984) and also the 1962 edition.

4. For an excellent historical review of Federal Gun control legislation, see *U.S. v. Lopez* (2 F.3d 1348–1360, 5th Cir.: 1993).

5. See data from Bureau of Alcohol, Tobacco, and Firearms and the United States Census Bureau. An analysis appears in *USA Today,* Wednesday, December 29, 1993, p. A8.

6. Based on data from the Bureau of Alcohol, Tobacco, and Firearms; Gallup Survey data; *Time/CNN* poll of gun owners.

7. Federal Election Commission Figures.

8. Adapted from "The Weapons of Crime," *USA Today,* Wednesday, 29 December 1993, p. 5A. The *USA Today* article contains highly useful illustrations of these weapons.

9. Adapted from *USA Today,* May 5, 1994. The *USA Today* article contains highly useful illustrations of these weapons.

10. *Soldier of Fortune Magazine* (October 1994), p. 91.

Directory of Organizations 5

The following list of organizations having some interest in the "gun control" issue is hardly exhaustive. It is merely representative of those groups that have, over time, expressed some type of opinion or interest on the subject.

The first section lists some of the most significant groups across the nation. The second lists some of the state organizations that are directly or indirectly involved with the general issue of guns and their use—whether for sporting purposes or other reasons. The third section provides a list of those organizations that are interested in the subject but at a more tangential level.

Telephone numbers and addresses change often, and entire organizations come and go. Consequently, there is no assurance that the following list is completely accurate. Every attempt has been made to provide current information.

National Organizations

Academics for the Second Amendment
P.O. Box 131254
St. Paul, Minnesota 55113
(612) 641-2142

Academics for the Second Amendment is a not-for-profit Minnesota corporation that encourages rigorous discussion and research on issues related to the constitutional provision dealing with the right to keep arms. Among its activities are the sponsoring of scholarship involving legal, philosophical, and historical questions related to the arms issue. It seeks in particular to further public knowledge of the scholarship so produced. It has sponsored professional meetings that examine in depth the many factors related to analysis of Second Amendment issues. A recent conference, held in 1995 in New Orleans drew scholars, lawyers, newspaper men and women, physicians, and students from throughout the United States and Canada.

Amateur Trapshooting Association
601 West National Road
Vandalia, OH 45377
(513) 898-4638

Established in 1923, this large-membership organization sets the rules that govern trapshooting associations on the local, state, and provincial levels. The organization keeps permanent records on individual performance in shooting competition and maintains a hall of fame, a museum, a library, and an exhibit hall. It publishes a monthly magazine, *Trap and Field Magazine,* and two annuals: *Official Trapshooting Rules* and *Trap and Official ATA Averages.* It holds an annual convention and tournament.

American Bar Association
Section of Criminal Justice
1800 M Street NW
Washington, DC 20035
(203) 331-2260

The American Bar Association consists of a diverse aggregation of lawyers, judges, professors, law students, and other individuals involved in the legal profession. It supports such objectives as the banning of assault weapons and a waiting period for the purchase of guns. The ABA argues that such measures are both constitutional and enforceable. The organization publishes a number of reference works, including course materials, reference books, and various legal analyses. Its major publication is *Criminal Justice,* a quarterly journal.

American Civil Liberties Union
132 West 43rd Street
New York, NY 10036
(212) 944-9800

The American Civil Liberties Union is a liberal organization that, depending on an individual's interpretation, can be said to both support and deny individual rights. For example, it will defend artists in their portrayal of what some persons feel is pornographic, using the First Amendment right of freedom of expression; but it also denies that the Second Amendment protects an individual's right to keep and bear arms. The organization argues that gun control is constitutional and that efforts should be enhanced to enforce gun control regulations and perhaps prohibit guns altogether.

The organization publishes journals such as *Civil Liberties* (a quarterly) and *Civil Liberties Alert* (a monthly). It also publishes periodical opinion/policy statements and various reports on subjects related to civil liberties.

American Custom Gunmakers Guild
P.O. Box 812
Burlington, IA 52601
(319) 752-6114

Established in 1983, this organization consists of persons interested in promoting and manufacturing custom weapons. Members encompass a variety of backgrounds, including stockmakers, engravers, and metalsmiths, among others. The group holds programs aimed at educating people about the production of custom guns. It publishes a bimonthly journal, *Gunmaker*, and brochures. It holds an annual convention.

American Jewish Congress
15 East 84th Street
New York, NY 10028
(212) 879-4500

Founded in 1918, this organization, consisting of over 50,000 people, is committed to the interests of Jews worldwide and vigorously opposes racism. According to its *Program Highlights, 1991*, "The American Jewish Congress . . . occupies a unique role among national Jewish community relations agencies. . . . It is in the forefront of American Jewish life in the impact it exerts on the most critical concerns of the Jewish community, domestically and internationally." The organization is willing to take positions on highly controversial issues. For example, a 22 April 1991 letter sent by its Office of the Washington Representative and hand-delivered to all members of the House Judiciary Committee over the signature of Robert J. Lifton, stated,

> On behalf of the American Jewish Congress and its national membership, I am writing you to urge you to support the Brady Handgun Violence Protection Act (HR. 7). . . . This vital legislation would establish a national 7-day waiting period to allow local law enforcement to conduct background checks on handgun purchasers. . . . It is long past time for effective governmental action on this subject. While we recognize that the Brady Bill will not eliminate handgun violence, we believe that it is a desperately needed step in the right direction.

The organization has also addressed such issues as the crisis in the Persian Gulf, loan guarantees for Israel, religious liberty, civil rights, academic freedom, and women's rights, among others. It publishes reports, sponsors conferences, maintains a library, and gives awards to those people who have represented the interests of the organization.

American Single Shot Rifle Association
709 Carolyn Drive
Delphos, OH 45833
(419) 692-3866

Founded in 1948, this group is made up of individuals interested in the collection, study, use, and historical preservation of single shot rifles manufactured between the Civil War and World War I. It is particularly interested in classic single shot rifles in the custom of the German-American Schuetzer and Creedmoor varieties. It opposes attempts to curtail the right to keep and bear arms, and serves as a conduit to the public for information about the illegal and harmful use of guns. It works with law enforcement agencies and gives instruction in the proper use of guns. It also has a program dealing with marksmanship. Among its other functions are the conduct of research about single shot rifles, the maintenance of a library and gun archives, and the sponsorship of competitions. It publishes the bimonthly *American Single Shot Rifle Association News* and holds an annual convention.

American Trap Shooting Association
P.O. Box 246
West National Road
Vendalia, OH 45377
(513) 898-4171

The American Trap Shooting Association establishes the rules for all trapshooting events and also sanctions the rules under which such events are governed. It maintains records for each participant in class competitions in state and provincial contests.

Americans for Democratic Action
1511 K Street, NW, Suite 941
Washington, DC 20005
(202) 638-6447

An independent liberal political organization founded in 1947 and made up of professionals, educators, labor union leaders, politicians, businesspersons, and others interested in establishing liberal foreign and domestic policies, Americans for Democratic Action holds conferences, has a campus program, and provides various publications and various legislative reports. Among its founders were Hubert H. Humphrey, the late Democratic senator from Minnesota and a former vice president, and former first lady Eleanor Roosevelt. The group supports gun control.

Association of Importers-Manufacturers for Muzzleloading
P.O. Box 684
Union City, TN 38261
(901) 885-0374

Established in 1976, this organization consists of individual members and companies that manufacture and distribute muzzle-loading guns and their accessories. To enhance its objectives, it engages in educational activities, advocates legislation on matters of interest, and advocates safety and rules relevant to the blackpowder sport. It also bestows awards in the sport, holds an annual convention with the National Shooting Sports Foundation, and publishes a booklet.

Browning Collectors Association
P.O. Box 526
Aurora, NE 68818
(402) 694-6602

This organization is affiliated with the National Rifle Association. It consists of individual collectors, gun dealers, and others who have an interest in Browning firearms, one of the classic weapons produced in the United States. It promotes the study of Browning history and supplies information on collecting Browning weapons. It engages in charitable events and maintains the Browning Museum. It publishes the *Newsletter,* a bimonthly, and holds an annual meeting.

Bureau of Alcohol, Tobacco, and Firearms
Department of the Treasury
15th Street and Pennsylvania Avenue
Washington, DC 20036
(202) 287-4097

The Bureau of Alcohol, Tobacco, and Firearms is a fully recognized bureau of the Department of the Treasury of the United States. Federal government concern over the use of firearms became particularly acute in 1934, when a wave of criminal violence engulfed the country in reaction to Prohibition. In 1942, the Alcohol Tax Unit (ATU) was established within the Bureau of Internal Revenue to deal with these problems. Several redesignations of titles and responsibilities followed—in 1952, the ATU was retitled the Alcohol and Tobacco Tax Division (ATTD) of the Internal Revenue Service, and in 1968, with the passage of the Omnibus Crime Control and Safe Streets Act and the Gun Control Act of 1968, the ATTD was retitled the Alcohol, Tobacco, and Firearms Division of the Internal Revenue Service. Today, as the acute need to deal with alcohol and tobacco violations have receded, the Alcohol, Tobacco, and Firearms Division has become particularly concerned with firearms. There are over 270,000 licensed gun dealers, importers, and manufacturers and an estimated 200,000,000-plus firearms in the United States, and the Bureau of Alcohol, Tobacco, and Firearms works mainly to deal with problems in this area. Although this bureau has jurisdiction in a number of areas relating to firearms, it is especially concerned with the Gun Control Act of 1968 (as amended), Title XI of the Organized Crime Control Act of 1970, certain sections of the Arms Export Control Act of 1978, the Anti-Arson Act of 1982, and the Armed Career Criminal Act of 1984.

Cast Bullet Association
1 Nantucket Lane
St. Louis, MO 63132
(314) 425-2466

This group is made up of individuals interested in improving accuracy when using cast lead alloy bullets in rifles and pistols, and in improving the quality and design of such bullets. It therefore encourages projects in casting lead alloy bullets and in hand loading, and conducts firing experiments. To further these and related objectives, the organization distributes technical data, compiles statistics, and gives awards. It is affiliated with the National Rifle Association and promotes the sport of rifle shooting by civilians. The organization publishes the bimonthly *Fouling Shot* and various newsletters and technical reports. It holds an annual convention.

Center to Prevent Handgun Violence
1225 I Street, NW, Suite 1150
Washington, DC 20005
(202) 289-7319

Established in 1983, this is a nonprofit organization especially concerned with educating people about the problems and dangers of handgun possession, ownership, and use. Through its national organization, it focuses on teaching young people and children about the dangers of handguns, holding programs for junior and senior high school students in particular. It conducts research in such areas as the constitutional guarantee of the right to keep and bear arms and the impact of gun control, and compiles statistics dealing with the impact of guns in society. The organization puts out news releases and audiovisual materials, and has a speakers bureau.

Central Conference of American Rabbis
192 Lexington Avenue
New York, NY 10016
(212) 684-4990

According to the "Summary of the Purposes and Goals of the Central Conference of American Rabbis," the Central Conference of American Rabbis was established in Detroit in 1889. It works with the Union of American Hebrew Congregations and the Hebrew Union College-Jewish Institute of Religion to effectuate and advocate various programs in which it is involved. Its rabbis are active in serving some 800 congregations, Hillel Foundations, hospitals, the armed services, and a variety of other institutions. Among its activities are "education, ritual, liturgy, publications, Reform Jewish practice, family, youth," and other social, literary, financial, and related activities. A gun control resolution was adopted by the 86th Annual Convention of the Central Conference of American Rabbis, 15-19 June 1975. Although the entire document cannot be included here, some relevant clauses may be quoted:

> Whereas we members of the Central Conference . . . have become increasingly aware of the great loss of human life in the United States due to the proliferation of handguns in so many sectors of society, . . . and Whereas the handgun has been accurately and positively identified as the weapon used most frequently in cases of rage and passion where one or more persons are killed or maimed, . . . Be it therefore resolved that the members of the Central Conference of American Rabbis call upon the Congress of the United States and all state legislatures to enact speedily legislation as will effectively ban the sale of handguns to all citizens except (1) the military, (2) duly authorized police officers, (3) qualified and competent security personnel who will have possession of such handguns only in direct performance of their duties, and (4) sports target shooters duly licensed by local authorities.

At its annual convention in Tarpon Springs, Florida, on 3–7 May 1987, the conference also adopted a resolution on gun control lobbying in which it called upon members of Congress to "eschew the support of the NRA [National Rifle Association] and to vote their support of stringent gun-control legislation." It publishes a quarterly journal, yearbooks, and prayer books, and holds an annual convention.

Church of the Brethren General Board
1451 Dundee Avenue
Elgin, IL 60120-1694
(708) 742-5100

The following resolution has been adopted by the General Brotherhood Board, Church of the Brethren:

The General Brotherhood Board of the Church of the Brethren, believing in the sacredness of human life and the obligation of the state for the safety of its citizens: 1. Calls for much stronger federal and state legislation in controlling the sale, ownership and use of firearms and ammunition; 2. Encourages our members and the general public to support such legislation; 3. Endorses the guidelines for legislation suggested by the General Board of the National Council of Churches on September 15, 1967 and again on June 7, 1968, as follows: A. Federal legislation to restrict the shipment and sale of firearms so as to eliminate mail-order sale to individual purchasers (shotguns and rifles as well as pistols). B. Federal legislation to prohibit individual importation of all firearms with the exception of collectors' antique items. C. Federal legislation to limit purchases of pistols to those persons over 21 years of age and of rifles to those over 18. D. Federal and state legislation to outlaw private possession and transportation of destructive devices such as bombs, fire bombs, bazookas, mortars and anti-tank guns. E. Federal legislation to require permits (where states have not taken appropriate action) for the purchase, ownership, possession and use of firearms, entailing a. Reliable identification of permit application (by fingerprint method if possible). b. Waiting period prior to issuance; allowing for verification of age, absence of mental illness and lack of a felony record. 4. Recognizes the need for ultimate total disarmament of the citizenry and discontinuance of arms bearing in normal police activity.

While control of firearms will not eliminate the causes of crime and social disorganization, it will prevent much tragic loss of life. All the private and government resources at our command must be used to rid our society of lethal violence.

The then executive of the Parish Ministries Commission, in a letter to the author, has expressed his concern about the datedness of this document, but at the same time he stated the information "reflect[s] the perspective of our denomination."

Citizens Committee for the Right to Keep and Bear Arms
Liberty Park
12500 NE 10th Place
Bellevue, WA 98004
(206) 454-4911

This is a nonprofit mass membership organization devoted to the right of individual Americans to keep and bear arms as guaranteed by the Second Amendment. Many members of its council are or have been members of Congress. It evolved as an ad hoc committee of the Young Americans for Freedom. It issues newsletters and other publications and is supported by membership fees and voluntary contributions. It conducts in-depth research on gun legislation and engages in weekend seminars. The organization lobbies legislative bodies and furthers efforts to educate the American people concerning the rights guaranteed under the Second Amendment, and is strongly opposed to gun control legislation. It has a Political Action Committee among whose objectives is support of political candidates who support pro-gun policies. Consisting of over 600,000 members, the organization has available on request various pamphlets and materials expressing its point of view: *The Rights of Gun Owners; Gun Rights Fact Book;* and *Point Blank,* a monthly newsletter. It has a speakers bureau and holds an annual conference.

Educational Fund to End Handgun Violence
P.O. Box 72
110 Maryland Avenue, NE
Washington, DC 20002
(202) 544-7227

The Educational Fund to End Handgun Violence is an organization founded in 1978 that is concerned particularly with doing away with gun violence among children. To that end, the organization conducts various educational programs and provides a variety of materials dealing with gun violence involving young people. The information is aimed especially at persons conducting research, but members of the press, lawyers, and legislators are also a focus of the organization's attention. The general public is also able to obtain the group's publications. Its materials focus on anti-handgun research and the design and manufacture of handguns. The organization conducts research into such areas as illegal use of handguns and provides films and videotapes to interested audiences. It maintains a library and has a speakers bureau and a database. The organization publishes *Firearms Litigation Reporter Newsletter,* a quarterly, *Assault Weapons and Accessories in America,* and *Kids and Guns* and provides a clearinghouse for gun litigation, assisting litigants, lawyers, professional scholars, and victims of gun violence. It is also concerned with the impact of firearms as a public health issue. The organization has been supported largely by private donations and by grants from foundations.

Firearms Policy Project
1300 N Street, NW
Washington, DC 20005
(202) 783-4071

Founded in 1989, the Firearms Policy Project conducts research and educational activities for the Violence Policy Center. It maintains a speakers bureau, reports statistics, gives information on gun violence, and conducts public policy research. The organization publishes various books, such as *Putting Guns Back in Criminals' Hands: 100 Case Studies of Felons Granted Relief from Disability Under Federal Firearms Laws; License to Kill: The Federal Firearms License; Assault Weapons: Analysis, New Research, and Legislation; Assault Weapons and Accessories in America; National Rifle Association: Money, Firepower, and Fear;* and occasional papers.

Firearms Research and Identification Association
17524 Colima Road, Suite 360
Rowland Heights, CA 91748
(714) 598-8919

This organization, founded in 1978, conducts research on subjects such as the history of firearms and defective weapons and performs weapons accident analysis. It provides expert witnesses to appropriate courts and authenticates and identifies weapons, both historical and contemporary. Its membership is made up largely of people in the professions of business, medicine, engineering, and safety-related occupations. It maintains a library and holds an annual convention.

Gun Owners Action Committee
862 Granite Circle
Anaheim, CA 92806
(714) 772-4867

This organization, established in 1989, vigorously supports the constitutional right to keep and bear arms and encourages citizen involvement in maintaining that right. It provides courses in marksmanship and gun safety, works with children, and offers competitions. It maintains a speakers bureau and publishes the monthly *We The People* and a newsletter.

Gun Owners Incorporated
3440 Viking Street, Suite 106
Sacramento, CA 95828
(916) 361-3109

This is a research and lobby organization seeking to elect pro-gun candidates to the national legislature. It has a gun owners Political Action Committee. The group also publishes various educational materials on subjects related to its focus of interest. The organization opposes gun control on constitutional grounds and argues that such control has very little if any impact on the level of crime. The organization strongly defends the right of law-abiding citizens to own firearms and to use them safely and within the limits of the law. It also advocates swift and harsh punishment for criminals. The organization was established in 1975 by then California State Senator Bill Richardson. It compiles statistics, attempts to keep its membership informed on legislation related to the gun issue, and bestows various awards.

Handgun Control Incorporated
1225 I Street, NW, Suite 1100
Washington, DC 20005
(202) 898-0792

Handgun Control Incorporated (HCI) is a full-time lobby group concerned with reducing handgun violence and adopting stronger gun laws in the United States. It advocates regulation of the importation, sale, transfer, and possession of handguns, and seeks controls over the manufacture of firearms. HCI represents a broad coalition of people and organizations, ranging from law enforcement officials to victims of handgun violence to celebrities. The organization was founded in 1974 under the leadership of Dr. Mark Borinsky, who had himself been the victim of a hold-up. He established the National Council to Control Handguns in Washington, D.C. N. T. Shields, an executive with the DuPont Corporation, later joined the organization; his own son had been murdered in San Francisco in 1974 during the notorious series of so-called Zebra killings. Shields later became chair of the organization. The organization was renamed Handgun Control, Inc., and in 1985 Sarah Brady, whose husband James Brady (former press secretary in the Reagan Administration) was seriously wounded during the attempted assassination of Reagan outside the Washington Hilton Hotel, joined the organization and served as its chair. According to the organization's brochure,

> Our agenda for a national gun policy contains legislation law enforcement experts have demanded for years. HCI lobbyists draft effective legislation, provide expert witnesses for testimony on the gun issue, track legislators' voting records and the contributions they receive from the gun lobby, and coordinate lobbying efforts with other national groups that share our goal of reducing gun violence.

The organization also works with the media and attempts to educate Americans about handgun violence in the United States. Among the organization's many objectives were enactment of the Brady Bill; elimination of private possession of military assault weapons; implementation of registration laws for the private sale of concealable handguns by individuals and at gun shows; establishment of mandatory sentencing laws for anyone convicted of misusing firearms; establishment of strong licensing procedures for those who manufacture and sell handguns; enactment of a national law requiring a waiting period for the purchase of handguns; introduction of a ban on the production and sale of Saturday Night Specials; and establishment of mandatory safety training programs for all of those who purchase handguns. To quote from another of its printed releases, "HCI does not support a ban on legitimate handguns, rifles or shotguns." Or, once again, "None of the laws HCI supports would deny a law-abiding citizen access to a handgun for any legitimate purpose. . . . Handgun Control, Inc., does not advocate a handgun ban. We are working for passage of a sensible national gun policy, including a federal waiting period for handgun sales, to help screen out criminals, and a ban on the sale and manufacture of non-sporting assault weapons." To this end, the group gathers and supplies up-to-date information on the issues surrounding the ownership and use of handguns. It also issues legislative reports and publishes various pamphlets. Among its publications are *Handgun Control: Washington Report*, a quarterly; *Action Guide*; and *Guns Don't Die: People Do*. It has also produced a film on the *American Handgun War*. It has a speakers bureau and holds an annual conference.

Hunter Education Association
P.O. Box 525
Draper, UT 84020
(801) 571-9461

This organization is made up of instructors in hunting education and other people with an interest in the field. One of its primary objectives is to encourage high standards of safety for hunters, and to encourage them to be knowledgeable and responsible in their hunting activities. It teaches international courses in addition to those in the United States. It publishes *Hunting Accident Report for North America,* a semiannual, and *Instructor,* which is published eight times a year. It holds an annual meeting.

International Association of Fish and Wildlife Agencies
444 North Capitol Street, NW, Suite 534
Washington, DC 20001
(202) 624-7890

The International Association of Fish and Wildlife Agencies was established in 1917 under the title National Association of Game Commissioners and Wardens. Its primary purpose is to conserve and manage wildlife so that it remains available for recreation and as an element in the food supply. To accomplish these objectives, the association has developed a variety of committees to educate the public on issues it deems relevant to its mission.

International Association of Law Enforcement Firearms Instructors
390 Union Avenue
Union Square
Laconia, NH 03246
(603) 524-8787

This organization was established in 1981. It advocates the acquisition of the finest firearms training and is made up of training officials from Australia, Canada, Europe, the South Pacific region, and the United States. It holds an annual training meeting and publishes an annual *Directory* and a quarterly journal.

International Benchrest Shooters
R.D. 1, Box 244A
Tunkhannock, PA 18657
(717) 833-2234

Established in 1970, this organization's primary objective is to achieve the epitome of firearm accuracy. The group is composed primarily of research engineers, people who write about guns and ammunition, and gunsmiths themselves. It provides a monthly publication, *Precision Shooting Magazine.* Inasmuch as the group is particularly concerned with accuracy in rifle shooting, it carries on registered shoots and gives awards. There are different divisions devoted to various types of rifles. The organization holds an annual meeting and presents seminars.

International Handgun Metallic Silhouette Association
P.O. Box 368
Burlington, IA 52601
(319) 752-9623

This group is composed of individuals who use handguns to shoot at metallic silhouettes of various animals, such as pigs and turkeys, from various range limits. It maintains the shooting scores of the participants and gives awards. It publishes a newspaper and the *IHMS News,* holds an annual convention, and maintains a museum and a hall of fame.

International Hunters Association
P.O. Box 820
Knightdale, NC 27545
(919) 365-7157

This organization engages in a number of activities, ranging from dispensing information to its members to arranging tours and safaris, providing education in wilderness survival and weapons safety, and organizing hunting outings. It is concerned with protecting the rights of hunters.

International Shooting Coaches Association
Internationale Schutzen Trainer Vereinigung
Association Internacional de Entrenadores de Tiro
P.O. Box 1114
Auburn, WA 98071
(206) 939-7857

The International Shooting Coaches Association is not "directly involved with the gun control controversy." The organization is primarily interested in the coaching aspect of the use of rifles, pistols, shotguns, and archery, and in "helping each other to coach better." According to its letterhead, the organization has national directors in Australia, Canada, Denmark, England, India, Ireland, Japan, Korea, Kuwait, Malaysia, Netherlands, New Zealand, Peru, Saudi Arabia, Singapore, Thailand, Trinidad/Tobago, Western Samoa, Gibraltar, Hong Kong, and Macao. The purpose of the organization is "to enhance the lives of others through the shooting sports," including rifle, pistol, and shotgun shooting, and archery. To quote from literature received from the organization, "Guns when used in a *safe* and *conscientious* manner, are a great source of freedom and recreation. . . . But one careless moment can result in tragedy. Don't you ever forget it!" In a statement on safety, the organization declares:

> Safety comes from man's mastery of his environment and of himself. It is won by individual effort and group cooperation. It can be achieved only by informed, alert, skillful people who respect themselves and have a regard for the welfare of others. Good housekeeping is the keynote to safety. Cleanliness, order and a place for everything are the essentials of safety.

Quoting from the Ontario, Canada, Soccer Coaches Association, the organization states, among other things, that "shooting is a game for enjoyment; the laws of shooting should be regarded as mutual agreements, the spirit or letter of which no one should try to evade or break; . . . officials and opponents should be treated and regarded as honest in intention; official decisions should be accepted without looking angry no matter how unfair they may seem; . . . in shooting, as in life, treat others as you have them treat you."

The organization is thus dedicated to keeping coaches updated in their training. It is also concerned with the enhancement of relations among shooting organizations, weapons manufacturers, athletes, and medicine. It publishes a quarterly, *On Target*, and a newsletter. It holds an annual convention.

Izaak Walton League
1401 Wilson Boulevard
Level B
Arlington, VA 22209
(703) 528-1818

This is a conservation and educational organization dedicated to the maintenance and preservation of soil, forests, water, and other natural resources. Maintaining a pro-sports, pro-hunting policy, it is particularly concerned with providing youth camps and purchasing land that will then be sold to the federal government. It has hundreds of local groups throughout the United States, and provides workshops on various subjects related to its interests.

Jews for the Preservation of Firearms Ownership
2872 South Wentworth Avenue
Milwaukee, WI 53207
(414) 769-0760

Founded in 1989, Jews for the Preservation of Firearms Ownership (JPFO) consists of individuals who wish to defend the right to keep and bear arms as stated in the Second Amendment, and especially to oppose the "anti-gunners," Jewish or otherwise. It regards those who advocate gun control as "elitist fascists" who seek to exercise domination over others' lives. Thus it opposes liberal organizations who advocate gun control, waiting periods when purchasing guns, banning handguns, and similar issues. A recent reprint of an article in *American Survival Guide* (June 1992), in which Aaron Zelman, executive director of the organization, was interviewed by Jim Benson, quotes Zelman as follows:

> JPFO members think that "gun control" is moral perversion because it treats the law-abiding person the same as the criminal. Such an approach clashes with America's basic legal doctrine that one is presumed innocent until proven guilty. It also clashes with Jewish law, a large part of which is devoted to ensuring that an innocent person shall not be wrongly convicted or punished.
>
> JPFO wants to educate Jews that Jewish law requires them to be able to defend their lives, and to educate Gentiles that most Jews who support "gun control" do so out of ignorance of Jewish law and not out of hatred for non-Jews. . . .
>
> JPFO members believe they have a duty to their misguided brothers and sisters, to point out to them the great harm that will result to the Jewish people and to all Americans if the government ends up with a monopoly of armed force.

The organization publishes a monthly periodical, *Maccabee*, and a newsletter.

Mannlicher Collectors Association
P.O. Box 7144
Salem, OR 97303
(503) 472-7710

Formed in 1984, this organization is affiliated with the National Rifle Association and is devoted to those collectors interested in sporting and military firearms based on the designs of Ferdinand Ritter von Mannlicher. The association holds competitions and gives awards, and engages in research and education in the area of Mannlicher-designed weapons. It compiles statistics and maintains a library, museum, and biographical collections. It has a speakers bureau and has developed a database pertaining to the interests of its members. It publishes the *Mannlicher Collector,* a quarterly, and holds an annual meeting.

National Association of Federally Licensed Firearms Dealers
2455 East Sunrise, Suite 916
Fort Lauderdale, FL 33304
(305) 561-3505

Founded in 1973, the organization consists of all individuals licensed by the national government to sell firearms. Essentially a trade association, it publishes various journals encompassing guns, knives, archery, and outdoor sports equipment. Among its publications are *Firearms Disposition and Requisition Log Book; AFI Shot Show Magazine* and *American Firearms Industry Buying Directory,* both annuals; and *American Firearms Industry,* a monthly. The organization exists primarily to protect the rights of firearms dealers and the firearms industry itself. It is a pro-firearms organization whose function is in part to distribute information and advice, and to engage in legislative influence pertaining to all aspects of its interests. An independent organization, it is supported essentially by membership fees and contributions from the firearms industry. It compiles statistics, maintains a database on weapons, and gives annual product awards to the makers of firearms, cutlery, archery, and optical devices.

National Association to Keep and Bear Arms
P.O. Box 78336
Seattle, WA 98178
(206) 246-1985

The objectives of this group, established in 1967, are to "support and defend" the American Constitution, particularly the Second Amendment and the rights of citizens to keep and bear arms. It is also concerned with the maintenance of law and order, impartial administration of the law, belief in God, and the American national heritage. The association compiles statistics, has a speakers bureau and library, and presents various awards. It publishes *Armed Citizen News*, a bimonthly, and various reports related to Second Amendment issues.

National Bench Rest Shooters Association
2027 Buffalo Drive
Levelland, TX 79336
(808) 894-4002

This organization, established in 1951, is concerned with precision in shooting, especially for rifle shooters. It keeps shooting statistics, presents awards, and has a hall of fame. It publishes *NBRSA News*, a monthly.

National Board for the Promotion of Rifle Practice
Pulaski Building, Room 1205
20 Massachusetts Avenue, NW
Washington, DC 20314
(202) 272-0810

Founded in 1903, this group consists of clubs in high schools and colleges; its activities there are focused on development of marksmanship in rifle shooting among the young. It carries out these activities under Title 10 of the United States Code as an agency of the Office of the Secretary of the Army. It is authorized to train citizens and others outside of the armed forces of the United States in firearms proficiency. The board provides the arms and ammunition to accomplish this objective, and awards trophies to those who meet its high standards. It holds an annual conference.

National Crime Prevention Council
Information Services
1700 K Street, NW, Second Floor
Washington, DC 20006
(202) 466-6272

A subunit of the United States Department of Justice, the council engages in activities that attempt to teach people about crime prevention and crime reduction. It publishes information for the public on gun control and weapons violence. People interested in information related to these and other subjects dealing with criminal behavior may contact this office to access its database and other extensive resources.

National Education Association
1201 16th Street, NW
Washington, DC 20036
(202) 833-4000

This is a national group of educators from all levels—elementary, secondary, college and university—and educational administrators. The organization deals with virtually all subjects related to education in the United States, ranging from curriculum to political and legislative matters. It has taken a position supporting gun control and waiting periods for the purchase of handguns. It publishes handbooks, newsletters, and various other materials, and holds an annual convention.

National Foundation for Firearms Education
440 Park South
New York, NY 10016
(800) 448-6529

Established in 1984 in New York as a nonprofit corporation, the National Foundation for Firearms Education's objective is to oppose the anti-gun movement. It became a federal tax-exempt organization in 1990. One of its most recent efforts has involved opposition to those who would ban semiautomatic weapons. The organization also attempts to educate people that gun ownership does not generally lead to crime: criminals who possess guns and other lethal weapons commit crime. One of the group's major objectives is to enhance the awareness of residents of urban areas of the various aspects of gun ownership and gun control.

National Hunters Association
P.O. Box 820
Knightdale, NC 27545
(919) 365-7157

Established in 1976, this organization exists to serve its members by providing information, including gun safety and survival instruction, and planning tours and safaris. It is concerned with protecting sportsmen's rights and with dispensing knowledge about survival in the wilderness.

National Mossberg Collectors Association
P.O. Box 22156
St. Louis, MO 63116
(314) 353-6401

Established in 1988, this National Rifle Association affiliate is composed of people interested in the preservation and exhibition of O. F. Mossberg firearms. The organization sends representation to National Rifle Association shows. It maintains a library and gives awards in fields of interest. It publishes the *NMCA News*, a bimonthly, and a newsletter.

National Muzzle Loading Rifle Association
Friendship, IN 47021
(812) 667-5131

Established in 1933, this group consists of those interested in black-powder shooting and firearm safety. More specifically, the organization aspires to preserve blackpowder shooting as a part of American heritage. It also offers programs aimed at safety in hunting. It has a national shooting range in Friendship, Indiana. It provides awards and holds a semiannual meeting, annual spring and fall shoots, and an annual turkey shoot. The association publishes *Muzzle Blasts*, a monthly.

National Reloading Manufacturers Association
1 Centerpointe Drive, Suite 300
Lake Oswego, OR 97035
(503) 639-9190

This organization is composed of manufacturers and suppliers who deal with handloading ammunition for handguns and long guns. It is concerned with improving reloading tools and handloading. It focuses on the standardization of reloading supplies, and presents programs and distributes literature aimed at educating the public on these issues. It holds an annual convention.

National Rifle Association (NRA)
11250 Waples Mills Road
Fairfax, VA 22030
(703) 267-1000

Founded in 1871, the National Rifle Association (NRA) is the largest association of gun owners in the United States, with membership exceeding 3 million people. Its membership consists largely of target shooters, gun collectors, hunters, police officers, and many other individuals interested in gun collecting, self-protection, firearms preservation, and other firearms-related matters. It has demonstrated over the years that it is perhaps the single most influential organization that resists gun control laws and advocates the rights of Americans to keep and bear arms. The NRA has consistently argued that gun control laws do not in general reduce the frequency or viciousness of crime. Although opposing most gun control measures, the organization does support laws that severely punish criminals and that would establish a computerized process by which the background of all gun purchasers would be examined.

The NRA has a program for police firearms instruction, keeps records of national and international shooting competitions, and sponsors teams to compete in international events. Its library and museum in Washington, D.C., are perhaps two of the finest of their type in the world. The organization encourages safety programs in shooting with pistols, rifles, and shotguns, and promotes hunting, gun collecting, and general safety in the use of firearms. It collects some of the most detailed statistics available anywhere on the subject of gun control, including legislation, use of guns, hunting, and wildlife preservation. The organization supports a speakers bureau and engages in intense lobbying activities when necessary. It publishes *American Hunter, American Rifleman, Insights, Shooting Sports, USA,* and *NRAction,* all monthlies. It holds an annual convention.

National Shooting Sports Foundation
555 Danbury Road
Wilton, CT 06897
(203) 762-1320

Established in 1961, this organization came into existence in order to create a better understanding of, and more involvement in, the shooting sports. It is made up largely of hunters and others who use guns for recreational purposes. The organization supports the firearms industry and sportsmen by publishing a variety of pamphlets and brochures, a bimonthly newsletter, booklets and reports, and *Gun Club Directory*. It also produces videotapes and maintains a book collection relevant to its interests. It engages in research relating to gun ownership, hunting, and conservation. It is in turn supported by the companies that manufacture firearms and ammunition, together with the accessories of such devices, and by the publishers of gun and outdoor magazines. It promotes safety in the use of firearms and works with various state and federal offices in promoting hunting, and with private organizations to establish recreational facilities for those interested in the safe use of firearms. The group is also concerned with delineating the history and development of guns. It underwrites the costs of various educational programs and keeps records of hunting and related activities. It holds an annual meeting and trade show, and sponsors a National Hunting and Fishing Day.

National Skeet Shooting Association
P.O. Box 680007
San Antonio, TX 78268
(210) 688-3371

This organization consists of amateur skeet shooters. Its primary goals are to regulate competitions and to formulate rules. It makes awards in both team and individual competitions, and maintains a Skeet Shooting Hall of Fame. It publishes *Skeet Shooting Review* and *Sporting Clays: The Shotgun Hunter Magazine,* both monthlies. It holds an annual meeting and sponsors an annual shoot.

National Urban League
500 East 62nd Street
New York, NY 10021
(212) 310-9000

Established in 1910, this organization is a community service agency made up of a number of subgroups, including community leaders, professionals, business and labor groups, and religious organizations. Its primary aim is to eliminate racial discrimination and segregation and to integrate African Americans into all facets of American political and social culture. It attempts to provide service to African Americans in areas such as housing, health, welfare, family planning, veteran counseling, youth and consumer problems, and many other related areas. It has taken a position in favor of gun control and waiting periods before the purchase of handguns. It publishes a number of reports, reviews, and journals, and holds an annual convention.

No Compromise Majority
2140 Wolverine Circle, No. E
Wasilla, AR 99654
(907) 376-8285

This organization was established in 1988 and consists of people who advocate gun rights for Americans. It lobbies in support of the right to keep and bear arms, and it maintains a speakers bureau.

Non-Powder Gun Products Association
200 Castlewood Drive
North Palm Beach, FL 33408
(407) 840-1137

This organization, founded in 1974, is composed of companies that manufacture and distribute non-powder guns and ammunition. It is interested in promoting correct use of air guns and related products. It encourages standardizing and simplifying non-powder guns. It publishes materials relating to safety in shooting, and holds an annual convention.

North American Hunting Club
12301 Whitewater Drive
P.O. Box 3401
Minnetonka, MN 55343
(612) 936-9333

Established in 1978, this organization is composed of hunters in North America. Its goals include enhancing the enjoyment of hunting and sharpening the necessary skills. The association compiles statistics and information, engages in charitable activities, and gives Big Game Awards as part of an organized program. Its publications include *North American Hunter*, a bimonthly; *Wild Game Cookbook*; and various reports concerning information for hunters. It conducts a biennial convention.

North-South Skirmish Association
9700 Royerton Drive
Richmond, VA 23228
(804) 266-0898

This organization, affiliated with the National Rifle Association, was established in 1950. Its major objective is to pay tribute to the memory of soldiers on both sides during the Civil War. During their mock "national skirmish," participants wear authentic uniforms and use weapons of the period. They also parade and fire weapons in authentic formations used during the Civil War era. The organization furthers the attainment of marksmanship with small arms and artillery used during the war. It holds a semiannual skirmish and a semiannual convention, and publishes *Skirmish Line,* a bimonthly.

Office for Church in Society (United Church of Christ)
700 Prospect Avenue
Cleveland, OH 44115
(216) 736-2174

110 Maryland Avenue, NE, Suite 504
Washington, DC 20002
(202) 543-1517

To quote from a brochure produced by the Office for Church in Society (OCIS), the organization was established by the General Synod

> to assume leadership functions for social action concerns in the United Church of Christ . . . , to provide resources to national, Conference, and local churches and to strengthen coordination of social action activities within the denomination.

On the matter of gun control, the Seventh General Synod of the United Church of Christ adopted a resolution that urged the protection of "the innocent and helpless against assault, to remove the needless temptation from potential assassins, and to delegate use of lethal weapons only to legitimate authority for protective or sporting purposes." It recognized that the Second Amendment has not been held to provide "unregulated private access to firearms," showed that opinion surveys support greater gun legislation, advocated licensing and examining of "all gun users" and the limiting of "handguns to persons whose occupation requires them to possess a handgun for self-defense."

The organization has continued to support strict gun controls and most recently lent its support to the Brady Bill. It publishes a number of newsletters, study books, videotapes, and pamphlets on a variety of social issues that also provides members with information about how to write to members of Congress and effectively influence them.

Pacific International Trapshooting Association
P.O. Box 847
Redmond, OR 97756
(503) 548-6621

The primary purpose of this organization is to hold state, provincial, and individual trapshoots. It publishes a yearbook and holds an annual meeting.

Police Foundation
1001 22nd Street, NW, Suite 200
Washington, DC 20037
(202) 833-1460

Founded in 1970, the Police Foundation is a service-oriented organization that attempts to increase the efficiency of crime control and protection to citizens through close relations with police departments, city officials, professionals, business people, scholars, and others interested in their work. It engages in research dealing with crime control (among other topics), sponsors forums, and in general tries to improve the police profession in the United States. It publishes a variety of books, reports, and other materials.

Police Management Association
1001 22nd Street, NW, Suite 200
Washington, DC 20037
(202) 833-1460

Established in 1980, the Police Management Association is made up of law enforcement personnel, civilians, and police officers, as well as criminal justice students who are granted associate membership. It focuses on the middle management levels of police departments and takes positions on various controversial issues of importance to the police mission in the United States. It conducts seminars for the improvement of police management, and publishes a newsletter and a membership directory.

Safari Club International
4800 West Gates Pass Road
Tucson, AZ 85745
(602) 620-1220

Founded in 1971, the Safari Club supports the preservation of wildlife. As a sporting organization, it encourages hunting as a means of managing wildlife. Thus, one of its major objectives is to support hunting rights. It has established the Safari Club

International Conservation Fund and carries on efforts with other conservation groups in their mutual concern with wildlife management and preservation.

Second Amendment Foundation
James Madison Building
12500 NE Tenth Place
Bellevue, WA 98005
(206) 454-7012

The Second Amendment Foundation, established in 1974, has a working relationship with the Citizens Committee for the Right to Keep and Bear Arms, and aims largely to do legal and educational research on the meaning and significance of the Second Amendment of the Constitution. It is a tax-exempt organization, and does not engage in lobbying activities. It works toward the preservation of American rights under the Second Amendment, strongly advocating the position that gun control laws violate these rights. The organization presents the James Madison Award to individuals who have demonstrated unusual commitment to areas with which it is concerned. It has a speakers bureau and holds annual meetings. It provides a legal reference service and hotline for gun owners who want current information on subjects of interest to them and to the organization. The foundation has produced videotapes and monographs dealing with gun control. It produces a radio program, provides media announcements, maintains a library that includes biographical materials, and publishes annual and periodical materials, among them *Gun Week,* a newspaper; *Second Amendment Reporter* and *Reporter,* both quarterlies; and *Women and Guns,* a monthly. The foundation conducts fundraising campaigns and holds an annual meeting.

Sons of Liberty
P.O. Box 503
Brisbane, CA 94005
(415) 468-2402

Founded in 1976, the Sons of Liberty is a nonprofit organization "dedicated to preservation of our Constitutional freedoms." Its membership consists of politically conservative people. To quote from a statement authored by Joseph W. Kerska, president of the organization:

> The Sons of Liberty speak for Thomas Jefferson, "NO FREE MAN SHALL EVER BE DEBARRED THE USE OF ARMS.". . . The liberties Our Founding Fathers

endowed us with are now in grave danger because we have taken them for granted, for many generations. . . . The Sons of Liberty are back to interpret the Second Amendment as it was intended by Thomas Jefferson and other Founding Fathers. The Second Amendment is the key to our freedom and was so intended by the framers of the Constitution.

The organization thus opposes gun control and restrictions on the ownership of semiautomatic weapons, and argues that gun control legislation—especially registration requirements—leads to gun confiscation. Arguing that 99 percent of guns are used for fully legal purposes and that only 1 percent are used illegally, the group maintains that any type of rigid gun control measure would only hamper law-abiding citizens. The organization maintains a library and dispenses information on the subject of the right to keep and bear arms as indicated in the Second Amendment. It also produces statistics, has a speakers' bureau, and publishes *News*, a monthly, and *Journal*.

United States Revolver Association
96 West Union Street
Ashland, MA 01721
(508) 881-2617

The United States Revolver Association exists to promote revolver and pistol shooting matches and keeps records of results. It seeks to encourage matches between members and the pistol clubs of the United States. It produces various publications. Founded in 1900, the organization rests on the belief that gun ownership is not only a right, but is necessary to self-protection and to defend oneself against foreign invasions and a potentially tyrannical government. It advocates stiff sentences for those who commit crimes with guns. It also provides information related to pending gun legislation regarding revolvers and threats to gun ownership in general. It publishes a bimonthly, *U.S. Handgunner*, and a newsletter. It holds an annual convention.

Violence Policy Center
1300 N Street, NW
Washington, DC 20005
(202) 783-4071

This organization is dedicated to research on violence committed using firearms. It is a national tax-exempt organization and seeks contributions from the general public and from foundations. It particularly opposes the National Rifle Association, and provides other information relevant to its position on the gun control issue. It supports rigorous gun controls. It has three main objectives: "examination of the role of violence within specific public policy areas, presentation of information not comprehensively addressed by other organizations or sources; and, development of violence reduction policy alternatives." Another of its objectives is education of the public on the hazards of guns in general and "mov[ing] beyond the popular but narrow perception of firearms violence as a crime issue to place it in its proper perspective: a widespread public health problem of which crime is merely the most recognized aspect." To all of these ends, the center compiles statistics, maintains a library, and serves as a clearinghouse of expert information. It conducts the Firearms Policy Project.

It has published *Assault Weapons Analysis: New Research and Legislation; The Federal Firearms License: License to Kill; Putting Guns Back into Criminals' Hands: 100 Case Studies of Felons Granted Relief from Disability under Federal Firearms Laws;* and *The National Rifle Association: Money, Firepower and Fear.*

Women's League for Conservative Judaism
48 East 74th Street
New York, NY 10021
(212) 628-1600

A member of the National Coalition to Ban Handguns and the National Jewish Community Relations Advocacy Council, the Women's League for Conservative Judaism advocates a number of policies on a number of issues. With respect to gun control, the group passed a resolution at its convention of November 1976 that read:

> The more than 40 million hand guns in circulation today are responsible for the staggering toll of one death per hour throughout the year! Despite the overwhelming public opinion in favor of gun control legislation, the National Rifle Association, with its powerful lobby, has effectively continued to block such legislation. Women's League for Conservative Judaism, mindful of the Jewish concept of the sanctity

of life, recommends that all its affiliated Sisterhood advocate and support Federal and State legislation:

1. [R]equiring registration and licensing of all guns privately owned;

2. Prohibiting the manufacture and importing of "Saturday Night Specials."

World Fast-Draw Association
924 Cedar
Wood River, IL 62095
(618) 259-1261

The primary purpose of this organization, affiliated with the National Rifle Association, is to encourage the sport of Western fast-draw. It therefore sponsors contests and grants awards, and gives instruction in fast-draw and safety advice to be employed in the process. It publishes *World Fast-Draw Association Newsletter,* a monthly periodical. The organization holds an annual convention.

Selected State Organizations Interested in Gun Issues

The following groups are composed primarily of persons interested in gun collecting; hunting, fishing, and general outdoors enthusiasts; antiquarians and weapons historians; target shooters; and those who, for a variety of other reasons, might have an interest in weapons. The list is hardly exhaustive. Only a sampling of such groups have been included. The organizations may or may not take a position on the issue of gun control. The reader is once again cautioned that some groups might have moved, changed their names, or become defunct since the list was compiled.

Alabama

Alabama Gun Collectors Association
P.O. Box 2131
Birmingham, AL 35201

Montgomery Gun Club
310 Burbank Drive
Montgomery, AL 36109

Arizona

Arizona Gun Collectors Association, Inc.
1129 South 6th Avenue
Tucson, AZ 85701

Arkansas

Petersburg Rod and Gun Club
P.O. Box 1034
Petersburg, AR 99833

California

California Hunters & Gun Association
2309 Cipriani Boulevard
Belmont, CA 94002

Greater California Arms & Collectors Association
8291 Carburton Street
Long Beach, CA 90808

Handgun Control, Inc.
10951 West Pico Boulevard, Suite 201
Los Angeles, CA 90064
(310) 446-0056

Northern California Historical Arms Collectors Association
25 Mizpah Street
San Francisco, CA 94131

San Bernardino Valley Arms Collectors, Inc.
1970 Mesa Street
San Bernardino, CA 92405

San Diego Committee Against Handgun Violence
705 12th Avenue
San Diego, CA 92101

Southern California Arms Collectors Association
4204 Elmer Avenue
North Hollywood, CA 91602

Colorado

Arapahoe Gun Collectors
2968 South Broadway
Englewood, CO 80110

Colorado State Rifle and Pistol Association
2123 Meyers Avenue
Colorado Springs, CO 80909

Pikes Peak Gun Collectors Guild
406 East Uintah Street
Colorado Springs, CO 80903

Connecticut

Antique Arms Collectors Association of Connecticut
17 Philip Road
Manchester, CT 06040

Ye Connecticut Gun Guild, Inc.
P.O. Box 67
Cornwall Bridge, CT 06754

Delaware

Delaware Antique Arms Collectors
2408 Duncan Road
Wilmington, DE 19808

Florida

American Heritage Hunting and Gun Club
P.O. Box 535
Riverview, FL 33539

Dade Citizens for Home Rule on Handguns
1450 NE 2nd
Miami, FL 33132
(305) 995-1334

Florida Gun Collectors Association
P.O. Box 470
Jasper, FL 32052

Georgia

Georgia Arms Collectors
P.O. Box 218
Conley, GA 30027

Georgians Against Gun Violence
1211 Timberland Drive
Marietta, GA 30067
(404) 952-4865

Hawaii

K-Bay Rod and Gun Club
Kaneohe Marine Corps Air Station
FPO San Francisco, CA 96615

Idaho

Idaho State Rifle and Pistol Association
P.O. Box 659
Nampa, ID 83653

Illinois

Illinois Council Against Handgun Violence
202 South State Street, #926
Chicago, IL 60604
(312) 341-0939

Illinois Gun Collectors Association
P.O. Box 1524
Chicago, IL 60690

Illinois State Rifle Association
224 South Michigan Avenue
Chicago, IL 60604

Safari Club International
1133 North Kilbourn Avenue
Chicago, IL 60651

Sauk Trail Gun Collectors
P.O. Box 645
Milan, IL 61264

Wabash Valley Gun Collectors Association, Inc.
1002 Lincoln Park Avenue
Danville, IL 61832

Indiana

Indiana Sportsman's Council
P.O. Box 93
Bloomington, IN 47401

Indiana State Rifle and Pistol Association
1321 Fletcher Street
Anderson, IN 46016

Northern Indiana Gun Collectors Association
16150 Ireland Road
Mishawaka, IN 46544

Southern Indiana Gun Collectors Association, Inc.
509 North 3rd Street
Boonville, IN 47601

Iowa

Central States Gun Collectors Association
1104 South 1st Avenue
Marshtown, IA 50158

I.O.P. Rifle and Pistol Club
413 South Gunnison
Burlington, IN 52601

Kansas

Four State Collectors Association
915 E. 10th
Pittsburgh, KS 66726

Missouri Valley Arms Collectors Association
P.O. Box 8204
Shawnee Mission, KS 66208

Kentucky

Citizens and Victims United for Sensible Gun Legislation
Council on Peacemaking
410 W. Chestnut Street
Louisville, KY 40202

Jefferson Gun Club
1418 Willow Avenue, Suite 220
Louisville, KY 40204

Kentucky Gun Collectors Association, Inc.
P.O. Box 64
Owensboro, KY 42301

Louisiana

Ark-La-Tex Gun Collectors Association
1521 Earl Street
Schreveport, LA 71108

Pelican Arms Collectors
8681 Sharon Hills Boulevard
Baton Rouge, LA 70811

Maryland

Appalachian Trail Arms Collectors, Inc.
College Estates, P.O. Box 1360
Frederick, MD 21701

Marylanders Against Handgun Abuse
2530 North Calvert Street
Baltimore, MD 21218

Massachusetts

Braintree Rifle and Pistol Club, Inc.
P.O. Box 24
Braintree, MA 02184

Citizens for Safety
95 Berkeley Street
Boston, MA 02116
(617) 695-9595

Massachusetts Arms Collectors
P.O. Box 1001
Worcester, MA 01613

State Rifle and Pistol Association of Massachusetts
MIT, Room 5-118
Cambridge, MA 02139

Michigan

Anti Handgun Association (AHA!)
11000 West McNichols
Detroit, MI 48221
(313) 341-0787

Detroit Coalition for A Freeze on Handguns
Detroit Catholic Pastoral Alliance
16000 Pembroke
Detroit, MI 48235

Michigan Antique Arms Collectors, Inc.
8914 Borgman Avenue
Huntington Woods, MI 48070

Michigan Rifle and Pistol Association
8384 Perrin
Westland, MI 48185

Organization United to Control Handguns
19171 Cardoni
Detroit, MI 48203

Royal Oak Historical Arms Collectors, Inc.
25487 Hereford
Huntington Woods, MI 48070

Save Our Sons and Daughters (SOSAD)
453 Martin Luther King Boulevard
Detroit, MI 48201
(313) 833-3030

Minnesota

Citizens for a Safer Minnesota
245 East 6th Street, Suite 461
St. Paul, MN 55101
(612) 292-8698

Minnesota Weapons Collectors
P.O. Box 662
Hopkins, MN 55343

Missouri

Edwardsville Gun Collectors
1055 Warson Woods Drive
St. Louis, MO 63122

Mineral Belt Gun Collectors Association
1110 East Cleveland Avenue
Monett, MO 65708

Missouri Committee for Firearms Safety
116 South Brent Avenue
Kirkwood, MO 63122
(314) 821-4705

Missouri Council to Control Handguns
2185 Danelle Drive
Florissant, MO 63031
(314) 837-2395

Montana

Montana Arms Collectors Association
308 Riverview Drive East
Great Falls, MT 59404

Nebraska

Nebraska Gun and Cartridge Collectors
710 West 6th Street
North Platte, NE 69101

Nebraskans for Responsible Gun Ownership
16512 Frederick Circle
Omaha, NE 68130
(402) 397-2641

New Hampshire

New Hampshire Arms Collectors, Inc.
Route 3
Windham, NH 03087

New Hampshire State Rifle and Pistol Association
Schoolhouse Road
Amherst, NH 03031

New Jersey

Emerson Fire Department Field and Target Club
207 Wortendyke Avenue
Emerson, NJ 07630

Emerson Police Reserve Gun Club
207 Wortendyke Avenue
Emerson, NJ 07630

Experimental Ballistics Associates
110 Kensington
Trenton, NJ 08618

Jersey Shore Antique Arms Collectors
P.O. Box 100
Bayville, NJ 08721

New Jersey Arms Collectors Club, Inc.
1 Towns End Road
Mendham, NJ 07945

United Sportsmans Association
R.D. 3, Box 144
Seville, NJ 08080

New Mexico

New Mexico Gun Collectors Association
P.O. Box 14145
Albuquerque, NM 87111

New York

Handgun Control, Inc., of New York
26 West 84th Street
New York, NY 10024
(212) 873-3361

Hudson-Mohawk Arms Collectors Association, Inc.
108 West Main Street
Frankfort, NY 13340

Iroquois Arms Collectors Association
McNeeley Road
Akron, NY 14001

Isle Shooting Club
2625 Fix Road
Grand Island, NY 14072

Mid-State Arms Collectors and Shooters Club
108 West Main Street
Frankfort, NY 13340

Nassau County Fish and Game Association, Inc.
49 Northridge Avenue
North Merrick, NY 11566

New York State Rifle and Pistol Association
Route 9
Nyack, NY 10960

Victory Rifle and Pistol Club
57 Carmel Avenue
Staten Island, NY 10314

Westchester Arms Collectors Club, Inc.
59 Pearsall Street
Staten Island, NY 10305

North Carolina

Carolina Gun Collectors Association
1020 Central Avenue
Charlotte, NC 28204

Mecklenburg Wildlife Club, Inc.
P.O. Box 2495
Charlotte, NC 28234

North Dakota

North Dakota Muzzle Loaders, Inc.
Courtenay, ND 58426

Ohio

Central Ohio Gun and Indian Relic Collectors Association
134 East Ohio Avenue
Washington, OH 43160

Gun Safety Institute
4614 Prospect Avenue, Room 421
Cleveland, OH 44103

Handgun Control Federation of Ohio
320 Leader Building
Cleveland, OH 44114

National Bench Rest Shooters Association, Inc.
607 West Line Street
Minerva, OH 44657

Ohio Gun Collectors Association, Inc.
130 South Main Street
Prospect, OH 43342

Ohio Rifle and Pistol Association
P.O. Box 39211
Solon, OH 44139

Safari Club International, Ohio Chapter
P.O. Box 5632
Cleveland, OH 44101

Oklahoma

Indian Territory Gun Collectors Association
P.O. Box 4491
Tulsa, OK 74104

Oklahoma Rifle Association
128 Blossom
Midwest City, OK 73110

Oregon

Four Corners Rod and Gun Club
P.O. Box 1105
Salem, OR 97308

Oregon Cartridge Collectors Association, Inc.
P.O. Box 25103
Portland, OR 97308

Oregon Handgun Alert
3509 SE Clayborn Street
Portland, OR 97292
(503) 231-5000

Oregonians Against Gun Violence
P.O. Box 82966
Portland, OR 97282
(503) 233-1224

Willamette Valley Arms Collectors Association
Route 3, Box 283
Springfield, OR 97477

Pennsylvania

Central Pennsylvania Antique Arms Association
549 West Lemon Street
Lancaster, PA 17603

Lancaster Muzzle Loading Association
R.D. 1, Box 447
Columbia, PA 17512

Pennsylvania Gun Collectors Association
37 Woodside Drive
Washington, PA 15301

Pennsylvania Rifle and Pistol Association
892 Farmdale Road
Mt. Joy, PA 17552

South Carolina

South Carolina Arms Collectors Association
3215 Lincoln Street
Columbia, SC 29201

South Carolina Shooting Association
1467 Battalion Drive
Charleston, SC 29412

South Dakota

Dakota Territory Gun Collectors Association, Inc.
1022 1st Street South
Moorhead, MN 56560

Tennessee

American Duck Hunters Association, Tennessee Wing
P.O. Box 17491
Memphis, TN 38127

Memphis Antique Weapons Association
4672 Barfield Road
Memphis, TN 38117

Tennessee Gun Collectors Association, Inc.
3556 Pleasant Valley Road
Nashville, TN 37204

Tennesseeans for Handgun Control
P.O. Box 150802
Nashville, TN 37215
(615) 385-2965

Texas

Alamo Arms Collectors
410 Rector
San Antonio, TX 78216

Houston Gun Collectors Association
P.O. Box 53435
Houston, TX 77052

Texas Gun Collectors Association
3119 Produce Row
Houston, TX 77023

Texas State Rifle Association
P.O. Drawer 43809
Dallas, TX 75234

Waco Gun Collectors
4021 North 26th
Waco, TX 76708

Utah

Defenders of Outdoor Heritage
P.O. Box 15135
Salt Lake City, UT 84111

Utah Gun Collectors Association
875 20th Street
Ogden, UT 84401

Vermont

Vermont State Rifle and Pistol Association
R.F.D. 1, Box 55
Springfield, VT 05156

Virginia

Virginia Arms Collectors Association
4601 Sylvan Road
Richmond, VA 23225

Virginia State Rifle and Revolver Association
6429 North 22nd Road
Arlington, VA 22205

Washington

Washington Arms Collectors, Inc.
446 Pelly Avenue
Renton, WA 98055

Washington Citizens for Rational Handgun Control
P.O. Box 9787
Seattle, WA 98119
(206) 283-9800

Yakima Valley Muzzle Loaders
Route 3, Box 3078
Selah, WA 98942

Wisconsin

Sportsmen for Firearms Responsibility
3300 Commercial Avenue
Madison, WI 53714

Wisconsin Gun Collectors Association, Inc.
West 180 N8996 Leona Lane
Menomonee Falls, WI 53051

Wyoming

National Shooters League
504 Lyons
Laramie, WY 82070

Wyoming Gun Collectors
P.O. Box 1805
Riverton, WY 82501

Other Organizations Interested in Gun Issues

American Association of Suicidology
2459 S. Ash
Denver, CO 80222

American Humane Education Society
180 Longwood Avenue
Boston, MA 02115

American Humanist Association
7 Harwood Drive
P.O. Box 146
Amherst, NY 14226-0146

American Jewish Committee
165 E. 56th Street
New York, NY 10022

American Medical Association
515 N. State Street
Chicago, IL 60610

American Pediatric Society
2650 Yale Boulevard, SE
Suite 104
Albuquerque, NM 87106

American Psychiatric Association
1400 K Street, NW
Washington, DC 20005

American Public Health Association
1015 15th Street, NW
Washington, DC 20005

Animal Charity League, Inc.
1747 Market Street
Youngstown, OH 44507

Animal Protection Institute
5894 South Land Park Drive
Sacramento, CA 95822

Animal Welfare Institute
P.O. Box 3650
Washington, DC 20036

B'Nai B'rith International
1640 Rhode Island Avenue, NW
Washington, DC 20036

Child Welfare League of America
440 1st Street, NW, Suite 310
Washington, DC 20001

Civic Disarmament Committee for Handgun Control
5532 South Shore Drive 15F
Chicago, IL 61637

Committee for Handgun Control
111 East Wacker Drive
Chicago, IL 60601

Committee for Humane Legislation, Incorporated
11 West 60th Street
New York, NY 10023

Committee for the Study of Handgun Misuse
111 East Wacker Drive
Chicago, IL 60601

Defenders of Wildlife
2000 North Street, NW
Washington, DC 20036

DISARM
175 5th Avenue
New York, NY 10010

Environmental Action Foundation, Inc.
732 Dupont Circle
Washington, DC 20036

Friends Committee on National Legislation
245 2nd Street, NE
Washington, DC
(202) 547-6000

Friends of Animals
11 West 60th Street
New York, NY 10023

Friends of the Earth Foundation, Inc.
529 Commercial Street
San Francisco, CA 94104

Fund for Animals
1765 P Street, NW
Washington, DC 20036

**General Board of Church and Society of the
United Methodist Church**
100 Maryland Avenue, NE
Washington, DC 20002

Handgun Alert, Inc.
P.O. Box 6771
Providence, RI 02940

Humane Information Services, Inc.
5421 4th Street
Saint Petersburg, FL 33705

Humane Society of the United States
1604 K Street, NW
Washington, DC 20006

International Ladies Garment Workers Union
1710 Broadway
New York, NY 10019

National Association of Social Workers
7981 Eastern Avenue
Silver Spring, MD

National Coalition Against Poisoning of Wildlife
P.O. Box 14156
San Francisco, CA 94114

National Coalition to Ban Handguns
100 Maryland Avenue, NE
Washington, DC 20002

National Council for a Responsible Firearms Policy, Inc.
826 First Street, SE
Minot, ND 58701

National Council of Negro Women
1211 Connecticut Avenue, NW Suite 702
Washington, DC 20036

National Council to Control Handguns
1910 K Street, NW
Washington, DC 20036

National Gun Control Center
1201 Connecticut Avenue, NW
Washington, DC 20036

National League of Cities
1301 Pennsylvania Avenue, NW
Washington, DC 20004

National Reloading Manufacturers Association
1 Centerpointe Drive, Suite 300
Lake Oswego, OR 97035

National Safety Council
444 N. Michigan Avenue
Chicago, IL 60611

People vs. Handguns
3 Joy Street
Boston, MA 02108

Sierra Club Foundation
1500 Hills Tower
220 Bush Street
San Francisco, CA 94104

Society for Animal Rights, Inc.
900 First Avenue
New York, NY 10022

Unexpected Wildlife Refuge
R.D. 1
P.O. Box 272
Newfield, NJ 08344

U.S. Conference of Mayors
1620 Eye Street, NW
Washington, DC 20006

Selected Victims Rights Groups

Families of Murder Victims, Inc.
1421 Arch Street, 7th Floor
Philadelphia, PA 19102
(215) 686-8078

Kentucky Voice for Crime Victims
P.O. Box 14123
Louisville, KY 40214
(502) 367-0638

National Organization for Victim Assistance
1757 Park Road, NW
Washington, DC 20010
(202) 232-6682

National Victim Center
2111 Wilson Boulevard, Suite 300
Arlington, VA 22201
(703) 276-2880

Parents of Murdered Children
100 East 8th Street, Room B-41
Cincinnati, OH 45202
(513) 721-5683

Texas Crime Victim Clearinghouse
Office of the Governor
P.O. Box 12428
Austin, TX 78711
(512) 463-1886

Selected Organizations Endorsing a National Waiting Period for the Purchase of Handguns

AFL-CIO
African Methodist Episcopal Church
Amalgamated Clothing and Textile Workers Union
American Academy of Pediatrics
American Academy of Physical Medicine and Rehabilitation
American Association of Retired Persons
American Bar Association
American College of Emergency Physicians
American Federation of Teachers
American Jewish Committee
American Jewish Congress
American Medical Association
American Medical Student Association
American Psychiatric Association
American Public Health Association
Americans for Democratic Action
Anti-Defamation League of B'nai B'rith
B'nai B'rith International
B'nai B'rith Women
Children's Defense Fund
Emergency Nurses Association
Episcopal Church, Washington Office
Federal Law Enforcement Officers Association
Fraternal Order of Police
International Association of Chiefs of Police
International Brotherhood of Police Officers
International Ladies' Garment Workers Union
League of Women Voters
Mennonite Central Committee, Washington Office
National Association for the Advancement of Colored People
National Association of Counties

National Association of Police Organizations
National Congress of Parents and Teachers
National Council of Jewish Women
National Education Association
National League of Cities
National Organization of Black Law Enforcement Executives
National Rainbow Coalition, Inc.
National Sheriffs' Association
National Urban League
Police Foundation
Police Management Association
Southern Christian Leadership Conference
Union of American Hebrew Congregations,
    Religious Action Center
Unitarian Universalist Association, Washington Office
United Church of Christ, Office for Church in Society
United States Catholic Conference
U.S. Conference of Mayors

Selected Print Resources

The literature on the subject of gun control—broadly defined—ranges from the most brilliantly scholarly to the most polemically biased. To attempt to sort through this staggering array of material is a rather daunting task. The following is a broad and eclectic sample of this literature, including some of the leading scholarly articles contained in both the law journals and the journals of social and medical science; the major books or chapters of books in the field; a series of references to the leading symposia dealing with a variety of topics related to gun control; a list of some relevant magazines; excerpts from some of the most useful scholarly papers presented at professional conferences; some of the more or less polemical materials published by vocal and even vitriolic organizations involved with the topic; and references to what might generally be referred to as "fugitive pieces"—undated flyers, pamphlets, mimeographed broadsides, and other materials.

No claim is made for comprehensive coverage, but the literature presented below provides the reader with a taste—perhaps even the flavor—of some of the types of references he or she is sure to encounter in a bibliographical search.

Articles

Ansell, S. T. **"Legal and Historical Aspects of the Militia."** *Yale Law Journal* 26, no. 5 (March 1917).

This article addresses the lack of knowledge "among eminent counsel and judges alike" of what constitutes the militia and where it stands in relation to the U.S. Army. Ansell briefly traces the Anglo-Saxon history of the militia and then discusses the development of the militia in the United States. He describes the "militia as distinguished from [the] federal army," stating that it "is not a federal army even when employed in federal service." (This has been changed in more recent law.) He also discusses the creation of the National Guard under the National Defense Act of 1916 and questions where the power originated "to impose . . . new and additional status of the militia of the several states." He argues that keeping the power of Congress within its scope when dealing with the militia will prove to be a difficult task.

Arrow, Paul S. **"Kelley v. R.G. Industries: California Caught in the Crossfire."** *Southwestern University Law Review* 17 (1988).

This is one of many articles dealing with manufacturers' product liability in relation to Saturday Night Specials. This article focuses on California and concludes that the court in the *Kelley* case misinterpreted the risk-benefit test (used to determine whether a handgun is defective in design) because it required that something be wrong as a prerequisite to applying the test. Instead, the test should be restricted to those instances where there are choices of other designs. Thus, inasmuch as the test in this case was based on an improper selection of design alternatives, California, given the statutory definition in that state, "would be conducive to a Kelley approach."

Ascione, Alfred M. **"The Federal Firearms Act."** *St. John's Law Review* 13 (April 1939).

This is a detailed discussion of the contents and application of the Federal Firearms Act, which became law on 30 June 1938 and went into effect one month later. The article discusses definitions, prohibitions, and administration of the act, and suggests that the Federal Firearms Act is well within the scope of the Congress to make all laws necessary for the regulation of interstate and foreign commerce. With respect to a possible infringement upon

Second Amendment rights, the author concludes: "The contention that the Act infringes upon this right [to keep and bear arms] has been answered about fifty years ago when it was held that 'to regulate a conceded right is not necessarily to infringe the same.' It would be absurd to hold that provisions requiring a license infringe the right to keep arms."

Ashbrook, John M. **"Against Comprehensive Gun Control."** *Current History* 71, no. 418 (July/August 1976).

At the time this article was written, Ashbrook was a Republican representative to the U.S. Congress from Ohio. It is his response to a renewed effort to pass firearms legislation. Gun control, he says, is viewed as crime control—a concept with which he disagrees. He briefly cites the historical context of the rights contained in the Second Amendment and speaks of the limited effects of gun legislation in the past. He also reasserts that depriving law-abiding citizens of guns will not reduce crime in America. The causes of crime must be examined and treated; depriving law-abiding citizens of their firearms will not solve the problem.

Barrett, Sidney R., Jr. **"The Right To Bear Arms and Handgun Prohibition: A Fundamental Rights Analysis."** *North Carolina Central Law Journal* 14 (1983).

Arguing that the Second Amendment "provides a deceptively clear guarantee," Barrett suggests that banning handgun ownership could clear the "rational basis" inspection under due process. Even if the Supreme Court gave a "fundamental right status" to the provisions of the Second Amendment, it would still be rational for legislatures to pass laws prohibiting handguns. Barrett states: "An analogy may be drawn between the second and first amendments, in that both may be said to contain a 'core content' of a political nature which justifies a lesser degree of protection to the exercise of that right outside of that scope. Thus, just as it is possible to regulate certain categories of speech due to their minimal contribution to the political process and their adverse effects on society, so may it be possible to regulate certain categories of weapons through the same considerations." Libertarianism might thusly be circumscribed to protect society from criminal use of firearms, especially those that might be easily concealed.

Batey, Robert. **"Techniques of Strict Construction: The Supreme Court and the Gun Control Act of 1968."** *American Journal of Criminal Law* 13 (Winter 1986).

This article, part of a debate with Professor John Calvin Jeffries, Jr., discusses the concept and applications of strict construction. It argues that courts should reject prosecution's interpretation of a criminal statute if it is not clear that the statute should be construed narrowly. Thus, the author argues for a reasonable doubt construction rather than a strict construction. The author examines samples from Supreme Court cases that come under provisions of the Gun Control Act of 1968, and presents four ways to construe a case for reasonable doubt: from "the language of the statute, from previous interpretation, from the legislative context . . . , and from proximity to an issue of constitutional law."

Benenson, Mark K. **"A Controlled Look at Gun Controls."** New *York Law Forum* 14 (1968).

Benenson examines the extent of gun ownership and the relationship of crime to that ownership and then looks at anti-gun arguments related to these figures. He suggests that "talking about the percentage of gun murders is essentially irrelevant; the core question is the homicide rate." Moreover, he states, "it is very difficult for a person unfamiliar with crime and firearms to understand how fewer guns cannot be followed, if not by less crime, at least by fewer homicides." He then discusses "cost effectiveness and gun controls" and the attitudes of sportsmen toward firearms regulations. He speculates about the possibility of constructing a "workable gun law—if any." He concludes: ". . . groups and legislators favoring strict gun controls have focused their attention on the firearm—the least important of all the congeries of influences that underly the commission of a crime."

Beschle, Donald L. **"Reconsidering the Second Amendment: Constitutional Protection for a Right of Security."** *Hamline Law Review* 9 (February 1986).

This examination of the Second Amendment suggests that firearms were a "means" by which American citizens could provide security for themselves. Individual ownership of weapons was necessary to accomplish this. Thus, the view that the Second Amendment does not apply to the states is justified, and the notion that the Second Amendment limits only federal intervention should be "modified." One must keep in mind that the objective of the Second Amendment is to make certain that American citizens are protected from specific threats, and one must keep in mind the "scope and effect" of the amendment's provisions so that it is not "belittled."

Bogus, Carl T. **"Pistols, Politics, and Products Liability."** *University of Cincinnati Law Review* 59 (Spring 1991).

This article discusses handguns and product liability, citing the "early doctrine" and the "risk-utility test" as applied to handguns. The article discusses practices in seven states, and then searches for explanations in applying—or not applying—product liability to handgun misuse and unsafe products. The author concludes as follows: "It is not possible to reach a definitive conclusion about whether the courts want to avoid imposing strict liability on handguns because they are afraid of provoking gun enthusiasts and prompting greater tort reform efforts. At this juncture, one can only suspect that the two may be related and hope that further research will throw more light on the subject. But, as a review of the cases has shown, the courts are going to extraordinary lengths to exempt handguns from the law of products liability."

———. **"Race, Riots, and Guns."** *Southern California Law Review* 66 (May 1993).

This article poses a challenge to the Cottrol-Diamond article, which argues that gun control has often been used to suppress minorities. Bogus suggests, instead, that African Americans have been the victims of guns and of the concept of the right to bear arms. The article examines the racial significance of the development of the Second Amendment and suggests that it might have been contrived in part as a means to control slaves. Bogus concludes by examining "the complex interactions among guns, race, riots, and urban history."

Bordenet, Bernard J. **"The Right To Possess Arms: The Intent of the Framers of the Second Amendment."** *UWLA Law Review* 21, no. 7 (1990).

The author argues that "the Constitution and Bill of Rights contain no superfluous language." Moreover, says the author, "The claim that the purpose of the Second Amendment was to guarantee the right of the states to maintain armed militia [that is, the right to bear arms belongs only to the militia itself], is not only contrary to historical fact, but demonstrates flawed reasoning or theory." The author contends that the purpose of the Second Amendment was to prevent creation of standing armies by providing the people with the right to keep and bear arms. This meant the right was not "collective," but "individual." "The only proper and logical approach is to interpret the Constitution as its drafters and adopters intended. The Constitution contains provisions for amending it. Amendment through judicial fiat is both unconstitutional and illegal."

Brabner-Smith, John. **"Firearm Regulation."** *Law and Contemporary Problems* 1, no. 4 (October 1934).

The author traces various forms of firearm regulations, including the carrying of weapons, their sale or disposal, licensing requirements, and penalties for their use and possession by criminals. He also touches upon gun laws in Britain and in Continental Europe, and the proposed Uniform Firearms Act in the United States. The Uniform Machine Gun Act is treated briefly, and the National Firearms Act is discussed. He also discusses the regulation of firearms and the provisions of the Second Amendment, taking the collective rights position on the subject. He discusses types of valid weapons legislation and then draws five conclusions based on information presented in his article.

Brands, Scot A. **"Casenotes: Tort Law—Strict Liability—Saturday Night Special Manufacturer Strictly Liable for Criminally Inflicted Injuries. *Kelley v. R.G. Industries*, 304 Md. 124, 497 A.2d 1143 (1985)."** *Cumberland Law Review* 16 (1985–1986).

This is another article discussing the much-reviewed *Kelley* case. The author states: "Although the *Kelley* court's holding constituted a modification of the common law, the public policy dictating the change was well justified. Since Saturday Night Specials serve no legitimate purpose, and since their criminal use is forseeable [sic], judicial removal of such weapons from the market was justified. . . . If *Kelley* does nothing more than force Saturday Night Special manufacturers to improve the gun in some way so that it will no longer be ideal for criminal use, the decision will have had a positive effect on society."

Breen, Victor, Virgil Garrett, William Kandt, and Frank Shinkle. **"Federal Revenue as a Limitation on State Police Power and the Right To Bear Arms—Purpose of Legislation as Affecting Its Validity."** *Journal of the Kansas Bar Association* 9 (November 1940).

This article deals with the extent to which Congress, through its power to tax, can regulate or suppress the item being taxed. The issue had to do with an indictment brought in the District Court of the Western District of Arkansas that charged Jack Miller and Frank Layton with unlawfully transporting a double-barreled shotgun with a barrel less than 18 inches long between Claremore, Oklahoma, and Siloam Springs, Arkansas. The gun was unregistered, and Miller and Layton did not procure a stamp-affixed written order as required under the National Firearms Act. The defendants alleged that the National Firearms Act is not a revenue law but an attempt to usurp the police power, is unconstitutional as such, and infringes on the right of the Second Amendment to keep and bear arms. Both charges were dismissed in *Miller v. U.S.* The authors conclude, "The Court . . . in the present case is manifestly justified when it states that The National Firearms Act cannot be held to violate the Second Amendment in absence of the showing of any reasonable relationship between such weapons and a well regulated militia. A sawed-off shotgun is not such a weapon."

Brown, Joe B. **"Firearms Legislation."** *Vanderbuilt Law Review* 18 (1965).

In this extensive note, the author discusses the gamut of firearms regulation in existence at the time it was written. He discusses the status of federal and state regulation, and the constitutional limitations on firearms regulation placed in the federal and state constitutions. The need for regulation of firearms is presented, with appropriate discussion of the individual interest in firearms, classifying firearms, and some criteria for legislation that might bridge the gap between those who feel that none is required to those who feel that only police officers should have guns. The Dodd and other proposed bills are discussed, and then proposed model state and federal statutes are presented as appendices. The author states that the model "is designed to prohibit harmful and illegal uses of firearms, not to prohibit the possession and reasonable use of firearms."

Brown, Tyler P. **"Ammunition for Victims of Saturday Night Specials: Manufacturer Liability under *Kelley v. R.G. Industries, Inc.*"** *Washington and Lee Law Review* 43 (Fall 1986).

This is another article on the *Kelley* case. It concludes that even though the court provided weak evidence to show that Saturday Night Specials have been mainly used in crime, ". . . courts properly can charge the manufacturers and distributors with knowledge of the injuries inflicted with their products. Unless and until the state legislatures or Congress decides to adopt legislation that addresses the problem posed by cheap, concealable handguns, by banning the sale of Saturday Night Specials or otherwise, American courts properly should consider holding Saturday Night Special manufacturers strictly liable for injuries resulting from products that the manufacturers design and market principally for criminal use."

Bruce-Briggs, B. **"The Great American Gun War."** *The Public Interest* 45 (Fall 1976).

The author discusses the prevalence of guns in American society and asks why Americans feel that they need firearms in order to protect themselves. He gives some treatment to existing gun laws and to federal gun control measures, and focuses on Saturday Night Specials. He gives attention to what he calls "crackpot schemes" of gun control and the limits of the interdiction process. He treats briefly the Second Amendment, speaks of "phallic narcissism," and points out that there simply are no reputable sources for such an interpretation of gun control. He concludes that "it would be useful . . . if some of the mindless passion . . . could be drained out of the gun-control issue. Gun control is no solution to the crime problem, to the assassination problem, to the terrorist problem."

Caggiano, Nicholas J. **"Handgun Manufacturers' Tort Liability to Victims of Criminal Shootings: A Summary of Recent Developments in the Push for a Judicial Ban of the 'Saturday Night Special.'"** *Villanova Law Review* 31 (September 1986).

This note summarizes recent cases on the liability of handgun manufacturers under traditional relief procedures. The first cases discussed concern "the rejection of the 'ultrahazardous activity' doctrine." Following that, the author presents "cases demonstrating the rejection of products liability theories." The last case presented is the *Kelley* case, which established a unique cause of action. The author states that "the decisions leading to *Kelley* properly recognized that the appropriate forum in which to balance the risks against the benefits of small handguns is the legislature" and that "the proper focus in a case such as *Kelley* should be on the *conduct* of the gun manufacturers, rather than on the physical characteristics of its *product*."

Callaghan, Michael O. **"State v. Buckner and the Right To Keep and Bear Arms in West Virginia."** *West Virginia Law Review* 91 (Winter 1988–1989).

In the words of the author: "*State v. Buckner* presented the West Virginia Supreme Court of Appeals the opportunity to assess the constitutionality of statutory provisions against carrying a dangerous or deadly weapon and to assess the extent to which the Legislature may regulate the keeping and bearing of arms in light of the 'Right to Keep and Bear Arms Amendment.'" The court held that the provisions at issue were unconstitutional but recognized that the right to keep and bear arms is not absolute."

Callahan, Charles M., and Frederick P. Rivara. **"Urban High School Youth and Handguns: A School-Based Survey."** *Journal of the American Medical Association* 267, no. 22 (10 June 1992).

The objective of this study was to determine the degree of ownership of handguns among high school students and to examine such relationships as "socioeconomic status, ethnicity, and deviant behaviors." Conducted in Seattle, Washington, the study deals with half "of the school district's 11th grade students." To quote from the summary: "Thirty-four percent of the students reported easy access to handguns . . . and 6.4% reported owning a handgun." Among other findings was that "handgun ownership was more common among students who reported deviant behaviors." They find, however, that such ownership "is not limited to high-risk groups."

Cantrell, Charles L. **"The Right To Bear Arms: A Reply."** *Wisconsin Bar Bulletin* 53 (October 1980).

This is a reply to an article by Robert L. Elliott, who, in the *Wisconsin Bar Bulletin*, took a collectivist view of the meaning of the Second Amendment. Cantrell refutes the Elliott argument, drawing on pre-Revolutionary historical events, discussing the "unorganized militia," and asserting that the courts have generally failed to confront the provisions of the Second Amendment head-on. He argues that the right has roots in the common law recognized by the framers of the Constitution and that Hamilton and Madison, among others, specifically intended that the Second Amendment would provide an individual right to keep and bear arms."

Caplan, David I. **"Restoring the Balance: The Second Amendment Revisited."** *Fordham Law Journal* 5 (1976).

Examining the background of the right to keep and bear arms from the perspective of the common law and developments in the American colonies, Caplan presents a legislative history of the Second Amendment and then examines the *Miller* case and other judicial decisions relevant to the amendment. He also treats the relevance of the Ninth Amendment to the right to keep and bear arms and then presents what he terms some "modern Second Amendment issues." He concludes by stating that the right to keep and bear arms does not imply wanton insurrection or secession from the contract made with the drawing of the Constitution. "What it does mean is that people are allowed by government to retain the ability to obtain, keep, and practice with arms, in order that they may always be in a position to exercise their right of self-preservation and defense, as well as to join and serve effectively in the appropriate militia to restore the Constitution, should the need ever arise."

————. **"Handgun Control: Constitutional or Unconstitutional? A Reply to Mayor Jackson."** *North Carolina Central Law Journal* 10 (1979).

In this article, the author criticizes comments concerning handgun control made by Mayor Maynard H. Jackson of Atlanta, Georgia. Mayor Jackson's article appeared in an earlier issue of the same law journal. Caplan remarks that Jackson's comments were "at best questionable," stating that "the limitation of the right of the people to keep arms solely for the organized militia was far from the minds of the Framers of the second amendment, simply because at the time of its framing in 1789, there was no such organized militia." He says that militias depend for their existence on statutes and that statutes "cannot create or destroy constitutional rights."

He adds, "If the National Guard really is the well regulated militia of the second amendment, then it would follow that every member of the Guard would have the constitutional right to keep his National Guard arms at home, and that he could own his National Guard arms."

————. **"Decisions Sound Death Knell for 'Collective Right' Theory."** *Gun Week* 24 (October 1980).
In this brief article, Caplan discusses cases from Indiana and Oregon that held, respectively, that a license to carry a pistol could not be denied merely because of the lack of a "proper reason" to have one, nor could ownership or possession of blackjacks and billy clubs be denied. In both instances, the constitutions of the states were cited as the underpinning rationale. Both Oregon and Indiana have constitutional provisions protecting the right to keep and bear arms. In the case of Indiana, the possible flouting of "administrative privilege" was also cited. According to Caplan, "The Oregon case is undoubtedly the most important 20th century case thus far explaining the origins, history, and current meaning of the right to keep arms under State constitutional provisions. . . ." He also draws an analogy with the Second Amendment.

————. **"The Right of the Individual To Bear Arms: A Recent Judicial Trend."** *Detroit College of Law Review* 1982, no. 4 (1982).

Pointing out that the "collective" interpretation of the right to bear arms had its origins in the *Salina v. Blaksley* decision in Kansas in 1905, Caplan states that this decision and this view were rejected in the Indiana *Schubert v. DeBard* and Oregon *State v. Kessler* decisions some 75 years later. Inasmuch as these latter decisions were consistent with the common law tradition and the historical development of the right to keep and bear arms, these two more recent cases may signal a "trend in favor of the right of the individual citizen to keep and carry arms, especially in those states that have constitutional provisions for the right to bear arms." These decisions will have an effect, he argues, on the interpretation of the Second Amendment.

Centerwall, Brandon S. **"Homicide and the Prevalence of Handguns: Canada and the United States, 1976 to 1980."** *American Journal of Epidemiology* 134, no. 11 (1 December 1991).

The article states that in the 1970s Canadians had one-tenth as many handguns per capita as Americans. In an effort to determine whether this difference in gun possession had an effect on the criminal homicide rate, the total mean criminal homicide rates of certain provinces of Canada were compared with the homicide rates of adjacent American states. There were no "consistent differences," and criminal homicide rates were sometimes higher in Canada's provinces and sometimes higher in the states with which they were compared. The author concludes: "Major differences in the prevalence of handguns have not resulted in differing total criminal homicide rates in Canadian provinces and adjoining U.S. states. The similar rates of criminal homicide are primarily attributable to underlying similar rates of aggravated assault." Canadians use other means to assault or to kill. Thus, "as regards homicide rates, it can be inferred that major efforts to reduce handgun prevalence in the United States would be of doubtful utility, even if successful."

Cottrol, Robert J., and Raymond T. Diamond. **"The Second Amendment: Toward an Afro-Americanist Reconsideration."** *Georgetown Law Journal* 80 (1991).

This analysis examines issues of the Second Amendment from the perspective of African Americans and takes the position that such issues should be examined in terms of how they have affected subcultures of American society, African Americans in particular, not just society as a whole. The analysis hinges on the notion that efforts have been made throughout American history to keep firearms and other weapons out of the hands of groups that have been defined as "socially undesirable"—blacks, Native Americans, Italians, labor union members, and so on. The authors conclude: "The history of blacks, firearms regulations, and the right to bear arms should cause us to ask new questions regarding the Second Amendment. . . ." The authors speculate that "a re-examination of this history can lead us to a modern realization of what the framers of the Second Amendment understood: that it is unwise to place the means of protection totally in the hands of the state, and that self-defense is also a civil right."

Council on Scientific Affairs, American Medical Association. **"Assault Weapons as a Public Health Hazard in the United States."** *Journal of the American Medical Association* 267, no. 22 (10 June 1992).

This article discusses assault weapons: their definition, the prevalence of their possession and use in crime, the incidence of death and injury as a result of their use, public opinion about them, their regulation, and barriers to legislation regarding them. The concluding sentence of the article states that "the AMA (American Medical Association) will continue to monitor the impact of assault weapons on public health and to support appropriate legislation to reduce this impact and save lives and scarce health care dollars."

Crago, Derrick D. **"The Problem of Counting to Three under the Armed Career Criminal Act."** *Case Western Reserve Law Review* 41 (1991).

The article abstract states: "The Armed Career Criminal Act [ACCA] provides sentence enhancement for those who have been convicted of three felonies. Confusion has arisen as to the sequence in which these convictions must take place in relation to the acts that gave rise to the convictions. The author proposes that each of the three previous convictions be required to precede the commission of the next offense." The author discusses the background of the act, attempts by Congress to clarify the act (focusing especially on *United States v. Balasckak,* which examined the three previous convictions requirement), and "the criminal episodes approach v. the intervening convictions approach," and then concludes that until Congress clearly defines its intent "courts should apply the intervening convictions approach."

Cress, Lawrence D. **"An Armed Community: The Origins and Meaning of the Right To Bear Arms."** *Journal of American History* 71 (1984).

Arguing that the Second Amendment does not guarantee the individual right to keep and bear arms—and that it was never intended to do so—Cress suggests that it referred to only a "citizenry ably drilled in arms." That is, the amendment referred to a fundamental principle of republicanism that involved reliance on a militia that could rise up against a tyrannical government, standing army, or a mob of persons bent on disrupting public order. Since the Constitution's inception, Cress argues, the courts have "seldom wavered" from Joseph Story, who, in his commentaries on the Constitution, had stated, "How it is practicable to keep the people duly armed without organization, it is difficult to see."

Dimos, James. **" 'Saturday Night Special' Manufacturers and Marketers Strictly Liable for Misuse of Their Products."** *Washington University Journal of Urban and Contemporary Law.* 32 (Summer 1987).

This article examines the Maryland case of *Kelley v. R.G. Industries,* in which the Maryland Court of Appeals decided that manufacturers and marketers of so-called Saturday Night Specials could be held liable to persons injured or killed by the criminal use of their products. Citing the "abnormally dangerous activity" theory together with the "abnormally dangerous product" argument (together with the consumer expectation test and the risk utility test), the author points out that "while rejecting strict liability for all handgun manufacturers and marketers in general, the *Kelley* court determined that an exception to the general public policy of controlled possession exists for the 'Saturday Night Special.'"

Dowlet, Robert. **"The Right to Arms: Does the Constitution or the Predilection of Judges Reign?"** *Oklahoma Law Review* 36 (Winter 1983).

Engaging in a largely historical analysis, Dowlet concludes that "the right to arms may not be undercut simply because some persons at the moment consider it a troublesome right." The author asserts that the Second Amendment should be made applicable to the states by incorporation through the Fourteenth Amendment, as has been done in the case of many other of the amendments, and that the rights under the Second Amendment have always existed, that they are part of the natural rights of humans to protect themselves and reach deep into the historical past. Dowlet proposes that courts should declare arms statutes unconstitutional if they violate the basic rights of the people as guaranteed, or if such laws infringe upon the people's right to bear arms for lawful purposes. He contends that judges appear to have abandoned their obligation to interpret the Constitution as it was intended and have permitted their own personal feelings—and those of a number of interest groups—to govern the decision process, causing the courts to appear to be increasingly political institutions.

Elliott, Robert L. **"The Right To Keep and Bear Arms."** *Wisconsin Bar Bulletin* 53 (May 1980).

Traversing his interpretation of the historical evolution of the Second Amendment and citing relevant Supreme Court cases, particularly the *Dennis* case, as constituting the "death knell" of the individualist interpretation of the amendment, Elliott concludes that "the Second Amendment was never intended by the framers of the Constitution to reserve to each individual the right to carry and use a weapon for his own purposes. The evolution of the Second Amendment in the executive and judicial branches of this government borne of revolution has clearly shown that the right to keep and bear arms was reserved to the 'people' where the 'people' are the individual states vis-à-vis the federal government."

Emery, Lucilius A. **"The Constitutional Right To Keep and Bear Arms."** *Harvard Law Review* 28 (1914–1915).

This early article takes an essentially collective view of the right to keep and bear arms. Emery argues that the rights guaranteed in the Second Amendment were not common law rights, and that those rights should be construed in the context of an opposition on the part of the entire people of the state to standing armies. The language used, he asserts, indicates more a military than a personal right. Thus, it does not include the keeping and bearing of weapons not useable in civilized warfare, and can be used to exclude from possessing weapons people who, among others, are incompetent, underage, or have bad habits. The author concludes, "I venture the opinion that, without violence to the constitutional guaranty of the right of the people to bear arms, the carrying of weapons by individuals may be regulated, restricted, and even prohibited according as conditions and circumstances may make it necessary for the protection of the people."

F. J. K. **"Restrictions on the Right To Bear Arms: State and Federal Firearms Legislation."** *University of Pennsylvania Law Review* 98 (1950).

This discussion of firearms legislation emphasizes pistols and revolvers, the types of weapons that are usually the objects of regulation. The author points out that every state recognizes that the regulation of firearms is constitutional to some extent, and that such regulations have become increasingly restrictive. The laws usually concern areas such as possession, carrying, purchase, sale, and "pledging" (that is, putting them up as security for a loan, for example) of firearms. The author points out that uniformity in the law may be forced by the federal government, and that it should include six points that are outlined in the conclusion of the article. The author states, "In general national welfare will be promoted by the encouragement of citizen training programs in the use of firearms, following the example of such organizations as the National Rifle Association, to develop a military asset, to help private persons to protect themselves against robbery and burglary, and to provide healthy recreation."

Feder, Donald. **"A Libertarian Looks at Gun Control."** *Reason* (March 1976).

The writer, neither a hunter nor a gun collector, has for years spoken out against firearms control. He is opposed to gun control from a purely libertarian point of view—he opposes gun control for the same reasons that he opposes such things as "censorship, antimarijuana legislation, or any other victimless crime laws. Government should protect individuals from the initiation of force." What a person otherwise does with his or her life is of no concern to government; laws that attempt to protect people from themselves interfere with their freedom and liberty. "Gun control . . . is far more dangerous than other forms of prohibition. It is a direct, and rather substantial, assault on the right to life itself. . . . Gun control . . . will leave the peaceable individual totally vulnerable to the criminal element."

Feller, Peter Buck, and Karl L. Gotting. **"The Second Amendment: A Second Look."** *Northwestern University Law Review* 61, no. 4 (1966).

The authors discuss the English Bill of Rights, the grievances of the U.S. colonists against the Crown, state bills of rights guaranteeing the right to keep and bear arms, the debates at the constitutional convention, the ratifying conventions in the states, and the development of the federal Bill of Rights. State and federal court decisions are examined. The authors conclude that the historic and contemporary periods are no longer comparable: "Since the emergence of the United States as a world leader and prime military power, the role of the federal government in maintaining a gigantic national defense capability has made that power overwhelming vis-à-vis the states. . . . The astounding march of technology has produced a spectrum of war weapons of immense destructive power. Under these circumstances the idea of a possible power struggle between state and federal government to insure state sovereignty is somewhat empty and absurd. It becomes apparent, then, that the ideal of the supremacy of state militia over federal military power is a fading echo. The second amendment as the embodiment of that ideal is therefore obsolete."

Fields, Samuel. **"Handgun Prohibition and Social Necessity."** *Saint Louis University Law Journal* 23, no. 1 (1979).

This is a reply to an article by Don B. Kates, Jr., that appeared in an earlier issue of the journal. Fields takes the position that the handgun has simply become "a menace to our society." The cost-benefit ratio "is overwhelmingly against a system that allows easy access to handguns." After critically analyzing many of the studies cited by Kates and addressing the issue of existing laws on the subject, Fields argues that the public wants severe handgun control. "Will effective federal handgun control come about? Those who believe otherwise are fighting the future and misreading the forces of history."

Fletcher, John G. **"The Corresponding Duty to the Right of Bearing Arms."** *The Florida Bar Journal* 39, no. 3 (March 1965).

Tracing the history of the right to keep and bear arms, Fletcher uses the example of a member of the Teutonic tribe, whose right to keep and bear arms "was based on his *duty* to defend the tribe and its chieftain." The same, he argues, was true in Saxon England and during the feudal period. The Assize of Arms of 1181 codified the principle, and required freemen to equip themselves with mail and weapons. Shifting to a discussion of the United States, Fletcher concludes: "The founders were aware of the unique Federation created and the interwoven authorities. The Federal government was the only body allowed to raise Troops— a standing army. To counter-balance this, the states were granted the right to allow their citizens to arm to avoid tyranny by Federal Troops. Thus the Second Amendment is a right granted to the States, not to the individuals of those states."

Forrester, David J. *"Halberstam v. Welch:* Economic Justice as a Means of Handgun Control?*"* *The American Journal of Trial Advocacy* 7 (1984).

This article deals with product liability and the redefinition of handguns as "abnormally dangerous instrumentalities." This area of product liability has become significantly more important in the last several years, especially with respect to an approach aimed at controlling the use and possession of handguns. This article suggests that the relative failure of handgun control on the basis of manufacturer liability can now be expanded, and therefore become more effective, to include "potentially all dangerous objects which are subject to abuse or misuse on a regular basis" and "aiding and abetting." The author suggests that the Halberstalm case, "with its emphasis on aiding-abetting's substantial assistance standard rather than conspiracy, would seem to be an excellent vehicle for imposing liability upon firearms manufacturers for the criminal misuse of their products."

Fingerhut, Lois A., Deborah D. Ingram, and Jacob J. Feldman. **"Firearm Homicide among Black Teenage Males in Metropolitan Counties."** *Journal of the American Medical Association* 267, no. 22 (10 June 1992).

The objective of this article was "to identify U.S. counties (1) that had either significantly high or significantly low firearm homicide rates among black males 15 through 19 years of age in 1983 through 1985 and in 1987 through 1989, and/or (2) that experienced a significant increase in the firearm homicide rate between 1983 through 1985 and 1987 through 1989." The counties of "Los Angeles, California; Wayne, Michigan; Kings, New York; St Louis City, Missouri; and Baltimore City, Maryland" were found to be "significantly high" in homicide rates during both time periods. The authors conclude that keeping watch over the rate of homicides in counties underlies the creation of programs aimed at preventing violence, and that more knowledge is required on the issue of nonfatal injuries by firearms.

Foster, Sarah E. **"Guns and Property."** *The Free Market* (Ludwig Von Mises Institute) 10, no. 7 (July 1992).

In this article, Sarah Foster describes how looters in the Los Angeles riots that occurred after the Rodney King trial were in fact kept at bay by armed citizens. Quoting a Neighborhood Watch leader, the article states, "You know, . . . I've supported every kind of anti-gun law that's come along. I thought those guys in my neighborhood with guns were nuts. But it was they and their guns that saved us." The historic Mann's Chinese Theatre and other structures were saved by the same means. Since then, the same individual stated, "Gun sales are way up."

Gardiner, Richard E. **"To Preserve Liberty—A Look at the Right To Keep and Bear Arms."** *Northern Kentucky Law Review* 10, no. 1 (1981).

Gardiner lays out the historical development of the right to keep and bear arms in the context of the intention of the Second Amendment's authors. He also critically analyzes the most important cases that have been decided in part on the basis of the Second Amendment. He emphasizes that, in any construction of the Constitution, it is of great significance that the values and mores of its writers and of those responsible for its ratification receive proper emphasis. After an in-depth analysis, the author concludes that the right to keep and bear arms "is indeed a fundamental individual right which no amount of historical revisionism can deny."

Garrigues, Gary. *"United States v. Martinez-Jimenez:* **Use a Toy Gun, Go to Prison."** *Golden Gate University Law Review,* 20 (Spring 1990).

The introduction to this article states: "In . . . [this case], the Ninth Circuit affirmed a conviction for armed bank robbery during which the defendant had displayed a toy gun." The court held that the toy gun was a "dangerous weapon" within the meaning of 18 U.S.C. Section 2113(d). That section provides an enhanced penalty for use of a dangerous weapon during a bank robbery. This decision continues a trend toward a broader interpretation of that section.

Geisel, Martin, Richard Roll, and R. Stanton Wettick, Jr. **"The Effectiveness of State and Local Regulation of Handguns: A Statistical Analysis."** *Duke Law Journal* (1969).

In this study the authors use data analysis to determine the effectiveness of state and local laws dealing with handguns. Reviewing gun control legislation—federal, state, and local—the authors present eight different categories of gun control legislation used for analysis. They describe in detail the techniques of data analysis they used, and then quantify gun control legislation. The results of the study are presented in terms of homicide, suicide, accidental deaths, aggravated assault, and robbery. The authors conclude with several observations and cite the limitations inherent in their analysis. They suggest that the results of their work serve to bring under suspicion the work of Alan Krug, whose work demonstrated that there is no relationship between the number of guns available and the actual crime rate. They suggest that many lives could probably be saved if states intensified their efforts on weapons control.

Gest, Ted. **"Firearms Follies: How the News Media Cover Gun Control."** *Media Studies Journal* (Winter 1992).

This article discusses the consistent display of media bias and carelessness in the coverage of news related to guns in American society. It asserts that, in general, the media are prejudicial in their coverage of the National Rifle Association, skeptical of law-abiding citizens who own guns, largely ignorant of the origins and meaning of the Second Amendment, and biased in their coverage of sports involving guns of various types. Claiming that the media are guilty of "inexcusable factual errors and general ignorance . . . [taking] editorial stands in news columns, . . . bias, . . . omitting crucial information, . . . questionable news judgment, . . . interest group tactics, . . . [and] personality journalism," Gest suggests that the media impact public policymaking, although to what extent is difficult to ascertain precisely, and that the media should focus on accuracy and objectivity.

Getchell, Richard. **"Carrying Concealed Weapons in Self-Defense: Florida Adopts Uniform Regulations for the Issuance of Concealed Weapons Permits."** *Florida State University Law Review* 15 (Winter 1987).

The Constitution of the State of Florida states that citizens have the right to keep and bear arms for self-defense and in defense of the state, and that such right "shall not be infringed," providing that "the manner of bearing arms may be regulated by law," however. In 1987, the state legislature adopted two laws that regulated the carrying of concealed weapons, thus preempting county and local jurisdictions from passing laws and creating statewide uniformity on the issue. Citizens of Florida may obtain permits to carry concealed weapons for self-defense under the new state provisions. The author provides a survey of other state laws on the subject, presents a brief history of relevant Florida law, and suggests how the Florida legislature might improve existing law in future considerations of the subject.

Gottlieb, Alan M. **"Gun Ownership: A Constitutional Right."** *Northern Kentucky Law Review* 10, no. 1 (1982).

The author states, "The evidence for the individual right interpretation is so overwhelming that the existence of an argument (by studiously ignoring that evidence) degrades the second amendment into a meaningless 'collective right' that is inexplicable." The evidence to which he refers includes the praise given by the framers to the individual ownership of firearms, their admiration for philosophers who consistently supported an individual right to oppose tyranny, the idea that the militia was to be made up of all able-bodied men who supplied their own arms, the fact that the English Bill of Rights and the common law guaranteed an individual right to arms, and the language used by the framers.

Grundeman, Arnold. **"Constitutional Limitations on Federal Firearms Control."** *Wasburn Law Journal* 8 (Winter 1969).

This note explores the constitutional issues raised by efforts to impose federal legislation on firearms. It examines the Tenth Amendment, the commerce clause, the power to tax, the impact of the Fifth Amendment, and the Second Amendment. Grundeman concludes: "The federal government has full power, under the Constitution, to control firearms in the United States. Recent court decisions have so broadened the taxing power and the powers under the commerce clause that there remains only for the Congress to find that the sale and possession of firearms affect interstate commerce or should be taxed and they may take whatever steps in regulation they desire."

Halbrook, Stephen P. **"The Jurisprudence of the Second and Fourteenth Amendments."** *George Mason University Law Review* 4 (1981).

In this lengthy article, Halbrook summarizes federal and state gun control laws in the context of the Constitution, and discusses the origins of the Second Amendment and its antebellum judicial interpretation, along with the intention of the writers of the Fourteenth Amendment. He discusses the relevant rulings of the Supreme Court and the reaction of state courts, and focuses on *United States v. Miller* as the point of departure for a discussion of federal and state court cases since that time. The final section of his article deals with "judicial policy and logic and the future of the right to keep and bear arms." Using the *Moore* and *Lewis* cases, which establish the right to keep and bear arms as a "specific guarantee" and a "fundamental" right, respectively, and the *Bivens* case, which refers to the right to recover against a federal agent who has engaged in a "constitutional violation," Halbrook suggests that this would include a violation of the Second Amendment as well.

————. **"To Keep and Bear Their Private Arms: The Adoption of the Second Amendment, 1787–1791."** *Northern Kentucky Law Review* 10, no. 1 (1982).

Halbrook traces the background of the fears of the framers of the Constitution with respect to the possible subjugation of the people because they might be unarmed or disarmed, and discusses this initially in a Federalist-Antifederalist context. Through a discussion of the arguments that raged over the ratification of the Constitution—including the insistence of delegates attending state ratification conventions that a right-to-bear arms provision be included, Madison's proposed amendments, and the ultimate adoption of the Second Amendment—Halbrook demonstrates that it was clear the framers who adopted the Constitution and those who voted both to submit the amendments and to approve them had an individual right in mind. "Artful misconstruction" of the Second Amendment might nevertheless be used to destroy the individual rights—including the right that every man be armed—intended by the writers of the document.

————. **"The Second Amendment as a Phenomenon of Classical Political Philosophy."** In *Firearms and Violence: Issues of Public Policy,* edited by Don B. Kates, Jr. San Francisco: Pacific Institute for Public Policy Research and Ballinger Publishing Company, 1984.

This is an examination of the origins of the Second Amendment in terms of classical political philosophy. The author concludes: "The two categorical imperatives of the Second Amendment— that a militia of the body of the people is necessary to guarantee a free state, and that all of the people have a right to keep and bear arms—were derived from the classical philosophical texts concerning the experiences of ancient Greece and Rome and seventeenth century England." He concludes: "In this sense the people's right to have their own swords was based on the sharpest intellectual swords known to the founding fathers."

————. **"The Right To Bear Arms in the First State Bills of Rights: Pennsylvania, North Carolina, Vermont, and Massachusetts."** *Vermont Law Review* 10 (Fall 1985).

This is an extraordinarily detailed analysis of arms guarantees in the bills of rights of Pennsylvania, North Carolina, Vermont, and Massachusetts. The author suggests that in order to understand the provisions of the federal Bill of Rights, it is necessary to examine and understand the state bills of rights, which were adopted before the federal. Examining judicial precedents; the declarations of rights of each of the states mentioned; the impact of such writers as Thomas Paine; and classical, republican, and contemporary (to the period) writers, the author concludes that "the arms guarantees of the four state bills of rights which preceded the federal second amendment were intended to protect the right to keep and to bear arms individually for self-defense and in groups for militia purposes. . . . The right of the citizen to have personal weapons was deemed fundamental and unquestioned."

———. "The Right of the People or the Power of the State: Bearing Arms, Arming Militias, and the Second Amendment." *Valparaiso Law Review* 26 (1991).

The last paragraph of this article states: "Every term in the Second Amendment's substantive guarantee—which is not negated by its philosophical declaration about a well regulated militia—demands an individual rights interpretation." Such concepts as "right," "people," "keep and bear," and "infringed" are applicable only to individuals, not to states. Citing historical evidence and the statements of contemporaries, the author concludes: "The language and historical intent of the Second Amendment mandates recognition of the individual right to keep and bear firearms and other personal weapons."

———. "What the Framers Intended: A Linguistic Analysis of the Right To 'Bear Arms.' " *Law and Contemporary Problems* 49, no. 1 (Winter 1986).

In this article, Halbrook attempts to answer the following questions: "Did the framers of the second amendment (as well as those of the fourteenth) intend constitutional protection of the right to 'bear' arms to encompass the private carrying of arms for self-defense? What 'arms' are protected under that guarantee? May licenses and registration be required for exercise of a constitutional right per se?" Through a careful analysis of the manner in which words were defined at the time of the writing of the Second Amendment (an analysis that is carried on in substantially greater detail in his book, *That Every Man Be Armed: The Evolution of a Constitutional Right,* 1984, annotated infra) and through the use of logical syllogism, the author concludes: "The framers of the second and fourteenth amendments intended to guarantee an individual right to carry firearms and other common hand-carried arms. It is inconceivable that they would have tolerated the suggestion that a free person has no right to bear arms without the permission of a state authority, much less the federal government, or that a person could be imprisoned for doing so. As the Founding Fathers realized, every right has its costs, but the alternatives are often more costly."

————. **"Firearms, the Fourth Amendment, and Air Carrier Security."** *Journal of Air Law and Commerce* 52 (Spring 1987).

In this detailed and lengthy article, the author points out that every day thousands of people legally transport firearms on air carriers in their checked luggage. This type of firearms transportation is a common part of daily commerce. Although the issues concerning such transport of weapons have been discussed only in terms of wrongful conduct, this article examines security programs in airports and the rights of individuals under the Fourth Amendment with respect to the transportation of firearms. The author provides an overview of air transportation of firearms and legislative histories of statutes prohibiting boarding an aircraft with a concealed weapon. Baggage screening and the relevance of the Fourth Amendment is discussed, as are Federal Aviation Administration regulations that pertain to baggage screening. Judicial construction of congressional legislation is examined, as are provisions related to air carrier transportation of firearms under the Gun Control Act of 1968. The article concludes with a look at whether the Fourth Amendment can survive future technologies in the development of firearms manufacture and airport screening procedures. The article is one of the definitive pieces on the subject.

Hardy, David T. **"Firearms Ownership and Regulation: Tackling an Old Problem with Renewed Vigor."** *William and Mary Law Review* 20, no. 2 (Winter 1978).

Hardy examines viewpoints on gun ownership, considering public opinion surveys, the Crime Control Research Project (which attempted to measure attitudes of law officers with respect to approaches to gun crimes), the extent to which criminals are armed and their use of weapons, the Police Foundation Report on Firearm Abuse, and firearms laws and enforcement programs. The author concludes that these studies reaffirm widespread gun ownership in the United States, and "that the application of this information to estimate the probable impact of firearm regulations should focus upon two issues: first, an assessment of the probability of evasion of firearm regulations, and, second, a determination of whether certain limited forms of regulation . . . are likely to produce significant results."

————. **"Legal Restriction of Firearm Ownership as an Answer to Violent Crime: What Was the Question?"** *Hamline Law Review* 6, no. 2 (July 1983).

Pointing out that attempts to regulate firearms ownership date back at least to the 1300s, Hardy maintains that "firearm regulation is inherently incapable of controlling criminal violence." He asserts that there is little compliance and enforcement of such laws, there is no true relationship between the ownership of guns and levels of violent crime, such laws have not had any affect on rates of violent crime, and, moreover, the use of handguns by the law-abiding in self defense has actually had beneficial social consequences. In any event, there would be "massive noncompliance" with laws that severely restricted or banned the use and possession of firearms. The best evidence to support this is that statutes attempting to regulate firearms have been as unsuccessful as statutes that once attempted to regulate alcohol.

————. **"Product Liability and Weapons Manufacture."** *Wake Forest Law Review* 20, no. 3 (Fall 1984).

Hardy suggests that few legal issues have been debated as heatedly as this one in the area of civil law. Because of the adversarial nature of the American legal system, attorneys may take their arguments to the "breaking point," even though those who advocate holding manufacturers responsible for misuse of their products rest upon "unsupportable assumptions." He concludes: There is little reason to conclude that handguns pose unreasonable risks *per se.* If the nature of risk is assessed on a consumer expectation test, the risk is clearly not unreasonable; handguns, like other firearms and explosives, behave as expected. If a broader test is employed, handguns are still clearly appreciably less dangerous than accepted products such as automobiles and alcohol."

————. **"The Firearms Owners' Protection Act: A Historical and Legal Perspective."** *Cumberland Law Review* 17 (1986–1987).

This article presents a detailed analysis of the Firearm Owners' Protection Act of 1986 in the context of pre-1986 legislation, notably the National Firearms Act of 1934 and the Federal Firearms Act of 1938, and the Gun Control Act of 1968. The author discusses the impact of the 1986 law on existing firearms statutes, and concludes, among other things, that Congress's "deliberations extensively reflect judgments that repudiated either the Gun Control Act in toto or its administration as a traditional regulatory system."

Hardy, David T., and John Stompoly. **"Of Arms and the Law."** *Chicago-Kent Law Review* 51 (1974).

In this lengthy article, the authors review federal firearms legislation in the context of the Constitution and examine the current status of the Second Amendment, reviewing the issue of whether its provisions point toward an individual or a collective right. Upon examination of the terms *well regulated militia, to keep and bear arms,* and *the people,* the authors conclude that the framers clearly had an individual right in mind, not a collective one. "The accepted interpretations of the second amendment thus turn upon distinctions not intended by the framers and create a grant of power which the framers sought specifically to negate."

Hayes, Stuart R. **"The Right To Bear Arms, A Study in Judicial Misinterpretation."** *William and Mary Law Review* 2 (1960).

The author points out that weapons have been used since the dawn of time for protection and defense. Covering historical ground, he discusses the common law of England and the right to bear arms, and then the American Revolution, the nation under the Articles of Confederation, and, finally, the Constitution. Hayes raises several questions, again in the historical context of the right to keep and bear arms, and suggests that the judicial interpretation has been incorrect. "The United States Supreme Court has admitted there are exceptions to the right to bear arms; and, then, refused to recognize the right itself. Isn't this a recognition of the right?" The author asserts that the framers of the Constitution had no idea that the state and local governments would even attempt to disarm the people. The people, he argues, have the right to bear arms "for their own self-defense and to preserve their forms of government."

Henigan, Dennis A. **"Arms, Anarchy and the Second Amendment."** *Valparaiso University Law Review* 26 (1991).

The general conclusions of this article may be indicated in terms of the first several paragraphs of the article itself. The author states: "An enduring feature of the contemporary debate over gun control is the effort to give the debate a constitutional dimension. Opponents of strict government regulation of private firearms invariably claim that regulation cannot be reconciled with the Second Amendment. . . . Federal and state courts in this century have reached a consensus interpretation of the amendment that permits government at all levels broad power to limit private access to firearms. The nation's strictest gun control laws have been upheld against Second Amendment challenge, including a local ban on private possession of handguns."

Herz, Andrew D. **"Gun Crazy: Constitutional False Consciousness and Dereliction of Dialogic Responsibility."** *Boston University Law Review* vol. 75, no. 1 (January 1995).

The objective of the article can be best summarized by the author himself; it is "about the causes and costs of false consciousness—false consciousness regarding the constitutional concept of the 'right to bear arms.' This is an article about the deceit, misperception, and dereliction of responsibility that have characterized America's dysfunctional gun control debate." The author argues that the individual right to bear arms "for all legal private purposes . . . is untenable." He attacks the "gun lobby" for feeding "an American psyche already rich in its reverence for the false gospel of a broad individual right to bear arms." And he chastises "political leaders, the media, and legal scholars" who "owe the public a special 'dialogic responsibility' " for not fulfilling it.

Hofstadter, Richard. **"America as a Gun Culture."** *American Heritage* 21, no. 6 (October 1970).

In this widely quoted article, the author asserts that "the United States is the only modern industrial nation in which the possession of rifles, shotguns, and handguns is lawfully prevalent among large numbers of its population. . . . Yet it remains, and is apparently determined to remain, the most passive of all the major countries in the matter of gun control." Quickly examining some of the historical evidence, particularly the violence of the 1960s, he asks: "One must wonder how grave a domestic gun catastrophe would have to be in order to persuade us. How far must things go?" The article is lavishly illustrated.

Horowitz, Edward J. **"Reflections on Gun Control: Does the Problem Have Solutions or Do the Solutions Have Problems?"** *Los Angeles Bar Journal* (November 1976).

Horowitz approaches the question by first examining the "problems of guns in our society" and then by examining "the problems with arguments against gun control laws." He then discusses the problems of gun control laws themselves from 13 different perspectives, examines states with strict gun control laws, and concludes that banning guns would not be enforceable any more than prohibition, for example. "Admittedly," he says, "the problem will never be eliminated; nevertheless, in view of the great cost guns impose on society in loss of life, limb and property, we must weigh the consequences of taking some action that would, regrettably, lead to less than ideal results."

Hunt, M. Truman. **"The Individual Right To Bear Arms: An Illusory Public Pacifier?"** *Utah Law Review* 4 (1986).

This article discusses a decision by the Utah Supreme Court that declared that the Second Amendment to the U.S. Constitution referred to a collective rather than an individual right to keep and bear arms. The author concludes, in part, that, even though the Utah constitution contains a provision guaranteeing an individual right to bear arms, the right can be limited by the power of the state legislature to determine which uses of arms are lawful. "In essence state constitutions guaranteeing an individual right to bear arms may be more of a public pacifier than a grant of significant substantive rights."

Jackson, Maynard Holbrook, Jr. **"Handgun Control: Constitutional and Critically Needed."** *North Carolina Central Law Journal* 8 (1977).

This is an emotional appeal for the elimination of handguns—except in very special instances—from American society. This objective, Jackson states, is within the scope of the government. The issue is, how is it to be accomplished? He advocates "a coordinated effort involving all levels of government." State and local governments should play an especially important role in initiating and enforcing handgun control efforts.

Jett, Rick L. **"Do Victims of Unlawful Handgun Violence Have a Remedy against Handgun Manufacturers?: An Overview and Analysis."** *University of Illinois Law Review* 4 (1985).

This note is concerned with the policy implications of permitting suits against the manufacturers of handguns. It is concerned also with whether courts have the ability to decide such cases. The author favors judicial action in this area, but suggests that "the theory of negligent entrustment" might be considered, as well as the traditional "products liability doctrine." Both concepts are found to lack sufficient rationale for purposes of recovery. A third alternative—that "the sale of handguns to the general public is an abnormally dangerous activity which creates strict liability for the manufacturer"—is presented. This alternative is found to provide not only a better rationale for such cases but advances policy objectives as well.

Kane, Jeffrey. **"The Case against Gun Control."** *The Forensics Quarterly* (September 1976).

Kane examines the right to keep and bear arms as a fundamental political freedom, and states that the Second Amendment guarantees against infringements of that individual right. He points out that registration requirements are a violation of the Second Amendment, that undue regulation of firearms violates the right to self-defense, and that there is no hard evidence to support the contention that firearms control reduces violence. Gun controls are fundamentally impracticable—attempts to implement and to enforce them are at best difficult and, ultimately, probably impossible. Laws, however, that deal with the abuse of firearms are valid, according to the author. "One need not contend that there are no restrictions on the bearing of arms in order to contest the position that the right does not exist."

Kaplan, John. **"The Wisdom of Gun Prohibition."** *Annals of the American Academy of Political and Social Science* 455 (May 1981).

Kaplan discusses gun control proposals from a number of perspectives. He speaks to the issue of voluntary compliance with such laws, the costs of prohibition of guns (citing as similar examples drugs and the failure of attempts to prohibit alcohol), and handgun prohibition, then presents what he calls the "vice model," which would prohibit the sale but not the ownership of guns. The article abstract provides a conclusion: "The fact that not everyone will obey a law is a very important determinant of the wisdom of its enactment. As applied to gun prohibition legislation, widespread violation of the law may place upon us unacceptable societal costs of enforcement, which would cast doubt upon the wisdom of enacting what might be thought to be a reasonable policy."

Kates, Don B., Jr. **"Why a Civil Libertarian Opposes Gun Control."** *The Civil Liberties Review* 3, no. 2 (June/July 1976).

The author summarizes his position as follows: "I am frequently asked: how can a civil libertarian oppose gun control? My reply is: how can a civil libertarian trust the military and the police with a monopoly on arms and with the power to determine which civilians may have them? I consider self-defense a human right. . . ." In this article Kates also argues that prohibiting handguns—even partially—would adversely affect personal freedom and stimulate police practices that would be "repugnant" and would greatly increase jail sentences.

———. **"Why Gun Control Won't Work."** *Commonweal* 58, no. 5 (1976).

Citing the immense social and economic costs of attempts to regulate guns, Kates comes to the conclusion that such controls simply will not work in the long run. Banning handguns would only result in the use of other weapons to kill or maim. "Real reduction in criminal violence cannot be accomplished by trying either to take away weapons or to frighten criminals out of using them. It will come only when economic, political, social, and cultural changes greatly reduce our production of people who *want* to misuse guns, knives, agricultural implements, etc. In this case, the long and difficult solution is the only solution, despite the illusory attraction of cosmetic shortcuts."

———. **"Reflections on the Relevancy of Gun Control."** *Criminal Law Bulletin* 13 (April/May 1977).

It is the author's contention that, on the basis of relevant studies, efforts to ban handguns in American society are "irrelevant" to eliminating violence in society. Banning handguns will simply drive those bent on violence toward the use of some other type of weapon. "Violence can be eliminated or reduced only by sweeping changes in the institutions and social and economic relationships, the ideologies and mores, which produce a violence-inclined people."

———. **"Some Remarks on the Prohibition of Handguns."** *St. Louis University Law Journal* 23, no. 1 (1979).

Reviewing existing studies from a critical point of view, Kates suggests that emphasis should be placed on what *effect* gun laws have had on the amount of violence in society. The cost and problems, including the legal and constitutional difficulties that would be involved in attempts to enforce handgun prohibition (especially those coming under the Fourth Amendment), would make such a ban largely unenforceable. Kates concludes by quoting a police officer referring to the Fourth Amendment: "I will never ask for or hope for any law which will give me or any other police officer the right to search and seize with any greater freedom than is already at hand. We should never ask for the elimination of a guaranteed right of the people. There aren't too many left anymore."

————. **"Handgun Prohibition and the Original Meaning of the Second Amendment."** *Michigan Law Review* 82 (November 1983).

This is one of the definitive studies of the right to keep and bear arms, the historical development of the Second Amendment, and the jurisprudence upon which its interpretation has been based. Juxtaposing the collective view of the Second Amendment against that of the individual view of gun ownership, Kates engages in what seems a virtually exhaustive examination of the subject. Discussing the "original understanding of the second amendment," the meaning of *militia,* the "right of the people" to keep and bear arms, and the leading Supreme Court and state litigation on the subject, Kates concludes that the framers clearly intended the right of the people to keep and bear arms to be an individual right. Since the other amendments constituting the Bill of Rights used the word *people* to refer to individuals, a consistent interpretation should be applied to the Second Amendment. The author believes that applying an exclusively states' rights (collective) view to this amendment would require a number of "textual incongruities" that "cumulatively . . . present a truly grotesque reading of the Bill of Rights." The precise parameters and ramifications of the framers' intent remain unclear, however.

————. **"The Second Amendment: A Dialogue."** *Law and Contemporary Problems* 49 (Winter 1986).

This is a dialogue between Stephen Halbrook and Don B. Kates, Jr. Halbrook had "reviled" certain of Kates's remarks in the latter's *University of Michigan Law Review* article in connection with the types of gun controls allowed under the Second Amendment. Reviewing the states' rights and individualistic concepts of the right to keep and bear arms, Kates asks the question "To what extent does the Second Amendment preclude 'gun control'?" Covering such topics as to whom the right extends, the types of arms covered by the amendment, and permits and registration requirements,

Kates concedes that the historical and linguistic analysis to which the Second Amendment was subjected by Halbrook does not negate Kates's point that "it should be clear that reasonable gun controls are no more foreclosed by the second amendment than is reasonable regulation of speech by the first amendment."

————. **"The Value of Civilian Handgun Possession as a Deterrent to Crime or a Defense against Crime."** *American Journal of Criminal Law* 18 (1991).

The author explores whether the civilian ownership of guns in fact leads to a reduction in crime. He addresses "non-empirical moral and philosophical considerations" of the gun control debate, analyzes "some non-empirical elements of anti-gun faith," discusses "the police as a source of personal protection for individual citizens," deterrence measures and benefits, "'vigilantism' and related concepts," the "defensive use of handguns," and the matter of "shifting criminals from confrontation to non-confrontation crime." He concludes, among other things, that the use of handguns for defense is far greater than has been thought and that they are used more often to prevent crime than to perpetrate crime. Thus, "evidence . . . cuts strongly against severe statutory restrictions based on the belief that handgun ownership offers few social benefits to offset the harms associated with it. Moreover, even if handguns offered no benefits whatsoever, neither does banning them—except as part of a policy of outlawing and confiscating guns of all kinds."

————. **"Bigotry, Symbolism and Ideology in the Battle over Gun Control."** *The Public Interest Law Review* (Carolina Academic Press, for the National Legal Center for the Public Interest) (1992).

Kates argues that anti-gun rhetoric has resulted in heated opposition to gun control on the part of those gun owners who might otherwise support controls and on the part of non–gun owners as well. He concludes: "It is not the innate strength of the gun lobby that defeats gun control proposals. Rather it is anti-gun zealots whose extreme proposals, and extremist arguments even for moderate controls, alienate a public that is open to ideas for rational control of firearms."

Kessler, Raymond G. **"Enforcement Problems of Gun Control: A Victimless Crimes Analysis,"** *Criminal Law Bulletin* 16 (March/April 1980).

Kessler discusses the problems of gun control from a "victimless" or "complainantless" law perspective, stating that such laws prohibit consensual behavior among people. He points out that "gun control laws deal primarily with goods rather than services and are thus more similar to liquor and narcotics offenses than to other victimless crimes," and actually create more victimless crimes. Citing eight categories of criticisms of victimless crimes, Kessler argues that his analysis "indicates that many of the problems that have led to an outcry against crimes traditionally termed 'victimless' may also result from gun control. . . ."

————. **"Gun Control and Political Power."** *Law and Policy Quarterly* 5, no. 3 (July 1983).

The author discusses five "political functions" of gun control laws, which are to: (1) "increase citizen reliance on government and tolerance of increased police powers and abuse; (2) help prevent opposition to government; (3) facilitate repressive action by government and its allies; (4) lessen the pressure for major or radical reform; and (5) . . . selectively enforce [gun control laws] against those perceived to be a threat to government," providing examples of each. The author believes that there may be political and ideological implications and objectives in attempting to impose gun control, and that greater research efforts should be expended in examining this question.

King, Wayne. **"Sarah and James Brady: Target: The Gun Lobby."** *The New York Times Magazine* (9 December 1990).

An account of how Sarah Brady came to be an anti-gun proponent. Her son pointed a gun, which he had found in the pickup truck of a friend, at her. She "calmly, carefully, took the gun from her son." She says, "I stormed about it for weeks. . . . And then back in Washington I picked up the paper and saw the Senate was getting ready to vote on the McClure-Volkmer bill," which had been introduced by James A. McClure (Dem., Idaho) and Harold Volkmer (Dem., Missouri) and was supported by the National Rifle Association.

Sarah Brady's husband James was shot while with President Reagan at the Washington Hilton; he has never fully recovered. Together they have become a major force in the anti-gun movement.

Kleck, Gary. **"Crime Control Through the Private Use of Armed Force."** *Social Problems* 15, no. 1 (February 1988).

Kleck argues that "defensive violence" is a major form of crime control in the United States. In his opinion it is "more prompt" and "about as frequent" as legal action by the authorities. He states: "Victim resistance with guns is associated with lower rates of both victim injury and crime completion for robberies and assaults than any other victim action, including nonresistance. Survey and quasi-experimental evidence is consistent with the hypothesis that the private ownership and use of firearms deters criminal behavior."

Knoerzer, Michael A. *"Kelley v. R.G. Industries, Inc.*: Maryland Court of Appeals Takes Shot in the Dark at Saturday Night Specials."* St. John's Law Review* 60 (Spring 1986).

Kelley, the plaintiff, was shot in the course of an armed robbery in a grocery store where he was working. The gun used was a handgun made in West Germany by Rohm Gesellschaft, the defendant, but was assembled and marketed in the United States by R.G. Industries, Inc., a subsidiary of Rohm Gesellschaft. While the court rejected both the plaintiff's claim of abnormally dangerous activity and the unreasonably dangerous product claim, it nevertheless argued that the common law permitted the court to impose strict liability on the manufacturers in conformity to that which it perceived as public policy goals. After detailed analysis of the case, the author concludes: "In an attempt to resolve a social problem in accordance with public policy, the *Kelley* court has developed a theory of strict liability without foundation in the common law. . . . It is clear that the *Kelley* court's attempt at regulation via the imposition of strict liability upon the manufacturers and marketers of Saturday Night Specials is of dubious merit in the short-run, is not the most efficient manner of handgun control, and does not reflect public opinion concerning handgun control."

Koop, C. Everett, and George D. Lundberg. **"Violence in America: A Public Health Emergency."** *Journal of the American Medical Association* 267, no. 22 (10 June 1992).

This editorial takes the position that it is "time to bite the bullet back." It focuses on the high number of manuscripts submitted to the nine American Medical Association specialty journals in response to the editors' call for papers on the subject of "interpersonal violence." The authors conclude that "this outpouring of manuscripts not only confirms what we all know—that violence in the United States is a major issue—it underscores that violence is also a medical/public health issue, which is keenly felt by innumerable physicians and subject to medical/epidemiologic research."

Krug, Alan S. **"The Relationship between Firearms Licensing Laws and Crime Rates."** *Congressional Record* 113, no. 115 (25 July 1967).

This study compares the crime rates of those states that have firearms licensing laws to those that do not. Krug finds "no statistically significant difference in crime rates between States that have firearms licensing laws and those that do not."

———. **"The Relationship between Firearms Ownership and Crime Rates: A Statistical Analysis."** *Congressional Record* 30 (January 1968).

Using a statistical analysis, Krug demonstrates that there is no positive correlation between the degree of gun ownership and crime rates in the United States, and that as the proportion of population owning guns decreases, crime rates actually go up. "Fewer people with guns do not mean less crime." Indeed, Krug's analysis is consistent with the thesis that gun ownership by law-abiding citizens may actually restrict or reduce "serious crime, aggravated assault and robbery."

———. **"The Misuse of Firearms in Crime,"** *Congressional Record* 114 (2 April 1968).

Assailing the misuse of statistics regarding gun use in crime, Krug says that in 1966 "serious crimes involving firearms constituted about 35/100 of one per cent (0.0035) of this total. Such crimes involving rifles and shotguns accounted for approximately 5/100 of one per cent (0.0005). What this means in practical terms is that if firearms were to be completely eliminated from society . . . and no criminal substituted any other type of weapon for a firearm, the United States would still have 96.6% of its serious crime, and 99.6% of its total crime." The author contends that, given the huge number of persons who lawfully own guns in the United States, those who advocate gun control laws should be required to demonstrate that they would reduce or prevent crime, using scientific evidence.

Laia, Chris. **"Supreme Court Shoots Down Proposition that the Design, Manufacture, and Marketing of Small, Easily Concealable Handguns Constitutes an Abnormally Dangerous Activity."** *Willamette Law Review* 22 (1986).

According to the article: "The Oregon Supreme Court, in *Burkett v. Freedom Arms, Inc.*, held that the design, manufacture, and marketing of small, easily concealable handguns is not an abnormally dangerous activity that would give rise to the manufacturer's strict liability under Oregon law." Oregon thus has joined those jurisdictions that state that those who make and dstribute non-defective weapons may not be held liable for injuries resulting from use of their products.

Leff, Carol Skalnik, and Mark H. Leff. **"The Politics of Ineffectiveness: Federal Firearms Legislation, 1919–38."** *Annals of the American Academy of Political and Social Science* 455 (May 1981).

This article summarizes the efforts by the federal government to enact firearms legislation between World War I and World War II. It explains that the federal laws had minimal impact because of an "individualist ethos" and the policymaking process.

Levine, Ronald B., and David B. Saxe. **"The Second Amendment: The Right To Bear Arms."** *Houston Law Review* 7, no. 1 (September 1969).

The article presents a historical overview of the development of the Second Amendment, using various arguments raised at the debates leading to the amendment and the various philosophical writings upon which its wording and philosophical orientations were based, and both federal and state cases are reviewed. The authors conclude that the holdings in the cases have not correctly interpreted the language of the Second Amendment and that, whether one uses an individual or a collective interpretation of the rights guaranteed under the amendment, "the basis for federal regulation would have to overcome very serious obstacles. Federal interference with the right would, in any event, have to be 'minimal.'"

Levinson, Sanford. **"The Embarrassing Second Amendment."** *Yale Law Journal* 99 (1989).

Discussing the politics of the Second Amendment, Levinson points out that scholars have, in general, not taken the amendment very seriously, relegating it to footnotes. He contends that many who are committed to the Bill of Rights and support gun control legislation may find the amendment "profoundly embarrassing." After tracing the history and jurisprudence of the Second Amendment, he suggests that legal scholars "have treated the Second Amendment as the equivalent of an embarrassing relative, whose mention brings a quick change of subject to other, more respectable, family members. That will no longer do. It is time for the Second Amendment to enter full scale into the consciousness of the legal academy."

Licitra, Edward. **"When Johnny Gets Your Gun: Felony Firearm Storage in Florida."** *Florida Law Review* 42 (July 1990).

This article discusses a Florida law, enacted in reaction to a disproportately high rate of accidental shootings of children by other children, requiring storage of firearms for child protection. It examines constitutional challenges to the law, including elements of cruel and unusual punishment, the equal protection clause, and issues related to substantive and procedural due process. The author concludes: "Florida's passage of a felony firearm storage measure has been a political success for the legislature. . . . An object of widespread criticism for its insensitivity to the public safety two years before, the Florida legislature has enacted a gun-safety measure which has been approved and emulated nationwide. . . . However, before emulating Florida's regulations too closely, other state legislators should consider both the process by which . . . [the Florida law] was enacted and the quality of the legislative product. . . ."

Lizotte, Alan J., and David J. Bordua. **"Firearms Ownership for Sport and Protection. Two Divergent Models."** *American Sociological Review* 45 (April 1980).

Two subsets of gun owners are examined in this article: those who own guns primarily for sporting purposes and those who own guns for personal defense. Family socialization seems of particular relevance for those who own guns for sporting purposes; these persons take on the trappings of a true subculture. Those who own guns for protection, however, do not have the characteristics of a subculture. Socialization and contact with others who own guns for protection do not seem of particular relevance. Moreover, and perhaps more importantly, "there is no indication of a subculture of violence among protective gun owners." Finally, "gun ownership for protection and gun ownership for sport were found to be independent events."

Loftin, Colin, David McDowall, Brian Wiersema, and Talbert J. Cottey. **"Effects of Restrictive Licensing of Handguns on Homicide and Suicide in the District of Columbia."** *New England Journal of Medicine* 325, no. 23 (5 December 1991).

This article suggests that licensing handguns resulted in lowering firearms homicides and suicides in the District of Columbia. The authors' "data suggest that restrictions on access to guns in the District of Columbia prevented an average of 47 deaths each year after the law was implemented."

Lund, Nelson. **"The Second Amendment, Political Liberty, and the Right to Self-Preservation."** *Alabama Law Review* 39 (1987).

Asserting that the Second Amendment has become "the most embarrassing provision of the Bill of Rights," Lund points to the warm support given to it by civil libertarians, the federal courts' shunning of a direct ruling on it, and state courts' interpretation of the amendment in a way that is "implausible on its face." He reviews the debate over the correct meaning of the amendment, reexamines some of the case law pertaining to it, and then addresses its "modern application." He concludes that the Second Amendment protects the individual's right to keep and bear arms, and involves self-defense and the right to resist tyranny. He suggests that viewing the Second Amendment as "outmoded" or as a "narrow provision with little or no relevance to modern problems" is incorrect. He believes that reasonable regulation of firearms is acceptable, saying that "a proper interpretation of the Second Amendment would protect the legitimate uses of firearms without making the possession of guns a sacrosanct and inviolable privilege."

McCabe, Michael K. **"To Bear or To Ban: Firearms Control and the 'Right To Bear Arms.'"** *Journal of the Missouri Bar* 27 (July 1971).

This article explores constitutional issues involved with federal firearms laws and presents an outline of existing federal laws on gun control. Its stated aim is to enlighten practicing attorneys about the tasks of defending clients and engaging in prosecutions under the law. The author expects that the passage of the Gun Control Act of 1968 will result in a significant increase in the amount of litigation in this area. He concludes that rights with respect to the Second Amendment will have to be decided case-by-case, and that the amendment "will not afford any basis for challenge in the courts to Federal controls on individual firearms possession, transfer, and use."

McClure, James A. **"Firearms and Federalism."** *Idaho Law Review* 7 (1970).

The author points out that scholars have attempted for many years to interpret the words of the framers of the Constitution, and that the Supreme Court has interpreted, revised, and re-revised its interpretations of the words of the framers. The actual meaning of the Second Amendment, however, has rarely been interpreted and has certainly not been settled by the Supreme Court. Examining historical evidence and court holdings, the author concludes that even though it has been asserted by many that "no thought was given to the principle of arms bearing as a *personal* right and that what was crucial was State control, [i]t appears to me that this construction of the word 'militia' is essentially incorrect when viewed by standard tests of determining intent. . . ."

McClurg, Andrew J. **"Handguns as Products Unreasonably Dangerous Per Se."** *University of Arkansas at Little Rock Law Journal* 13, no. 4 (Summer 1991).

This article is one of two constituting a debate between McClurg and Philip D. Oliver over the question of "whether handgun manufacturers should be held strictly liable when one of their products is used to kill or injure someone." McClurg argues that "manufacturers should be strictly liable for handgun inflicted deaths and injuries," and concludes by stating, "I oppose the policy in this country which favors ready access to this weapon of destruction which, while it may provide solace and recreation for many people, inflicts untold misery and suffering upon many others."

McClurg, Andrew Jay. **"The Rhetoric of Gun Control."** *American University Law Review* 42 (Fall 1992).

This is an article dealing with the nature of rhetoric in the gun control controversy. Major topics include: Reason: The Missing Link in Gun Control Rhetoric; Fallacies of Emotion (appealing to "fear and sympathy," "pride and popular opinion," "improper sources of authority," and *"ad hominem"*); Fallacies of Diversion (including "hyperbole," "slippery slope," "straw man and . . . red herring," and "faulty analogies"); and Fallacies of Proof (including "one-sided assessment," "causal fallacies," and "arguments from ignorance").

McKenna, Daniel J. **"The Right To Keep and Bear Arms."** *Marquette Law Review* 12 (1928).

McKenna reviews the various state constitutional provisions dealing with the right to keep and bear arms and declares that the Second Amendment applies only to Congress. Exactly what the amendment forbids Congress from doing remains unclear, however; it would appear that it "only forbids Congress so to disarm citizens as to prevent them from functioning as state militiamen." The regulation of weapons in other areas—such as the carrying of concealed weapons—has long been accepted. He closes his article with the question: "Will the courts ever say that the Constitutions [*sic*] would protect the right to keep and bear arms, if there were such a right, but that it does not exist and never did exist except in the minds of discredited theorists?"

Malcolm, Joyce Lee. **"The Right of the People To Keep and Bear Arms: The Common Law Tradition."** *Hastings Constitutional Law Quarterly* 10 (1983).

The author summarizes the article as follows: "If one applies English rights and practices to the construction of the Second Amendment to the United States Constitution, it is clear that the Amendment's first clause is an amplifying rather than a qualifying clause, and that a general rather than a select militia was intended. In fact, every American colony formed a militia that, like its English model, comprised all able-bodied male citizens. This continued to be the practice when the young republic passed its militia act under its new constitution in 1792. Such a militia implied a people armed and trained to arms. The Second Amendment should properly be read to extend to every citizen the right to have arms for personal defense. . . ." This served to extend the English Bill of Rights to America with the objective of reaffirming that government should be "by and for the people."

Mann, James L., II. **"The Right To Bear Arms."** *South Carolina Law Review* 19 (1967).

Mann discusses the relevance of the common law to the development of the right to keep and bear arms, and then briefly presents an overview of the constitutional origins of the Second Amendment. He examines the "judicial fate of the amendment" and the "present day 'well regulated militia.'" After a brief discussion of federal and state regulation, he concludes that "the

amendment is declarative of a collective right. The state governments may regulate arms in any way and to any extent they
choose without infringing on second amendment rights. . . . Federal control of arms is violative of the second amendment only
when it impairs the functioning of a state militia."

Martire, P. V. **"In Defense of the Second Amendment: Constitutional and Historical Perspectives."** *Lincoln Law Review* 21
(1993).

Martire examines the opposing interpretations of the Second
Amendment (the exclusively state's right view and the individual
right view), discusses the intent of the amendment's framers, analyzes the language, provides case histories, and concludes, "Examination of the Second Amendment, in its historical context,
clearly demonstrates the guarantee of an individual right to keep
and bear arms. Concurrence with the views of the exclusively
state's rights proponents would be tantamount to disregarding
the historical intent of the Framers, the language of its text, and
interpretations by the Supreme Court."

Miller, Richard C. **"New Perspectives in Litigation: Smoking
Guns."** *Trial* (July 1991).

This article discusses injuries caused by firearm use. "It is hard to
imagine a more lethal consumer product. Yet litigation involving
firearms has not been nearly as effective in preventing injury and
death as litigation involving other dangerous and defective products." The article suggests that the firearms industry is largely unregulated and has been allowed to regulate itself. "Manufacturers
defend themselves on the grounds of loss of the original condition
of the weapon, misuse of the weapon, and violation of safety rules."
The author cites examples of unsafe firearms and the victims of their
existence as rebuttals to these arguments. Seven categories of some
problem firearms are listed. The author concludes, "Unless con-
sumers demand safer firearms, legislators provide regulation, or the
industry regulates itself, litigation will continue to provide the only
spur to firearms manufacturers to produce safer products."

———. **"A Call to Arms: Trends in Firearms Litigation."** *Trial* 29
(November 1993).

Miller states, "Sadly, there will always be firearms accidents and
intentional shootings that will require judicial attention to assess

fault and provide compensation." He argues that the law must change so that the injured continue to receive compensation. He refers at length to situations that have focused on gun manufacturers and the constitutionality of weapons regulation, particularly of assault weapons, and ordinances that ban "the sale, display, transfer, acquisition, or possession" of such weapons.

Moncure, T. M., Jr. **"The Second Amendment Ain't about Hunting."** *Howard Law Journal* 34 (1991).

This article can be summarized best by using the author's own words that open his remarks by referring to a bumper sticker: "The Second Amendment ain't about hunting." He states, "The current debate concerning whether a particular gun is better suited for a hunting or sporting purpose completely misses the aim of the Second Amendment. The Second Amendment recognized a common law and natural law right, taken for granted as inalienable, to keep and bear arms. Additionally, the Second Amendment was directed at maintaining an armed citizenry for mutual defense, and perhaps most significantly, to protect against the tyranny of our own government."

Morgan, E. C. **"Assault Rifle Legislation: Unwise and Unconstitutional."** *American Journal of Criminal Law* 17 (Winter 1990).

The author states: "It is the purpose of this note to show that, first, legislation of this 'anti-assault weapon' genre is unnecessary and will be ineffective. Second, this note will argue that, even if legislatures choose to pass such unwise legislation, the results of their efforts will be unconstitutional. Third, this note will propose solutions to the problems associated with the criminal misuse of semiautomatic firearms." Among the solutions advocated are the funding of additional assistant U.S. attorneys to prosecute possession by felons under federal law, funding new prisons, and establishing a task force that will exert "informal pressure" on the entertainment business to de-emphasize criminal misuse of so-called assault weapons. The author points out that assault rifle laws are unconstitutional under the Second Amendment and will be found so if constitutionally challenged.

Murray, Douglas R. **"Handguns, Gun Control Laws, and Firearms Violence."** *Social Problems* 80 (1975).

This article examines the relationship between handgun access, firearms laws, and violence linked to firearms. Using multiple regression analysis on data collected from the Federal Bureau of Investigation, the census, public opinion surveys, and vital statistics, the author concludes that "gun control laws have no significant effect on rates of violence beyond what can be attributed to background social conditions." Moreover, "differential access to handguns seems to have no effect on rates of violent crime and firearms accidents, another reason why gun control laws are ineffective."

O'Donnell, Michael T. **"The Second Amendment: A Study of Recent Trends."** *University of Richmond Law Review* 25 (Spring 1991).

In this law review article, the author states his objective, which is to "give an overview of how the Supreme Court has interpreted the [Second A]mendment. This note will then examine the recent trend towards restricting the individual's right to own certain firearms that has been taking place in both the courts and the legislatures."

Olds, Nicholas V. **"The Second Amendment and the Right To Keep and Bear Arms."** *Michigan State Bar Journal* 46 (October 1967).

Olds discusses whether private individuals continue to retain the constitutional right to keep and bear arms for purposes other than a state militia. He touches briefly on standing armies, the English origins of the right, private armies, and constitutional guarantees, and concludes that "the second amendment applies not only to the states, but also protects the individual citizen in his right 'to keep and bear arms' for the defense of himself, his property and his country."

Oliver, Philip D. **"Rejecting the 'Whipping-Boy' Approach to Tort Law: Well-Made Handguns Are Not Defective Products."** *University of Arkansas at Little Rock Law Journal* 14, no. 1 (Fall 1991).

The author opposes court decisions that declare well-made handguns to be "products sold in 'a defective condition unreasonably dangerous' and imposing strict liability on their manufacturers and sellers" and challenges an article written by Andrew McClurg in which he argues that handguns are unreasonably dangerous per se. The thrust of Oliver's argument is that courts should resist the extention of tort law in liability cases because this violates the appropriate role of the courts, ignores the mistakes of common-law policymaking, and ignores the fact that existing principles of tort law have been wrongly interpreted. "The underlying principles of products liability law require a defect before liability is to be imposed. Simply stated, a well-made handgun is free from defect."

Pacheco, Michael M. **"The Armed Career Criminal Act: When Burglary Is Not Burglary."** *Willamette Law Review* 26, no. 1 (Winter 1989).

The Armed Career Criminal Act did not retain the 1984 definition of burglary; thus, various interpretations are possible. In Pacheco's opinion, the best interpretation is that the act is meant to be a sentence enhancement device. "It is difficult to imagine how Congress could have meant to say, 'We want enhanced punishment for crimes which we have not defined.' It is much easier and reasonable to accept the probability that by omitting a definition of burglary, Congress intended to use state definitions of burglary."

R. T. G. **"The Federal Firearms Act."** *Temple University Law Quarterly* 17 (May 1943).

The author points out that the constitutionality of the Federal Firearms Act was upheld by a lower court but that the Supreme Court had not yet acted on the issue. The objective of the article was to indicate the "controversial elements in the statute and to analyze them in the light of previous Supreme Court decisions and also basic constitutional law principles to determine their constitutionality."

"Regulation of Firearms." *Journal of Criminal Law, Criminology and Police Science* 17 (November 1926).

The author argues for "a law in every state regulating the sale and ownership of deadly weapons. There should also be a federal act regulating interstate traffic for without such supplementary legislation a State law is of little use." The author cites an over-emphasis of legislation directed at the foreign-born. "We have already too many laws that discriminate against the alien and punish him more harshly than the citizen."

Richard, Leonce Armand, III. **"Strict Products Liability: Application to Gun Dealers Who Sell to Incompetent Purchasers."** *Arizona Law Review* 26 (1984).

The author concludes this article by stating that handgun dealers should be liable if they do not exercise care to prevent sales of handguns to those who are incompetent. Such sales result in a danger beyond consumer expectation. "The gun is therefore defective and unreasonably dangerous, subjecting the handgun dealer to strict liability for any resulting injury."

Ridberg, Michael D. **"The Impact of State Constitutional Right To Bear Arms Provisions on State Gun Control Legislation."** *The University of Chicago Law Review* 38, no. 1 (Fall 1970).

The article deals with the "sources and limits of state power to regulate arms," a "categorization of the state arms provisions" (in which the purposes of arms provisions and a classification of state arms provisions are discussed), and the "extent to which state arms provisions limit the range of permissible gun control legislation." The author concludes: "While most of the familiar forms of arms regulation seem valid even under arms provisions guaranteeing a right to private possession, those provisions restrict to some extent the scope of permissible gun control. Thus, the analysis set forth establishes a threshold level of constitutionality."

Riley, Robert J. **"Shooting To Kill the Handgun: Time To Martyr Another American 'Hero.'"** *Journal of Urban Law* 51 (1974).

The author argues that there is little justification for individual private possession of handguns in the United States, and that their legitimate use is far overshadowed by the violence they bring. He argues that Americans have neither a natural nor constitutional right to own such weapons, but that substantial gun control will result only from some future horrible incident that will at long last perhaps provide the rationale for establishing truly effective legislation dealing with handguns.

Riordan, Michael J. **"Using a Firearm during and in Relation to a Drug Trafficking Crime: Defining the Elements of the**

Mandatory Sentencing Provision of 18 USC 924 (c) (1)."
Duquesne Law Review 30 (1991).

Riordan presents the background of the mandatory sentencing portion of the statute, revised in 1986 under the Firearm Owners' Protection Act, which mandates a five-year prison sentence for those who have used or have carried a firearm during or in relation to any drug trafficking offense. The issue of defining "during or in relation to" is discussed, and the elements required to bring the possession of a firearm within the "uses" language of the law is examined. Some relevant court decisions are discussed. Other aspects of the law involving "the fortress theory . . . underlying predicate drug trafficking offenses," and "aiding and abetting" are analyzed. Finally, the constitutional implications of this section of the law are examined, and the author concludes that the law's provisions involve a "spider's web" of interconnections and are so complex that "whether there exists a web sturdy enough to support convictions under [this section] . . . is ultimately a question for the trier of fact."

Riseley, Richard F., Jr. **"The Right To Keep and Bear Arms: A Necessary Constitutional Guarantee or an Outmoded Provision of the Bill of Rights?"** *Albany Law Review* 31 (March/April 1966).

Riseley discusses legal interpretations of the right of citizens to keep and bear their individual and private arms for the defense of their country, citing the *Cruikshank, Presser, Miller v. Texas,* and *United States v. Miller* cases. According to the author, "In admitting that there are certain well-recognized exceptions to the right to bear arms, the Supreme Court has perhaps by negative inference admitted that there exists a fundamental right to which these exceptions are taken." Risely discusses some significant state court cases that address the issue and examines federal legislation on the subject. The author concludes that "any legislation, federal or otherwise, that unreasonably infringes upon the purchase, possession, or use by individuals of legitimate firearms must be struck down in its inception as an undue restraint on the right to bear arms." Thus, although regulation of firearms is lawful, the denial to citizens of the right to keep and bear arms for legitimate purposes is considered by the author to be distinctly unconstitutional.

Rohner, Ralph J. **"The Right To Bear Arms: A Phenomenon of Constitutional History."** *Catholic University Law Review* 16 (1966).

Rohner discusses the constitutional and historical background of the Second Amendment, the historical development of weapons regulation, and legal and judicial developments since 1791, and proposes a "purposes doctrine" or test to determine for what purposes a weapon is actually going to be used. His proposal hopes to avoid the argument over whether the right to keep and bear arms is collective or individual "and also furnishes a means of evaluating the constitutionality of proposed regulations ahead of time through the legislative (data-gathering) process."

Rosenberg, Mark L., Patrick W. O'Carroll, and Kenneth E. Powell. **"Let's Be Clear: Violence Is a Public Health Problem."** *Journal of the American Medical Association,* 267, no. 22 (10 June 1992).

The article discusses efforts "to clarify the patterns of violence through surveillance and research and to identify and evaluate interventions to prevent and reduce the impact of violence," the reasons public health practitioners should be concerned with violence, whether those "in public health know how to prevent violence," and the commitment of the public health service to make "the prevention of violence one of its highest priorities."

Santarelli, Donald E., and Nicholas E. Calio. **"Turning the Gun on Tort Law: Aiming at Courts To Take Products Liability to the Limit."** *St. Mary's Law Journal* 14, no. 3 (1983).

The article suggests that the notion of product liability with respect to the manufacturer of guns is based on a series of false premises, including (1) that "handgun manufacturers know and intend that their products will be used for criminal purposes," (2) that "handguns lack social utility in the hands of the general public," and (3) that "holding handgun manufacturers strictly liable for the criminal acts of a third party will reduce crime." The article argues that criminal misuse of a product does not make it defective or dangerous and that manufacturing or selling a gun "cannot be held the proximate cause of an injury which results from the criminal act of a third party." The authors conclude that criminals themselves must be held accountable for their antisocial activities. "Civil liability must be based upon solid legal principle, not political emotionalism."

Santee, John C. **"The Right To Keep and Bear Arms."** *Drake Law Review* 26 (1976–1977).

Santee traces the English background of the American tradition to keep and bear arms and then discusses the American origins of the Second Amendment. The amendment proposed by James Madison is given careful attention, followed by judicial interpretation of the Second Amendment since its adoption. The author concludes: "It is submitted that on the basis of the few cases which have considered the nature and scope of the second amendment and in light of the purposes which the second amendment was intended to further, it is improbable that any type of federal regulation will or should be held by the courts to infringe upon the second amendment."

Seitz, Steven Thomas. **"Firearms, Homicides and Gun Control Effectiveness."** *Law and Society Review* 6, no. 4 (May 1972).

The author argues that reducing the extent of gun ownership will reduce crime, and that one of the best ways to reduce gun ownership is to pass laws regulating their possession and use. Seitz uses an empirical model to demonstrate the point. He concludes that "it does appear . . . that gun control legislation is an effective means of reducing the incidence of criminal homicide, particularly in the larger white culture." He concludes, however, that "it is probably better to treat the underlying causes of crime than to attempt to deal with it exclusively by use of gun control legislation."

Shalhope, Robert E. **"The Ideological Origins of the Second Amendment."** *The Journal of American History* 69, no. 3 (December 1982).

The author makes "an attempt to understand the origins of the [Second A]mendment within the perspective of the late eighteenth, rather than that of the late twentieth, century." He argues that the writers of the amendment intended Americans to have arms for their personal defense, defense of the state, and defense against governmental tyranny. He also argues that "whether the armed citizen is relevant to late-twentieth century American life is something that only the American people—through the Supreme Court, their state legislatures, and Congress—can decide."

———. **"The Armed Citizen in the Early Republic.** *Law and Contemporary Problems* 49 (Winter 1986).

Tracing the history of the evolution of the right to keep and bear arms from the period of republican thought through the eighteenth century and later, Shalhope examines the background of the Bill of Rights and the importance of the individual as construed in post-Revolutionary America. He concludes that the contentiousness on both sides of the argument pertaining to the proper interpretation of the Second Amendment should not result in confusion about the framers' intentions. He states: "It may very well be true that *neither* the militia nor the armed citizen is appropriate for modern society. The second amendment included *both* of its provisions because the Founders intended both of them to be taken seriously. They intended to balance as best they could individual rights with communal responsibilities."

Sprecher, Robert A. **"The Lost Amendment."** *American Bar Association Journal* 51 (June/July 1963).

This article was the winner of the 1965 Samuel Pool Weaver Constitutional Law Essay Competition, an annual contest sponsored by the American Bar Foundation. Sprecher traces the history of the development of the provisions in the Second Amendment, citing the amendment's philosophical underpinnings and making reference to relevant case law. He concludes by referring to the Universal Declaration of Human Rights of the United Nations, which, although not referring to a right to keep and bear arms, declares certain objectives relating to the "life, liberty and security of [the] person." Sprecher states: "If we can ever be certain that we have for all time reached the ideal of universal existence based upon law, world disarmament would follow and the Second Amendment would be without any meaning. Until that happens, the Second Amendment may prove to have been another remarkable insight by the Founding Fathers into our needs for a long period of history. We should find the lost Second [A]mendment, broaden its scope and determine that it affords the right to arm a state militia and also the right of the individual to keep and bear arms."

Steffey, Matthew S. **"Torts—Strict Liability—Manufacturers' or Marketers' Liability for the Criminal Use of Saturday Night Specials: A New Common Law Approach—*Kelley v. R.G. Industries*, 497 A.2d 1143 (Md. 1985)."** *Florida State University Law Review* 14 (1986).

This note analyzes the impact of the *Kelley* case on application of traditional strict liability theories with respect to manufacturer liability. It discusses the court's establishment of a new "common law cause of action" against those who manufacture or market cheap handguns. The note also evaluates the court's decision and offers some comparisons with strict liability law and policy with respect to handguns in the State of Florida. The author concludes as follows: "The *Kelley* court did not overstep its judicial authority and make law inconsistent with legislative policy or prerogative. Instead, the court decided an issue traditionally within the purview of its role as the arbiter of the common law. It saw an injustice and found that its goal in providing a remedy was within the established policy of the state."

Stevens, Susan M. *"Kelley v. R.G. Industries:* **When Hard Cases Make Good Law."** *Maryland Law Review* 46 (Winter 1987).

The author concludes that "the Court of Appeals took a bold step in *Kelley.*" In this case, the court established a different and new genre of strict liability. Indeed, "noting a Saturday Night Special's lack of legitimate societal purpose and a legislative policy against such handguns, the court held that strict liability in tort may be imposed upon the manufacturer or marketer of a Saturday Night Special causing injury to an innocent victim during the course of a crime." The author feels that "the long-term effect of this decision may well be a better system of handgun distribution." Finally, the author contends that Second Amendment provisions are not violated by this construction of the law.

Teret, Stephen P., Garen J. Wintemute, and Peter L. Beilenson. **"The Firearm Fatality Reporting System: A Proposal."** *Journal of the American Medical Association* 267, no. 22 (10 June 1992).

The authors argue that a "Firearm Fatality Reporting System" should be implemented and that it should include information on the type of weapon (e.g., caliber, serial number, model, etc.) used in the killing; whether the death was by suicide, homicide, or some other cause; data on the deceased (e.g., sex, race, the impact of drugs and alcohol, etc.); data describing the person who shot the victim; "information on the circumstances of the shooting"; and whether emergency medical attention was required. The authors conclude that "the Firearm Fatality Reporting System would bring important, new, and needed information to help with the resolution of difficult issues. The creation of such a system should be recognized as a national health priority."

Thompson, Thomas R. **"Form or Substance? Definitional Aspects of Assault Weapon Legislation."** *Florida State University Law Review* 17 (Spring 1990).

The author discusses reactions to the fatal shootings of five schoolchildren in Stockton, California, by Patrick Purdy in 1989, and the subsequent calls for restrictions on the sale and purchase of so-called assault weapons. Thompson examines relevant federal law, Florida law, and law in other jurisdictions, and discusses a 1989 Florida legislative session with respect to debates on assault weapons and the Bureau of Alcohol, Tobacco, and Firearms' enforcement of relevant laws from a variety of perspectives. The article focuses on "an analysis of assault weapon legislation definitions," giving various approaches to the issue. Thompson concludes: "If the Commission on Assault Weapons determines that no problem with illegal assault weapon use exists in this state [Florida], less need for further legislation will exist. However, if the Commission recommends further legislation in this area, the broad purpose statement appears to offer the best hope for a reasonable, workable definitional form."

Udulutch, Mark. **"The Constitutional Implications of Gun Control and Several Realistic Gun Control Proposals."** *American Journal of Criminal Law* 17 (Fall 1989).

Udulutch considers gun laws necessary, asserts that people's concerns about constitutional restrictions on gun laws are incorrect, and examines the constitutional foundations for federal gun laws and the relevance of the Fourth and Fifth Amendments to firearms legislation. He presents various gun control proposals that involve federal legislation, licensing, an educational program, registration of weapons, investigation of the transferees of guns, the institution of a waiting period before gun purchases can be completed, and the banning of automatic and semiautomatic weapons. "To be most effective, these proposals should be adopted together and they should be addressed by the federal government."

Waybright, Roger J. **"The Right To Bear Arms."** *Florida Law Journal* 13, no. 7 (July 1939).

This is an examination of federal and Florida laws that regulate the possession, carrying, and use of firearms. The major question considered is "To what extent does a person, assuming that he is not a peace officer or otherwise entitled by reason of his duties as an employee of some governmental agency, or by reason of special exemption, to do so, have the right to bear serviceable arms in Florida?" Ten detailed answers are given to this question in the summary, and the notation made that if a Floridian passes the various tests provided in the laws, then he can exercise his right to keep and bear arms, "except that he must not *use* his firearms in violation of any of the many criminal laws of the United States or Florida regulating the manner in which they may and may not be used." The author cynically concludes: "Truly, the days when 'Judge Colt' administered the laws are gone. If it were not for the increasing numbers of those whose shiny badges give them the right to ignore most of the laws above cited, the 'Merchants of Death' would be paunchless."

Weatherup, Roy G. **"Standing Armies and Armed Citizens: An Historical Analysis of the Second Amendment."** *Hastings Constitutional Law Quarterly* 2 (Fall 1975).

Stating that the controversy over an individual and a collective interpretation of the provisions of the Second Amendment has not been resolved and that there has been little case law interpreting the meaning of the Second Amendment, the author reviews the British and colonial history preceding the adoption of the amendment and then discusses its implications. The author examines the controversy over constitutional ratification and the Bill of Rights and discusses the purpose of the amendment and the Supreme Court's interpretation of it. He concludes that the Second Amendment "was designed solely to protect the states against the general government, not to create a personal right which either state or federal authorities are bound to respect."

Weil, Douglas S., and David Hemenway. **"Loaded Guns in the Home. Analysis of a National Random Survey of Gun Owners."** *Journal of the American Medical Association* 267, no. 22 (10 June 1992).

This article examines the reasons people keep loaded guns in their homes. Based on a 1989 telephone survey, the study found that people are more likely to keep their guns loaded if they plan to use them for defense, if they are handguns, and if there are no children in the house. Training or no training in the use of guns apparently had no effect.

Weiss, Jonathan A. **"A Reply to Advocates of Gun-Control Law."** *Journal of Urban Law* 52, no. 3 (Winter 1974).

This is a reply to Robert Riley's piece in the same journal. Weiss points out many fallacies in Riley's presentation, suggesting that the figures cited may be inaccurate. The author takes the position that doing away with handguns will not prevent violent crime, since it is obvious that other weapons can be used as effectively. Weiss notes that the Constitution does not distinguish between handguns and other types of firearms. He also argues that the words of the Second Amendment are clear and that other amendments add to its validity. "Let us not chip at the constitutional absolutes in hysteria over dramatic tragedies. Now is the time to keep constitutional commands clear."

Whisker, James B. **"Historical Development and Subsequent Erosion of the Right To Keep and Bear Arms."** *West Virginia Law Review* 78 (1976).

Whisker examines the historical foundations of the Second Amendment, noting that the right to keep and bear arms for hunting and defense is an ancient one and can thus be considered a "natural right." He then focuses on the "controls" over the Second Amendment, citing taxation and revenue-raising devices to regulate various gangster weapons, and the National Firearms Act of 1934 and the Federal Firearms Act of 1938. He also discusses the Federal Gun Control Act of 1968 and the proclivity of the courts to "reinterpret" the provisions of the Second Amendment so that citizens are not only prevented from bearing arms, but also from possessing them. Whisker concludes with a discussion of the "prior restraint" issue and the right of the citizen against self-incrimination. He states that "the right against self-incrimination could be more significant in the protection of the right to keep and bear arms than the second amendment" itself.

Williams, David C. **"Civic Republicanism and the Citizen Militia: the Terrifying Second Amendment."** *Yale Law Journal* 101 (December 1991).

Williams argues that under republican principles the right to bear arms was a collective right not an individual right. Thus, he suggests, the Second Amendment was founded on the aspiration that the "means of force could be vested in those who would express universal good." In other words, it attempted to balance "hope against fear." The appropriate structures must exist to provide the people with a sense of virtue. Without such structures, placing full reliance on the people to bear arms would probably be naive.

Wright, James D. **"Public Opinion and Gun Control: A Comparison of Results from Two Recent National Surveys."** *Annals of the American Academy of Political and Social Science* 455 (May 1981).

This article reviews data drawn from two national public opinion surveys on gun control and other issues related to weapons. The surveys analyzed were commissioned by the National Rifle Association and the Center for the Study and Prevention of Handgun Violence, two organizations whose gun control positions are generally diametrically opposed. The fact that these two organizations are so different did not seem to have much of an impact on the outcome of the surveys, at least where direct comparisons could be made. In those instances, "the results from both surveys are nearly identical." The author concludes, "Together, the two surveys thus provide a very detailed empirical portrait of the state of popular thinking on the regulation of private arms in the United States."

Wright, James D., and Linda L. Marston. **"The Ownership of the Means of Destruction: Weapons in the United States."** *Social Problems* 23, no. 1 (October 1975).

Even though the number of weapons owned by the people in the United States far exceeds that of any other industrial nation, little effort has been undertaken to study the implications of this fact. The social and political characteristics of firearms owners are examined, data dealing with the number of guns in cities are presented, and comments relevant to "guns, gun owners, and gun control" are made. The authors conclude that "perhaps the most significant finding reported here is the sizable amount of pro-gun-control sentiment registered by the people who own guns."

Zimring, Franklin E. **"Firearms and Federal Law: The Gun Control Act of 1968."** *Journal of Legal Studies* 4, no. 1 (January 1975).

This article attempts "to increase our rather modest knowledge of the effects of governmental efforts to control firearms violence." The study is also "an effort to gain some perspective on

the difficulties and promise of empirical studies of 'legal impact.'"
Zimring provides an overview of the history preceding passage of
the Gun Control Act of 1968, an analysis of the act, some data on the
effects of the law, and a final discussion of some of the "broader implications" of the study. "There is . . . reason to believe that the potential impact of the act is quite limited when measured against the
problems it sought to alleviate."

————. **"Handguns in the Twenty-First Century: Alternative
Policy Futures."** *The Annals of the American Academy of Political
and Social Science* 435 (May 1981).

This is a speculative article dealing with future handgun policy
in the United States. Zimring discusses two alternatives: "federal
support for state and local variation in handgun control," which
he describes as a "logical extension of historical trends in federal
firearms control since the 1930s," and "federal commitment to reduce substantially the availability of handguns nationwide,"
which, he states, "would represent a significant departure from
previous federal regulatory approaches." The development of
this latter policy could grow out of changes in public perception
about handguns and their appropriate use as self-defense instruments. On the other hand, if a loaded handgun is viewed in the
future as an appropriate and "respectable means of self-defense,
restrictive proposals at the national level are probably doomed."

————. **"The Problem of Assault Firearms."** *Crime and Delinquency* 35, no. 4 (October 1989).

Zimring defines an assault rifle and reviews the major laws dealing with them. He suggests that a "rational discussion" about
these weapons can revolve around a definition of assault rifles,
reasons why such weapons present a "special problem," and the
relevancy of the discussion of these weapons to the wider debate
over gun control. He concludes that a "concealed Smith and Wesson handgun" is a much greater threat than, for example, the AK-
47. He states: "There is probably no city in the United States
where semi-automatic rifles pose one-tenth the crime problem of
handguns. Control proposals that restrict the growth of civilian
ownership of semi-automatic rifles might help keep a small problem from growing larger. Any more grandiose expectations will
only prove self-defeating. The tiresome debate about handguns
is, and will continue to be, the main issue of gun control in the
American future."

Bibliographies

Some of the best bibliographies of gun control literature are found in the leading books and monographs on the subject. To select the "best" of them is to be arbitrary to some extent, but serious students of the subject should consult the bibliographies in Stephen P. Halbrook, *That Every Man Be Armed: The Evolution of a Constitutional Right* (in this case, actually a series of extensive footnotes to each subject covered), and the bibliography in his *Right To Bear Arms: State and Federal Bills of Rights and Constitutional Guarantees;* James D. Wright and Peter H. Rossi, *Armed and Considered Dangerous: A Survey of Felons and Their Firearms;* Gary Kleck, *Point Blank: Guns and Violence in America;* Don B. Kates, Jr., ed., *Firearms and Violence: Issues of Public Policy,* which contains extensive bibliographies for each section covered; Joyce Lee Malcolm, *To Keep and Bear Arms: Origins of an Anglo-American Right* (detailed footnotes to each subject); and Earl R. Kruschke, *The Right To Keep and Bear Arms: A Continuing American Dilemma.* (See Books, Monographs, Theses, Symposia for publication information.)

Many articles in law journals—a sampling of which has been presented in this book—are major treatises in themselves and present an extraordinary documentation in both breadth and depth by way of footnotes.

Other bibliographies of periodical literature can be found in the *Index to Legal Periodicals* under the subjects "Weapons" and "Right to Bear Arms." This resource enables researchers to keep up with some of the most recent work in the field.

For bibliographies of legal cases dealing with the subject, consult *Corpus Juris Secundum* and its pocket supplements, and (perhaps more importantly because it is more recent) *American Jurisprudence* and its pocket supplement. *West's Federal Practice Digest 2d* and its pocket supplement and *United States Code Annotated* also supply both historical and recent cases and codification on the subject. These are not bibliographies in the traditional sense; one must keep up with them if one wants to have the most authoritative information on the subject up to the time of their publication.

Other useful bibliographies are included in the following listing.

Campbell, C. **Firearms Control Pro and Con—A Revised, Selected, Annotated Bibliography.** Albany: State University of

New York at Albany, 1976. The works cited in this bibliography were published between 1966 and 1976. Books, articles, periodicals of various types, and documents dealing with both sides of the gun control issue are cited. References contained are those held by the New York Public Library.

Chunn, D. E. **Firearms Control: A Selected Bibliography.** Washington, DC: Law Enforcement Assistance Administration Library, 1977.

This bibliography treats various aspects of the gun control issue: general problems of control, statutes and commentaries on firearms legislation, and such aspects of firearms control as the constitutional issues involved, firearms and police, and guns and violence. An appendix deals with organizations and other publications relevant to the gun control issue.

Cook, Earleen H., and Joseph Lee Cook. **Gun Control and the Second Amendment** (Public Administration Series, Bibliography Number P544). Monticello, IL: Vance Bibliographies, 1980.

This is an extensive bibliography covering the major literature of the subject.

Dardick, Nathan. **A Comprehensive Bibliography on Gun Control.** Chicago: University of Chicago, 1972.

This bibliography is divided into six sections: magazines, periodicals, and bulletins; law reviews and journals; books, pamphlets, and reports; hearings from Washington, New Jersey, and New York on various gun issues; firearms laws, regulations, and ordinances; and governors' messages dealing with their recommendations.

Garrison, William L., Jr. **Bibliography of Pro-Gun Literature: The Decades 1960–1980.** Bellevue, WA: The Second Amendment Foundation, 1981.

This excellent bibliography contains well over 1,000 references, doubling the number contained in the 1979 edition. Asterisks preceding titles indicate articles more likely to be accessible to the general public. The range of citations runs from *Accident Facts,* an annual published by the National Safety Council in Chicago, to an article by Don Zutz, "The Intellectual Origins of the Second Amendment," which appeared in *Rifle* (January/February 1972). The bibliography also contains a brief list of journals that frequently contain "pro-gun" literature, and a list of data sources.

Hasko, John J. **"Gun Control: A Selective Bibliography."** *Law and Contemporary Problems* (1986).

This bibliography contains citations for symposia, monographs, congressional documents, and articles. It is highly useful for anyone who seeks a firm foundation in the study of the gun control problem and its relation to the Second Amendment.

Jones, K. **Bibliography on Personal Violence—An Index for Understanding and Prevention, 1950–1971.** Galveston: Moddy Foundation, 1971.

This bibliography pertains to the literature of psychiatry, psychology, sociology, criminology, law, and behavioral sciences. It covers a gamut of topics: individual violence, homicide, aggravated assault, robbery with use of a dangerous weapon, juvenile delinquency, and the impact of television, drugs, and alcohol on violence are also covered. It also includes sources dealing with health and violent crime and predicting violent crime, and an index to journals and authors.

Manheim, J., and M. Wallace. **Political Violence in the United States 1875–1974—A Bibliography.** New York: Garland Publishing, 1975.
The literature included in this bibliography is divided into strikes and labor strife; race, riots, and urban riots; anarchism and terrorism; assassinations; vigilantism, lynching and police violence; and the general issue of gun control. Both popular and scholarly sources are included.

U.S. Conference of Mayors. 1978. **U.S. Conference of Mayors—Handgun Control Clearinghouse Resource Publication.** Washington, DC: U.S. Conference of Mayors.

This bibliography contains a list of other bibliographies on a variety of gun issues and then discusses the effectiveness of gun control legislation; the criminal justice system; statistics on homicide, suicide, and the role of handguns; politics and public opinion surveys as they relate to handguns; gun ownership demographics;

the "psychology" of gun ownership; the Police Foundation; comparison of statistics from foreign countries; cost effectiveness of gun control; the Second Amendment and its implications on gun control; accidents and guns; editorials and other opinion; gun control and the police; interstate commerce and handgun control; firearm fact sheets; and the safe use of firearms.

U.S. Department of Justice. Law Enforcement Assistance Administration. 1978. **Firearm Use in Violent Crime.** Washington, DC: National Institute of Law Enforcement and Criminal Justice, 1978.

A bibliography that treats the topics of firearms and violent crime, legislation on the books and hearings, issues in regulation of firearms, research done on the effects of gun regulation, surveys related to gun control, and additional reference sources. The bibliography also lists resource agencies from which additional information can be obtained.

Wright, James D., Huey-tsey Chen, Joseph Pereira, Kathleen Daly, and Peter H. Rossi. **Weapons, Crime, and Violence in America: An Annotated Bibliography.** Washington, DC: National Institute of Justice, 1981.

This is an extensive bibliography covering the major works in the field and is highly useful for both the introductory reader and the more advanced specialist in the field.

Books, Monographs, Theses, Symposia

Alviani, Joseph D., and William R. Drake. **Handgun Control: Issues and Alternatives.** Washington, DC: United States Conference of Mayors, 1975.

This book attempts to address the growing concern in the United States about the role of the handgun as a weapon of death. The authors' concern is that Americans in general and policymakers in particular have not sufficiently addressed the problem. It is the purpose of the book, therefore, as a voice for the United States Conference of Mayors, to provoke a national debate on handguns through an examination of objective facts. The Conference argues for the elimination of handguns from private ownership and possession in the United States and suggests several alternatives that could come into effect before that ultimate goal is reached. The book has a very brief selected bibliography.

American Enterprise Institute for Public Policy Research. **Gun Control.** Washington, DC: American Enterprise Institute for Public Policy Research, 1976.

This short book outlines the legislative history of firearms control efforts and includes summaries of the specific bills introduced during the 94th Congress. The book also deals with the fundamental points that have been debated in Congress and among groups and individuals, giving a brief account of both sides of the gun control issue. Particular attention is focused on the effectiveness of gun control and the significance of the Saturday Night Special. The two major bills before Congress at the time are examined in some detail.

Asbury, Charles J. **The Right To Keep and Bear Arms: The Origins and Application of the Second Amendment to the Constitution.** Ph.D. diss., University of Michigan, 1974.

This is an overview of the development of the right to keep and bear arms. Included are chapters on the early English system, the colonial experience and the American Revolution, the debates and arguments in the Constitutional Convention, the debates leading to the adoption of the Second Amendment, its meaning, and the interpretation of the amendment by way of the Constitution, the Supreme Court, and the state courts. There are comments dealing with the national government and weapons laws and then a summary of the Second Amendment, as viewed at the time of Asbury's writing. A relatively brief bibliography is included. In the preface to his work, the author suggests that there had not been a historical analysis of the Second Amendment up to the time he did his research; actually, law journal articles had begun to examine the question decades before, even though the definitive monograph had not been written.

Ayoob, Massad F. **In the Gravest Extreme: The Role of the Firearm in Personal Protection.** Massad and Dorothy Ayoob, 1980.

This book provides an overview of the use of guns in self-defense in a variety of settings. It discusses the use of lethal force in self-defense, "samaritans" and the use of guns, the use of guns by women, and having a gun at one's store, home, in the street, or in one's car. Ayoob examines the deterrent effect of handguns and provides common sense ideas about carrying such weapons. Other chapters are devoted to how to choose a weapon, the choice of caliber, techniques of gunfighting, and basic lessons in firearms safety. It is a useful introduction to these subjects. The author takes the reader through a detailed and systematic accounting of how one can survive in today's high-crime society.

Bakal, Carl. **The Right To Bear Arms.** New York: McGraw-Hill Book Company, 1966.

Arguing that pro-gun enthusiasts invariably read the Second Amendment out of context, Bakal takes the position that the amendment protects a collective, not an individual right. The author briefly examines each of the elements of the wording of the Second Amendment, asserting that reference to a well-regulated militia means that weapons may be used only to maintain such an organization; that "the people" refers to citizens in a collective sense; that "to bear arms" is a military phrase and does not apply to individuals who use guns for other purposes; and that "shall not be infringed" has to do with disarming citizens to prevent them from serving in the militia. Other chapters deal with other aspects and issues related to the firearms issue.

Barnes Company. **Handgun Laws of the U.S.** Fairfield, CT: Barnes Company, 1974.

This book is a brief but useful attempt to summarize laws pertaining to the purchase, ownership, and carrying of handguns in the United States at the time of publication. The book aims to show the differences and inconsistencies in the law among the various states and to answer some of the major questions often raised by the owners of handguns with respect to their rights. It gives a list of the states and a brief summary of the law for each relevant to the purposes of the book. There are several appendices containing tabular data and maps.

Bell, Bob, ed. **1995 Handloader's Digest,** 14th ed. Northbrook, IL: DBI Books, 1994.

This book consists of a series of articles by some of the leading experts in the field of handloading. Among the topics covered are screw-in chokes and sporting clays, assembling compressed loads in order to achieve maximum velocity and accuracy, black powder cartridge rifle silhouette shooting, the British experience with hand-loading, and types of benchrests. There is a complete catalog of materials relevant to the subject at the end of the book. Ballistics charts and a handloader's marketplace are also included.

Bloomgarden, Henry S. **The Gun: A "Biography" of the Gun that Killed John F. Kennedy.** New York: Grossman Publishers, 1975.

This book traces the history of the gun (a Mannlicher-Carcano) that killed President John F. Kennedy from its origins in the Royal Arms Works in Terni in 1940 to the day of the assassination. It is written from the perspective of an advocate of gun control and it often condemns the National Rifle Association. The book includes a collection of documents, including invoices and customs papers.

Bovard, James. **Lost Rights: The Destruction of American Liberty.** New York: St. Martin's Press, 1994.

The major thesis of this book is that American freedom and liberty are being largely destroyed under the weight of an increasingly powerful government at all levels, a government that is taking citizens' property, destroying their opportunities to succeed, and quashing their rights under the Constitution. In Chapter 7, Brovard points out that the more gun control laws that are passed, the greater the likelihood that crime will increase and sentences for criminals will be reduced—as has already happened. "The creeping political repeal of the right to self-defense is a huge decrease in the modern American's liberty because the government has completely failed to fill the void. . . . Gun bans are one of the best cases of laws that corner private citizens—forcing them either to put themselves into danger or to be a law-breaker." Bovard contends that individual liberty, not the state, must be the new driving force in society.

Burdick, Charles K. **The Law of the American Constitution.** New York: G. P. Putnam's Sons, 1922.

The Second and Third Amendments are briefly discussed in Chapter 2. Discussing the Second Amendment in conjunction with Section 8 of Article I of the Constitution, Burdick concludes that Congress is ultimately supreme, and that "the right to keep and bear arms is not granted by this amendment; it constitutes only a denial of the power to limit that right. And this limitation, like those contained in all the others of the first ten amendments, is directed only against the national government. . . . It is well settled that the right is not unqualified, but is subject to the police power of the States. . . . The right guarantied [*sic*] is that to bear arms in the common defense, not to carry such arms as the individual may choose to be used in private affrays."

Center for the Study of Firearms and Public Policy. **"Guns in America."** *Journal on Firearms and Public Policy* 3, no. 1 (Summer 1990). Sponsored by the Second Amendment Foundation. Bellevue, WA: Merril Press, 1990.

This is from a symposium dealing with an overview of issues related to the gun control controversy. It contains articles, most of them reprints, by Sanford Levinson, Paul H. Blackman, David I. Kaplan, David B. Kopel, Lance K. Stell, and Charles H. Chandler. Despite its brevity, it is an excellent collection that provides a general introduction to some of the most interesting aspects of the firearms controversy.

Corwin, G. Lester. **The Right To Keep and Bear Arms: America's Legacy through the Common Law.** A Thesis in Fulfillment of the Law and Liberty Fellowship, Institute for Humane Studies, Menlo Park, CA, 1975.

Lester says that the Second Amendment came to the United States through English common law and cites various early English statutes and some of the basic writers and codifiers, such as Blackstone. He presents legal cases supporting the argument and relevant statements from the framers of the Constitution.

Cottrol, Robert J., ed. **Gun Control and the Constitution: Sources and Explorations of the Second Amendment.** New York and London: Garland Publishing, 1994.

This book provides a superb overview of some of the major court decisions and recent acts of Congress (the Brady Bill and the Firearms Owners Protection Act) in the area of gun control and the Second Amendment, general issues of concern in the gun control debate, a treatment of the historical context of the issue, and articles by leading scholars who set the philosophical foundations for the debate on the right to keep and bear arms. The author's introductory essay is particularly useful.

Cozic, Charles P., and Carol Wekesser, eds. **Gun Control.** San Diego: Greenhaven Press, 1992.

Various aspects of the gun control issue are addressed by individuals presenting both sides of the controversy. Among the topics discussed are the effect of gun control on crime, the constitutionality of gun control, gun ownershp as an effective method of self-defense, a discussion of the measures that would reduce violence, and the efficacy of gun control measures in other nations. There is a brief bibliography and a very brief list of organizations from which further information may be obtained.

Davidson, Bill R. **To Keep and Bear Arms.** Boulder, CO: Sycamore Island Books, 1978.

This book argues for the creation of a true militia for purposes of maintaining civil defense, and for use of the military and police in the case of riots, "panic, disorder, subversion, and helplessness" that would follow a direct attack on the United States by a foreign aggressor or as the result of internal subversion. A militia could also be used to harvest crops and reconstruct the infrastructure—railways, water systems, power lines, and so on—under adverse conditions. A detailed proposal, ranging from marksmanship programs to recruitment procedures, is made for the establishment and maintenance of such an organization. The book has a very useful appendix, "Major Conclusions and Recommendations of 'A Study of the Activities and Missions of the National Board for the Promotion of Rifle Practice,'" conducted by Arthur D. Little, Inc., which could provide a foundation for procedures of a militia and the training of manpower in safety practices and proper uses of weapons.

Davidson, Osha Gray. **Under Fire: The NRA and the Battle for Gun Control.** New York: Henry Holt and Company, 1993.

This is a journalistic and largely anti-gun account of the gun lobby as led by the National Rifle Association. It discusses the gun lobby's origin, development, objectives, and methods, as well as its impact on policy. The author purports to examine both sides of the "battle for gun control," and the book does, indeed, offer some useful insights into the subject, but the references upon which the author relies are often superficial and sometimes relatively sensational newspaper accounts. The book does bring to the lay public an account of one of the leading controversies of our time, written in a breezy, readable style.

Defensor, H. Charles. **Gun Registration Now—Confiscation Later?** New York: Vantage Press, 1970.

This book presents a case against the registration of firearms on the grounds that once government has a record of all of those persons who own weapons, it can easily begin the process of confiscation. In Chapter 2, the author lists 15 conclusions related to the erosion of the Second Amendment's right to keep and bear arms.

Draper, Thomas, ed. **The Issue of Gun Control.** The Reference Shelf, vol. 53, no. 1. New York: The H. H. Wilson Company, 1981.

This book contains articles written by a variety of authors with a wide range of professional and journalistic expertise. Both pro-gun and anti-gun arguments are presented. The book touches upon the history of the gun controversy, examines methods of controlling guns, and explores the concept of gun registration. It also discusses the differences in the results of public opinion polls, demonstrates that politicians have mixed points of view on the issue of how to solve the gun problem, and points out that the legislation enacted on both the state/local and national levels have had mixed success at best, but most often have failed to reduce violence by the use of guns. A bibliography is included. Although more than a decade has passed since this book was published, the basic controversies remain largely the same.

Edwards, James E. **Myths about Guns.** Coral Springs, FL: Peninsula Press, 1978.

This book examines the various proposals made with respect to gun control. The author provides a list of nine tests to determine whether a proposed gun law stands up, and examines various myths about guns. These include the beliefs that the presence of more guns in society causes more crime, that registering guns and issuing permits to carry them reduces crime, that gun registration reduces crime because it makes felons easier to trace, that stringent laws such as New York's Sullivan Law reduce crime, that the people in general should be disarmed, that the right to keep and bear arms belongs only to the militias, that reducing the number of firearms would reduce accidents, and that capital punishment is cruel and unusual punishment. Each chapter is well documented.

"Firearms and Firearms Regulation: Old Premises, New Research." A Symposium. *Law and Policy Quarterly* 5, no. 3 (1983).

See the preceding section for citations of some of the articles appearing in this symposium.

Flayderman, Norm. **Flayderman's Guide to Antique American Firearms and Their Values.** 6th ed. Northbrook, IL: DBI Books, 1994.

Over 3,600 models of antique firearms are described in this volume, the authoritative book in the field. It provides the marks and specifications of these firearms for easy identification, and the large-scale photographs accompanying the descriptions are extremely helpful. The book is cross-referenced and has a comprehensive index.

Gottlieb, Alan M. **The Rights of Gun Owners.** Aurora, IL: Caroline House Publishers, 1981.

Gottlieb presents a brief constitutional history of the right of the individual to keep and bear arms, citing the Second Amendment, the rationale underlying its inclusion in the Bill of Rights, its common law origins, and the meaning of the amendment's various terms. A bibliography of readily available literature is included.

———. **The Gun Grabbers.** Bellevue, WA: Merril Press, 1986.

This book is about what the author calls the "gun grabber elite." It discusses Handgun Control, Incorporated, the National Coalition to Ban Handguns, and the media bias against guns. The author describes activities of anti-gun groups and individuals throughout the United States and lists their sources of funding. The book is something of a Who's Who of gun control groups in the United States, providing a readable introduction to the most important figures and organizations in that network.

———. **Gun Rights Factbook.** Bellevue, WA: Merril Press, 1988.

This brief book consists of three parts. The first, titled "Political Action," discusses the means by which individuals and groups can engage in political action activities; the second, titled "Gun Facts," discusses several topics, including constitutional rights, foreign gun laws, the media, product liability, self-defense, and violent crime; the third section contains a "radio show fact sheet" and a list of references.

Graham, Hugh Davis, and Ted Robert Gurr. **Violence in America: Historical and Comparative Perspectives.** A Report to the National Commission on the Causes and Prevention of Violence. A New York Times Book. New York: Bantam Books, 1969.

This is probably the most complete report ever published on violence in the United States. It provides a detailed historical overview of the subject and extraordinarily useful figures and tables on various aspects of crime, including statistics on violent events over ten-year periods, vigilantism, the crime rate, and the number of individuals killed and wounded in militia interventions. The many authors who have contributed to the volume are recognized authorities in their respective fields, and Graham and Gurr provide a very useful conclusion.

"Gun Control." **A Symposium.** *The Annals of the American Academy of Political and Social Science,* no. 455 (1981).

Some of the articles included in this symposium are cited in the preceding section.

Halbrook, Stephen P. **That Every Man Be Armed: The Evolution of a Constitutional Right.** Albuquerque: University of New Mexico Press, 1979.

This is probably one of—if not the—definitive works in the entire range of understanding of the origins and meaning of the Second Amendment. Using meticulous scholarship, Halbrook examines what Thomas Jefferson called "the elementary books of public right," taking the reader from the Greek and Roman periods through republican Italy, the absolutism of the seventeenth century, and the reforms of the eighteenth century. A detailed examination of English common law follows, and the underpinnings of the Second Amendment are discussed in terms of the literature and politics that preceded its adoption. Halbrook examines in detail the gamut of American jurisprudence as it pertains to the amendment, with particular focus on antebellum interpretations, the Dred Scott case, and the definition of "the people" and of "the militia." He dissects Supreme Court cases, especially the *United States v. Miller,* and state cases and other federal judicial holdings. His linguistic analysis of the meaning of the terms contained in the Second Amendment suggests that the framers had in mind an individual, not a collective, right when they drafted the amendment.

————. **The Right To Bear Arms: State and Federal Bills of Rights and Constitutional Guarantees.** Westport, CT: Greenwood Press, 1989.

This monograph can be described as a historic first in its coverage of the development of right-to-keep-and-bear-arms provisions in the states. Halbrook begins by looking at the disarming of the Boston citizenry in the eighteenth century and the political implications and reactions to that event by both the Americans and the British, then examines "the right to bear arms" provisions in the Declarations of Rights of Pennsylvania, North Carolina, Vermont, and Massachusetts and the concept of a "well regulated militia" in Virginia, Maryland, Delaware, and New Hampshire. He then focuses on the constitutions of New York, New Jersey, South Carolina, and Georgia—which did not have bills of rights—and the charters of Connecticut and Rhode Island, states that did not have constitutions. The book concludes with an epilogue about "state constitutional conventions in the nineteenth and twentieth centuries." The volume is heavily documented and contains a useful selected bibliography.

Hardy, David T., ed. **Origin and Development of the Second Amendment.** Southport, CT: Blacksmith Corporation, 1986.

This is a brief book that is useful to the beginning investigator of the gun control issue. It is largely documentary and "quotational" in nature, drawing upon documents, debates, speeches, and opinions from Saxon times (before 1640) to the drafting of bills of rights, contemporary discussion of the Second Amendment, and various state and federal court opinions laying out interpretations of the right to keep and bear arms. This is an excellent review of basic documents and attitudes.

Hogg, Ian, and John Weeks, eds. **Pistols of the World,** 3rd ed. Northbrook, IL: DBI Books.

This book describes well over 2,500 handguns manufactured between 1870 and 1991. It is said to be the most complete and authoritative reference book available on the subject.

Kates, Don B., Jr., ed. **Restricting Handguns: The Liberal Skeptics Speak Out.** Croton-on-Hudson, NY: North River Press, 1979.

Topics covered include a study of the history of handguns in the United States, cross-cultural data, a critique of handgun prohibition, the impact of prohibiting handguns on violent crime, self-defense and the use of handguns by women, and the constitutional and civil liberties aspects of efforts to ban handguns. Biographies of each of the contributors and extensive notes are provided.

————. **Firearms and Violence: Issues of Public Policy.** Cambridge: Ballinger Publishing Company, 1984.

This is a superb overview of the public policy issues related to gun control from the perspectives of leading legal, constitutional, and criminological experts. The topics covered include: constitutional difficulties in writing gun control legislation; five major assumptions underlying gun control; public opinion; the relationship between firearms ownership and violence in the United States; the likely effects of banning handguns; the so-called Saturday Night Special; an analysis of state and national gun laws and a market analysis of handguns; owning guns for protection against rising crime; the philosophical underpinnings of the Second Amendment; and the common law foundations of the right to keep and bear arms. Each of the book's 17 chapters contains a brief bibliography.

Kennett, Lee, and James LaVerne Anderson. **The Gun in America: The Origins of a National Dilemma.** Westport, CT: Greenwood Press, 1975.

This book explores the role of the gun in American society. Its authors disclaim to have written a history of the gun or to have provided a solution to the gun problem in the United States. They do conclude, however, that, notwithstanding the deep cultural attachments Americans have had with firearms, "in the long run, time works against the gun. Increased social consciousness finds its excesses intolerable, whereas they were once accepted without thought. The era of thermonuclear war has made the citizen-soldier harder to defend. The war against crime has mobilized the computer and other sophisticated techniques. . . . In megalopolis the gun as necessity seems doomed; what can be salvaged of it as sport and diversion remains to be seen. In some attenuated form it will no doubt linger, the distinctive heritage of a nation that began with a shot heard 'round the world.'"

Kleck, Gary. **Point Blank: Guns and Violence in America.** New York: Aldine de Gruyter, 1991.

In one of the leading books on guns and violence in the United States, Kleck deals with the issues of the gun control controversy; the involvement of guns in self-defense, violent crime, suicides, and accidents; and gun regulation. There are lessons for policy-making: "the shape of effective gun controls" and "a workable gun control strategy," six appendices relating to technical aspects of gun control, and one of the finest bibliographies available on the subject.

Kopel, David B. **The Samurai, the Mountie, and the Cowboy: Should America Adopt the Gun Controls of Other Democracies?** A Cato Institute Book. Buffalo: Prometheus Books, 1994.

This is an excellent overview of gun control laws in Japan, Great Britain, Canada, Australia, New Zealand, Jamaica, Switzerland, and the United States. Kopel examines the cultural nature of each of these societies and cites an array of data and findings related to the use of guns in each nation. Kopel draws conclusions based on the historical role of violence in American culture, the conquest of the continent, the American militia tradition, vigilantism, and social conditions that have ultimately determined the role of guns in this society. The book is extraordinarily well-documented for having examined so many different cultures.

Kruschke, Earl R. **The Right To Keep and Bear Arms: A Continuing American Dilemma.** Springfield, IL: Charles C Thomas, Publisher, 1985.

This book provides a broad overview of the gun issue that attempts to bridge the gap between scholars and legal experts, on the one hand, and sophisticated laypersons on the other. It discusses the historical foundations of the natural right to keep and bear arms and the practical implications of regulation; explains the differences between the individual and collective interpretations of the right, using edited versions of state and national court cases to illustrate the two sides; and summarizes the issue in the current political context. Its two appendices cite state constitutional provisions on the right to keep and bear arms and a list of selected cases on the subject. It has a selected bibliography that is still relatively extensive.

LaPierre, Wayne. **Guns, Crime, and Freedom.** Washington, DC: Regnery Publishing, An Eagle Publishing Company, 1994.

LaPierre provides a fine overview of gun control and its ramifications, covering a broad range of topics. A useful appendix lists the law review articles published on both sides of the issue. This is perhaps the most useful, easy-to-read volume on the subject, and will be of great utility to both the beginning researcher and the seasoned scholar.

Leddy, Edward F. **Magnum Force Lobby: The National Rifle Association Fights Gun Control.** Lanham, MD: University Press of America, 1987.

This book offers a synopsis of the National Rifle Association's political opposition to gun control laws. The analysis covers the years from 1926 through 1983. Congress began to seriously focus its attention on the gun issue during the 1960s. With this development, the National Rifle Association began to shift its own efforts, focusing more on political objectives. Especially useful is the analysis of the contents of the *American Rifleman*. The magazine began to deal more with legislation after 1965, and the percentage of space devoted to target shooting declined after World War II.

LeFave, Donald George. **The Will To Arm: The National Rifle Association in American Society, 1871–1970.** Ph.D. thesis, University of Colorado, 1970.

In his discussion of the Second Amendment, LeFave states that the amendment's provisions guaranteed the right to keep and bear arms only for militia purposes, not as a protection for individuals in situations outside of that function. He also discusses the establishment of a militia, the development of rifle marksmanship training, and the relationship of these to military preparedness. The role of the National Rifle Association is discussed, particularly in terms of its historical evolution and lobbying efforts.

Lester, David. **Gun Control: Issues and Answers.** Springfield, IL: Charles C Thomas, Publisher, 1984.

Lester provides an overview of some aspects of the gun control problem, including the proliferation of guns in American society, the social and personality correlates of gun ownership, the criminal use of guns, the influence of gun control laws on the commission of crimes of personal violence, and attitudes toward gun control. The author concludes that stricter gun control laws have no impact on the homicide rate. "If Americans decide that the dangers from widespread ownership of guns outweigh the benefits, then they will support major restrictions of gun ownership, and then the impact of such restrictions on violent crime and death involving firearms may be examined."

Lewis, Jack, ed. **Assault Weapons,** 3rd ed. Northbrook, IL: DBI Books.

This book describes essentially all fully automatic and select-fire rifles, machine guns, submachine guns, combat shotguns, and sniper rifles.

Lipinski, Andrew. **The Future of Hunting and Gun Control: An Experiment in Communicating.** Menlo Park, CA: Institute for the Future, June 1975.

This brief monograph is divided into two sections, one on the future of hunting and the other on the future of gun control. Examining the image of hunting from pro and con viewpoints, the author concludes that the outlook for hunting is "neither rosy nor gloomy." In examining gun control as it relates to hunting, he concludes that there will be a "troubled future" in this area, even if handgun production is ultimately phased out. The monograph concludes by discussing possible cooperation between the two sides.

Malcolm, Joyce Lee. **To Keep and Bear Arms: The Origins of an Anglo-American Right.** Cambridge: Harvard University Press, 1994.

In this book Malcolm portrays the history underlying the current debate over gun control. Examining the fundamentals in seventeenth-century England, Malcolm explores why the possession of arms was deemed a necessity. She especially discusses the evolutionary process by which the *duty* to keep and bear arms evolved into the *right* to keep and bear arms. She then explores the relevance of the English experience to the "right" as it developed in the United States. The book increases understanding of how the Second Amendment developed and why it plays an important role in the current debate over gun control.

Murtz, Harold A., ed. **1995 Guns Illustrated.** 27th ed. Northbrook, IL: DBI Books, 1994.

This volume contains highly technical articles useful to gun buffs on subjects such as ammunition, ballistics, reloading, gunsmithing, customizing, and hunting. Both long guns and hand guns are discussed. The book contains a complete catalog describing all firearms made in the United States or imported into the country, including prices and full specifications for each.

National Rifle Association. **The Basics of Personal Protection: A Practical Handgun Handbook.** Washington, DC: National Rifle Association (Safety and Education Division and Recreational Shooting, Training, and Ranges Division), 1988.

As stated in the book itself: "This handbook has been written to provide a practical understanding of handguns and the fundamentals of shooting them. Key objectives are to . . . (1) Teach the rules of safe handling and shooting of handguns. (2) Provide guidelines for selecting handguns and ammunition. (3) Provide general guidelines for safe loading, unloading and firing of handguns. (4) Review procedures for the care and storage of firearms. (5) Teach the fundamentals of handgun marksmanship. (6) Introduce ways to maintain shooting skills. (7) Offer suggestions for avoiding or controlling criminal attack. (8) Highlight federal, state and local laws pertaining to the purchase, ownership, possession and transportation of handguns." The book fulfills these objectives clearly and adequately.

Newton, George D., and Franklin E. Zimring. **Firearms and Violence in American Life: A Staff Report to the National Commission on the Causes and Prevention of Violence in American Life.** Washington, DC: U.S. Government Printing Office, 1970.

In this useful survey, the authors discuss the number of guns owned by civilians, the "patterns of firearms ownership," the ways in which guns are acquired, trends in the sale of guns, and accidents resulting from firearms. They also examine topics such as suicide by the use of guns, crime committed with firearms, collective violence, the use of guns in self-defense, violence resulting from increased numbers of weapons in society, and some "strategies of firearms control." The volume presents information on local, state, and federal laws dealing with firearms, issues of firearms regulation arising from constitutional provisions, the costs of controlling firearms, and technological advancements in tracing and detection of guns, as well as developments in weapons technology itself.

Nisbet, Lee, ed. **The Gun Control Debate: You Decide.** Buffalo, NY: Prometheus Books, 1990.

This is a well-balanced collection of articles on gun control, including policies espoused by various groups and the government, and the constitutional issues involved. The book emphasizes the deep divisions in discussions related to the conflict.

Rosenberg, Mark L., and Mary Ann Fenley. **Violence in America: A Public Health Approach.** New York: Oxford University Press, 1991.

A general summary of research on personal violence, this relatively brief book provides a comprehensive examination of violence since 1969. The editors cover child abuse, child sexual abuse, spouse abuse, violence against senior citizens, violence by assault, rape and sexual assault, and suicide. The editors do not make many conclusions about the complex subject matter, and perhaps raise more questions than they answer.

"Second Amendment Symposium: Rights in Conflict in the 1980's." *Northern Kentucky Law Review* 10, no. 1 (1982).

Some of the articles included in this symposium are cited in the preceding section.

Sherrill, Robert. **The Saturday Night Special, and Other Guns with which Americans Won the West, Protected Bootleg Franchises, Slew Wildlife, Robbed Countless Banks, Shot Husbands Purposely and by Mistake, and Killed Presidents together with the Debate over Continuing Same.** Baltimore: Penguin Books, 1975.

This generally anti-gun book discusses the many types of guns present in American history, particularly the Saturday Night Special, and the circumstances surrounding their use. Sherrill points out that after the assassination of John F. Kennedy sales of the type of rifle used by Lee Harvey Oswald increased dramatically. In his opinion, gun violence is something Americans "enjoy . . . more than we will admit."

Spitzer, Robert J. **The Politics of Gun Control.** Chatham, NJ: Chatham House Publishers, 1995.

In this book, Spitzer examines such issues as the reason why Americans are so divided on the gun control issue, the possible interpretations of the Second Amendment, the impact of the National Rifle Association on the course of events surrounding the gun control issue, and suggestions for a more reasoned approach to dealing with the issue of guns and crime in America. In his introduction, Spitzer goes to the fundamental concern of his book: "At its heart, the gun debate is a question about the relationship between the citizen, the state's power to regulate, and the maintenance of public order. All these relationships come together under the public policy umbrella and are thus amenable to a policy analysis that has as its central question: Should gun possession and use be significantly regulated?"

Swiggett, Hal, ed. **Handguns '95**. 7th ed. Northbrook, IL: DBI Books, 1994.

This book contains complete reports on developments in the area of handguns and speculates about future developments. It provides results of tests for new handguns and treats historical subjects. There is a complete catalog of handguns currently manufactured in or imported into the United States, with a price list and all specifications.

"Symposium." *Behavioral Science and Law* 11 (Autumn 1993).

This publication consists of articles about community policing, motivations for owning and carrying guns among juveniles, homicides among juveniles, weapons used by juveniles to kill parents, and guns and the mentally ill. It has a useful introduction.

"Symposium on Firearms Legislation and Litigation." *Hamline Law Review* 6, no. 2 (1983).

See the preceding section for a synopsis of some of the articles included in this publication.

Tonso, William R. **Guns and Society: The Social and Existential Roots of the American Attachment to Firearms.** Washington, DC: University Press of America, 1982.

Tonso argues that objective and sociocultural conditions have fostered widespread use of firearms in the United States and that guns have taken on symbolic as well as recreational importance. He contends that deeply rooted cultural factors continue to cause Americans to maintain their attachment to guns, while cultural conditions in some other parts of the world have not created this phenomenon.

Tonso, William R., ed. **The Gun Culture and Its Enemies.** Bellevue, WA: Second Amendment Foundation, 1990.

This book is divided into two sections, "The Gun Culture" and "Its Enemies," each containing seven articles written by experts in the field. It provides a cohesive view of various aspects of the widespread existence and use of guns in America. Biographies of the authors are given at the end of the book.

U.S. Library of Congress. **Gun Control Laws in Foreign Countries.** Washington, DC: Library of Congress, Law Library, 1981.

Laws and regulations regarding ownership and use of guns in countries other than the United States are reviewed in this book. Although now somewhat dated, this volume provides a useful introduction to the regulating provisions on weapons, primarily in European nations.

Wallack, Louis Robert. **The Anatomy of Firearms.** New York: Simon and Schuster, 1965.

This is an overview of what actually happens inside firearms used by sportsmen. It covers topics such as actions, gunstocks, barrels, sights, ammunition and ballistics, and other aspects of firearms and shooting relevant to understanding the construction and use of both long guns and handguns. The book is not written for the expert but, as Larry Koller says in the introduction, for the "intelligent shooter who wants to know more about his guns, how the different types operate, what makes them tick, and why." It is well illustrated and has an index to definitions and explanations.

Warner, Ken, ed. **1995 Gun Digest.** 49th ed. Northbrook, IL: DBI Books, 1994.

This is one of the best-selling outdoor books published in the United States. Articles cover all aspects of guns and related subjects, and there are charts of currently manufactured ammunition; a catalog of scopes, sights, and mounts; a bibliography of books and periodicals related to arms; and a complete list of every American manufacturer in the gunmaking business.

Whisker, James B. **Our Vanishing Freedom: The Right To Keep and Bear Arms.** McLean, VA: Heritage House, 1972.

This is a defense of the right to keep and bear arms. Whisker points out that, although the Constitution did not specifically require the right, Congress very soon found it necessary to pass the Militia Act of 1792, which required that each white, able-bodied male citizen have available his own firearm—described as a musket or flintlock—when he was called to service. Whisker maintains that when the Second Amendment was written, the framers did not intend to merely reiterate what was already in the Constitution; they intended to grant power to individuals, just as they had in the other amendments. The author contends that the historical evidence clearly demonstrates that the right to keep and bear arms was considered a basic right. The book also discusses court interpretation, self-defense, who may bear arms, and other issues relevant to the author's objectives.

Wilson, James Q., and Richard J. Herrnstein. **Crime and Human Nature.** New York, NY: Touchstone Books, 1986.

The authors argue that the responsibility for crime in society should be placed on the criminal, not on the weapons used. This lengthy book provides an excellent introduction to and discussion of the major reasons people engage in aberrant criminal behavior.

Wright, James D., and Peter H. Rossi. **Armed and Considered Dangerous. A Survey of Felons and Their Firearms.** New York: Aldine De Gruyter, 1986.

This may be the best book available on "the criminal acquisition and use of firearms." It discusses how criminals acquire and use firearms and describes the methods, procedures, and data resulting from the authors' "felon survey," in which over 2,000 felons were interviewed. It provides a typology of various armed criminals and discusses "patterns of weapons ownership and use on the circumstances of criminal violence," the impact of socialization on felons' use of weapons, the motivations of criminals who use guns and of those who don't, and felons' "patterns of [weapon] acquisition." A bibliography is provided, and the tables alone could provide the careful reader with an insider's view of this subject's scholarship.

————. **The Armed Criminal in America: A Survey of Incarcerated Felons.** Washington, DC: U.S. Department of Justice, National Institute of Justice, 1981.

This government publication presents the results of a government-funded survey of criminals in prison. It examines the acquisition and use of weapons in criminal situations. It is focused on felons in state prisons located throughout the United States.

Wright, James D., Peter H. Rossi, and Kathleen Daly. **Under the Gun: Weapons, Crime, and Violence in America.** New York: Aldine Publishing Co., 1983.

A well-prepared survey of the use of guns and other weapons in assault, murder, and robbery situations in the United States. It deals with the number of guns in private hands; trends in ownership for sports, recreation, and policing; mass demands; characteristics of owners; firearms used in crime; and regulations and their effect. Policy implications are also discussed.

Wright, James D., Peter H. Rossi, Kathleen Daly, and Eleanor Weber-Burdin. **Weapons, Crime, and Violence in America: A Literature Review and Research Agenda.** Washington, DC: U.S. Department of Justice, National Institute of Justice, 1981.

This thoroughly researched publication is an excellent starting point for research on the issue of criminal gun usage. It provides the reader with commentaries on the most important literature in the field. It annotates virtually every book and article of relevance up to the date of its publication and suggests avenues of study leading to implementation of public policy.

Zimring, Franklin E., and Gordon Hawkins. **The Citizen's Guide to Gun Control.** New York: Macmillan Publishing Company, 1987.

This book contains 20 chapters on the many-faceted aspects of the gun control debate in the United States. The volume attempts to examine the relationship between guns and violence in American society, drawing upon statistics, economic data, surveys of public opinion, and many research studies conducted over recent decades. It is a good introduction to the subject for the sophisticated lay reader, and provides a partial foundation of knowledge for the scholar.

Periodicals

The following is a list of selected periodicals in both magazine and tabloid/newspaper format that pertain to guns and weapons and that are available either by subscription or on the shelves of magazine dealers. The magazines contained in this list are devoted for the most part to sporting interests, and their editors and authors may or may not take a position with respect to the issue of gun control. It should be noted that periodicals taking an anti-gun stance are not available in the marketplace.

American Firearms Industry
National Association of Federally Licensed Firearms Dealers
2455 E. Sunrise Boulevard, Ninth Floor
Ft. Lauderdale, FL 33304-3118

A monthly periodical oriented toward gun dealers and the gun trade.

American Handgunner
Publishers Development Corp.
591 Camino de la Reina, Suite 200
San Diego, CA 92108

A monthly periodical devoted to the handgunning sport, self-defense, hunting, and shooting competition.

The American Hunter
National Rifle Association Publications
470 Spring Park Place, Suite 1000
Herndon, VA 22070

A monthly magazine distributed to members of the National Rifle Association who are interested in hunting activities.

The American Rifleman
National Rifle Association Publications
470 Spring Park Place, Suite 1000
Herndon, VA 22070

A monthly magazine that contains a wide variety of articles dealing with firearms of all types.

Armed Citizen News
National Association to Keep and Bear Arms
P.O. Box 78336
Seattle, WA 98178

This is a bimonthly tabloid newspaper. It contains a variety of articles and advertisments of interest to those concerned with protecting Second Amendment rights. Its coverage is not confined to the State of Washington; it includes material and advertising from around the United States.

Banned Guns
Challenge Publications, Inc.
7950 Deering Avenue
Canoga Park, CA 91304

This magazine deals with weapons that have been banned from manufacture and importation.

Double Gun Journal
Box 550
East Jordan, MI 49727-9636

This is a magazine of interest to owners of double-barreled shotguns and rifles.

Ducks Unlimited
Ducks Unlimited, Inc.
1 Waterfowl Way
Long Grove, IL 60047

A monthly magazine devoted to publishing articles on waterfowl and their conservation.

Field and Stream
Times Mirror Magazines, Inc.
2 Park Avenue
New York, NY 10016

A monthly periodical devoting itself to articles dealing with firearms, hunting, and fishing.

Gun Digest
4092 Commercial Avenue
Northbrook, IL 60062-1890

An annual publication dealing with developments on all aspects of guns and their use.

Gun Report
World Wide Gun Report, Inc.
Box 38
Aledo, IL 61231-0038

A monthly magazine for the gun collector.

Gun World
Gallant/Challenge Publications, Inc.
34249 Camino Capistrano
Capistrano Beach, CA 92624

A monthly periodical of interest to the hunter and shooting enthusiast.

Guns
Publisher's Development Corp.
591 Camino de la Reina, Suite 200
San Diego, CA 92108

A monthly periodical containing articles for gun collectors and those engaged in the shooting sports.

Guns and Ammo
Petersen Publishing Company
8490 Sunset Boulevard
Los Angeles, CA 90069

This is a monthly magazine publishing somewhat technical articles dealing with weapons and shooting.

Guns and Weapons for Law Enforcement
Harris Publications
1115 Broadway
New York, NY 10010

This bimonthly magazine deals with weapons used both on-duty and off-duty, and contains a wide variety of related articles.

The Handgunner
Handgunner
591 Camino de la Reina, No. 200
San Diego, CA 92108-3192

A monthly magazine devoted to articles dealing with handguns and handgun competitions.

Handgunning
PJS Publications, Inc.
No. 2 News Plaza
P.O. Box 1790
Peoria, IL 61656

This magazine is published six times a year and is devoted to detailed discussions of handguns and their use.

Handguns, Rifles, Shotguns
Gallant/Challenge Publications, Inc.
34249 Camino Capistrano
Capistrano Beach, CA 92624

This is a quarterly publication dealing with all aspects of weapons falling within these categories.

Handloader
Wolfe Publishing Company
6471 Airpark Drive
Prescott, AZ 86301

This is a journal on ammunition reloading.

Journal of Firearms and Public Policy
Center for the Study of Firearms and Public Policy
P.O. Box 2002
Tarleton Station
Stephenville, TX 76402

This journal is the official publication of the Center for the Study of Firearms and Public Policy. It is sponsored by the Second Amendment Foundation (James Madison Building, 12500 Tenth Place, Bellevue, Washington 98005).

Man at Arms
Andrew Mowbray
Box 460
Lincoln, RI 02865

This is the National Rifle Association journal devoted to the American arms collector.

Muzzle Blasts
National Muzzle Loading Rifle Association
Box 67
Friendship, IN 47021

A monthly publication for those interested in blackpowder shooting.

Muzzleloader
Rebel Publishing Company, Inc.
Route 5, Box 347M
Texarkana, TX 75501-9805

A periodical for blackpowder shooters.

New Gun Week
Second Amendment Foundation
Box 488
Station C
Buffalo, NY 14209-0488

This weekly tabloid newspaper is of interest to gun owners, hunters, and the public. It deals with all aspects of gun ownership, including hunting, sporting competition, gun legislation, and other related topics.

North American Hunter
12301 Whitewater Drive, Suite 260
Minnetonka, MN 55343-4100

This periodical deals with bow hunting and the use of rifles, shotguns, muzzleloaders, and pistols for the hunting of game, birds, and waterfowl.

North-South Skirmish Association Newsletter
9700 Royenton Drive
Richmond, VA 23228-1218

This journal contains articles, news items, and materials related to muzzleloading guns.

NRAction
National Rifle Association
Institute for Legislative Action
1600 Rhode Island Avenue
Washington, DC 20036-6326

This publication contains feature articles on firearms, crime statistics, and laws—either impending or enacted—that have an effect on law-abiding citizens who own guns.

Outdoor Life
Times Mirror Magazines, Inc.
2 Park Avenue
New York, NY 10016

A monthly magazine devoted to many aspects of life in the outdoors, this magazine has special columns on shooting and hunting.

Petersen's Hunting
Petersen Publishing Company
8490 Sunset Boulevard
Los Angeles, CA 90069

A monthly devoted to the sport of hunting.

Point Blank
Citizens Committee for the Right to Keep and Bear Arms
12500 N.E. 10th Place
Bellevue, WA 98005

This is a monthly journal dedicated to the preservation of the right to keep and bear arms.

Precision Shooting
Precision Shooting, Inc.
37 Burnham Street
East Hartford, CT 06108-1009

A monthly periodical on general target shooting published by the International Benchrest Shooters.

Shooters Bible
Stoeger Publishing Company
55 Ruta Court
South Hackensack, NJ 07606-1799

An annual publication reviewing major developments, guns and their types, and both general and detailed information related to the interests of firearms users.

Shooting Industry
591 Camino de la Reina, No. 200
San Diego, CA 92108-3192

A journal for firearms retailers, jobbers, manufacturers, and others interested in the general shooting industry.

Shooting Sports USA
1600 Rhode Island Avenue, NW
Washington, DC 20036-3240

This publication features articles on competitive shooting events, scores, and evaluation of equipment. It also contains a calendar of shooting events.

Shooting Times
PJS Publications, Inc.
News Plaza, Box 1790
Peoria, IL 61656

This is a monthly publication that carries articles on all aspects of guns and activities with guns, shooting, reloading, and so on.

Skeet Shooting Review
National Skeet Shooting Association
Box 680007
San Antonio, TX 78268-0007

A monthly journal dedicated to reporting scores and averages in skeet shooting and to publishing general articles on skeet shooting.

Soldier of Fortune
Omega Group, Ltd.
Box 693
Boulder, CO 80306

This is a monthly magazine devoted to all aspects of weaponry and material related to mercenaries, exotic weapons, and world events.

Sports Afield
Hearst Magazines
250 W. 55th Street
New York, NY 10019

A monthly devoted to hunting and fishing articles, with special sections on firearms.

Trap and Field
Curtis Publishing Company
1200 Waterway Boulevard
Indianapolis, IN 46202

This periodical is the official monthly publication of the Amateur Trapshooters Association. It contains articles dealing with trap-shooting as well as shooting scores and averages.

Women and Guns
12500 N.E. Tenth Street
Bellevue, WA 98005

Subjects covered in this publication include self-defense, general shooting sports, products, and legal issues.

Scholarly Papers and Government Reports

Blackman, Paul H. **"Civil Liberties and Gun-Law Enforcement: Some Implications of Expanding the Powers of Police To Enforce a 'Liberal' Victimless Crime."** Paper presented at the annual meeting of the American Society of Criminology, Cincinnati, OH, 7–11 November 1984.

This paper deals extensively with the issue of protections under the Fourth Amendment regarding searches and seizures with respect to bearing guns. One of the paper's major points is that the courts have not opposed vigorous enforcement that violates the protection against unreasonable search and seizure. Both liberals and conservatives have thus put those who own guns in jeopardy of having their premises unreasonably searched and their guns confiscated. In fact, evidence indicates that both restrictive gun laws and the case against handguns are weak in terms of their results. Nevertheless, some criminologists are using the current conservative mood of the courts to reduce the degree to which handguns are carried or transported.

————. **"Carrying Handguns for Personal Protection: Issues of Research and Public Policy."** Paper presented at the annual meeting of the American Society of Criminology, San Diego, CA, 13–16 November 1985.

Blackman examines "carrying and carry laws in the American Constitutional context," citing the background of the common law of England, the influences on the "criminological understanding" of the framers of the Constitution, and other constitutional issues, such as slaves and racism, privacy, due process, equal protection, and "the right not to be a victim." Other sections of the paper deal with "carry laws and their enforcement and effects" and "the effects of carrying for protection." The author concludes that the existing data "do not support the conclusion that restrictive policies are either necessary or effective." The paper has an extensive bibliography and useful tabular data.

————. **"Law Enforcement Lobbying and Policymaking on 'Gun Control': An Essay."** Paper presented at the annual meeting of the Academy of Criminal Justice Sciences, Washington, DC, 1 April 1989.

Blackman discusses some of the aspects and implications of gun control lobbying by law enforcement officials, including application of the first amendment, possible police intimidation and/or abuse of opponents exercising their rights under the first amendment, the potential for increased violation of the law, legislating by police, and "the credibility of law enforcement" who engage in lobbying activities. One of the author's primary conclusions is that law enforcement officers, given the potential that they may abuse their authority, should exercise particular restraint in the lobbying process so that the liberties of ordinary citizens are not infringed.

————. **"Criminology's Astrology: An Evaluation of Public Health Research on Firearms and Violence."** A paper presented at the annual meeting of the Academy of Criminal Justice Sciences, Denver, CO, 13–17 March 1990.

Blackman suggests that, like astrology—which wishes to predict the future—those in the public health field have a predisposition to use their data—in this case, on mortality—to "prove something." Inasmuch as it is impossible to disprove claims in either field, no proof is therefore necessary. "The mere statement is believed enough to make firearms and violence a public health problem, subject to epidemiological analysis, with prescription forthcoming—however unrelated to the lists of figures given."

Blackman, Paul H., and Richard E. Gardiner. **"Flaws in the Current and Proposed Uniform Crime Reporting Programs Regarding Homicide and Weapons Use in Violent Crime."** Paper presented at the annual meeting of the American Society of Criminology, Atlanta, GA, 29 October–1 November 1986.

This paper's major topics are "Murder and Nonnegligent Manslaughter" and "Weapons Use in Crime." The concluding section deals with "Policy Implications," suggesting that the *Uniform Crime Report (UCR)* data of the Federal Bureau of Investigation will always be, to some extent, limited because "different jurisdictions will report crimes different ways." The authors suggest that improvements could be made in terms of how data are acquired from local police officials. Budgetary difficulties may intervene in this effort, however. In the meantime, "statistical criminologists would be wise, in studies based on *UCR* data, to emphasize those crimes providing the largest data bases rather than the smallest." The paper contains a useful bibliography.

Blackman, Paul H., and the Research and Information Division, National Rifle Association Institute for Legislative Action. **"Firearms and Violence, 1986: An Analysis of the FBI's Uniform Crime Reports and Other Data."** January 1988.

This paper discusses homicide; violent crime, gun availability, and the issue of gun control; robbery and related offenses; and gun control efforts in specific jurisdictions, such as Washington, D.C., New York City, Massachusetts, and South Carolina. It also examines the effectiveness of police, courts, and prosecutors; the impact of mandatory sentencing laws; and the safety of the shooting sports.

Davis, E. Duane, and Laura J. Moriarty. **"Citizens' Attitudes Concerning Firearms, Self-Protection and Crime Prevention."** Academy of Criminal Justice Sciences annual meeting, n.d.

While handguns are owned mainly for purposes of self-defense, this study found that people own shotguns and rifles because they enjoy hunting, the weapons were a gift, or because their families had always had one. Other findings support the argument that gun ownership does not increase the danger of their misuse in the home; that gun owners are most-often married, have reached middle age, and are employed professionally; that owners of handguns are not "unstable, irresponsible individuals endangering their homes"; that most gun-owners have in fact rarely if ever used their weapons to protect themselves; and that "fifty-five percent of the sample felt their right to use deadly force should be expanded" with respect to defending themselves from criminals and rapists. The authors conclude that because police protection cannot be guaranteed, the public desires more power to protect themselves in various criminal situations that threaten their security.

Kates, Don B., Jr. **"Guns, Murders, and the Constitution: A Realistic Assessment of Gun Control."** A Policy Briefing of the Pacific Research Institute for Public Policy, San Francisco, CA, February 1990.

This is a detailed and highly scholarly overview of the many problems in an analysis of gun control policy and constitutional rights, divided into the following sections: "Pejorative Characterizations of Gun Ownership"; "Defensive Gun Ownership as a Response to Crime"; "Comparisons Among Nations and Over Time"; "The Law-Abiding Gun Owner as Domestic and Acquaintance Murderer"; "Gun Accidents"; "Control All Guns, Not Just Handguns"; "Basic Principles of Gun Control"; and a conclusion that presents "Seven Rational Gun Control Proposals." An epilogue is titled "Futility of Gun Controls in an Overloaded System."

Kleck, Gary. **"The Mass Media and Information Management: News Media Bias in Covering Gun Control Issues."** Paper to be read at the annual meetings of the American Society of Criminology, San Francisco, CA, 20–23 November 1991.

This paper portrays aspects of media bias in reporting events about guns and gun control. Kleck cites at least four significant examples: "lack of skepticism" by the media with respect to claims made by pro-control groups; "selective and one-sided exclusion" of anti-control data; "differing amounts of 'play'" given to news stories about guns, and favoring pro-control opinions; and newspaper editorial policies. The conclusion discusses the political implications and effects of this alleged bias.

Kopel, David B. **"Why Gun Waiting Periods Threaten Public Safety."** Independence Issue Paper. Independence Institute, Golden, CO, 25 March 1991.

This paper presents detailed discussion of proposals before the Congress and various state legislatures to require waiting periods before a consumer is issued a handgun. Suggesting that waiting periods appeal to the public, Kopel's findings indicate that such waiting periods may actually be a threat to public safety. The cost of administering waiting periods may very well cancel out the few benefits to be derived. The author contends that it would prove more cost-effective to concentrate efforts on black market activities through which most criminals acquire their weapons.

Mauser, Gary A., and Michael Margolis. **"The Politics of Gun Control: Comparing Canadian and American Patterns."** Paper presented to the American Political Science Association, San Francisco, CA, August/September 1990.

This paper suggests that although there are many similarities between American and Canadian cultures, important differences remain. History and the impact of the media are seen as particularly important in explaining these differences. Majorities in both Canada and the United States support more stringent gun control measures, yet they also insist that the right to own guns be maintained. Use of guns in self-defense is considered justifiable. Canadians are more likely to support firearms legislation than are Americans; ideology, fears about safety, or "evaluation of police" played no role in this supportive attitude. Thus, mixed feelings exist in both cultures. There is support for legitimate use of firearms despite uneasiness about the misuse of weapons in both populations.

Morgan, Eric, and David Kopel. **"The Assault Weapon Panic: 'Political Correctness' Takes Aim at the Constitution."** Independence Issue Paper. Independence Institute, Golden, CO, 10 October 1991.

This is an analysis of efforts to prohibit so-called "assault weapons" among the American public. The authors argue that just as "political correctness" undermines the foundations of the First Amendment, the concern about assault weapons likewise undermines the strictures of the Second Amendment. The authors conclude that assault weapons regulation is unconstitutional and that analysis has been replaced by public and politician hysteria. Measures to address crime problems should be substituted for this hysteria, even though they will undoubtedly prove more costly. This alternative will also preserve basic constitutional rights.

Tesoriero, James M. **"Handgun Ownership for Sport and Protection."** Paper presented at the annual meetings of the American Society of Criminology, Baltimore, MD, November 1990.
Tesoriero was a graduate student at the University of Albany when this paper was presented. He examines the relationship between membership in given subcultures and gun ownership. Ordinary least squares regression analysis is used to make predictions about legal handgun ownership in selected subgroups. As was the case in the Bordua and Lizotte analysis, a "sporting culture" was found to be a good predictor of firearms ownership, as was the effects of socialization. There was also evidence to support a racial correlation with respect to the applications for handguns. Fear of crime did not seem very important as a variable related to gun ownership.

U.S. Congress. Senate. Committee on the Judiciary. Subcommittee on the Constitution. **The Right To Keep and Bear Arms.** Report from the U.S. Senate, 97th Cong., 2d sess., 1982.

This is an official document of the U.S. Senate Committee that contains articles on both sides of the gun control issue. It essentially endorses the individual right to keep and bear arms as stated in the Second Amendment. Senators Orrin Hatch (Republican, Utah) and Dennis DeConcini (Democrat, Arizona) provide introductory statements, after which there are sections dealing with the history of the amendment, enforcement of federal firearms laws in the context of Second Amendment provisions, and articles dealing with the pros and cons of the amendment's language. Reference is also made to the Fourteenth Amendment and the fear of standing armies, gun control legislation, and case law on the subject. On the whole, the report provides a useful introduction to the study of the gun issue.

U.S. Treasury Department. Bureau of Alcohol, Tobacco, and Firearms. **Project Identification: A Study of Crime Handguns.** Washington, DC: U.S. Government Printing Office, 1976.

This brief study discusses barrel length and caliber of the guns most frequently submitted for tracing; the role of pawnshops in the gun dealing process; interstate purchases of handguns; the number of stolen handguns involved in crime; the types of crime handguns; and the value of the weapons successfully traced. The findings are considered preliminary. The study contains illustrations of various handguns and data about them.

————. **Your Guide to Firearms Regulation.** Washington, DC: U.S. Government Printing Office, 1978.

This is an overview of the regulations that apply to the sale, purchase, and use of firearms in the United States. It deals with such matters as providing a basic and somewhat detailed guide to gun dealers on gun control requirements, federal laws relating to firearms and ammunition, and United States Code requirements, and it supplies a list of typical questions and their answers with respect to manufacturing, dealing, selling, purchasing, licensing, and using firearms. Reference is made to some state laws, and copies of forms and relevant maps are included.

————. **Firearms State Laws and Published Ordinances.** 20th ed. Washington, DC: U.S. Government Printing Office, 1994.

This is an excellent summary of state laws and ordinances governing the purchase, sale, ownership, and rules regulating the use of firearms under certain circumstances. It is intended to serve as a guide to licensed firearms dealers in the United States. The book contains sections dealing with age restrictions, the Brady Bill, forms and publications used in the firearms industry, so-called relevancy criteria, a list of criminal enforcement field offices and summary lists, and a map indicating the states that must conform to the provisions of the Brady Bill.

Pamphlets, Booklets, and Reprints

Ayoob, Massad. *Handgun Primer* and *Gun Proof Your Children.* Concord, NH: Police Bookshelf, 1986.

This publication is two booklets in one. The first half, *Handgun Primer*, discusses gun safety and provides excellent advice about deadly force, how to choose a handgun and ammunition, how to shoot, carrying a firearm, keeping a gun in one's home, defense strategy, and training. Turn the booklet over and upside down to read the second half, *Gun Proof Your Children,* in which Ayoob provides excellent advice on childproofing a gun and gunproofing a child. Ayoob discusses the responsibilities of possessing a gun and what this means for keeping children safe. Ayoob is a former police officer.

Blackman, Paul H. **"Study of Armed Criminals Blasts Anti-Gun Myths."** Reprinted from American Rifleman, August 1985.

This reprint from *American Rifleman,* one of the official magazines published by the National Rifle Association (NRA), is largely a review of the Wright-Rossi study of the armed criminal in America. The author is the research coordinator and deputy director of the National Rifle Association Institute for Legislative Action (NRA-ILA) Information and Member Services Division. These reprints are published intermittently.

California Office of the Attorney General. Department of Justice. Division of Law Enforcement. **Dangerous Weapons' Control Law.** Distributed by the Bureau of Criminal Information and Analysis. Sacramento, CA, n.d.

This publication includes laws through the 1991 portion of the 1990-91 session of the California state legislature, as well as discussions of general legal provisions relating to firearms, machine guns, the Roberti-Roos Assault Weapons Control Act, destructive devices, metal- and armor-penetrating ammunition, body armor, tear gas weapons, and firearm devices. Relevant sections of the welfare and institutions code are also examined.

Citizens Committee for the Right to Keep and Bear Arms. **The Failure of Gun Control. A Task Force Report to the President of the United States, the U.S. Congress and the American People.** Bellevue, WA: Citizens Committee for the Right to Keep and Bear Arms, 1989.

This report deals with the failure of gun control laws. It cites the major studies that have dealt with the subject on the local, state, and national levels. It speculates that gun control may actually lead to increased crime because the innocent are disarmed while the criminal element is not. Moreover, gun control efforts tread heavily on civil rights and individual liberties. The report suggests that causes of crime themselves should be studied and resolved, and that controlling the weapons that a small portion of

Americans use in the commission of crimes will have little or no effect.

————. **Issues and Answers.** Bellevue, WA: Citizens Committee for the Right to Keep and Bear Arms, n.d.

These flyers, published intermittently, address issues of relevance to the organization and to gun owners, such as one on efforts to ban semiautomatic rifles. It presented a series of questions and answers, concluding that the nation's law enforcement officers do not "favor a ban on semi-automatic sporting rifles as portrayed by the media and the anti-gun groups." Other flyer topics have included "State Pre-emption of Firearms Legislation," "Waiting Periods: Myth Exposed," and "The Police View of Gun Control."

————. **"Keynote Comments: Inspiring Words from America's True Defenders of Freedom."** Bellevue, WA: Citizens Committee for the Right to Keep and Bear Arms, n.d.

This flyer highlights remarks by Congresswoman Jolene Unsoeld of Washington made before the 1991 Gun Rights Policy Conference on 21 September 1991 in Philadelphia. After giving a brief history of the development of the Bill of Rights and focusing on the Second Amendment, Unsoeld remarks that the hysteria that frequently follows tragic shootings that make headlines often forces politicians into making decisions that erode the basic right to keep and bear arms. It is Unsoeld's belief that a citizen should not have to submit to a waiting period to enjoy his or her rights.

————. **Point Blank.** Bellevue, WA: Citizens Committee for the Right to Keep and Bear Arms (published intermittently).

This pamphlet aims to keep its readers abreast of major developments in the gun control controversy. It publishes news briefs from around the country and information on members of Congress and their positions on gun legislation, as well as information about personalities in the pro-gun and anti-gun movements. It provides registration forms for meetings of interest to firearms supporters.

Gottlieb, Alan M. **"Gun Ownership: A Constitutional Right."** Reprinted by the Citizens Committee for the Right To Keep and Bear Arms, Bellevue, WA (n.d.) with permission of the Salmon P.

Chase College of Law, Northern Kentucky University, from the *Northern Kentucky Law Review*, "Second Amendment Symposium: Rights in Conflict in the 1980's," Volume 10, Number 1, 1982.

This reprint traces the historical roots of the development of the right to keep and bear arms as expressed in the Second Amendment, defining each of the terms and then discussing as an example the Morton Grove case, which the author describes as "an assault on the Second Amendment" and an ordinance that "outrages constitutional federalism."

Halbrook, Stephen P. **"The Arms of All the People Should Be Taken Away."** Reprinted from *American Rifleman*, March 1989.

This is a six-page reprint of an article tracing the history of the origins of the Second Amendment, which was in part provoked by British plans to disarm all Americans. It was written in part to commemorate the celebration of the bicentennial of the Bill of Rights, and is a good introduction to this aspect of understanding the Second Amendment.

Handgun Control, Inc. **Facts You Should Know about Guns and Violence in America.** Washington, DC: Handgun Control (published intermittently).

This one-page flyer, using statistics from the Bureau of Alcohol, Tobacco, and Firearms or those compiled by the Senate Judiciary Committee, lists some of the facts related to murder, handgun crimes, the probability of becoming a murder victim, where guns tend to be purchased, and assault weapons, among other categories.

————. **Issue Paper.** Washington, DC: Handgun Control, n.d.

This pamphlet, issued periodically, deals with specific issues related to the gun control problem. One, for example, deals with assault pistols and large-capacity ammunition magazines, and includes a list of the votes cast by members of the House of Representatives when the issue came before it as a part of the Volkmer Amendment.

————. **"You *Can* Do Something about Handgun Violence."** Washington, DC: Handgun Control, n.d.

This brief pamphlet extols the virtues of Handgun Control, Inc., stating that "Handgun Control, Inc., has taken on the NRA

[National Rifle Association] . . . and we have made tremendous progress!" It describes its membership and tactics before Congress and its educational efforts among civic clubs, schools, and state and local legislative groups. It lists its legislative agenda and advocates a national gun policy. A membership application is printed in the flyer and a message from Sarah Brady appears on the last page.

Jews for the Preservation of Firearms Ownership. **American Survival Guide.** Milwaukee, WI: Jews for the Preservation of Firearms Ownership (published intermittently).

This is one of several publications by Jews for the Preservation of Firearms Ownership, which calls itself "America's Aggressive Civil Rights Organization." It staunchly favors the rights of gun owners and opposes regulating and banning guns, citing the lessons of dictatorial governments that seized firearms and totally disarmed citizens, such as that of Adolph Hitler. The organization publishes a number of flyers and pamphlets on the issue.

Kates, Don B., Jr. **"The Second Amendment and the Ideology of Self-Protection."** Reprinted from *Constitutional Commentary* 9, no. 1 (Winter 1992).

This reprint is a heavily documented defense of the right to self-defense and the right to protect oneself from a tyrannous government. Citing an array of historical and contemporary authors and publications, Kates concludes that "those examples confirmed both the criminologically based worldview of classical philosophy and its foundation in the even more ancient dictum that just and popular governments rest upon widespread popular possession of arms."

Kleck, Gary. **The Good Side of Guns: The Role of Firearms in Self Defense.** Reprinted from Kleck, "Crime Control through the Private Use of Armed Force." *Social Problems* 35, no. 1 (February 1988). Second Amendment Foundation Monograph Series. Bellevue, WA: Second Amendment Foundation, n.d.

Citizens using firearms in legal defensive violence is described as a "significant form of social control in the United States." Kleck points out that research has demonstrated that private use of firearms against criminals is common and frequent; it is roughly comparable in frequency to arrests by police. It is, however, "a more prompt negative consequence of crime than legal punishment and is often far more severe." There is a correlation between armed resistance by crime victims and lower injury rates and lower levels of crime completion, especially for robberies and assaults. "Survey and quasi-experimental evidence is consistent with the hypothesis that the private ownership and use of firearms deters criminal behavior."

Kopel, David B. **"The Violence of Gun Control."** *Policy Review* no. 63 (Winter 1993).

This is a reprint of an article covering topics such as "what criminals have to say about gun control" and "how guns prevent crime" and concluding with an argument that the justice system must control criminals, not guns, since the latter would have a deleterious effect on law-abiding citizens. *Policy Review* is the flagship publication of the Heritage Foundation, Washington, DC.

Malcolm, Joyce Lee. **Disarmed: The Loss of the Right To Bear Arms in England.** Radcliffe College: The Mary Ingraham Bunting Institute, 1980.

This well-researched and scholarly treatise, reprinted with permission by the National Rifle Association Institute for Legislative Action, Washington, DC, deals with the disarmament of English Protestants. It examines how the disarmament was accomplished, how the people reacted, whether they gave up their arms willingly, and when they decided that the right to keep and bear arms was a fundamental right of every Englishman.

National Association to Keep and Bear Arms. **Armed Citizen News.** Seattle, WA: National Association to Keep and Bear Arms, n.d.

This bimonthly newspaper contains articles of relevance to all those with an interest in firearms and in preserving their rights under the Second Amendment. Sometimes a bit vitriolic, it nevertheless presents its point of view in a wide-ranging and hard-hitting style.

National Rifle Association. **"A Call to Arms. Don't Wait To Protect Your Gun Owner Rights. They Are at Risk in the U.S. Congress."** Washington, DC: National Rifle Association, 1991.

This is a one-page flyer directed at all people who were interested in defeating the Brady Bill. It urged readers to call or write their senators and representatives and oppose the legislation. It spelled out the major provisions of the bill and its impact on gun owners, and maintained that it would have no real effect on future criminal activity. Such sheets are published on various issues at various times.

————. **How Media Misinformation Threatens Your Rights. A Special Report to Gun Owners on Media Treatment of the Second Amendment.** Washington, DC: National Rifle Association, n.d.

This four-page brochure attacks what the National Rifle Association (NRA) alleges is misleading information and falsehoods spread by the media about the gun problem in the United States. The following are declared "all lies": that the "NRA supported cop-killer bullets"; "that more and more criminals use assault weapons that spray bullets"; "that plastic guns can defeat airport security systems"; and that "a national waiting period would curb gun crime if Congress will just pass it."

————. **It's Time You Faced the Cold-Blooded Killers of the Second Amendment.** Washington, DC: National Rifle Association, n.d.

This is both an informational brochure and an invitation to support CrimeStrike, a division of the National Rifle Association. It cites statistics and makes various statements about criminals and the efforts that CrimeStrike has undertaken to thwart crime. Other titles include "Let Armed Criminals Be Warned" and "What's the First Step to a Police State?"

————. **NRA Fact Sheet.** Washington, DC: National Rifle Association (published intermittently).

This is a one-page flyer published by the National Rifle Association (NRA) on various issues related to the gun control lobby. An example is "What Is the Gun Lobby? The Gun Lobby is People," which explains the functions of the Institute for Legislative Action, the lobbying arm of the NRA. Other fact sheets have dealt with topics such as semiautomatic firearms and "cop killer" teflon-coated bullets.

National Rifle Association Institute for Legislative Action. **Criminals Don't Wait—Why Should You? The Case against Waiting Periods.** Washington, DC: National Rifle Association Institute for Legislative Action, 1991.

This pamphlet argues that waiting periods and background checks are probably unworkable under current procedures and are likely to be inaccurate. It also points out that criminologists have found that such procedures do not reduce crime or homicide, and maintains that the criminal justice system has not been performing its functions diligently: the focus should be on criminals, not on the law-abiding. A bibliography is provided.

————. **Freedom's Legacy: The Bill of Rights.** Washington, DC: National Rifle Association Institute for Legislative Action, 1991.

This pamphlet contains the Virginia Declaration of Rights of 1776, and three articles: "Virginia's Great Dissenters" by Thomas M. Concure, Jr., "Madison & the Bill of Rights" by Michael K. McCabe, and "The Bill of Rights & the States" by Stefan Tahmassebi. It is a highly instructive document with a good introductory bibliography to the Second Amendment. It was reprinted from the *American Rifleman,* February, March, and April 1991.

————. **Gun Law Failures.** Washington, DC: National Rifle Association Institute for Legislative Action, 1992.

This booklet discusses the impact of gun laws on the crime rate in the United States and concludes that gun laws have little or no effect on reducing crime. It cites some of the major studies that have empirically demonstrated the validity of its assertions. The booklet has references to support the data presented. This is one of the booklets published intermittently by the National Rifle Association.

————. **Myth of the "Saturday Night Special."** Washington, DC: National Rifle Association Institute for Legislative Action, 1991.

This pamphlet examines the various arguments for banning so-called Saturday Night Specials and declares many of the assertions about them myths. Most street guns are, simply, not the cheap guns typified by this term, but are often weapons that were originally developed for use by law enforcement officers. Criminals use whatever weapons they can get, and to focus on this relatively cheap weapon may constitute the first step toward elimination of all handguns and, ultimately, all guns in the United States.

————. **Myths about Guns.** Washington, DC: National Rifle Association Institute for Legislative Action, 1991.

This booklet discusses ten "myths" about gun control, including topics such as public opinion about gun ownership and use, citizen deterrence of crime, the Second Amendment, and the relationship of gun laws to crime. Similar pamphlets are published frequently by the National Rifle Association.

————. **NRA Fact Card.** Washington, DC: National Rifle Association Institute for Legislative Action (published intermittently).

This card can be folded and carried in a wallet. It provides statistical information and commentary on many gun-related issues.

————. **A Question of Self-Defense.** Washington, DC: National Rifle Association Institute for Legislative Action, 1992.

This brochure is intended to supply information to the individual concerned about self-protection. It is not legal advice; one must consult local and state jurisdictions to determine the law on the subject. It discusses various approaches to self-defense and examines the safety measures involved. This is one of a series of publications of this type issued by the National Rifle Association.

————. **Twelve Tall Tales: Media Myths about Guns, Gun Laws and the National Rifle Association.** Washington, DC: National Rifle Association Institute for Legislative Action, 1990.

In this pamphlet, 12 "media myths" are exposed, including misstatements about the National Rifle Association's alleged opposition to reasonable restrictions on "cop-killer bullets" and "plastic guns," myths about assault weapons and waiting periods, and misinterpretation of the provisions of the Second Amendment.

Second Amendment Foundation. **"Founding Fathers Bicentennial of the Bill of Rights Booklet of Gun Quotes."** Bellevue, WA: Second Amendment Foundation, n.d.

This brief pamphlet consists of quotations from various eminent American historic figures, such as Thomas Jefferson, Albert Gallatin, Patrick Henry, George Mason, Samuel Adams, and George Washington, all of whom defended the individual right to keep and bear arms and defined a militia as "the people themselves."

————. **Research Reports.** Bellevue, WA: Second Amendment Foundation, n.d.

These reports are brief discussions of some of the major issues related to the gun control controversy. One recent example is "Bans on Semi-Automatics: Unconstitutional Hysteria," by David B. Kopel, in which Kopel discusses the frenzy over possession of assault rifles and the need for gun owners to take a "sober look at the facts." Kopel maintains that the proposed ban would affect only the law-abiding, not criminals, who will procure them whenever they want, even though the amount of crime actually committed with them is minuscule.

The Sporting Arms and Ammunition Manufacturers' Institute. **"A Responsible Approach to Firearms Safety for Children."** Newtown, CT: The Sporting Arms and Ammunition Manufacturers' Institute. n.d.

This brief brochure lists ten key safety points that should always be observed when handling weapons, and discusses ways to reduce firearms injuries and deaths among children. This brochure is Number 3 in a series of background papers produced by the institute, such as "Market Size and Economic Impact of the Sporting Firearms and Ammunition Industry in America," "A Century of Success in Reducing Firearms Accidents," "Ammunition Types and Characteristics—Handgun," "A Responsible Approach to Legislation Regulating 'Assault Weapons,'" and "Excise Taxes on Firearms and Ammunition."

————. **A Responsible Approach to Public Firearms Ownership and Use: An Industry Perspective.** Newtown, CT: The Sporting Arms and Ammunition Manufacturers' Institute. n.d.

This brief booklet affirms a commitment to firearms safety and responsibility in gun use on the part of manufacturers of sporting firearms and ammunition. The institute emphasizes safety education and endorses background checks, intensification of the prosecution of illegal gun sales, and sales to legitimate gun dealers only. It also appeals to the entertainment industry to cease portraying guns as instruments of destruction, and seeks the elimination of guns in schools and the secure storage of firearms, among other objectives.

Tahmassebi, Stefan B. **Gun Control and Racism.** Reprinted from *George Mason University Civil Rights Law Journal* 2, no. 1 (Summer 1991).

This paper argues that gun control efforts in the United States have historically involved suppression of blacks and other racial and ethnic minorities, as well as such "unwanted elements" as foreign immigrants, reformers, and union organizers. "Firearms laws were often enacted to disarm and facilitate repressive action against these groups." Thus, those in positions of political power used—and continue to use—gun control legislation to dominate the underclass and to maintain their power monopoly on the instruments of force in society. "In the final analysis, citizens must protect themselves and their families and homes. The need for self-defense is far more critical in the poor and minority neighborhoods ravaged by crime and without adequate police protection." Violations of the Fourth Amendment have also followed quickly on the heels of racial repression, especially in the urban ghettos.

Treanor, William W., and Marjolijn Bijlefeld. **Kids and Guns: A Child Safety Scandal.** 2d ed. Washington, DC: The American Youth Work Center and the Educational Fund to End Handgun Violence, June 1989.

This brief booklet discusses the increasing homicide rate among children using handguns, accidents with handguns, and attacks on children by mentally and otherwise deranged or distraught individuals. The pamphlet contains cartoons illustrating the problem, statistical tables and data, and reproductions of relevant letters, editorials, and other related materials. Sources and a BB Gun Bibliography are included.

U.S. Congress. Senate. Committee on the Judiciary. Subcommittee on the Constitution. Citizens Committee for the Right to Keep and Bear Arms. . . . **An Individual Right.** Report from the U.S. Senate, 97th Cong., 2d sess., 1982. Reprinted courtesy of the Citizens Committee for the Right to Keep and Bear Arms, Bellevue, WA.

This reprint is largely a history of the evolution of the right to keep and bear arms as provided for in the Second Amendment. It has a preface by Senator Orrin Hatch, chair of the subcommittee. The Citizens Committee publishes these booklets intermittently.

U.S. Department of Justice. National Institute of Justice. **Research in Brief.** Washington, DC: United States Department of Justice, November 1986.

Research in Brief is an intermittent publication of the National Institute of Justice. The issues covered are related to crime and other topics in the United States, such as a piece that reviews and reports on James D. Wright's study, *The Armed Criminal in America.* Other topics have included discussions of AIDS in prison, the role of the private sector in crime and corrections, problem-oriented policing, and violence in schools.

Young Americans for Freedom. **"Right To Keep and Bear Arms."** Young Americans for Freedom, n.d.

This one-page flyer, written by Young Americans for Freedom National Director James D. Bieber, discusses recent oppressive events in China and other countries where dictatorships have eliminated the right to keep and bear arms, comparing it to the opposite American tradition. Quotations from Thomas Jefferson, Patrick Henry, James Madison, and Samuel Adams are given.

Selected Nonprint Resources 7

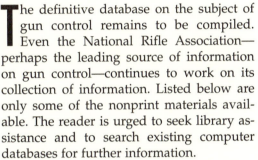

The definitive database on the subject of gun control remains to be compiled. Even the National Rifle Association—perhaps the leading source of information on gun control—continues to work on its collection of information. Listed below are only some of the nonprint materials available. The reader is urged to seek library assistance and to search existing computer databases for further information.

Films and Videocassettes

America Needs a National Gun Policy
Type: Video
Length: 20 min.
Date: 1991
Source: Handgun Control, Inc.
          1225 I Street
          Suite 1100
          Washington, DC 20005

This video looks at handgun violence in the United States and suggests alternatives aimed at reducing the severity of the problem. It is narrated by Sarah Brady and Pete Shields of Handgun Control, Incorporated.

The Constitution: That Delicate Balance: School Prayer, Gun Control and the Right To Assemble
Type: Video
Length: 56 min.
Date: 1984
Source: Public Media, Inc.
5547 Ravenswood Avenue
Chicago, IL 60640

This color program discusses issues related to the Bill of Rights. It is moderated by Harvard Law Professor Arthur Miller, and includes guests Fred Friendly, Potter Stewart, Griffen Bell, Shirley Hufstedlere, and Jean Baker, who focus on rights under the Second Amendment, among other topics. A teacher's guide is also available.

Crime
Type: 16mm film
Length: 19 min.
Date: 1976
Source: Documents Associates, Inc.
211 East 43rd Street
New York, NY 10017

This color film is a general look at crime—from the fact that most crime in the United States is not reported to the low conviction rates of those who are brought before the courts. The film particularly focuses on so-called white collar crime, more specifically, embezzlement. Former Attorney General Ramsey Clark is featured. Sophisticated technology and its relation to the success of crime are discussed.

The Crime
Type: 16mm film
Length: 25 min.
Date: 1973
Source: Kent State University
Audio-Visual Services
Kent, Ohio 44242

This is a color movie narrated by F. Lee Bailey, the nationally known defense attorney, on the subject of arrest, arraignment, trial, and sentencing in a drug-related incident. Bailey's major point is that more attention must be paid to the rehabilitation of criminals. The focus is on both Ohio and the United States.

Crime and Delinquency

Type: 16mm film
Length: 29 min.
Date: 1959
Source: National Educational Television, Inc.
Indiana University
Bloomington, IN 97401

This black-and-white film features Dr. Margaret Mead and Dr. Bertram Beck, who are interviewed on the issues of delinquency and violence in the United States. A primary topic of discussion is the rising crime rate and what might be done to stem it.

Crime and Human Nature

Type: 16 mm film
Length: 28 min.
Date: NA
Source: Films for the Humanities & Sciences
P.O. Box 2053
Princeton, NJ 08543

This color program addresses the nature-nurture argument with respect to whether crime is natural or socially induced. Anthropologist Ashley Montagu and others appear with Phil Donahue.

Crime and the Courts

Type: 16mm film
Length: 38 min.
Date: 1971
Source: Columbia Broadcast System
383 Madison Avenue
New York, NY 10017

This black-and-white film has to do with the nature of the judicial decision: does a judge send an offender to jail (where the offender is likely to learn more about crime) or does the judge release the offender, thus placing him or her back into the social environment that was possibly the major initial cause of the commission of crime? Professor James Vorenberg is interviewed.

Crime and the Criminal

Type: 16mm film
Length: 33 min.
Date: 1973

Source: Columbia Pictures
711 5th Avenue
New York, NY 10022

Learning Corp. of America
Distributed by Simon & Schuster Communications
108 Wilmot Road
Deerfield, IL 60015

This color and black-and-white film is an edited version of Truman Capote's film (adapted from his novel) *In Cold Blood.* Perry Smith, convicted of the murder of the Clutter family in Kansas, discusses his family background, his personal loneliness, and his alternating love and hate for his father. Orson Welles is the narrator. Smith is ultimately portrayed as not responsible for what he did because he lacked understanding of his actions.

Crime at Home: What To Do
Type: 16mm film
Length: 21 min.
Date: 1976
Source: Teleprograms, Inc.
Division of Simon & Schuster Communications
108 Wilmot Road
Deerfield, IL 60015

This brief color film demonstrates measures one might take to secure one's home from burglary and various incursions by criminals and others. It is an elementary "how to" lesson on home safety.

Crime, Criminals and the System
Type: 16mm film
Length: 27 min.
Date: 1974
Source: Coronet
Division of Simon & Schuster Communications
108 Wilmot Road
Deerfield, IL 60015

This color film examines the criminal justice system in the United States and the reasons that it apparently is not accomplishing its objectives. The film looks at who is a criminal and what constitutes a crime from the perspectives of the police officer, the lawyer, the judge, the warden, the prisoner, and the average citizen. The subjects of street crimes, victimless crimes, white collar crimes, and violent crimes are dramatized.

Crime: Dye Guns, Lasers, Justice?
Type: 16mm film
Length: 22 min.
Date: 1970
Source: Document Associates, Inc.
            211 East 43rd Street
            New York, NY 10017

This color film examines police technology such as voiceprint, eavesdropping, so-called dye guns, laser weapons, and, in general, highly sophisticated devices used against crime in the United States. Ramsey Clark comments on rising crime in the United States. Ralph Salerno, who discusses crime syndicates, is also interviewed.

Crime in the Cities
Type: 16mm film
Length: 25 min.
Date: 1966
Source: National Broadcasting Company
            30 Rockefeller Plaza
            New York, NY 10020

            Films, Inc., Public Media Inc.
            5547 Ravenswood Avenue
            Chicago, IL 60640

This black-and-white film examines crime in both a contemporary and historical context. Interviews are conducted with individuals from a variety of backgrounds, and some of the circumstances under which crime occurs are examined. One of the film's highlights is a comparison of criminal statistics from the past to the present.

Crime in the Home
Type: 16mm film
Length: 22 min.
Date: 1973
Source: AIMS Media, Inc.
            6901 Woodley Avenue
            Van Nuys, CA 91406

This color film deals with crimes in homes and apartments, discussing ways to deal with potential burglaries and methods of protection.

Crime Lab

Type: 16mm film
Length: 18 min.
Date: 1948
Source: RKO Radio Pictures
         129 North Vermont
         Los Angeles, CA 90004

This black-and-white film briefly explains the modern devices used by police to detect and solve crime. The film suggests that modern technology and sophisticated techniques make solutions to crime far more possible, and thus the criminal's chances of succeeding are significantly decreasing.

A Crime of Violence

Type: 35mm film
Length: 17 min.
Date: 1976
Source: University of Minnesota
         Audio-Visual Library
         3300 South East University Avenue
         Minneapolis, MN 55414

This is a color slide-tape program dealing with rape as a violent crime, not as a crime of passion. The presentation suggests methods to protect against this type of violent crime and what to do if attacked. Various elements of the Minnesota Criminal Sexual Conduct Law are covered.

Crime on the Streets

Type: 16mm film
Length: 19 min.
Date: 1972
Source: AIMS Media, Inc.
         6901 Woodley Avenue
         Van Nuys, CA 91406

Theft, burglary, assault, and rape are discussed in this color film, which was made with the cooperation of the Pasadena (California) Police Department. Suggested defenses against such criminal possibilities are provided, and the film makes the point that prevention is the best defense.

Crime on the Streets (2nd Edition)
Type: 16mm film
Length: 16 min.
Date: 1984
Source: AIMS Media, Inc.
            6901 Woodley Avenue
            Van Nuys, CA 91406

This color film features a former mugger and thief who offers advice to viewers about how to avoid being attacked on the streets. "Angelo" suggests that there are certain "landmarks"—persons who are more or less likely than others to be mugged or attacked. One, he says, is the person who is "just asking for it" because of his or her outright careless behavior patterns; the other is the person who sends signals that he or she will be "easy" for the would-be attacker. All of this, he says, has to do with how one walks, carries one's purse, briefcase, packages, or other objects.

Crime Prevention: It's Elementary
Type: 16mm film
Length: 12 min.
Date: 1983
Source: AIMS Media, Inc.
            6901 Woodley Avenue
            Van Nuys, CA 91406

This color film is directed at young people. It provides lessons by McGruff, a crime prevention mascot, regarding crimes that children might experience. The film underscores the lesson that even children can do something to prevent crime.

Crime: Senior Alert
Type: 16mm film
Length: 18 min.
Date: 1978
Source: AIMS Media, Inc.
            6901 Woodley Avenue
            Van Nuys, CA 91406

This color film describes ways in which senior citizens can avoid (if not totally prevent) being criminally victimized in their homes or in other environments, such as their cars. The film also discusses high-risk crime areas—hallways, parking areas, and laundry facilities—and how to cope with an attacker who displays a weapon.

Crime under Twenty-One
Type: 16mm film
Length: 30 min.
Date: 1958
Source: National Educational Television, Inc.
Indiana University
Bloomington, IN 97401

This black-and-white film focuses on teenage criminal behavior. It suggests that the amount of teenage crime might be overstated and that gathering statistical evidence might change the image Americans have of crime among the young. Young people discuss their lives and the types of problems they face.

Crimebusters
Type: 16mm film
Length: 26 min.
Date: 1995
Source: Films for the Humanities & Sciences
P.O. Box 2053
Princeton, NJ 08543

This color film discusses progress in the area of criminal investigation, with special emphasis on DNA techniques, lasers in the detection of fingerprints and palm prints, computer graphics, and artificial legal reasoning.

Crimes in Progress
Type: 16mm film
Length: 24 min.
Date: 1973
Source: Motorola Teleprograms
Division of Simon & Schuster Communications
108 Wilmot Road
Deerfield, IL 60015

This color film, made for law enforcement personnel, depicts a burglary and safe-cracking, an armed robbery, and a so-called Peeping Tom, and demonstrates how police respond to these criminal and deviant episodes as they are occurring. Scenes discussing police communications, driving and unit responses to the events, single and two-person police responses, observation techniques, and lookouts are included, as well as legal definitions of the methods involved.

The Criminal
Type: 16mm film
Length: 30 min.
Date: 1958
Source: National Educational Television, Inc.
Indiana University
Bloomington, IN 97401

This black-and-white film discusses definitions of the terms *crime* and *criminal*, and it makes a superficial attempt to come to grips with the problems of cultural, locational, and other matters that have an impact on crime. The film also briefly addresses the topic of criminal law.

The Criminal and How To Neutralize Him
Type: 16mm film
Length: 30 min.
Date: 1958
Source: National Educational Television, Inc.
Indiana University
Bloomington, IN 97401

This black-and-white film asserts that a series of principles involving criminal correction have not yet been fully developed, and it discusses the need for criminal rehabilitation. Its particular focus is the evaluation and treatment of criminals.

The Criminal and Punishment
Type: 16mm film
Length: 30 min.
Date: 1958
Source: National Educational Television, Inc.
Indiana University
Bloomington, IN 97401

This black-and-white film is about the rehabilitation of the criminal and the concept of punishment. Five inmates at San Quentin Prison in California are interviewed.

A Criminal Is Born
Type: 16mm film
Length: 22 min.
Date: 1938
Source: Metro Goldwyn Mayer
1350 Avenue of the Americas
New York, NY 10019

Indiana University
Audio-Visual Center
Bloomington, IN 47405

This somewhat dated classroom film in black and white follows a gang of four boys who enter into criminal activity. One of the boys leaves the gang, one of the remaining three is ultimately killed during a holdup, and the other two are taken into custody.

Criminal Justice in the United States
Type: 16mm film
Length: 32 min.
Date: 1966
Source: National Broadcasting Company
30 Rockefeller Plaza
New York, NY 10020

Encyclopaedia Britannica Educational Corporation
425 North Michigan Avenue
Chicago, IL 60611

This black-and-white film studies 12 men who were imprisoned for crimes they did not commit. Forced confessions, mistaken identities, unsubstantiated alibis, excessive bail, withheld evidence, and the question of poverty and its impact on criminal events are examined. The film also looks at the impact of mass media on the public demand for the conviction of criminals. Chet Huntley narrates.

The Criminal Justice System
Type: 16mm film
Length: 18 min.
Date: 1974
Source: Paramount Communications
Distributed by AIMS Media
6901 Woodley Avenue
Van Nuys, CA 91406

This color film uses animation to explain the criminal justice system in the United States. It takes the viewer from the arrest of a suspect through rehabilitation in the penal system. The film examines misdemeanors, felonies, and violations of the law by juveniles, and discusses the concepts of fairness and equality.

Criminology: Lead Us Not into Temptation
Type: 16mm film
Length: 22 min.
Date: 1972
Source: Document Associates, Inc.
211 East 43rd Street
New York, NY 10017

This color film examines crime detection and the notion of crime as a game, including the psychology underlying such an idea.

Criminology Research
Type: 16mm film
Length: 27 min.
Date: 1955
Source: University of California
Extension Media Center
2223 Fulton Street
Berkeley, CA 94720

CRM/McGraw-Hill Films
674 Via de la Valle
P.O. Box 641
Del Mar, CA 92014

This black-and-white film shows graduate students examining prisoners in California's San Quentin Prison. They take photographs and study prison authorities and prison life in general. Rehabilitation is discussed from various perspectives.

Deadly Decisions: The Right To Protect Yourself
Type: 16mm film
Length: 28 min.
Date: 1995
Source: Films for the Humanities & Sciences
P.O. Box 2053
Princeton, NJ 08543

This color film discusses whether a person has the right to shoot an intruder in his or her home or someone threatening in the workplace. Police cases illustrate decisions made by individuals under such circumstances and examine whether individuals are within their rights to defend themselves with firearms.

Ever Changing, Ever Free
Type: 16mm film
Length: 11 min.
Date: 1974
Source: United States National Audiovisual Center
           General Services Administration
           Reference Section
           Washington, DC 20409

This color film examines the Bill of Rights, emphasizing the freedoms it guarantees and the system of order and rules within which it must function if it is to provide its widest application.

Firearm Safety
Type: Video
Length: 30 min.
Date: 1987
Source: Educational Resources Foundation
           5534 Bush River Road
           Columbia, SC 29212

Though brief, this is a very useful and quite complete introduction on handling firearms safely. It is aimed at an audience from junior high school through adult.

Firearm Safety Begins in the Home
Type: Video, 8mm film
Length: 22 min.
Date: 1982
Source: Coronet/MTI Film & Video
           Division of Simon & Schuster Communications
           108 Wilmot Road
           Deerfield, IL 60015

This film, directed at senior high school and adult audiences, suggests that guns in the home should be used for protection and that they should therefore be regarded as off-limits except for that purpose. Above all, guns should be kept out of the way of children.

George Mason
Type: Video
Length: 51 min.
Date: 1965
Source: Social Studies Schools Service
           10000 Culver Boulevard
           Culver City, CA 90232

This color video constitutes a partial biography of George Mason, a leading Virginia statesman during the time of the adoption of the Constitution. Mason was a prime mover on behalf of the Bill of Rights, and was a particularly strong supporter of the right to keep and bear arms.

Gun Control
Type: Filmstrip (90 frames)
Length: 19 ½ min.
Date: 1984
Source: Encyclopaedia Britannica Educational Corporation
           425 North Michigan Avenue
           Chicago, IL 60611

This is one of the programs in the Contemporary Issues Series produced by Encyclopedia Britannica. Speakers from each organization present the viewpoints of the National Rifle Association and the National Coalition to Ban Handguns.

Gun Control: A Target for Controversy
Type: Filmstrip (87 frames)
Length: 14 min.
Date: 1979
Source: New York Times Education Enrichment Materials
           Filmstrip Subscription Series on Current Affairs
           229 West 43rd Street
           New York, NY 10036

This color filmstrip discusses a range of gun control laws, beginning with the 1930s. It analyzes the issue of gun control and presents the views of hunters and those who advocate greater legislative control of guns. It also presents contemporary legislative analyses and proposals dealing with the subject.

Gun Control: Pro and Con
Type: 16mm film, video
Length: 51 min.

Date: 1976
Source: CRM/McGraw-Hill Films
674 Via de la Valle
P.O. Box 641
Del Mar, CA 92014

This color film examines both sides of the handgun control issue. Police officers, criminals, judges, and others present their opinions. The film points out that most gun crimes are committed by recidivists (repeat offenders) or persons on parole or probation. Howard K. Smith and John Scali are featured.

Gun Control: The Right To Bear Arms
Type: Filmstrip (74 frames)
Length: 17 min.
Date: 1977
Source: Current Affairs Films
Address unavailable

This color filmstrip attempts to provide an objective discussion of the issues related to the gun control controversy by presenting both sides.

Gun Dogs and Ringnecks
Type: Video
Length: 30 min.
Date: 1989
Source: Video Treasures
1767 Morris Avenue
Union, NJ 07083

Ted Dewey narrates this production and takes the viewer on a pheasant hunt with his bird dog. The aficionado will find this film, which is entertaining and somewhat instructional, interesting and useful.

A Gun for Mandy
Type: Video
Length: 27 min.
Date: 1982
Source: Paulist Productions
P.O. Box 1057
Pacific Palisades, CA 90272

This video examines private gun owners. It is directed at senior high school and religious audiences.

Gun Handling

Type: ¾" U-matic
Length: 29 min.
Date: 1976
Source: University Division of Media and Learning Resources
Special Services Building
Pennsylvania State University
University Park, PA 16802

This production, directed at college and adult audiences, is about safe hunting. It demonstrates a number of techniques for storage of guns and ammunition, the correct method to clean a rifle, and the appropriate use of a rifle in the field and during transportation.

Gun Safety

Type: 16mm film
Length: 12 min.
Date: 1967
Source: Moreland-Latchford Productions, Ltd.
299 West Queen Street
Toronto, Ontario
Canada

Sterling Educational Films, Inc.
241 East 34th Street
New York, NY 10016

In this color film, hunters demonstrate the basics of gun safety while hunting. It is filmed on location and is part of the Survival In the Winter Wilderness Series.

Gun Wise

Type: Video
Length: 17 min.
Date: 1977
Source: AIMS Media, Inc.
6901 Woodley Avenue
Van Nuys, CA 91406

This brief video presents the basic lessons of firearm safety, from handling and storage to the dangers of keeping guns. It is aimed at a senior high and adult audience.

Gunfight, USA

Type: Video

Length: 58 min.
Date: 1983
Source: PBS Video
50 North La Cienega Boulevard
Beverly Hills, CA 90211

This documentary concerns the range of issues surrounding the gun control controversy in the United States. It is aimed at a junior high through adult audience.

Gunning the Flyways
Type: 16mm film
Length: 30 min.
Date: 1951
Source: Remington Arms Company
939 Barnum
Bridgeport, CT 06602

This color film discusses hunting of waterfowl from Canada to North Carolina and California. Discussion of duck blinds and working retriever dogs constitutes a major element of the film.

Guns: A Day in the Death of America
Type: Television film
Length: 20 min.
Date: 1989
Source: Handgun Control, Inc.
1225 I Street
Suite 1100
Washington, DC 20005

This documentary discusses the deaths of 61 people in one day as a result of gun incidents. The film's introduction features Democratic Senator Howard Metzenbaum of Ohio.

Guns Are Different
Type: Video
Length: 20 min.
Date: 1980
Source: National Archives and Records Administration
Customer Service Section P2
8700 Edgeworth Drive
Capitol Heights, MD 20743

The underlying message of this program, aimed at senior high and adult audiences, is that guns are in and of themselves safe, but their misuse may lead to tragedy. Many gun injuries or deaths are the result of unfortunate unintentional acts.

Guns: Be Safe Not Sorry
Type: 16mm film
Length: 14 min.
Date: 1975
Source: Universal Education and Visual Arts
Division of Universal Studios, Inc.
100 Universal City Plaza
Universal City, CA 91608

Focusing on children between the ages of 10 and 18, this color film argues that the careless use of guns leads to destructiveness, and that appropriate techniques to store and handle guns must be learned.

Guns, Drugs, and the CIA
Type: Video
Length: 60 min.
Date: 1989
Source: PBS Video
50 North La Cienega Boulevard
Beverly Hills, CA 90211

This program explores the notion that the Central Intelligence Agency (CIA) has employed drug leaders and used drug money to engage in "secret" wars in various parts of the world for many years. It is directed toward junior high school through adult audiences.

Guns of Autumn
Type: 16 mm film
Length: 77 min.
Date: 1975
Source: Focus On Animals
P.O. Box 150
Trumbull, CT 06611

This color documentary film, considered to be highly controversial, discusses the philosophy of hunting—the reasons why people hunt, the type of person who hunts, and how hunting is conducted.

Guns of the Old West, Volume 1, 1803–1861
Type: Video
Length: 60 min.
Date: 1991
Source: Cassel Productions
1249 Point View Street
Los Angeles, CA 90035

This film examines the guns of choice used by outlaws and law enforcers between 1803 and 1861 in American history. The program features Hoyt Axton. It is aimed at junior high through adult audiences.

Guns of the Old West, Volume 2, 1862–1898
Type: Video
Length: 60 min.
Date: 1991
Source: Cassel Productions
1249 Point View Street
Los Angeles, CA 90035

This film examines guns that were especially popular from 1862 through 1898 in American history. It is aimed at junior high through adult audiences.

Gunshot Wound of Hand
Type: Video
Length: 12 min.
Date: 1975
Source: Ohio State University
Medical Audio-Visual Center
1583 Perry Street
Columbus, OH 43210

This is a medically oriented depiction of injury to the carpals, distal ulna, and radius as a result of a gunshot wound. It is intended for college and adult audiences, and is useful in understanding traumatic wounds resulting from firearms use.

Gunsmith of Williamsburg
Type: 16mm film
Length: 62 min.
Date: 1969

Source: Colonial Williamsburg, Inc.
Film Distribution Section
Goodwin Building, Box C
Williamsburg, VA 23185

Master Gunsmith Wallace Gusler of Williamsburg, Virginia, takes the viewer through the actual creation of a flintlock rifle of the 1770s. A useful and interesting color documentary for the collector and maker of guns, it shows the viewer the step-by-step process by which a rifle is constructed. The film discusses the history of guns of the period and shows examples of costumes, tools, and traditions of the time. The gunmaker's skill is portrayed in detail.

Kids and Guns
Type: Video
Length: 28 min.
Date: 1995
Source: Films for the Humanities & Sciences
P.O. Box 2053
Princeton, NJ 08543

This color production concerns youth violence and the number of deaths and accidents related to the use of guns in the United States. It argues that the gun has become the "weapon of choice" among youthful offenders.

Law and Order
Type: Video
Length: 56 min.
Date: 1988
Source: Films for the Humanities & Sciences
P.O. Box 2053
Princeton, NJ 08543

This color production examines police rights under the Fourth Amendment, which deals with unreasonable searches and seizures. The basic issue addressed in the film is whether the constitutional rights of the accused interfere with the work of the police or whether such rights help to create better police forces throughout the country.

Prayer, Gun Control and the Right to Assemble 3
Type: Video
Length: 60 min.

Date: 1984
Source: Films, Inc., Public Media Inc.
5547 Ravenswood Ave.,
Chicago, IL 60640

This color video examines political and social issues growing out of the application of the provisions of the First and Second Amendments. It refers to the Supreme Court and the manner in which it determines basic public policy through its decisions on these issues.

The Right To Bear Arms
Type: Filmstrip (77 frames)
Length: 12 min.
Date: 1974
Source: Xerox Films
Department of Xerox Education Publications
Distributed by Center for Humanities, Inc.
Communications Park
Box 1000
Mount Kisco, NY 10549

This is a detailed color filmstrip kit in which eight concepts fundamental to understanding the Second Amendment are examined. The kit includes books for students and duplicate masters.

A Shooting Gallery Called America
Type: 16mm film
Length: 52 min.
Date: 1975
Source: Public Media Incorporated
5547 Ravenswood Avenue
Chicago, IL 60640

In this program an NBC reporter interviews owners of handguns, focusing on the impact that handgun ownership might have on American society.

So Violent a Nation
Type: Video
Length: 60 min.
Date: 1992
Source: Films for the Humanities & Sciences
P.O. Box 2053
Princeton, NJ 08543

This color program is about violent crime in America, focusing on rape, robbery, assaults, and murder. Dallas, Texas, is featured. The film is part of the Listening to America with Bill Moyers series, and was produced by Public Affairs Television and Station KERA, Dallas/Fort Worth/Denton.

Street Gangs of Los Angeles
Type: 16mm film
Length: 44 min.
Date: 1995
Source: Films for the Humanities & Sciences
            P.O. Box 2053
            Princeton, NJ 08543

This color film examines Los Angeles youth gangs, the sheer ruthlessness of their behavior, and the underlying drug difficulties involved. Youth gangs might constitute a type of omen for future American urban life. The program also portrays the efforts some parents have made to protect their children from such violence.

Sweet Sorrow
Type: 16mm film, video
Length: 8 min.
Date: 1988
Source: Pyramid Film & Video
            Box 1048
            Santa Monica, CA 90405

This program is about a teenage boy who accidentally shoots another person. Its message is that handguns should not be misused and, especially, are not toys.

Three American Guns
Type: 16mm film, video
Length: 35 min.
Date: 1982
Source: Motorola Teleprograms
            Division of Simon & Schuster Communications
            108 Wilmot Road
            Deerfield, IL 60015

This program examines three events in which guns were used: a woman who shot two men who had murdered her husband after holding up their store; a man who mistakenly shot his wife when the home alarm system sounded; and a widow who was killed with her own gun by an intruder.

"To Keep and Bear Arms": Gun Control
and the Second Amendment
Type: Video
Length: 30 min.
Date: 1994
Source: Close-up Publishing
            Department C75
            44 Canal Center Plaza
            Alexandria, VA 22314

This video explores both sides of the gun control controversy. Experts on both sides of the issue present their legal and political arguments, and advocates of gun control and those who oppose it give their opinions.

Weapons: Part I (Prohibited Weapons)
Type: Video
Length: 26 min.
Date: 1974
Source: AIMS Media, Inc.
            6901 Woodley Avenue
            Van Nuys, CA 91406

This presentation is about possession of weapons, concealed weapons, various handguns, and so-called switchblade knives. It is of particular use in police training.

Weapons: Part II (Deadly and Concealed Weapons)
Type: Video
Length: 22 min.
Date: 1975
Source: AIMS Media, Inc.
            6901 Woodley Avenue
            Van Nuys, CA 91406

This production is a companion piece to *Weapons: Part I: (Prohibited Weapons)*, above. It deals specifically with unloaded guns, prohibited weapons, concealed weapons, and the public handling of weapons. It is intended for an adult audience, and has been particularly useful in the training of police.

Databases

BNA ONLINE
Bureau of National Affairs, Inc.
1231 25th Street, NW
Washington, DC 20037
(202) 452-4132

This database contains information on federal laws, current political and social issues, and business affairs contained in the publications of the Bureau of National Affairs (BNA), and is available to any user. Especially helpful for this topic are the BNA California Case Law Daily and the BNA New York Case Law Daily databases (both of which contain information on court cases on the state and national levels), the BNA Washington Insider (which contains Supreme Court opinions, the Federal Register, and congressional hearings and actions), and U.S. Law Week, an excellent source of information on the actions of the Supreme Court.

BNA PLUS
Bureau of National Affairs, Inc.
1231 25th Street, NW
Washington, DC 20037
(202) 452-4323

This database is available to subscribers for a fee or free of charge, and to nonsubscribers for a fee. Its delivery service includes, among other things, annotated bibliographies, current affairs, analytical reports, and government information. Rush delivery service is available.

Congressional Information Service, CIS/Index
4520 East-West Highway, Suite 800
Bethesda, MD 20814-3389
(301) 654-1550

This database is accessible through DIALOG Information Services. It provides access to all publications and laws of Congress, documents related to Supreme Court briefs and decisions, and documents related to state constitutional revisions.

DIALOG Information Services
3460 Hillview Avenue
Palo Alto, CA 94304
(415) 858-3785

Available in many libraries to subscribers and those who provide a purchase order, DIALOG offers access to over 370 databases. For those interested in the Bill of Rights, America History and Life, CIS/Index, Legal Resource Index, SOCIALSCI SEARCH, and U.S. Political Science Documents are especially recommended.

LEGAL FORUM
CompuServe Information Service
5000 Arlington Centre Boulevard
P.O. Box 20212
Columbus, OH 43220
(614) 457-8600

Available through CompuServe, Inc., this database serves the legal fraternity and anyone else interested in its materials. Its data library on current legal problems is particularly useful.

LEGI-SLATE
111 Massachusetts Avenue
Washington, DC 20001
(202) 898-2300

Available on a subscription basis, this service tracks congressional bills, offering the full text of bills and resolutions, member profiles and ratings, and news journal articles (references to the *Washington Post, National Journal,* and *Congressional Quarterly Weekly Report*). It also offers the Press Briefing Service and the Federal Register Service.

LEXIS
Reed Elsenier—LEXIS
P.O. Box 933
Dayton, Ohio 45401
(800) 253-5624, ext. 1286

LEXIS is a leading online service available to those in the legal profession. It includes federal and state case law, and it is accessible under contract with Mead Data Central. More than 60 million articles are stored in LEXIS; over 3 million federal and state legal cases, American Bar Association and American Law Reports, legislation, state laws, and some foreign materials, especially those from France and the United Kingdom.

PAIS INTERNATIONAL
Public Affairs Information Service
521 West 43rd Street
New York, NY 10036-4396

This is a useful general guide to information sources relevant to government and research in the social sciences. It is a compilation of information contained in the *PAIS Bulletin* and *PAIS Foreign Language Index*. It can be accessed through BRS Information Technologies, BRS/After Dark, Data-Star, DIALOG, or DIALOG'S KNOWLEDGE INDEX.

WESTLAW
West Publishing Company
50 West Kellogg Boulevard
P.O. Box 64526
St. Paul, MN 55164-0526
(612) 228-2500

This is the leading service offering legal information. It holds all federal and state case law and includes the Index to Legal Periodicals. It is accessible under contract with the West Publishing Company.

WILSONLINE
H. W. Wilson Company
950 University Avenue
Bronx, NY 10452
(800) 367-6770

The databases Index to Legal Periodicals and Social Sciences Index are especially valuable to researchers on this topic. Services are available to all users.

CD-ROMs

Congressional Masterfile 1 and Congressional Masterfile 2
Source: Congressional Information Service, CIS/Index
4520 East-West Highway
Bethesda, MD 20814-3389

This service offers complete indexing and abstracting of congressional hearings, relevant documents and reports, and committee prints. It is perhaps the most complete CD-ROM available on the subject. Masterfile 1 contains publications from 1789 through 1969; Masterfile 2 contains publications from 1970. It is updated quarterly. An IBM PC-AT or compatible equipment, a drive meeting High Sierra standard, and Quantum Access software are required. There is a subscription fee.

The Constitution Papers
Source: Electronic Text Corporation, Publisher Software
Resources; CALI, Inc., Distributor
526 East Quail Road
Orem, UT 84057

This CD-ROM contains the texts of the constitutions of the original 13 states, the entire Constitution of the United States, the Magna Carta, the Federalist Papers, Thomas Paine's *Common Sense*, and documents dealing with the constitutional convention, colonial history, the Revolutionary War, and the Codfishery Debates. An IBM PC-XT/AT or compatible; a Hitachi, NEC, Sony, or Toshiba drive; and Word Cruncher software are required.

Social Science Index
Source: H. W. Wilson Company
950 University Avenue
Bronx, NY 10452

This CD-ROM contains the leading index to over 300 social science publications in the English language. It is updated quarterly. An IBM PC with hard disk and 640K RAM; a Hitachi, Sony, or Phillips drive; and H. W. Wilson software are required. There is a charge.

Educational Software

The Amendments to the Constitution
Source: Classroom Consortia Media, Inc.
57 Bay Street
Statem Island, NY 10301

Designed for young people in grades 6 through 12, this program is an introduction to the amendments to the U.S. Constitution and the process of formal constitutional amendment. The Bill of Rights is emphasized, and interactive situations are provided.

The software consists of a 5¼" or 3½" floppy disk, and requires an IBM PC, PC XT, PCjr, PC AT, or compatible, and a color graphics adapter. It requires 16K of memory and a PC-DOS 2.0 or greater operating system.

U.S. Constitution

Source: Classroom Consortia Media, Inc.
57 Bay Street
Staten Island, NY 10301

This package is intended for students in grades 6 through 12. It focuses on the amendments to the U.S. Constitution, and includes case studies aimed at creating court trials based on the amendments themselves. After weighing the evidence, the student must come to a decision. The student must complete crossword puzzles and multiple choice questions concerning each amendment. Software involves a 5¼" or 3½" disk; IBM PC, PCjr, PC XT, PC AT, or compatible; a color graphics adapter and a PC-DOS 2.0 or greater operating system.

Glossary

abusive use of raids The use by the U.S. Bureau of Alcohol, Tobacco, and Firearms of raids that do not fully take into account the safety or constitutional rights of those occupying the businesses or homes being raided. The February 1993 raid of the Branch Davidian complex in Waco, Texas, is often used as an example.

action The mechanism by which a firearm works. Action mechanisms include single-shot, revolver, multi-barrel, slide action, pump action, lever action, semiautomatic action, and automatic action.

air resistance The resistance of the air encountered by a bullet as it emerges from the muzzle of a gun. For example, if a .30/06 bullet emerges from a rifle at 2,700 feet per second, it encounters a wind of 1,841 miles per hour. This resistance slows the bullet to only 2,460 feet per second after it has traveled only 100 yards. The shape of a bullet has much to do with the way it slices through the air, and resistance is reduced or increased accordingly.

airguns Strictly speaking, these are not firearms, but guns using compressed air or carbon dioxide for propulsion of the projectile. Typical examples are the BB gun and the pellet gun.

AK-47 A semiautomatic rifle that chambers the same types of cartridges as some of its military counterparts. It is often incorrectly referred to as an assault rifle, but the assault rifle, first developed by Germans for use in World War II, has the capability of being fired in both a semiautomatic and a fully automatic mode.

Alliance against Handguns This group, although not widely known nor highly active on the gun control issue, is an organization seeking enactment of a variety of anti-weapons legislation.

American Protective Association One of several organizations that came into existence to urge a flat ban on gun ownership by aliens. The fear of immigrants and labor organizations led to this organization's rise.

American Rifleman The most widely known publication of the National Rifle Association, available by subscription to members of the organization. It contains articles and analyses of the pro-gun and anti-gun movements in the United States, often written by widely recognized experts in the field. The magazine is well-illustrated and contains a variety of articles pertaining to guns and gun safety and to training in gun use. It is largely dedicated to the sporting use of guns, gun collecting, and the right of Americans to keep and bear arms.

ammunition The components of cartridges of one type or another, including a primer, gunpowder, and projectiles (such as bullets used in handguns and rifles, or multiple or single projectiles used in shotguns).

anti-control argument An argument that avers that gun control laws are essentially useless. Some of the points raised in the argument are that all laws are violated and thus are not completely enforceable; that the costs to enforce them would significantly exceed the benefits of gun control laws; that criminals will ignore these laws and procure weapons anyway—whether guns or alternative weapons; that, as such, law-abiding citizens would suffer most from such laws; that limited restrictions will ultimately lead to a complete ban on guns; and that the only way to reduce crime is to "get tough" on criminals, not to inflict further restrictions on law-abiding citizens.

antique An antique firearm is defined by the national government as one manufactured before 1899 and for which ammunition is difficult or impossible to obtain. It is also defined as a weapon that cannot fire fixed ammunition.

application to purchase system This is a process relating to the purchase of firearms whereby the consumer is required to fill out an application that the seller then sends to a regulatory agency. If the seller has not heard from the regulatory agency after a specified period of time, the sale is made. The silence of the agency implies consent to the sale.

armed crime A crime during which a weapon is carried or used.

armed criminals typology A criminal model based on the type of weapon or weapons used during the commission of a crime.

armed victims of crime Those persons who arm themselves for protection against possible crime. There is some disagreement among scholars and law enforcement officials as to whether arming oneself in fact reduces the probability of being victimized by criminals.

armor-piercing ammunition The national government defines armor-piercing ammunition as "a projectile or projectile core which may be used in a handgun and which is constructed . . . from one or a combination of tungsten alloys, steel, iron, brass, bronze, beryllium copper, or depleted uranium." Certain exceptions to laws prohibiting their manufacture or import are made; for example, shotgun shells coming under game regulations for hunting, target shooting, sporting use, or industrial use are not subject to such laws.

assassinate A killing by sudden, often secret, assault. Premeditation usually precedes assassination.

assault An attempt to threaten or hurt someone with the apparent ability to effectuate injury or threat. National Crime Survey statistics indicate that about half of all assaults are threats without attack, and only about half of assaults involving attacks culminate in injury, with only 1 percent resulting in death.

assault rifle The Department of Defense defines an assault rifle as a military rifle capable of "selective fire." That is, it is capable of being fired semiautomatically or fully automatically. Journalists during the 1980s and 1990s changed the definition to mean firearms that can be fired in an automatic mode alone, thus seriously misleading the public.

assault weapon This can be any weapon used in an assault upon another individual or other type of target. It is a vague term that is often misused, especially by journalists, and misunderstood by the public because the weapon has erroneously been identified as including almost exclusively semiautomatic pistols, some shotguns, and so-called assault rifles.

automatic pistol A handgun in which, when its trigger is pulled, releases a continuous stream of bullets. The term is misleading in that it is usually applied to what is in fact a semiautomatic pistol, auto-loading pistol, or self-loading pistol.

automatic weapon Any firearm that feeds cartridges, fires them, and empties their cases, and is designed to repeat this process as long as the trigger is depressed and the weapon contains cartridges. The most common examples are machine guns, submachine guns, and certain types of military and police rifles.

ball This term is most often used in the military. It originally described a spherical projectile, but in present times it relates to a bullet with a jacket having a cylindrical shape and a round or pointed nose.

BB gun An airgun that fires a BB, a round projectile .175 inches in diameter.

blackpowder The earliest firearms propellant. Today it is generally used in muzzleloaders and fixed-cartridge weapons requiring lower pressure.

blank A round containing blackpowder or some smokeless powder, but no projectile. Blanks are most often used to start races, in the theater or filmmaking, and to acclimate dogs to guns and gunfire.

bolt action A manually operated gun mechanism similar to a door bolt.

bore The interior of a firearm's barrel. The term does not include the chamber.

brass An expression used to describe metallic cartridge cases once they have been expended.

bullet A term often confused with cartridge. It is the projectile fired from a gun and can consist of various materials, and may be of many different shapes and weights. A bullet can be made of lead inside a jacket, and can be round-nosed, flat, or hollow-pointed, among other configurations.

Bureau of Alcohol, Tobacco, and Firearms An agency of the national government that attempts to oversee gun transactions and the use of guns, and whose primary purpose it is to enforce national gun laws in the United States.

burglary Under current law, burglary is defined as the unlawful breaking or entering into a building during the night to commit a felony or to steal. Although most dictionary definitions confine it to the night, some state laws as well as the *Uniform Crime Reports* have expanded it to include such activities that occur during daylight hours.

burst fire A characteristic of some weapons used in the military that enables them to fire a predetermined number of rounds each time the trigger is pulled.

caliber Generally, the diameter of a projectile of a rifle or the diameter between bands in a rifle that has been barreled. In the United States this dimension is usually stated in hundredths of an inch. Expression of caliber may vary in other countries: in the United Kingdom, for example, it is expressed in thousandths of an inch, and in millimeters in the countries of continental Europe and elsewhere.

carbine A type of rifle with a comparatively short barrel. Rifles with barrels shorter than sixteen inches and shotguns with barrels shorter than eighteen inches are required to be registered with the U.S. Bureau of Alcohol, Tobacco, and Firearms.

career criminals Adults who have had a history of juvenile or extended previous criminality; their repeated participation in crime is therefore often considered to be "career" behavior.

carry laws Laws that regulate the carrying of firearms. The strictness of such laws varies from state to state.

cartridge One round of ammunition.

case, or casing The container, known as the envelope, of a cartridge. Handgun and rifle casing is generally made of brass or some other metal, while shotgun casing is generally made of paper or plastic and has a metal head. In the latter instance, it is commonly called a shell.

chamber That part of the barrel of a firearm designed to hold the cartridge that is to be fired. In a revolver, for example, the chamber is a rotating device that accommodates the number of cartridges for which the weapon has been designed.

Chicago school A series of criminological ethnologies presented during the 1920s and 1930s that viewed crime from a microsocial approach and suggested that crime was both a learned activity (stemming from an individual's social environment) and a social activity reinforced by that social environment.

choke A device located at or near the muzzle of a shotgun that affects the actual dispersion of shot.

civilian justifiable homicide Generally, homicide committed as an act of self-defense. Guns are perhaps the most frequently used weapon in this type of act. The act must be in the course of the lawful defense of one's person or property.

civilian legal defensive homicide Homicide committed as an act of self-defense. Such acts are most often classified by the Federal Bureau of Investigation as excusable, rather than justified.

clip A mechanism designed to hold a group of cartridges. The word is also sometimes used to describe a distinct device used to hold and transport a group of cartridges to a magazine—either fixed or detached—or one that can be inserted into the firearm itself, thus essentially becoming a part of the mechanism.

collective right theory A theory that asserts that the right to keep and bear arms is a collective right for the purpose of serving in a state militia. Most opponents of this theory believe the argument has little foundation in fact, since the state militia—known generally as the National Guard—has been taken over by the national government and because a militia originally referred to every able-bodied male, who would supply his own weapons when called into service.

conflict theory A theory that defines crime as a consequence of social inequalities that are said by some to be particularly inherent to capitalism and societies having capitalistic economies.

cooling-off period A period of time between the point when an application to purchase a gun is filled out and when the consumer actually gains possession of the gun. It is used by police and other agencies to examine the applicant's record, and is based in part on the assumption that angry people may rush out to purchase a gun; it is assumed that the waiting period will allow such persons to "cool-off."

"cop-killer bullets" A pejorative term used by those in the anti-gun movement to describe certain types of bullets sometimes used in the killing of police officers. The term, in and of itself, has no historical, legal, or technical basis.

cylinder bore A term referring to the barrel of a shotgun that has neither a muzzle constriction nor a choke.

defective firearms Although the word *defective* is somewhat ambiguous, in this case it refers to the defects in weapons that could cause their discharge through accidental or negligent misuse. For example, a single-action revolver or derringer that does not have a safety device (such as a hammer block or rotating firing pin, which would prevent the weapon's hammer from striking the primer of a cartridge) could fire if the weapon were to be accidentally dropped on its hammer. Most defects of this type can be prevented with the purchase of appropriate regulatory devices.

derringer A small pistol designed to be carried in the pocket and made up of one barrel or two, but rarely more.

deterrence theory A theory that maintains that crime can generally be deterred or prevented if swift, harsh punishment is given.

detonate An act of exploding in a violent manner, usually by use of TNT or dynamite.

double action A mechanism in a handgun where the hammer or firing pin is retracted and released to create discharge when the trigger is pulled.

dumdum bullet A bullet developed by the British in the Dumdum arsenal of India. It was widely used on the Northwest Frontier of India and in the Sudan. Its jacket was left open and the lead core exposed to make it more effective. It was outlawed by the Hague Convention for war use in 1899 (not by the Geneva Convention of 1925, as is often erroneously cited). The term is often incorrectly used to describe other soft-nosed or hollow-pointed bullets.

entrapment A government agency's luring, tricking, or encouraging a person to commit a crime for the purpose of then arresting that person. Several types of entrapment have been used by the U.S. Bureau of Alcohol, Tobacco, and Firearms: buying guns from collectors or private sellers and then arresting the seller for dealing without a license; attempting to get a licensed dealer to sell a weapon to an individual prohibited from owning it; or providing information different from that required for the deactivation of machine guns, arresting the seller for violating these rules, and then introducing the actual legal requirements at the defendant's trial.

expanding bullet A bullet that expands upon impact with its target. Virtually all rifle bullets used for hunting expand when entering their targets.

exploding bullet A projectile that is intended to explode upon impact with its target. It is generally considered ineffective because it lacks the penetration capacity necessary for both hunting and defense.

explosive A substance, such as TNT, that as a result of a chemical reaction violently detonates or changes to a gas accompanied by both heat and pressure.

fatal gun accident Death as a result of the accidental discharge of a firearm. It has been estimated that fewer than 5 percent of gun deaths result from firearms accidents. The term is often miscalculated and used ambiguously.

firearm A rifle, shotgun, or handgun that can fire a projectile by controlled explosion or chemical reaction. Devices such as BB guns and carbon dioxide pellet guns are not considered firearms. The 1968 Gun Control Act also exempts antique weapons from this definition.

flash hider or flash suppressor A device attached to the muzzle of a weapon to reduce the flash ignited by the burning repellent.

gauge The size of the bore of a shotgun. It is calculated by tabulating the number of round lead balls of bore diameter equal to a pound.

gravity One of the forces that works upon a bullet during its passage through the air. As soon as it leaves the muzzle of a gun, a bullet begins to drop as a consequence of the gravitational laws that govern all falling bodies.

gun control The notion that imposing limitations on the use of guns and on those who own guns will prevent or reduce crime. Studies dealing with this problem have been inconclusive in their findings; criminals always seem able to obtain weapons, legally or illegally, while law-abiding citizens who own guns are most often those who are penalized under gun control efforts. Control of guns may be classified into many categories, e.g., gun-related activities (such as manufacturing, importing, sale, purchase or transfer, or possession or use); type of gun; persons to whom given regulations apply; the level of government actually imposing given regulations; and the degree to which controls restrict the use of guns, among others.

gun culture A term used to describe a theory of social behavior in which fathers who own guns teach their children—particularly their sons—about firearms and expose them to their use. These children acquire their own guns as adults as an allegedly predictable result of their early learning experiences. The term is also used pejoratively to suggest that Americans are obsessed with owning and using guns.

gun decontrol An effort to decrease existing detailed laws that control guns, based largely on evidence that stringent gun control laws do not work and that law-abiding citizens do not generally commit felonious crimes with guns.

gun ownership The private possession of firearms. The two most important ways of estimating the extent of U.S. gun ownership are (1) to attempt to determine the number of guns manufactured domestically and the number imported, then subtract those exported, and (2) to actually conduct a random survey of Americans and simply ask whether they own guns and, if so, how many. Both methods have deficiencies.

gun powder Material made up of various chemical compositions, shapes, particle sizes, and colors that, when ignited, propels a projectile. There is also so-called smokeless gunpowder, which emits only a limited amount of smoke from the weapon's muzzle. Blackpowder (q.v.) dispenses a large amount of smoke upon ignition.

guns In the United States, a rather ambiguous term that refers to airguns, handguns, shotguns and rifles, and even cannons. The definition differs in the United Kingdom.

handgun A gun designed to be fired by hand (not from the shoulder). Its barrel generally does not exceed eight inches in length. The term usually refers to a pistol.

high-capacity magazine A somewhat imprecise term suggesting a magazine that holds more rounds than might be deemed average.

hollow-point bullet A bullet with a concave nose designed to increase expansion upon penetration of its target.

homicide The killing of one human being by another human being. An unlawful homicide may be viewed as either murder or manslaughter.

individual right theory The belief that the right to keep and bear arms is an individual right based upon natural law, English common law, and the Second Amendment, which refers to all able-bodied males responsible for owning their own guns and bringing them for use in a militia. It also rests upon the right to keep and bear arms for self-defense.

instant records check A proposal requiring that, during the process of purchasing a gun, a prospective purchaser fill out an application at a licensed gun dealer and present two pieces of identification, one of which has a photograph. The gun dealer would be required to call the toll-free number of a state or federal agency that would then use its computer system to scan arrest records for any felonies and major misdemeanors that might have been committed by the applicant. This process would presumably take only a few minutes to complete. If no negative information was found, the sale could be made immediately.

jacket That cover, referred to as the envelope, that encloses the core of the bullet itself.

Kennesaw A city in Georgia where in 1981 the council passed a law requiring every noncriminal head of the household to own a gun for the common defense of the social community. This was in response to an act adopted by the village of Morton Grove, Illinois, that banned possession of handguns within its jurisdiction. Other cities have since passed legislation similar to the Kennesaw law.

labeling theory A theory that explains deviant or criminal activity by ascribing deviant labels to the activity and the person engaging in it.

lever action Activation of a gun mechanism by manual use of a lever.

licensing laws Laws that screen applicants, collect fees, and provide for procedural administration for the purchase, sale, possession, or carrying of guns. Such laws can be highly discretionary or essentially nondiscretionary, depending on the jurisdiction. Licenses may be expensive and the time required to get them may be long. In some cases, administrative discretion may be overriding, and in other cases specific provisions of the law must be adhered to rigidly.

long gun A firearm with a long barrel. It is to be fired from the shoulder by use of a buttstock. Shotguns and rifles fall into this category.

M-1 Garand A semiautomatic rifle that became famous during World War II. At the end of the war, Americans could readily obtain it in surplus stores.

M-16 machine gun A fully automatic weapon capable of firing continuous rounds as long as the trigger is being pulled and the ammunition supply does not run out. It fires rifle-caliber bullets. Civilian use of this weapon has been severely regulated.

machine pistol This term usually refers to a submachine gun; the term is widely used in Europe.

magazine A container for cartridges that is spring loaded and that may be either part of the mechanism of the gun or detachable. Magazines may be labeled box, tube or tubular, and drum. The term may also refer to a storage place for ammunition or explosives of all kinds.

magnum A heavily loaded cartridge or shotshell and a weapon constructed to fire it.

mandatory sentences Sentences required for anyone who uses a gun in a crime. Because such laws do not necessarily differentiate between criminal and victim, these sentences could punish someone who uses a gun for self-defense.

microeconomic theory As it relates to gun issues, this is a theory asserting that crime results from individual economic decisions to engage in either criminal or legitimate behavior. It relies heavily on cost-benefit analysis and personal choice.

military bullets These types of bullets have been defined by the Hague Convention as having a "full metal jacket," that is, they may not have any lead exposed at the tip and they must not be of the expanding variety.

militia That body of able-bodied men who, under the Second Amendment of the American Constitution, were guaranteed the right to keep and bear arms both within and outside their homes. At the writing of the Constitution, the term *militia* did not mean a select militia, such as that of the National Guard; it referred to every able-bodied man in each state. Even today, Section 10, Title 10 of the U.S. Code declares that the militia consists of "all able-bodied males at least 17 years of age and . . . under 45 years of age who are, or have made declaration of intention to become, citizens."

Mortality Detail File A file on victims of fatal gun accidents, calculated by the U.S. Bureau of the Census, that includes marital status, size of place of residence, and area of occurrence.

Morton Grove A village in Illinois that voted in 1981 to outlaw—with certain exceptions—the possession of handguns within its jurisdiction.

multi-barrel Generally speaking, this most commonly refers to a shotgun having more than a single barrel, as the double-barreled shotgun.

mushroom bullet A bullet whose forward section expands upon penetration of its target.

muzzle The end of the barrel from which a projectile leaves a firearm.

muzzle brake The part of the barrel of a weapon that, by trapping and diverting expanding gases, tends to reduce recoil upon firing.

muzzleloader A gun, now produced mostly as a historic replica, in which blackpowder and a projectile are individually loaded into the muzzle of the weapon. In the case of so-called cap-and-ball revolvers, the weapons are loaded by way of the open ends of the chambers of the cylinder.

National Crime Surveys Surveys that report crime statistics compiled by the U.S. Bureau of Justice Statistics. The bureau estimates that some 83 percent of Americans will be victims of violent crime at least once during their lifetimes. Its estimates are based on interviews of representative samples of Americans aged 12 and over and deal with estimates of crimes, deemed to be major or nonmajor, involving both reported and non-reported guns.

over-under Generally speaking, a shotgun having two barrels stacked upon each other rather than parallel to each other.

pellet gun A gun, whether rifle or pistol, that uses compressed air or carbon dioxide to propel a pellet. It differs from a BB gun and is not classified as a firearm.

pellets Most often called shot, these are spherical projectiles contained in shotshells or used in pellet guns.

permits Laws that allow one to have a gun in one's home or to carry a gun on one's person in a public place.

personality traits It is sometimes argued that certain personality traits—such as aggressiveness, low control of hostility, low self-esteem, and low estimation of the value of life—lead to both accidental and intentional use of weapons. Many people believe that dealing with these and other characteristics on a sound medical, sociological, or psychological basis might reduce or limit much of the accidental or intentional use of weapons in an antisocial manner.

pistol This term generally refers to a gun that can be held in one hand, thus it is usually referred to as a handgun. A pistol may be of the single-shot, multi-barrel, repeating, or semiautomatic variety. The term includes revolvers.

pistol grip That part of a pistol that serves as its handle. It also refers to that protrusion on the fore-end of a shoulder-held gun that resembles the handle of a pistol.

plastic guns Weapons that are largely undetectable by metal detectors like those commonly used in airports, courtrooms, prisons, and so on. A 1988 federal law requires that all guns be made of a minimum amount of metal and bans guns made of entirely non-metallic materials. Ironically, no weapon of this completely plastic type had yet been made when this law was passed. Much discussion related to plastic guns focuses on the Glock 17, an official pistol of the Austrian army.

plinking Informally firing at inanimate targets. Of all shooting sports in the United States, plinking is most frequently engaged in.

police power A power that enables the government to legislate in the interests of the health, safety, and morals of the people.

possession laws Laws under which some jurisdictions may require that guns be registered to be possessed. Some states have laws that require persons possessing guns to have a license, even if they keep the gun only in their own homes. Persons in so-called high-risk groups (felons or misdemeanants, for example) may be prohibited from gun possession, and carrying regulations may be imposed.

power In general, refers to the magnification power of the scope used on a gun. Actually, it has been found that an increase in the power of magnification tends to reduce the field of view and the concomitant gathering of light, thus decreasing both the area the shooter is able to see and the illumination of the target.

primer Metallic fulminate or lead styphnate that serves as the ignition element of a cartridge.

procontrol argument The argument that guns are good only for killing. Handguns (and, more recently and especially, Saturday Night Specials), assault rifles (often misidentified—see the entry above), machine guns, and plastic guns are the usual focus of the argument. Proponents argue that gun control, and even elimination of guns, is worthwhile if even one life can be saved.

product liability The field of tort law that deals with holding manufacturers or sellers of a product liable for the misuse or injury that product might cause when used by a consumer.

proficiency screening Testing of individuals to determine their ability to handle firearms, their competency in using firearms safely, and their general knowledge of how firearms work. Very few states require such tests, and those that do limit them to a narrow segment of purchases and applications for carry permits. There is considerable expense involved in implementing such a program, and no state currently requires mandatory training of all those who possess guns.

propellent Generally speaking, the chemical composition, ignited by the primer, that generates gas. Compressed air and carbon dioxide in air or pellet guns are examples of propellent.

pump action A motion by which shells are hand-pumped for firing into a long gun. Also called slide action.

purchase permit laws Laws, in existence in some states, that require individuals who wish to purchase guns to obtain a purchase permit. Such a permit cannot be issued until the purchaser's record is closely examined. Such laws have existed since at least 1911.

rape Unlawful sexual intercourse between a man and a woman without her consent and as a result of the use of force on the part of the male or the fear of force on the part of the female. Guns are sometimes used in such assaults and greatly increase the likelihood that the crime will be completed.

registration A process by which records of gun purchases are maintained. This process may range from relatively stringent programs that require that all guns possessed be recorded with some government agency to the most common and least repressive program, in which retail sales of weapons be so recorded. Under the 1968 Gun Control Act, all gun sales by licensed dealers must be recorded; it should be noted, however, that such records are kept by the dealers, not by a government agency. Registration procedures do not prevent a person from getting or possessing a gun, and it is virtually assured that criminals will not register their own guns.

revolver A handgun with a revolving cylinder that rotates cartridges to the barrel, from which they may be fired repeatedly (usually from five to nine in sequence).

rifle A long gun having a barrel with spiraling grooves—rifling—on the inside. Cartridges can be entered into the firing position by use of a bolt action device, a lever, or a pump action. Some are also semiautomatic.

rifling The spiral grooves in the bore of a gun that spin the projectile in its flight. These grooves are present in the bore of all rifles, virtually all handguns, and in some shotguns where greater accuracy is desired.

right of the people to keep and bear arms A right guaranteed under the Second Amendment to the Constitution of the United States. There is disagreement about whether this right pertains to the individual or exists for the purpose of serving in a militia. See **collective right theory, individual right theory,** and **militia.**

robbery Forcible stealing through use of fear or violence. It has been estimated that guns are used by the thief in only about 20 percent of robberies. Nevertheless, individual robbers armed with guns are more likely to succeed.

round See **cartridge.**

safety training Training programs to educate firearms users about safe use of their weapons. Technical instruction, such as how to place the safety on the gun and how to safely determine whether a gun is loaded, are also part of the program. Safety training is not intended to alter a weapon owner's underlying personality or medical conditions.

Saturday Night Specials Small, cheap, low-caliber handguns readily available to those who wish to purchase them. The term itself has no legal or technical definition, but can be traced to a racial slur once used in the South.

sawed-off shotgun Generally described as a conventional shotgun with a barrel less than 18 inches long, or a rifle with a barrel less than 16 inches long or having an overall length of less than 26 inches. These are restricted by federal law.

seizures of property In the context of the gun controversy, this refers to the taking of firearms or other property by the U.S. Bureau of Alcohol, Tobacco, and Firearms and other government agencies.

selective fire A firearm with the capacity to be fired automatically, semiautomatically, or in bursts, depending on the wishes of the person using the weapon.

self-defense The right to defend oneself, one's family, or one's property by use of a weapon, if necessary, against those who threaten forcibly to attack and to commit a crime against any of these. Even though gun owners have expressed a willingness to use their guns against marauders, burglars, or others who might threaten them, it has been found that no shooting is in fact involved in most cases where guns are used in a defensive manner. Most often, the gun was mentioned to the assailant or was merely displayed. Generally, the person engaging in self-defense must not be at fault and or have provoked his assailant, there must have been no relatively convenient mode of escape or opportunity to decline the confrontation, and there must have been impending peril to the victim.

semiautomatic A term used to describe a firearm that fires a single cartridge, then ejects the case and reloads the firing chamber after each pull of the trigger.

semiautomatic pistol A handgun with a special spring-loaded device that files cartridges into the firing chamber. Each trigger pull causes another cartridge to be loaded, ready to be fired. The magazine of such a gun usually contains up to 17 cartridges.

sentence enhancement laws Laws that provide additional penalties for certain crimes, usually felonies, when a gun is used in their commission. Although some judicial discretion may be allowed in sentencing, some minimal length of term is usually involved.

shot spread The spread, or diameter, of the pattern left by a shot.

shotgun A long, shoulder-held gun that might have one or two barrels. The barrels, whose interior is smooth, discharge shotshells (containing a large number of pellets). Hunting shotguns most commonly hold from two to five rounds of ammunition. Unusual varieties of shotguns may hold 20 or more rounds.

silencer A device that can be attached to the muzzle of a gun in order to reduce—but not entirely eliminate—the sound made when the weapon is fired. The attachment is virtually prohibited.

single-shot A gun requiring the manual insertion of ammunition into the chamber before each firing of the weapon.

slide action See **pump action**.

snubbies, snub-nosed A handgun whose barrel is three inches long or shorter.

social control theory A theory that firm discipline in the family and schools will prevent criminal behavior.

spin and yaw A term that describes the phenomenon of a bullet taking on a somewhat wobbly flight (called yaw) before settling into a smoothly spinning stage, known as its sleep stage.

starter pistol A handgun using blank cartridges, generally employed to start sporting events.

submachine gun A fully automatic weapon that can be fired by one person. The weapon discharges handgun ammunition.

substitution theory A theory that argues that a reduction in or complete ban of handguns would result in the substitution of handguns with other weapons—such as rifles, shotguns, sawed-off shotguns, and knives—by those bent on committing crime.

suicide The voluntary and intentional killing of oneself. Firearms are frequently the weapon of choice.

Supplementary Homicide Reports (SHR) A reporting program maintained by the Federal Bureau of Investigation that provides data on civilian legal defensive homicides and civilian justifiable homicides, among other statistics.

technological modification of guns Alteration of firearms after manufacture. Weapons can be modified so that, for example, they do not "go off" when they are accidentally dropped; so that they must be unlocked with a key or are in some other way made unusable; to increase or decrease their fire power; to shorten or lengthen their barrels; and in other ways, many of which are illegal.

theft "The felonious taking and carrying away from any place the personal property of another, without his consent, by a person not entitled to possession thereof, with the intent to deprive the owner of the property and to convert it to the use of the taker or some person other than the owner." 53 So. 2d. 533, 536.

traits of shooters This is a finding that suggests that those involved in intentional homicides, both perpetrators and victims, tend to resemble each other on such variables as race, age, and social class. Thus, persons involved in gun accidents tend to be from the same groups, and likewise share such characteristics as reduced capacity to control aggression, impulsiveness, risk-taking tendencies, and even some physical characteristics.

trajectory The path taken by a bullet after it leaves the muzzle of a gun. Trajectory will vary depending upon the velocity of the bullet; slow bullets will go higher and fast bullets will go lower.

transfer of guns The sale and exchange of guns between private individuals. It is estimated that about 64 percent of guns acquired are purchased from gun dealers by law-abiding citizens, and that most felons acquire their weapons by means other than from licensed dealers. It has been proposed that the private transfer of weapons be routed through licensed dealers, who would act as brokers.

trombone See **pump action.**

Uniform Crime Reports Published under the title of *Crime in the United States,* this annual report provides a nationwide view of crime compiled from statistics supplied by state and local law enforcement agencies. Crimes covered range from arson to violent crime. Such reports are published by the Federal Bureau of Investigation, U.S. Department of Justice, Washington, D.C. 20535.

unlawful carrying of guns Having in one's possession a firearm that has not been licensed or that it is otherwise unlawful to carry. A violation requires a mandatory penalty. There is some debate about such laws, as the mere carrying of a gun constitutes a so-called victimless crime.

unlawful transfer of guns Knowingly transferring guns to ineligible persons. It has been proposed that individuals who engage in this activity be made liable under civil laws for any harm or injury perpetrated with these guns. These proposals aim to keep guns out of the hands of ineligibles rather than to reduce the actual number of guns or ammunition available for them.

Uzi This term is a shortened form of Uziel Gal, the name of an Israeli army officer, and it is used to designate a type of Israeli machine pistol that is able to discharge 25 rounds from a detachable magazine. Uzis are generally considered to be some of the deadliest of military weapons.

velocity The speed of a bullet during the course of its flight. It is measured by very sensitive instruments known as chronographs.

Victim Risk Supplement A survey administered to over 14,000 households in February 1984 that supplemented National Crime Survey data. One of its conclusions was that unarmed resistance to a crime is likely to provoke attack by the offender, whereas resistance with a gun will deter attack.

vigilantism Originally, the collective use of private force to maintain social norms. It was widely practiced in frontier America. Today it involves action by private citizens to maintain law and order, especially in those areas where police protection is less visible and applicable, such as densely populated urban areas and private neighborhoods.

waiting periods A period of time between purchase and delivery of a firearm, designed to enable law enforcement officials to examine the background of the purchaser. The Brady Handgun Violence Prevention Act, passed by Congress in 1994, requires a five-day waiting period for the purchase of a handgun.

warden's survey fallacy The suggestion by wardens of American prisons that the death penalty did not deter murderers from committing their crimes. This conclusion is based on discussions wardens had with prisoners on death row, all of whom attested to this. Scholars are divided on these findings.

weapon Any device used for offensive or defensive behavior. Virtually any object can thus become a weapon—a baseball bat, a knife, a rake or shovel, an ice pick, a gun, or dozens of other items.

weapons effect hypothesis A hypothesis that asserts that angry individuals could be driven to aggression by just the sight of a weapon.

wind deflection The action of wind upon a bullet that causes it to deviate from its path. Even gentle winds can cause serious error in striking a target. Since wind is variable, a gun hunter or marksman will observe the movement of grass or foliage before firing at a target.

Index

Abnormally dangerous
    products/activities, 254, 257
Aborn, Richard, 99–100
Academics for the Second
    Amendment, 189–190
ACCA. *See* Armed Career
    Criminal Act
An Act for the Better Preservation
    of Game, 67
Adams, John, 70
Adams, Samuel, 73, 109, 340, 343
    Declaration of Rights and, 76
    Faneuil Hall meeting and, 71
    use of arms and, 13
*Additional Letters from the Federal
    Farmer* (Lee), 78
African Americans. *See* Blacks
AHA. *See* Anti Handgun
    Association
Alabama Gun Collectors
    Association, 218
Alamo Arms Collectors, 231
Alcohol, Tobacco, and Firearms
    Division of the IRS, 88
Alfred, King, 11, 61–62
Alviani, Joseph D., 299
AMA. *See* American Medical
    Association
Amateur Trapshooting
    Association, 190
*The Amendments to the
    Constitution*, (software), 370
*America Needs a National Gun
    Policy*, 345
American Association of
    Suicidology, 233
American Bar Association, 190

Magna Carta memorial by, 62
American Bar Foundation, 289
An American Citizen (Coxe), 77
American Civil Liberties Union,
    109, 191
American Custom Gunmakers
    Guild, 191
*An American Dictionary of the
    English Language* (Webster), 80
American Duck Hunters
    Association, Tennessee Wing,
    230
American Enterprise Institute for
    Public Policy Research, 300
American Federation of Police,
    39, 113, 120
American Firearms Industry, 319
American Handgunner, 319
American Heritage Hunting and
    Gun Club, 220
American Humane Education
    Society, 233
American Humanist Association,
    233
The American Hunter, 319
American Jewish Committee, 233
American Jewish Congress,
    191–192
American Medical Association
    (AMA), 233, 252–253
American Pediatric Society, 233
American Protective Association,
    27
American Psychiatric Association,
    233
American Public Health
    Association, 234

The American Rifleman, 120, 311, 319, 333
American Single Shot Rifle Association, 192–193
American Trap Shooting Association, 193
Americans for Democratic Action, 193
Ammunition
    armor-piercing, 93, 333
    choosing, 313, 332
    "cop-killer," 41, 338, 340
    hollow-point, 119
Anderson, James LaVerne, 309
Animal Charity League, Inc., 234
Animal Protection Institute, 234
Animal Welfare Institute, 234
Ansell, S. T., 242
Anti Assault-Weapons Bill, Feinstein and, 106
Anti Handgun Association (AHA!), 224
Anti-Drug Abuse Act, 93
Anti-Federalists, 77
Anti-Ku Klux Klan Act, 95
Antique Arms Collectors Association of Connecticut, 220
Appalachian Trail Arms Collectors, Inc., 223
Application of Atkinson, 136–137
Arapahoe Gun Collectors, 220
An Argument Showing That a Standing Army Is Inconsistent with a Free Government (Trenchard and Moyle), 69
Aristotle, 65
    natural rights and, 9
    on tyranny, 60
Arizona Gun Collectors Association, Inc., 219
Ark-La-Tex Gun Collectors Association, 223
Armed Career Criminal Act (ACCA), 91–92, 93, 174, 253
Armed Citizen News, 320
Army-Navy Journal, 82
Arrow, Paul S., 242
Arthur D. Little, Inc. study, 304
Articles of Confederation, 266
The Art of War (Machiavelli), 64
Asbury, Charles J., 300

Ascione, Alfred M., 242–243
Ashbrook, John M., 243
Assault weapons, 252–253
    banning, 94, 104, 105, 106, 119, 330–331
    manufacturer liability for, 44
    problems with, 295
    waiting periods for, 94, 95
Assault Weapons Ban Bill, 96, 127
Assize of Arms (1181), 12, 62–63, 257
Association International de Entrenadores de Tiro, 203–204
Association of Importers-Manufacturers for Muzzleloading, 193
Austerman, Wayne R., 20
Australia, gun control in, 24
Automatic weapons, 18
    banning, 92, 291
    licensing, 85
Aymette v. The State, 127–128
Ayoob, Massad F., 300–301, 332–333

Background checks, 84–85, 94, 95, 115–116, 121
Bakal, Carl, 301
Baker, James Jay, 100
Banned Guns, 320
Barnes Company, 301
Barrett, Sidney R., Jr., 243
Bartley-Fox law, 22–23
Batey, Robert, 244
Bayh, Birch, 88
Beard, Michael K., 101
Beccaria, Cesare, 9, 71
Beilenson, Peter L., 290
Bell, Bob, 301
Benenson, Mark K., 244
Beschle, Donald L., 244–245
Biden, Joseph R., Jr., 101–102
Bieber, James D., 343
Bijlefeld, Marjolijn, 342
Bill of Rights, English, 12, 69, 72, 104, 256, 261
Bill of Rights, federal, 2, 11, 245–246, 256, 262, 288, 292, 306, 335
    approval of, 79
    changes in, 13

Madison and, 117–118
right to bear arms and, 109–110
roots of, 60, 61, 67, 69
Bill of rights, state, 74
arms guarantees in, 262–263
Black Codes, 25, 81
Blackman, Paul H., 326–328, 333
gun control and, 303
on Sloan research, 22
on women/guns, 33
Blacks, guns and, 24–29, 80, 81,
82, 245, 252
Blackstone, William, 102, 303
auxiliary subordinate rights
and, 12
natural rights and, 9
Bliss v. Commonwealth, 140–141
Bloomgarden, Henry S., 302
BNA ONLINE (database), 367
BNA PLUS (database), 367
B'Nai B'rith International, 234
Bodin, Jean
natural rights and, 9
on political absolutism, 65
Bogus, Carl T., 245
Bordenet, Bernard J., 245–246
Boston Massacre, 72
Boston Police Department, 39
Bovard, James, 302
Boxer, Barbara, 102–103
Brabner-Smith, John, 246
Brady, James, 103
Brady, Sarah, 103, 335
Brady Handgun Violence
Prevention Act, 42, 96,
176–177, 303, 332, 337–338
supporters/opponents of, 101,
103, 106–107, 115, 116– 117,
119–120
Brady II, 99–100
Braintree Rifle and Pistol Club,
Inc., 224
Branch Davidians, 119
Brands, Scot A., 246
Breen, Victor, 247
Bristow v. State, 139
Brown, Joe B., 247
Brown, Tyler P., 248
Browning Collectors Association,
194
Bruce-Briggs, B., 248
Buford, Justice

Florida gun control and, 26–27
Bullets. *See* Ammunition
Bundy, Ted, 117
Burdick, Charles K., 302–303
Bureau of Alcohol, Tobacco, and
Firearms (BATF), 101, 115,
121, 127, 194, 331–332
Branch Davidians and, 119
data from, 102, 335
detectable firearms and,
112–113
enforcement by, 291
firearms manufacture/sale and,
89
Gun Control Act and, 124
licensing and, 85
publication by, 179
Burger, Warren E., 7
Burgh, James
natural rights and, 9
on standing armies, 72
Burton v. Sills, 132–133
Bush, George, 19

Caggiano, Nicholas J., 248–249
California Hunters & Gun
Association, 219
Calio, Nicholas E., 287
Callaghan, Michael O., 249
Callahan, Charles M., 249
Campbell, C., 296–297
Cantrell, Charles L., 249–250
Caplan, David I., 250–251
Carolina Gun Collectors
Association, 228
Cases v. United States, 130–131
Cast Bullet Association, 195
Cato's Letters (Trenchard and
Gordon), 69–70
Center for the Study and
Prevention of Handgun
Violence, survey by, 294
Center for the Study of Firearms
and Public Policy, 303
Center to Prevent Handgun
Violence, 195
Legal Action Project and, 45
U.S. v. Miller and, 6
Centerwall, Brandon S., 251–
252
Central Conference of American
Rabbis, 195–196

Central Ohio Gun and Indian Relic
  Collectors Association, 228
Central Pennsylvania Antique
  Arms Association, 230
Central States Gun Collectors
  Association, 222
Chandler, Charles H., 303
Charles II, 66, 67
Chen, Huey-tsey, 299
Child Welfare League of America,
  234
Children, guns and, 16, 94, 249,
  292, 342
Chunn, D. E., 296–297
Church, William C., 82
Church of the Brethren General
  Board, 196–197
Cicero, 60–61
  natural rights and, 9
Citizens and Victims United for
  Sensible Gun Legislation, 223
Citizens Committee for the Right
  to Keep and Bear Arms, 107,
  120, 198, 333–334, 342
Citizens for a Safer Minnesota,
  225
Citizens for Safety, 224
City of Las Vegas v. Moberg,
  148–149
City of Salina v. Blaksley, 128–129,
  251
Civic Disarmament Committee
  for Handgun Control, 234
Civil Rights Act (1866), 26, 81
Civil Rights Act (1871), 95
Clinton, William Jefferson,
  103–104, 116, 117
Cnut, King, 11, 62
Coalition to Stop Gun Violence,
  22–23
Coffey, Judge, 91
Coke, Sir Edward
  natural rights and, 9
  self-defense and, 12
Colorado State Rifle and Pistol
  Association, 220
*Commentaries on the House of
  England* (Blackstone), 102
Commission on Assault Weapons,
  291
Committee for Handgun Control,
  234

Committee for Humane
  Legislation, Incorporated,
  234
Committee for the Study of
  Handgun Misuse, 234
Commonwealth v. Davis, 133–134
*Compendious Dictionary of the
  English Language* (Webster),
  79
Comprehensive Crime Control
  Act, 96
Concealed weapons, 83
  licensing for, 37
Concure, Thomas M., Jr., 339
Congressional Information
  Service, CIS/Index
  (database), 367
Congressional Masterfiles 1 and 2
  (CD-ROM), 369–370
Conservatives, guns and, 2–3
Constitution. *See* United States
  Constitution
*The Constitution: That Delicate
  Balance: School Prayer, Gun
  Control and Right To Assemble*,
  346
The Constitution Papers,
  (CD-ROM), 370
Cook, Earleen H., 297
Cook, Joseph Lee, 297
Cooley, Thomas M., 14, 104
"Cop-killer" bullets, 41, 338, 340
Corwin, G. Lester, 303
Cottrol, Robert J., 252, 303
  on blacks/guns, 28–29
Council of Scientific Affairs,
  252–253
Coxe, Tench, 77
Cozic, Charles P., 303
Crago, Derrick D., 253
Cress, Lawrence D., 253
Crime
  controlling, 39, 46, 114
  guns/gun control and, 21–24,
  28, 46–48, 84, 118, 243, 293,
  313, 318, 336–337, 339–340
  See also Violent crime
Crime, 346
The Crime, 346
Crime: Dye Guns, Lasers, Justice?,
  349
Crime: Senior Alert, 351–352

Crime and Delinquency, 347
Crime and Human Nature, 347
Crime and the Courts, 347
Crime and the Criminal, 347–348
Crime at Home: What To Do, 348
Crime Bill, 106, 119
Crime Control Act, 95
Crime Control Research Project, 264
Crime Control Research Survey, 39
Crime, Criminals and the System, 348–349
Crime in the Cities, 349
Crime in the Home, 349–350
Crime Lab, 350
A Crime of Violence, 350
Crime on the Streets, 350–351
Crime on the Streets (2nd Edition), 351
Crime Prevention: It's Elementary, 351
Crime under Twenty-One, 352
Crimebusters, 352
Crimes in Progress, 352–353
Crimes of passion, 106
CrimeStrike, 338
The Criminal, 353
The Criminal and How To Neutralize Him, 353
The Criminal and Punishment, 353–354
A Criminal Is Born, 354
Criminal justice, 2, 17, 244, 354–355
Criminal Justice in the United States, 354
The Criminal Justice System, 354–355
Criminality, causes of, 46–47
Criminology: Lead Us Not into Temptation, 355
Criminology Research, 355
Cromwell, Oliver, 66
Cushing, Samuel, 71

Dade Citizens for Home Rule on Handguns, 220
Dakota Territory Gun Collectors Association, Inc., 230
Daly, Kathleen, 299, 318

Dardick, Nathan, 297
Davidson, Bill R., 304
Davidson, Osha Gray, 304
Davis, E. Duane, 37, 328–329
Deadly Decisions: The Right To Protect Yourself, 355–356
Declaration of Causes of Taking up Arms (1775), 73
Declaration of Independence (1776), 74, 110
    roots of, 65, 67
Declaration of Rights (various states), 13, 74–77, 308, 339
Declaration of Rights, an Act of Parliament, 68–69, 72
DeConcini, Dennis, 331
Defenders of Outdoor Heritage, 231
Defenders of Wildlife, 234
Defensor, H. Charles, 305
Delaware Antique Arms Collectors, 220
Detroit Coalition for A Freeze on Handguns, 224
DIALOG Information Services (database), 367–368
Diamond, Raymond T., 252
    on blacks/guns, 29
Dimos, James, 253–254
DISARM, 235
Disarmament, 40–41, 67, 73, 289, 337
Discourse of Government with Relation to Militias (Fletcher), 69
Discourses concerning Government (Sidney), 69
Discourses on the First Ten Books of Titus Livy (Machiavelli), 64
Dole, Robert, 105
Double Gun Journal, 320
Dowlet, Robert, 254
Drake, William R., 299–300
Draper, Thomas, 305
Dred Scott v. Sanford, 25, 80–81, 307
Drug-trafficking, guns and, 92, 100
Ducks Unlimited, 320
Dunne v. People, 82
Durkheim, Emile, 47

Eadric, proclamation of, 11
Early doctrine, applying, 245
Eckert v. City of Philadelphia, 7
Educational Fund to End
    Handgun Violence, 198–199
Edward I, Statute of Winchester
    and, 12, 63
Edward III, Statute of
    Northampton and, 12, 63
Edwards, James E., 305
Edwardsville Gun Collectors, 225
Elliott, Robert L., 249, 254–255
Emerson Police Reserve Gun
    Club, 226
Emery, Lucilius A., 255
*Encyclopedia of the American
    Constitution*, Kates and, 112
Environmental Action
    Foundation, Inc., 235
*Espinosa v. Superior Court of San
    Joaquin County*, 149–150
Ethelbert, King, 11
Evanston, Illinois, 90
Ever Changing, Ever Free, 356
*An Examination of the Leading
    Principles of the Federal
    Constitution* (Webster), 77
Experimental Ballistics
    Associates, 226

Fairfax County, Virginia, Militia
    Association, 73
Families of Murder Victims, Inc.,
    237
Fass, Barbara, 105–106
FBI. *See* Federal Bureau of
    Investigation
Feder, Donald, 256
Federal Aviation Act, 87, 171
Federal Aviation Administration,
    264
Federal Bureau of Investigation
    (FBI), 119
    background checks by, 84–85
    Uniform Crime Report data from,
        328
Federal Communications
    Commission, 5
Federal Firearms Act, 86, 171,
    242–243, 265, 293
Federal Militia Act, 80
The Federalist (Hamilton,

Madison, and Jay), 13, 77–78,
    117
Feinstein, Dianne, 106
Feldman, Jacob J., 258
Feller, Peter Buck, 256
Felons
    guns and, 89, 93
    identification programs for, 93,
        94
Fenley, Mary Ann, 314
Ferri, Enrico, 46
Ferri, Gian Luigi, 44
Field and Stream, 320
Fields, Samuel, 256–257
Fifth Amendment, 3, 85, 89, 108,
    113, 261, 291
Fingerhut, Lois A., 258
Firearm Fatality Reporting
    System, proposed, 290
Firearm Safety, 356
Firearm Safety Begins in the Home,
    356–357
Firearms. *See* Guns
*Firearms and Violence: Issues of
    Public Policy* (Kates), 112
Firearms Owners Protection Act.
    See McClure-Volkmer Bill
Firearms Policy Project, 199
Firearms Research and
    Identification Association,
    199
First Amendment, 2, 3, 14, 109,
    330
    limits on, 5
    roots of, 69
Flayderman, Norm, 306
Fletcher, Andrew, 69
Fletcher, John G., 257–258
Florida Gun Collectors
    Association, 221
Forrester, David J., 257
Foster, Sarah E., 258
Four Corners Rod and Gun Club,
    229
Four State Collectors Association,
    223
Fourteenth Amendment, 26, 83,
    125, 254, 261, 263, 331
    adoption of, 81
    interpreting, 85
Fourth Amendment, 3, 13–15, 85,
    104, 108, 113, 264, 270–271

firearms legislation and, 291
  interpreting, 95, 326
  violation of, 342
Fraternal Order of Police
  Gun Control Act and, 116
  waiting periods and, 42
Freedman's Bureau Act, 81
Friends Committee on National
  Legislation, 235
Friends of Animals, 235
Friends of the Earth Foundation,
  Inc., 235
Fund for Animals, 235

Gage, General, 73, 75
Galen, 65
  natural rights and, 9
  on self-defense, 61
Gallatin, Albert, 340
Gallup Poll, on handgun ban,
  20–21
Gardiner, Richard E., 258–259, 328
  on Bill of Rights, 11
Garfield, James, 82
Garofalo, Raffaele, 46
Garrett, Virgil, 247
Garrigues, Gary, 259
Garrison, William L., Jr., 297–298
Geisel, Martin, 259
Gekas, George, 106–107
General Board of Church and
  Society of the United
  Methodist Church, 235
Genocide, gun control and, 24–25
George Mason, 357
Georgia Arms Collectors, 221
Georgians Against Gun Violence,
  221
Gest, Ted, 259–260
Getchell, Richard, 260
Glock 17, controversy over, 100,
  108, 118
Glorious Revolution, 68, 75
Goddard, Calvin C., 84
Gordon, Thomas, 69–70
  natural rights and, 9
Gotting, Karl L., 256
Gottlieb, Alan M., 107, 260–261,
  306
Graham, Hugh Davis, 307
Great Britain, gun control in,
  23–24

Greater California Arms &
  Collectors Association, 219
Grotius, Hugo
  natural rights and, 9
  self-defense and, 65
Grundeman, Arnold, 261
Guatemala, gun control in, 25
Gun Control, 357
*Gun Control: A Target for
  Controversy*, 357
Gun Control: Pro and Con, 357–358
*Gun Control: The Right To Bear
  Arms*, 358
Gun Control Act, 87, 105, 108,
  120, 121, 172–174, 179, 244,
  264, 265, 293, 295
  amendments to, 91–92, 101,
  114–115, 116, 124
  sporting purposes, test of, 96
Gun control groups, 2, 3
  handgun control and, 22–23
Gun control laws, 104, 255, 310,
  331
  analysis of, 309
  effectiveness of, 21–24, 118,
  298–299, 339
  major federal, 170–179
  opposition to, 23–24, 311
  problems with, 267–268,
  333–334
  selected state/local, 179–182
  support for, 20–21
  underclass and, 342
  violations of, 65
Gun Digest, 320
Gun Dogs and Ringnecks, 358
A Gun for Mandy, 359
The Gun Grabbers (Gottlieb), 107
Gun Handling, 359
Gun Owners Action Committee,
  199–200
Gun Owners Incorporated, 200
Gun Report, 321
Gun Safety Institute, 228
Gun shop owners, litigation for,
  43–44
Gun Week, 107
Gun Wise, 359
Gun World, 321
Gunfight, USA, 359–360
Gun-Free School Zone Act, 97
Gunning the Flyways, 360

Guns
  antique, 306
  banning, 39, 302
  handling, 254, 313, 332–33, 341
  laws/regulations regarding,
    316
  patterns of ownership of, 313
  plastic, 93, 112–113
  registering, 305
  sales of, 332
  self-defense and, 114, 309, 313,
    330
  social control and, 336
  survey on, 292, 317–318
  transporting, 84–85, 261
  types of, 18–20
  See also Handguns
Guns, 107, 321
Guns: A Day in the Death of
  America, 360
Guns: Be Safe Not Sorry, 361
Gun Safety, 359
Guns and Ammo, 107, 321
Guns and Weapons for Law
  Enforcement, 321
Guns Are Different, 360–361
Guns, Crime, and Freedom
  (LaPierre), 114
Guns, Drugs, and the CIA, 361
Guns of Autumn, 361
Guns of the Old West, Volume 1,
  1803–1861, 362
Guns of the Old West, Volume 2,
  1862–1898, 362
Gunshot Wound of Hand, 362
Gunsmith of Williamsburg, 362–363
Gurr, Ted Robert, 307

Halbrook, Stephen P., 107–108,
  261–264, 296, 307–308, 335
  on Bill of Rights, 15
Hamilton, Alexander
  Federalist and, 77–78
  Second Amendment and, 250
Hancock, John, 10–11, 71, 73
Handgun Alert, Inc., 235
Handgun Control Federation of
  Ohio, 228
Handgun Control, Inc., 99, 103,
  120, 200–201, 219, 227, 306
  NRA and, 335–336
  self-defense and, 34

Handgun Review Board
  (Maryland), 43
The Handgunner, 321
Handgunning, 322
Handguns, 17, 328
  banning, 1, 20–21, 26, 80, 243,
    270, 339
  choosing, 313, 332
  controlling, 18–19, 23–24, 89,
    118, 257, 268, 294–295, 299
  handling, 313
  history of, 308, 315
  legislative policy against, 290
  market analysis of, 309
  problems with, 295
  risk from, 245, 265
  support for, 111
  training for, 292
  types of, 332
  See also Guns
Handguns, Rifles, Shotguns, 322
Handloader, 322
Hardy, David T., 108–109,
  264–266, 308
Harper, Robert Berkley
  on banning handguns, 18–19
  on black violence, 29
Harrington, natural rights and, 8
Harris v. State, 132
Hasko, John J., 298
Hatch, Orrin, 109–110, 331, 342
Hawkins, Gordon, 318
  self-defense and, 12
Hayes, Stuart R., 266
Hemenway, David, 292
Henigan, Dennis A., 5–6, 266–
  267
Henry, Patrick, 12–13, 109, 340,
  343
  standing armies and, 78
Henry II, Assize of Arms and, 12,
  62
Henry III, Assize of Arms and,
  62–63
Henry VII, hunting and, 63
Henry VIII, gun limitations by,
  64–65
Heritage Foundation, 337
Herrnstein, Richard J., 317
Herz, Andrew D., 267
Hlothhere, proclamation of, 11
Hobbes, Thomas, 66

natural rights and, 9
Hofstadter, Richard, 267
Hogg, Ian, 308
Homicides
in Canada, 251–252
criminal/self-defense, 35
guns and, 16, 17, 18, 22–23, 244,
251–252, 259, 288, 290, 317,
328, 342
rate of, 258
Horowitz, Edward J., 267–268
House of Commons, 72
House of Lords, 72
right to keep and bear arms
and, 70
Houston Gun Collectors
Association, 231
Houston v. Moore, 80
Howard, Jacob M., 81
Hudson-Mohawk Arms
Collectors Association, Inc.,
227
Hughes, William, 92
Humane Information Services,
Inc., 235
Humane Society of the United
States, 235
Hume, David, 9
Hunt, M. Truman, 268
Hunter Education Association,
202
Hunting, 86, 109, 123
future of, 312
licenses for, 83, 85
as natural right, 102

Idaho State Rifle and Pistol
Association, 221
Illinois Council Against Handgun
Violence, 221
Illinois Gun Collectors
Association, 221
Illinois State Rifle Association,
221
Immigration Protective League,
handguns/aliens and, 27
In re Brickley, 143–144
Indian Territory Gun Collectors
Association, 229
Indiana Sportsman's Council, 222
Indiana State Rifle and Pistol
Association, 222

Ingram, Deborah D., 258
Institute for Legislative Action
(NRA-ILA), 100, 328, 333,
337, 338–339
Internal Revenue Service
bombings/arsons and, 88
licensing and, 86
International Association of
Chiefs of Police, waiting
periods and, 42
International Association of Fish
and Wildlife Agencies, 202
International Association of Law
Enforcement Firearms
Instructors, 202
International Benchrest Shooters,
202–203
International Handgun Metallic
Silhouette Association, 203
International Hunters
Association, 203
International Ladies Garment
Workers Union, 235
International Shooting Coaches
Association, 203–204
Internationale Schutzen Trainer
Vereinigung, 203–204
Interstate commerce, firearms
and, 261
I.O.P. Rifle and Pistol Club, 222
Iroquois Arms Collectors
Association, 227
Isle Shooting Club, 227
Izaak Walton League, 204–205

Jackson, Maynard Holbrook, Jr.,
250–251, 268
Jacobs, James B., 41
on self-defense, 40
Jamaica, gun control in, 24
James II, 67, 68
Japan, violent crime in, 23–24
Jay, John, 77–78
Jefferson, Thomas, 70, 109,
110–111, 340, 343
Second Amendment and, 307
use of arms and, 13
Jefferson Gun Club, 223
Jeffries, John Calvin, Jr., 244
Jersey Shore Antique Arms
Collectors, 226
Jett, Rick L., 268–269

Jews for the Preservation of
Firearms Ownership (JPFO),
205–206, 336
John, King, 62
Jones, K., 298
*Journal of Firearms and Public
Policy*, 322
Judiciary Committee (U.S.
House), 100, 105, 108, 112,
119, 122, 124
Judiciary Committee (U.S.
Senate), 101, 102, 109, 113,
331, 342
on Second Amendment, 15
statistics from, 335

*Kalodimos v. Village of Morton
Grove*. See *Michael Kalodimos
et al., Appellants, v. The
Village of Morton Grove,
Appellee*
Kandt, William, 247
Kane, Jeffrey, 269
Kapelsohn, Emanuel, 111
Kaplan, David I., 303
Kaplan, John, 269
Kates, Don B., Jr., 28, 111–112,
269–272, 296, 309, 329, 336
on Bill of Rights, 15
reply to, 256–257
on women/guns, 33
K-Bay Rod and Gun Club, 221
Kelley v. R.G. Industries, 43, 45,
242, 246, 248, 249, 253–254,
289–290
Kennedy, John F., 87, 314
Kennedy, Robert, 87
Kennesaw, Georgia, 23, 90
Kennett, Lee, 309–310
Kentucky Gun Collectors
Association, Inc., 223
Kentucky Voice for Crime
Victims, 237
Kids and Guns, 363
King, Martin Luther, 87
Kleck, Gary, 296, 310, 329,
336–337
on self-defense, 37
studies by, 36
on women/guns, 33
Knight, John, 67
Knox, Neal, 17, 112–113

Knox, William, 10, 75
Koller, Larry, 316
Kopel, David B., 101–102,
113–114, 303, 310, 330, 337,
341
Krug, Alan, 259
Kruschke, Earl R., 296, 310
Ku Klux Klan, 29, 82

Ladies' Home Journal, on
women/guns, 33
Lancaster Muzzle Loading
Association, 230
LaPierre, Wayne, 114, 311
Law and Contemporary Problems,
Kates and, 112
Law and Order, 363
Law & Policy Quarterly, Kates and,
112
Law enforcement. *See* Police
Law Enforcement Assistance
Administration, 299
Law Enforcement Officers
Protection Act, 93, 176
Laws (Plato), 59
Laws of Alfred, 61–62
Laws of Cnut, 62
Layton, Frank, 247
Leddy, Edward F., 311
on guns/self-defense, 36–37
Lee, Richard Henry, 77, 78
LeFave, Donald George, 311
Legal Action Project, 45
LEGAL FORUM (database), 368
LEGI-SLATE (database), 368
Lester, David, 311–312
Letters from the Federal Farmer
(Lee), 77
Leviathan (Hobbes), 66
Levinson, Sanford, 303
Lewis, Jack, 312
Lewis v. United States, 6–7, 89,
261
LEXIS (database), 368
Liability
manufacturers'/product, 2,
42–45, 248–249, 257, 265, 269,
287, 306
strict, 44–45, 244, 269, 289–290
Liberals, guns and, 3
Libertarians, guns and, 3, 243,
269–270

Licensing, 83, 85, 86, 126
Lincoln, Abraham, 81
Lipinski, Andrew, 312
Livy, , 9
Locke, John
　human rights and, 67–68
　natural rights and, 9
Lombroso, Cesare, 46
Lopez, Alfonso, Jr, 97

Macaulay, Thomas, 9
McCabe, Michael K., 339
McClure, James A., 105, 114–115, 120, 124
　Gun Control Act and, 114–115
McClure-Volkmer Bill (Firearms Owners Protection Act), 39, 92, 101, 108, 114–115, 116, 120, 124, 175–176, 303
McClurg, Andrew J., 44–45
McCollum, Ira William "Bill," Jr., 115–116
McGoldrick, Vince, 116
Machiavelli, Niccolo, 9, 64, 71
McKevitt, Mike, 103
McKinley, William, 83
McNamara, Joseph, 116–117
McNulty, Paul J., 117
Madison, James, 117–118, 123, 343
　constitutional amendment by, 78–79
　Federalist and, 77–78
　Second Amendment and, 8–9, 13, 109, 250, 262, 288
Magna Carta, influence of, 62
Malcolm, Joyce Lee, 12, 296, 312, 337
Malloch v. Eastly, 70
Man at Arms, 322
Manheim, J., 298
Mannlicher Collectors Association, 206
Maraziti, Joseph J., 103
Margolis, Michael, 330
Marston, Linda L., 294
Maryland Council, 75
Maryland for the Use of Levin v. United States, 87
Marylanders Against Handgun Abuse, 224
Mason, George, 73, 78, 340

Massachusetts Arms Collectors, 224
Mauser, Gary A., 330
Mecklenburg Wildlife Club, Inc., 228
Media, 306, 330
　gun control and, 329
　NRA and, 260
Memphis Antique Weapons Association, 230
Michael Kalodimos et al., Appellants, v. The Village of Morton Grove, Appellee (1984), 92, 153–156
Michigan Antique Arms Collectors, Inc., 224
Michigan Law Review, Kates and, 112
Michigan Rifle and Pistol Association, 224
Mid-State Arms Collectors and Shooters Club, 227
Migratory Bird Hunting Stamp Act, 85
Militia Act (1663), 66
Militia Act (1792), 14, 79, 317
Militias, 6, 12, 14, 15, 69, 77, 79, 82, 86, 102, 104, 110, 118, 126, 246, 247, 250, 256, 260, 263, 289, 304, 307
　blacks and, 28
　establishment of, 73, 311
　federal army and, 242
　maintaining, 4, 73, 81, 87
　unorganized, 249
　well-regulated, 4, 7, 10, 13, 74, 75, 76, 78, 266
Miller, Jack, 161–162, 247
Miller v. Texas, 160–161
Milo, Titus Annius, 60
Mineral Belt Gun Collectors Association, 225
Minnesota Weapons Collectors, 225
Minorities, guns and, 24–29, 80, 81, 82, 245, 252
Missouri Committee for Firearms Safety, 225
Missouri Council to Control Handguns, 225
Missouri Valley Arms Collectors Association, 223

Montana Arms Collectors
Association, 226
Montesquieu, Baron de la Brede
et de, 9, 70
Montgomery Gun Club, 219
Moore v. East Cleveland, 89, 261
Morgan, Eric, 330–331
Moriarty, Laura J., 37, 328–329
Morn, Frank T., 38
Morton Grove, Illinois, 7, 23, 40,
90, 91
Moyle, Walter, 69
Murder. *See* Homicide
Murtz, Harold A., 312
Mutual Security Act, 86–87, 171
Muzzle Blasts, 323
Muzzleloaders, 323

Nassau County Fish and Game
Association, Inc., 227
National Academy of Sciences, on
violence/neurobiological
markers, 47
National Advisory Commission
on Criminal Justice
Standards and Goals, 88
National Association of Chiefs of
Police, Kopel and, 113
National Association of Federally
Licensed Firearms Dealers,
206
National Association of Social
Workers, 236
National Association to Keep and
Bear Arms, 206–207, 337
National Bench Rest Shooters
Association, Inc., 207, 228
National Black Law Journal, 18
National Board for the Promotion
of Rifle Practice, 207
National Coalition Against
Poisoning of Wildlife, 236
National Coalition to Ban
Handguns, 101, 236, 306
National Commission on the
Causes and Prevention of
Violence, 88
National Council for a
Responsible Firearms Policy,
Inc., 122, 236
National Council of Negro
Women, 236

National Council to Control
Handguns, 236
National Crime Prevention
Council, 207–208
National Defense Act, National
Guard and, 242
National Education Association,
208
National Firearms Act, 84–85,
170–171, 246, 247, 265, 293
registration provisions of, 126
National Foundation for Firearms
Education, 208
National Guard, 14, 87, 95
creation of, 242
Second Amendment and,
250–251
National Gun Control Center, 236
National Hunters Association,
208–209
National Institute of Justice, 343
National League of Cities, 236
National Mossberg Collectors
Association, 209
National Muzzle Loading Rifle
Association, 209
National Organization for Victim
Assistance, 237
National Reloading
Manufacturers Association,
209, 236
National Research Opinion
Center, 33
National Rifle Association (NRA),
109, 114, 209–210, 313, 333,
335–338
Brady Bill and, 99, 103
criticism of, 302
establishment of, 81–82
gun control and, 255, 304, 311,
338
hunter safety program by, 86
law enforcement groups and,
41
media and, 260
self-defense and, 34
survey by, 294
U.S. v. Miller and, 6
National Safety Council, 236,
297–298
National Sheriffs' Association, 39
National Shooters League, 233

National Shooting Sports
Foundation, 210–211
National Skeet Shooting
Association, 211
National Urban League, 211
National Victim Center, 237
Natural rights, 8–9, 102
Navegard, Inc., 44
Nebraska Gun and Cartridge
Collectors, 226
Nebraskans for Responsible Gun
Ownership, 226
Nedham, Marchamont, 66
New Gun Week, 323
New Hampshire Arms Collectors,
Inc., 226
New Hampshire State Rifle and
Pistol Association, 226
New Jersey Arms Collectors Club,
Inc., 227
New Mexico Gun Collectors
Association, 227
New York State Rifle and Pistol
Association, 227
New York Transit Authority, suit
against, 30–31
Newton, George D., 313
Ninth Amendment, 3, 15, 95, 250
Nisbet, Lee, 314
No Compromise Majority, 212
Non-Powder Gun Products
Association, 212
North American Hunter, 323
North American Hunting Club,
212
North Dakota Muzzle Loaders,
Inc., 228
Northern California Historical
Arms Collectors Association,
219
Northern Indiana Gun Collectors
Association, 222
North-South Skirmish
Association, 212–213
*North-South Skirmish Association
Newsletter*, 323
NRA. *See* National Rifle
Association
NRAction, 323
NRA-ILA. *See* Institute for
Legislative Action
Nunn v. State, 80

Oak Park, Illinois, 90
*Observations on the Importance of
the American Revolution*
(Price), 76
Office for Church in Society
(United Church of Christ),
213
Office of Munitions Control, 87
Ohio Gun Collectors Association,
Inc., 228
Ohio Rifle and Pistol Association,
229
Oklahoma Rifle Association, 229
Oliver, Peter D., 44–45
Omnibus Crime Control and Safe
Streets Act, 87, 171–172
Omnibus Violent Crime Control
and Prevention Act, 177–179
On Crime and Punishments
(Beccaria), 71
On the Law of War and Peace
(Grotius), 65
Ordinance No. 81-11, 90, 91
Oregon Cartridge Collectors
Association, Inc., 229
Oregon Handgun Alert, 229
Oregonians Against Gun
Violence, 229
Organization United to Control
Handguns, 225
Organized Crime Control Act, 88,
174
Oswald, Lee Harvey, 314
Otis, James, 10, 71
Ottoman Turkish Penal Code, 25
Outdoor Life, 324

Pacific International Trapshooting
Association, 214
Paine, Thomas, 262
PAIS INTERNATIONAL
(database), 369
Palko v. Connecticut, 85
Parents of Murdered Children,
237
Pelican Arms Collectors, 223
Pennsylvania Gun Collectors
Association, 230
Pennsylvania Rifle and Pistol
Association, 230
People v. Barela, 139
People vs. Handguns, 236

People v. Zerillo, 147–148
Pereira, Joseph, 299
Permits, 83, 305
Perpich v. Department of Defense,
95–96, 157
Personality types, criminal, 47
Petersburg Rod and Gun Club,
219
Petersen's Hunting, 324
Pikes Peak Gun Collectors Guild,
220
Plastic guns, 93, 112–113
Plato
armed populace and, 59, 60
natural rights and, 9
Point Blank, 120, 324
Police, 2, 329
credibility of, 327
gun control and, 38–42, 90–91,
327
NRA and, 41
self-defense and, 39–40
Police Foundation, 214, 299
Police Foundation Report on
Firearm Abuse, 264
Police Management Association,
214
Political Disquisitions (Burgh), 72
Politics (Aristotle), 60
Pratt, Lawrence D., 118
*Prayer, Gun Control and the Right
To Assemble 3*, 363–364
Precision Shooting, 324
President's Commission on Law
Enforcement and
Administration, 87
Presser v. Illinois, 82–83, 159–160
Price, Richard, 76
The Prince, (Machiavelli), 64
Prison reform movement, 71
Product liability, 2, 257, 287, 306
gun control policy and, 42–45
rejection of, 248–249
See also Liability
Proposition 15, defeat of, 91
Public health
firearms and, 327–328
violence and, 287
Pufendorf, Samuel von, natural
rights and, 9
Purdy, Patrick Edward, 18–19,
105, 121, 290

Quigley, Paxton, 32, 33
Quilici v. Village of Morton Grove.
See *Victor D. Quilici, Robert
Stentl, et al., George Reichert,
and Robert E. Miller, Plaintiffs-
Appellants, v. Village of Morton
Grove, et al., Defendants-
Appellees*

Race, 327
gun control and, 24–29
Rawle, William, 14
Reagan, Ronald, 103
BATF and, 121
crime control and, 92
gun control and, 93
Registration, 21, 84, 91, 103, 126,
305
Reno, Janet, 116, 118–119
Republic (Plato), 59
Responsibility, consumer, 42–43
*Restricting Handguns: The Liberal
Skeptics Speak Out* (Kates), 112
Revolutionary War, 73
Rex v. Dewhurst, 79
Rex v. Gardner, 70
Rex v. Knight, 67
*The Right Constitution of a
Commonwealth*, (Nedham), 66
The Right To Bear Arms, 364
*A Right To Bear Arms: State and
Federal Bills of Rights and
Constitutional Guarantees*,
(Halbrook), 108
Right to keep and bear arms, 11,
74–82, 125, 126, 243, 246,
249–251, 253, 255, 257, 259,
260–263, 266, 267, 303, 304,
306, 309, 310, 331, 343
analysis of, 311, 312
Bill of Rights and, 109–110
constitutional provisions for
(by state), 162–170
development of, 13–14, 77,
287–289, 300, 307–308
guaranteeing, 93
interpreting, 4–15, 95, 104, 127,
268, 293, 300, 301
limits on, 106
militias and, 305
roots of, 61–62, 64, 68, 70
Second Amendment and, 95

self-defense and, 34
as specific guarantee, 89
women and, 32
The Rights of Gun Owners,
  (Gottlieb), 107
Riley, Robert, 293
Risk-utility test, applying, 245
Rivara, Frederick P., 249
Roberti-Roos Assault Weapons
  Control Act, 94, 333
Roll, Richard, 259
Roosevelt, Franklin Delano, 3, 84
Rosenberg, Mark L., 314
Rossi, Peter H., 296, 299, 317–318
  on women/guns, 33
Rousseau, Jean-Jacques, 9, 71
Royal Oak Historical Arms
  Collectors, Inc., 225
Rwanda, gun control in, 25

Safari Club International,
  214–215, 222, 229
*The Samurai, the Mountie, and the
  Cowboy: Should America Adopt
  the Gun Control of Other
  Democracies,* (Kopel), 113
San Bernardino Valley Arms
  Collectors, Inc., 219
San Diego Committee Against
  Handgun Violence, 219
Santarelli, Donald E., 287
Santee, John C., 287–288
Saturday Night Specials, 120, 242,
  254, 290, 300, 309, 314, 339
  controlling, 1, 18, 103
  crime and, 246, 248
  manufacturer liability for, 43, 45
  right to, 7
  self-defense and, 26
Sauk Trail Gun Collectors, 222
Save Our Sons and Daughters
  (SOSAD), 225
Saxon law, 61
Schubert v. DeBard, 150–151, 251
Schumer, Charles, 119–120
Searches and seizures, 14, 66, 326
Seattle, Washington, 22
Second Amendment, 108, 112,
  113, 125, 243, 246, 247, 252–
  255, 257, 258, 261, 263, 266,
  268, 269, 290, 298, 302–303,
  305, 306, 309, 330–331, 337,

339–340, 342
  adoption of, 79
  blacks and, 26–27
  changes in, 13–14, 260
  controls over, 109–110, 293
  debate over, 3–15, 308
  development of, 13, 244–245,
    250, 289, 300, 311, 312
  gun control and, 2, 7–8, 84, 267,
    298
  interpreting, 4, 5–8, 29, 85, 86,
    96, 104, 249–250, 289, 292,
    300, 308, 314–315, 317
  militias and, 246
  origins of, 60, 69, 287–288, 293,
    303, 307, 335
  provisions of, 11, 95, 331
Second Amendment Foundation,
  107, 120, 215
Seitz, Steven Thomas, 288
Self-defense, 2, 11, 26, 28, 29, 102,
  252, 260, 263, 266, 295,
  300–301, 304, 306, 310, 317,
  340, 342
  concept of, 34–38
  guns and, 114, 309, 313, 330
  natural right of, 9, 12
  police and, 39
  right to, 29, 34, 269, 270, 302,
    336
  roots of, 61, 62, 63, 65, 68, 70, 71
  women and, 31–33
Semiautomatic weapons, 18
  banning, 1, 19–21, 93–94, 95, 96,
    103, 113, 291, 334
  problems with, 295
  spread of, 41
  support for, 19–20, 111
Shalhope, Robert E., 288
Sherrill, Robert, 314
Shettle v. Shearer, 152–153
Shields, Nelson T. "Pete," 120
Shinkle, Frank, 247
Shooters Bible, 324
A Shooting Gallery Called America,
  364
Shooting Industry, 325
Shooting Sports USA, 325
Shooting Times, 325
Shotguns, 18, 111, 328–329
Sidney, Algernon, 9, 69
Sierra Club Foundation, 237

Six Bookes of a Commonweale (Bodin), 65
Sixth Amendment, 3, 85
Skeet Shooting Review, 325
Sklar v. Byrne, 139
Sloan, John H., 22
Smith, Adam, 9, 73–74
Snyder, John M., 120–121
So Violent a Nation, 364–365
The Social Contract (Rousseau), 71
Social Science Index (CD-ROM), 370
Society for Animal Rights, Inc., 237
Soldier of Fortune, 325
Sons of Liberty, 215–216
SOSAD. *See* Save Our Sons and Daughters
South Carolina Arms Collectors Association, 230
South Carolina Shooting Association, 230
Southern California Arms Collectors Association, 220
Southern Indiana Gun Collectors Association, Inc., 222
Spirit of the Laws (Montesquieu), 70
Spitzer, Robert J., 314–315
Sporting Arms and Ammunition Manufacturers' Institute, 341
Sporting culture, gun ownership and, 331
Sports Afield, 326
Sportsmen for Firearms Responsibility, 232
Sprecher, Robert A., 289
Staggers, Harley O., Jr., 121–122
Standing armies, 7, 75–76
criticism of, 72, 73, 78
dangers of, 76–77
State Rifle and Pistol Association of Massachusetts, 224
State v. Buckner, 249
State v. Buzzard, 141–143
State v. Delgado, 156
State v. Kerner, 145–147
State v. Kessler, 151–152, 251
State v. Rosenthal, 144–145
State v. Rupp, 136
State v. Stevens, 157
Statute of Northampton (1328), 12, 63, 67

Statute of Winchester (1285), 12, 63
Steffey, Matthew S., 289–290
Steinberg, David J., 121
on handguns, 16–17
Stell, Lance K., 303
Stevens, Susan M., 290
Stompoly, John, 266
Story, Joseph, 122–123, 253
Street Gangs of Los Angeles, 365
Strickland v. State, 129–130
Subcommittee on Crime (U.S. House), 100, 105, 108, 111, 112, 119, 122, 124
waiting periods and, 42
Subcommittee on Crime (U.S. Senate), 113
Subcommittee on Criminal Law (U.S. Senate), 16–17
Subcommittee on the Constitution (U.S. Senate), 331, 342
on Second Amendment, 15
Suicide, guns and, 16, 35, 259, 290, 313
Sullivan Law, 27, 83, 305
Sutherland, differential association theory of, 47
Sweet Sorrow, 365
Swiggett, Hal, 315
Symms, Steven D., 123

Tahmassebi, Stefan B., 339, 342
on gun control, 29
Tammany Hall, 83
Taney, Chief Justice: *Dred Scott* and, 25, 80–81
Tannenbaum, labeling theory of, 47
Tennesseeans for Handgun Control, 231
Tennessee Gun Collectors Association, Inc., 231
Tenth Amendment, 15, 95, 261
Teret, Stephen P., 290
Terrorism, gun control and, 100
Terrorist Firearms Detection Act, 93
Tesoriero, James M., 331
Texas Crime Victim Clearinghouse, 238

Texas Gun Collectors Association, 231
Texas State Rifle Association, 231
That Every Man Be Armed: The Evolution of a Constitutional Right (Halbrook), 108, 263
Thompson, Thomas R., 291
Three American Guns, 365–366
Time, survey by, 21
"To Keep and Bear Arms": Gun Control and the Second Amendment, 366
Tonso, William R., 315–316
Trap and Field, 326
Treanor, William W., 342
Trenchard, John, 9, 69–70
Triggers
  exotic mechanisms for, 94, 95
  locks for, 94
Trust the People: The Case against Gun Control (Kopel), 113
Tucker, St. George, 14
20 Questions and Answers, 22
Two Treatises on Government (Locke), 67

UCR. *See Uniform Crime Report*
Udulutch, Mark, 291
Ultrahazardous activity doctrine, rejection of, 248
Unexpected Wildlife Refuge, 237
Uniform Crime Report (UCR), 328
Uniform Firearms Act, 246
United Sportsmans Association, 227
United States Attorney General's Task Force on Violent Crime, report by, 90–91
United States Code, 14, 332
United States Conference of Mayors, 105, 106, 237, 298
  handguns and, 299
United States Constitution, 245–246
  adoption of, 77–78, 79
  amending, 246
  right to keep and bear arms and, 266
  roots of, 61, 65, 67, 69
U.S. Constitution (software), 371
United States Department of Justice, 299, 343

background checks by, 121
felon identification and, 93
studies by, 36
on violent crime/guns, 15
United States Department of the Treasury, 331
  bombings/arsons and, 88
  serial numbering system by, 89
United States Library of Congress, 316
United States Revolver Association, 216
United States Supreme Court
  gun control and, 59
  right to keep and bear arms and, 127
United States v. Balasckak, 253
United States v. Cruikshank, 82, 157–159
United States v. Lopez, 96–97
United States v. Miller, 6, 14, 86, 161–162, 247, 250, 261, 307
United States v. Oakes, 135–136
United States v. Tot, 131–132
United States v. Verdugo-Urquidez, 95, 156–157
United States v. Warin, 134–135
Universal Declaration of Human Rights (United Nations), 289
Unting Act, 67
Utah Gun Collectors Association, 231

Vancouver, British Columbia, 22
Vatel, natural rights and, 9
Vermont State Rifle and Pistol Association, 232
Victims rights groups, 237–238
Victor D. Quilici, Robert Stentl, et al., George Reichert, and Robert E. Miller, Plaintiffs-Appellants, v. Village of Morton Grove, et al., Defendants-Appellees, 91, 137–139
Victory Rifle and Pistol Club, 228
Violence
  causes of, 46–47
  patterns of, 287
Violence Policy Center, 216–217
Violent crime
  guns and, 1, 15–18, 22, 23, 28, 293, 309, 328

Violent crime *(cont.)*
  impulsive nature of, 17
Violent Crime Control and
  Enforcement Act, 96
Virginia Arms Collectors
  Association, 232
Virginia Declaration of Rights, 74,
  339
  Madison and, 13
Virginia Instantaneous Firearms
  Transaction Program, 122
Virginia State Rifle and Revolver
  Association, 232
Volkmer, Harold L., 105, 114,
  123–124
Voltaire, 9

Wabash Valley Gun Collectors
  Association, Inc., 222
Waco Gun Collectors, 231
Waiting periods, 1, 5, 21, 92, 94,
  95, 101, 103, 330
  support for, 41–42
Wallace, M., 298
Wallack, Louis Robert, 316
Warner, Ken, 316
Washington, George, 73, 340
Washington Arms Collectors, Inc.,
  232
Washington Citizens for Rational
  Handgun Control, 232
Waybright, Roger J., 291–292
*Weapons: Part I (Prohibited
  Weapons)*, 366
*Weapons: Part II (Deadly and
  Concealed Weapons)*, 366
Weatherup, Roy G., 292
Weber-Burdin, Eleanor, 318
Webster, Noah, 77
  definitions by, 79, 80
Weeks, John, 308–309
Weil, Douglas S., 292
Weiss, Jonathan A., 293

Wekesser, Carol, 304
Westchester Arms Collectors
  Club, Inc., 228
WESTLAW (database), 369
Wettick, R. Stanton, Jr., 259
"What Is Fit To Be Done with
  America?" (Knox), 10, 75
Whisker, James B., 293, 317
Wildlife management, 83, 85
Wildlife Restoration Act, 85
Willamette Valley Arms
  Collectors Association, 229
William and Mary, 67, 68, 72
Williams, David C., 293–294
Wilson, James Q., 317
WILSONLINE (database), 369
Winchester Repeating Arms
  Company, semiautomatic
  rifles by, 19
Wingfield v. Stratford, 70–71
Wintemute, Garen J., 290
Wisconsin Gun Collectors
  Association, Inc., 232
Women, 30–34
Women and Guns, 326
Women's League for
  Conservative Judaism,
  217–218
World Fast-Draw Association, 218
Wright, James D., 294, 296, 299,
  317–318, 343
  on women/guns, 33
Wyoming Gun Collectors, 233

Yakima Valley Muzzle Loaders,
  232
Ye Connecticut Gun Guild, Inc.,
  220
Young Americans for Freedom, 343
Yugoslavia, gun control in, 25

Zimring, Franklin E., 294–295,
  313, 318

Earl R. Kruschke holds a B.S. from the University of Wisconsin, Madison; an M.A. from the University of Wyoming, Laramie; and a Ph.D. from the University of Wisconsin, Madison. He also holds a law degree. He has authored or coauthored seven scholarly books and dozens of papers and articles, and he has received many honors, including the prestigious California State University Foundation's Trustees Statewide Outstanding Professor Award. He is Professor Emeritus of Political Science at California State University, Chico.